THE SS

A WARNING
FROM HISTORY

Dedicated to the victims of the SS

THE SS

A WARNING FROM HISTORY

GUIDO KNOPP

TRANSLATED BY ANGUS MCGEOCH

This book was first published in 2002 by C. Bertelsmann Verlag GmbH, Munich, under the title *Die SS: Eine Warnung der Geschichte*.

This English translation first published in 2003 by Sutton Publishing Limited

This paperback edition first published in 2005

Reprinted in 2008 by
The History Press
The Mill, Brimscombe Port,
Stroud, Gloucestershire, GL5 2QG
www.thehistorypress.co.uk

In collaboration with Jens Afflerbach, Stefan Brauburger, Christian Deick, Jöng Müllner, Sönke Neitzel, Ricarda Schlosshan.

Research: Alexander Berkel, Mario Sporn
Translation: Angus McGeoch

British Library Cataloguing in Publication Data
A catalogue record for this book is available from the British Library.

ISBN 978 0 7509 4046 7

Typeset in 10/12.5pt Galliard.
Typesetting and origination by
Sutton Publishing Limited.
Printed and bound in England.

CONTENTS

Picture Credits   vi
List of Illustrations   vii
Introduction   ix

1   *The Struggle for Power*   1
    Knopp/Afflerbeck

2   *Himmler's Mania*   60
    Knopp/Dieck

3   *Heydrich's Ascendancy*   112
    Knopp/Müllner

4   *Death's Head*   170
    Knopp/Brauburger

5   *The* Waffen-*SS*   229
    Knopp/Neitzel

6   *The 'Odessa' Myth*   284
    Knopp/Schlosshan

    Appendix: SS Ranks and Their Equivalents   344
    Index   345

Picture Credits

AKG London: 12, 17, 18
Bildarchiv Preussischer Kulturbesitz: 6, 7, 9, 19, 21, 22, 23, 24
Bilderdienst Süddeutscher Verlag: 8, 27
Bundesarchiv Koblenz: 1 (80/31/16 A), 11 (152152/4), 13
   (146/72/39/44), 20 (183/H29077)
Corbis: 28
Karl-Bernt Karwasz: 30
Kreismuseum Wewelsburg: 5
Ullstein: 2, 3, 4, 10, 14, 15, 25, 29
United States Holocaust Memorial Museum: 16

LIST OF ILLUSTRATIONS

THE STRUGGLE FOR POWER
1. An SA Brigade on the march, 1931
2. *Stosstrupp* Hitler in 1923
3. Röhm and Hitler on 31 January 1934

HIMMLER'S MANIA
4. Himmler and Hitler in 1939
5. Wewelsburg castle
6. Himmler plucks flowers
7. Gudrun Himmler with her father
8. Himmler in Auschwitz, 1942

HEYDRICH'S ASCENDANCY
9. Heydrich with Hacha
10. Huber, Nebe, Himmler, Heydrich and Müller in 1939
11. The Heydrich family in 1934
12. Wannsee in 1942
13. Heydrich's destroyed car
14. Lidice, 10 June 1942

DEATH'S HEAD
15. Theodor Eicke
16. German policemen shoot Jewish women
17. Unbridled sadism
18. Höss in captivity

THE *WAFFEN*-SS
19. The 'Black Corps' in 1933
20. Mustering recruits in 1938
21. *Totenkopf* soldiers in France, 1940
22. Sepp Dietrich in 1943

23. Bosnian Muslims of the *Waffen*-SS
24. Child soldiers captured by the Americans

THE 'ODESSA' MYTH
25. Forged banknotes, 1959
26. Skorzeny with Hitler, 1943
27. Bishop Alois Hudal
28. Simon Wiesenthal in 1983
29. Klaus Barbie in 1987
30. Honouring fallen SS men at Ulrichsberg

INTRODUCTION

Its very name epitomised terror. Its assignment was mass murder. More than any other organisation in Hitler's Reich, it embodied the deadly delusion of the 'master-race'. The double 'S' – like two flashes of lightning – were in fact runic letters, the ancient Germanic script. They stood for *Schutz-Staffel* or 'Protection Squadron'. In only a few years it grew from an unimportant bodyguard into a state within Hitler's state, and one that was built on slavery.

'Loyalty is thine honour' – under this motto, propagated by Heinrich Himmler, SS men were to act as 'fire-fighters', plugging gaps in the front line, pitilessly exploiting prisoners and slave labour, and cold-bloodedly killing tens of thousands in mobile murder-squads and in the death-camps of the Nazi regime. And when it came to the Holocaust, of all the organisations that made up the Nazi state, only the SS was capable, and above all, willing to carry out Hitler's orders.

This book is not an attempt to add to the many useful and detailed studies concerning the history of the SS. Instead, at a time when the last of the perpetrators and their surviving victims are still alive, we offer a final summing-up. Accompanying an internationally financed television series, this book is aimed at a wide readership. We have drawn on many hitherto unpublished sources, consulted archives as far apart as Washington and Moscow – and we have talked to witnesses to the history of the SS: victims, perpetrators and opponents, who have never spoken out publicly before. In another five years, such personal evidence from people involved at the time will no longer be available. Now is therefore the time to put it on record.

The SS began in a small way. It was born in May 1923, in the bowling-alley of a Munich beer-house, the Torbräu. Under the name of *Stosstrupp Hitler* (Hitler Shock Force), twenty-two men formed the nucleus of the black order. In meeting-hall punch-ups their job was to protect the life of the agitator who wanted to be 'Führer'. On their black caps they wore a skull, the death's-head symbol they had borrowed from the 1st Guard Reserve Pioneer Regiment which, in the First World War, operated with flame-throwers in advance of the front line. The mentality of 'death-defying relish for battle', which had grown up in the trenches, would now be turned by the shock troops against the hated new republic.

After Hitler's amateurish and unsuccessful attempt to overthrow the Bavarian government in November 1923, he was tried and imprisoned. But on his premature release in 1925 he set up a new *Stosstrupp*, known as the *Schutzstaffel*, or SS. Like its predecessor, the SS saw itself from the outset as a totally dedicated Praetorian Guard, the 'elite' of the Party, subject to the unquestioned authority of the Führer. Applicants for the SS had to be aged between twenty-three and thirty-five, were required to give the names of two personal guarantors, to be 'healthy and powerfully built', at least 1.7 metres (5 ft 7 in) tall and, needless to say, of 'Aryan extraction'.

Yet in the years before Hitler sneaked into power, the tiny band of SS were all but invisible among the million-strong SA, the 'brown-shirt battalions' that dominated the fighting in the streets. Even when Himmler pointed the way forward with the phrase, 'The SA are the line infantry, the SS are the regiment of Guards', it was the SA, led by Ernst Röhm, who were instrumental in clearing Hitler's path to the Reich Chancellery and who became increasingly vehement in their demands for a share in power and government.

For them the fatal hour struck on 30 June 1934. In a hitherto unprecedented killing operation SS squads, acting on Hitler's orders, murdered the entire SA leadership, including Röhm, one of his own oldest colleagues. With this German equivalent of the Massacre of St Bartholomew in sixteenth-century France, the SS began its rise to become the most powerful weapon of organised terror in the Third Reich. It was not just that the frustrated brownshirt revolutionaries had been standing in Hitler's way; the undisciplined violence of the SA cohorts, which followed the Nazis' seizure of power, had struck fear into the middle classes, who were anxious to see a strong central government. But Röhm, the head of the SA, was disappointed by Hitler's alliance with the forces of conservatism, and called for a 'National Socialist revolution', to follow the national revolution. What is more, he wanted to call in the still unpaid debt to his brownshirt brigades, for their 'sacrifices in the campaigning years'.

All this was endangering the pact that the new Chancellor had made with the *Reichswehr*, the regular army, which he needed if he was to realise his imperial ambitions. That is why Himmler's accomplice Reinhard Heydrich, and the Gestapo boss, Rudolf Diels, gathered evidence against the supposedly mutinous Röhm. Yet there was never any danger of Röhm staging a coup against Hitler. The 'Röhm putsch' was a putsch *against* Röhm. A sinister concoction of rumour, doctored evidence and falsified information provided the pretext for removing Hitler's troublesome rival.

SS units and police squads, equipped with arms supplied by the Reichswehr, not only murdered the leaders of the SA, but made a thorough job of liquidating opponents of the Nazi regime, such as Hitler's former associate Gregor Strasser, and the former Reich Chancellor, Kurt von Schleicher, whose wife was also slain.

However, the real winner in this internecine power-struggle within the Nazi Party was the SS, under its hitherto almost unknown 'Reichsführer', Heinrich Himmler. The rise of the SS was inseparably bound up with Himmler's own career.

His secret motto was one he had presumptuously borrowed from the Prussia of Frederick the Great: 'Be more than you seem'. No-one would ever have supposed that, of all people, this unprepossessing man would become Hitler's most powerful henchman.

Indescribable as are the crimes associated with his name, the man who had them committed was merely banal. His contemporaries described him as 'a completely insignificant personality', 'a man without qualities', at best 'a typical schoolmaster, excessively frugal by nature'. In any other age he would probably have employed his talents as a bureaucrat. In fact, Himmler performed his tasks like a revenue official signing off so many tax-returns.

To him, genocide was simply a matter of organisation.

The fact that the Holocaust was carried out with such systematic, mechanical thoroughness, was above all the work of Himmler. He personally inspected the death factories. He ensured that the dreadful statistics were reported to him on a daily basis.

Yet the SS chief was no intellectual; he was maladroit, timid and indecisive. He did not derive his authority from any convincing force of personality, but from a purposeful and single-minded expansion of his power. A talent for organisation combined with the consciously cultivated image of a ruthless hardliner turned him into Hitler's indispensable executor – and executioner. By the end, Himmler was Reichsführer-SS, chief of the German police and Reich Minister of the Interior, as well as commander-in-chief of the Reserve Army. After Hitler he was the most powerful man in the Reich.

Himmler's ideal of manhood was one of cold brutality and a willingness to die for the cause; and his aim was to breed such men. He preached honour and morality to his troops, while in the same breath ordering violence and mass murder. To him ruthlessness was a virtue, pitiless murder a sign of strength. Ultimately, Himmler cared nothing for the suffering of his victims, only for the mental trauma of those who inflicted it. Cold and austere rationality was of course only one side of his contradictory character. At the same time he got carried away by an absurd but potent brew of racial theory, naturopathy and neo-Germanic occultism.

Yet on the political front, it was this same willing executioner, this 'faithful Heinrich', who in the last months of the war played a desperate double game. On one hand he organised the largely illusory *Volkssturm* and *Werwolf* brigades, while on the other he was holding secret talks in which he offered the Western Allies a negotiated surrender – without apparently realising that his name had long been synonymous with mass murder. Thus he was betraying his Führer just as, eleven years earlier, he had betrayed his first two mentors, Ernst Röhm and Gregor Strasser. 'Loyalty is thine honour' – in the end he himself showed how much value could be placed in the motto he had given to the SS.

In the 1930s the top Nazi leadership had a joke at Himmler's expense: 'HHHH–*Himmlers Hirn heisst Heydrich*' ('Himmler's brain's called

Heydrich'; the four Hs are pronounced 'Ha ha ha ha' in German). And indeed Reinhard Heydrich, despite having been dishonourably discharged from the German navy, achieved a comet-like rise through the SS hierarchy. Under Himmler he built up the security service (SD) of the SS, and turned the name 'Gestapo' into a synonym for Nazi Germany, for the possibility of violent death at any time. He created the *Reichsicherheitshauptamt*, the Central Office of Reich Security, a vast bureaucracy that spread out an invisible network of systematised terror.

Nevertheless, it is important here to cut one legend down to size – that of the Gestapo as an all-knowing, all-powerful secret police. In Hitler's Reich it was spoken of as a medusa-like super-authority, whose mere existence was intended to show everyone that resistance was futile. In the decades after the war, it came to stand for the terrorising of Germany's civil population. In fact the Gestapo was very much smaller than legend would have us believe. In the last analysis, Heydrich could only wield his power by commanding an army of informers: the narks and stool-pigeons of the Nazi Reich. Without these cohorts of slanderers the Gestapo would have remained blind and deaf. Never before in the history of Germany had it been so easy to denounce unpopular neighbours, competitors or simply people one loathed, to make them helpless victims of an arbitrary authority, to deprive them of employment and a future, and finally to deliver them to the executioner's guillotine. Waves of malice swept across the country. The traces of this deluge lived on in thousands of files.

Heydrich owed his rise to Himmler, and he repaid the debt with unquestioning loyalty and an amoral callousness. Himmler's obsession with racial cleansing and Heydrich's ice-cold sense of the macabre formed a lethal combination.

Heydrich was the prototype of the power manager, who picked up Hitler's vaguely formulated intentions and read into them his future plans and developments, even before the dictator needed to issue orders. If anyone was 'second-guessing the Führer', it was Reinhard Heydrich. As SD chief under Himmler's protection, he tackled the organisation of the 'Final Solution' with the energy he did, not least because he was eagerly courting the Führer's favour, in order to became Reichsführer one day himself.

Even before the war, the Swiss academic and Red Cross representative, Carl Burckhardt, saw him as a 'young, evil god of death'. A former victim of the Gestapo, Ralph Giordano,* wrote that 'Heydrich was the prototype of the New Man, as envisaged by National Socialism. He spearheaded the generation of the Absolute. No form of inhumanity was beyond his capacity. Everything was possible, including the murder of millions of men, women and children.' Reinhard Heydrich had organised this genocide, but did not live to see it carried out. In June 1942 he was attacked by Czech partisans in Prague and died of his injuries.

What might have happened if Heydrich had remained alive? In a way Heydrich foreshadowed the future of Hitler's Germany: an SS state. In a Greater German Reich stretching from the Atlantic to the Urals, criss-crossed by autobahns, dominated by temples to the dead, 90 million souls would have been the slaves of Nazi violence. As many as 14 million were already being used as forced labour, some 30 million were to be killed, and the rest driven eastward beyond the Urals – into the wilderness of Siberia. Reinhard Heydrich, the 'coming man' of the SS, would not have hesitated in making this terrible vision come true.

At the war crimes tribunal in Nuremberg Heydrich was not standing in the dock. There can be no doubt that he would have been condemned to death.

At Nuremberg one organisation was comprehensively classed as criminal; in the closing phase of the war, with nearly 900,000 men under arms, it was numerically the largest section of the SS – the *Waffen*-SS.

To this day opinions are divided about the military arm of the SS. Was it an elite force or a gang of criminals? Were its men 'soldiers like any others'? Simply the epitome of martial courage and aggression? Or were they Nazi ruffians and killers, who had been

---

* Journalist and author, born in Hamburg in 1923 of a German-Jewish mother and Sicilian father. Forced to leave his high school in 1940, he was interrogated and maltreated by the Gestapo. In 1944 the family hid in the cellar of a bombed building and thus escaped deportation and death. His recent writings about the revival of right-wing extremism in Germany have caused considerable controversy.

so thoroughly brutalised that they were willing and eager to hack down everything and everyone?

Evidence can be found to support either thesis. In the hot-spots of the eastern front, especially after Stalingrad, the panzer divisions of the *Waffen*-SS fought in the role of a 'fire brigade', often with huge losses. Of course, the regular Wehrmacht suffered such losses as well. On the other hand, when it came to war crimes, the *Waffen*-SS were notoriously prominent: certainly they were not unique in their brutal behaviour, and the difference between the Wehrmacht and the *Waffen*-SS was by no means as great as is often claimed. Nevertheless, the excesses of SS units usually outstripped those of the Wehrmacht in their repulsive horror. The name of Oradour, the French village burnt to the ground with all its inhabitants, stands as a symbol for countless other war crimes.

After the war, veterans of the *Waffen*-SS attempted to prove the unprovable: that the soldiers of the *Waffen*-SS had been no more than men of battle, who had nothing to do with the crimes of the SS death-squads and the extermination camps. This may have been how it seemed to some SS men, especially those who were compelled to enlist. Yet the reality looked very different. The links between the *Waffen*-SS and the regular SS were extremely close. The officers were trained together, regardless of where they would later serve: in concentration camps, in administration or at the front. In no way were they 'soldiers like any others'.

In the case of the Death's Head units of the SS, the question of individual guilt at the sites of the worst horrors, in general, never even arose. They were the core of the perpetrators' forces, those who carried the Holocaust through to its ghastly conclusion. For the world that came after, it might well have been comforting to brand those and also the other members of the *Schutzstaffel* indiscriminately as criminals, as born sadists. For that would of course mean that we could regard them as an aberrant product of human society.

Yet the men who served in the SS were very often 'perfectly normal people' drawn from the social mainstream. The SS was anything but a monolithic bloc, sworn to loyalty to a higher cause. It was a complex and dynamic structure, which was constantly changing throughout its twenty years of existence. The men (and women) who served in the SS were extremely diverse. Some were 'faithful disciples', who ascribed an almost religious mission to the 'Order of the Death's Head'. Others picked the aspects of Himmler's armoury that suited them and tried, as far as they were able, to ignore much else that they rather disapproved of. Still others saw the SS above all as offering an opportunity to make a career; while they paid lip-service to the ideology of the Black Order, inwardly they were pretty indifferent to it. In the early days, it was the unemployed intellectuals who thought they could find in the *Schutzstaffel* the one chance of giving meaning and direction to their lives. But at the same time some of the recruits, and not only those in the Death's Head units, were the scum of society: criminals, drop-outs, murderers. At the outset, the skeleton of the SS was provided by veterans of the First World War, who had won their spurs in meeting- hall brawls, but once Hitler had parleyed his way into power, men of a 'better class' queued up to join the Black Guard. Himmler took over complete organisations of the social elite, such as the 'Gentlemen's Riding Club' or the 'Kyffhäuser League'.* There was a disproportionately large representation of the aristocracy in the upper ranks of the SS. Academics and men from the liberal professions were recruited, especially for secret service work and to run the SS's business empire. Officers in the regular army were drafted into the SS to train the *Verfügungstruppe*, the 'Rapid Response Force'. In addition, Himmler awarded 'honorary' ranks in the SS to hundreds of captains of industry, diplomats and civil servants. A German prince of the blood could be an SS man, just as much as a Rhineland farm-worker who, as a concentration camp guard, was an accomplice in the murder of Jews.

In short, the SS was in every respect a mirror of German society. The great majority were 'perfectly normal people', many of whom became criminals under very abnormal circumstances, because they were encouraged to do so by a criminal regime. If a

---

* An ex-army association that took its name from the Kyffhäuser rocks in the Harz Mountains where, according to legend, the medieval emperor Friedrich Barbarossa sleeps, until the moment when he will reawaken and save Germany.

government declared that killing people, though in itself harsh and inhuman, nonetheless served a higher purpose that was 'good', then the bonds of human morality were clearly not strong enough to prevent hundreds of thousands from behaving like criminals. Most of those who turned into criminals were unaware that they were doing wrong.

So what is the moral of this story? Anyone could have become a perpetrator. Everyone is under threat when a criminal state breaks down the barriers between right and wrong. Human nature is inherently weak. There's something of a Himmler or a Mengele, an Eichmann or a Heydrich in all of us. At other times, under different circumstances, all those men might have pursued 'perfectly normal' careers as inconspicuous private citizens. Himmler as a headmaster, perhaps? Heydrich as a naval officer? Mengele as a paediatrician?

It would be irresponsible simply to put one's trust in the humanity of mankind, in all its frailness and instability. Only a free state with clear norms and standards, based on a humane society, can effectively prevent right from becoming wrong. We must never again allow a criminal state, which makes possible an organisation like the SS, to come into being. To this extent, the story of the SS is, more than anything, a warning from history.

CHAPTER ONE

THE STRUGGLE FOR POWER

On 30 June 1934 the terror of the Third Reich took on a new hue. Black replaced brown and blended with blood-red. These perpetrators did not bawl slogans, nor did they brandish cudgels. They drove around in black limousines.

On that day, in Berlin, three men from the Gestapo HQ hustled Paul Schulz, formerly a senior official in the Nazi Party, into a four-seater coupé. They then closed the roof of the car. 'It exuded an unpleasant smell of spilt blood, which removed any lingering doubts I might have had about the purpose of this journey', Schulz recalled later. The car was driven at high speed through Steglitz and into the Grunewald forest. It raced on towards the lake at Wannsee, But as it was a weekend there were a lot of hikers on the roads. Not until they had passed the village of Seddin, half an hour from Potsdam, did the men find a secluded part of the forest, suitable for administering what they called the 'shot'.

They ordered their victim out of the car and told him to walk a few paces. Schulz only had a few seconds left. He knocked the gun from the hand of one of the SS men. A shot from the second man hit him before he could reach the cover of the undergrowth. 'When I came round I was lying on my stomach, with my head down. I felt a severe pain in my spine. My body was wet with blood. I immediately began to utter a death-rattle and imitated the twitching of a dying man. Then I kept absolutely still – as still as a dead body.' The killers felt there was no need to finish him off. When they went to fetch a ground-sheet to roll up the presumed corpse, Schulz, though seriously wounded, jumped up and fled down a forest path. He only just made it.

This was the only instance, on that fateful 30 June 1934, when the men in black uniforms failed to carry out an assignment as ordered. On every other occasion they killed in the manner expected of them: meticulously, obediently, ruthlessly, intelligently and unobtrusively. On that sultry summer Saturday there was no outward sign that the SS were carrying out the Third Reich's first mass murder. Calm reigned over the country. No-one got very excited about the conflicts that had been seething for weeks between the Nazi Party and its most important wing, the SA. Conversation turned to another kind of drama; a week earlier the football team FC Schalke 04 had beaten First Nuremberg 2–1 to win the German Cup Final, the decisive goal being scored just before the final whistle.

The public had little inkling about the pitiless power-struggle that had broken out within the Nazi leadership. It was a face-off in which the two elements of the Party, which both promoted themselves as the centre of power, lined up behind Hitler in a hypocritical masquerade, praising loyalty and obedience, at the same time fighting each other to the death. It was a deadly duel, which the new masters exploited to settle old scores.

There was a danger that Röhm's SA was developing into a state within the state, so to speak, and that was a threat to Hitler and his cronies.

Eberhard Richter, who lived in Berlin at that time

Ultimately it was, more than anything, a dispute between the SS and SA, in which many people who had nothing to do with the coup were removed by the SS.

Albert Speer, under US interrogation, May 1945

The criminal trial was staged, evidence was falsified, and the verdict decided from the start. Under the pretext of smashing a threatened coup by the SA, the SS chiefs, Himmler and Heydrich, worked from death-lists that had been drawn up well in advance. On that day an alliance forged with top Nazis like Göring and Bormann proved its solidity. It was to become the foundation of the Nazi dictatorship. The black battalions were its obedient enforcers. It was in Munich's Stadelheim prison that the senior officers of the SA died in a hail of bullets from the SS *Leibstandarte Adolf Hitler*. In the *Leibstandarte*'s Lichterfelde barracks in Berlin firing-squads of the Führer's Praetorian Guard executed the personal enemies of the Party elite. As Hans Fischach, a former member of the *Leibstandarte*, remembers: 'The platoons were made up of young men who had been told: "These are men who planned to overthrow Hitler. They'll be executed, and that's it." Then: "Fall in. First row kneel. Second row stand." And the orders were carried out. Individual SS men didn't give it a second thought. It was simply a national emergency.'

You will take on the Klausener case. Klausener is to be shot immediately, in his office at the Ministry. Then call me on his office phone.

Gestapo chief Reinhard Heydrich, speaking to SS man Kurt Gildisch, who murdered the senior civil servant, Erich Klausener

During the Röhm putsch on 30 June, it was when [former Chancellor] General Schleicher was shot that I began to worry for the first time.

Horst Zank, former Wehrmacht officer

For other assignments the SS despatched professional killers. Shortly before 1 p.m. *Hauptsturmführer* Kurt Gildisch parked his car in front of the Reich Ministry of Transport. Gildisch asked for the office of a departmental head, Dr Erich Klausener. His department was shipping, but more important to the men in power was what he did outside working hours. As leader of 'Catholic Action' he had organised a demonstration of more than 60,000 people the previous week, in Berlin's Hoppegarten. He had closed the meeting with an impromptu speech that had moved those who heard it: it was in these times, most of all, he said, that no-one should be excluded from the love of God. What is more, the civil servant had a background that did not appeal to Göring and Heydrich. Under the Weimar Republic Klausener had worked in the police department of the Prussian Ministry of the Interior. No-one knew the criminal records of old Nazis better than he. Klausener was just leaving his office when his murderer confronted him. Gildisch told him he was under arrest. As the official reached for his jacket, his killer fired two shots into his head. An SS guard took up position outside the victim's office. Without looking round, Gildisch left the ministry building. Other assignments awaited him.

On the evening of 30 June 1934, black limousines were gliding through the streets of Munich. One stopped at no. 3 Schackstrasse, very near the Victory Arch. Unlike Paul Schulz, Dr Willi Schmid suspected nothing. His family were very surprised at the brusque tone of the four men in black uniform, but Schmid reassured his wife and children: it would be cleared up in no time, and he would soon be back. What could the SS possibly want with him, a music critic? Before getting into the car, Schmid grabbed his hat. This mundane thing that they had watched him do countless times, was the last memory his daughter Renate has of her father. She now knows that 'the limousine headed for Dachau, where he was immediately shot'.

All over the Reich nearly a hundred people died in an unparalleled wave of terror – they included conservative opposition politicians like Kurt von Schleicher, and Hitler's old party colleague, Gregor Strasser. Starting with the 'Night of the Long Knives' the SS rose to become the most feared institution of the Nazi regime. As the Munich lawyer Otto Gritschneder puts it, it was on that day that the SS completed its 'apprenticeship in murder'. Within a few years the *Schutzstaffel* grew from being Hitler's personal bodyguard to become a monstrous network of terror, which penetrated the whole state and the nation. The events of that summer were transformed by SS mythology into a legendary 'blood-cleansing'. That assignment was the touchstone by which they measured their own reputation. As early as 1933 the SS house journal, *Das Schwarze Korps*, exhorted its readers to cultivate '. . . all the virtues and all the qualities that the SS has cherished through the long years of its existence and through which it has proved its worth: loyalty to the Führer, subordination and discipline'.

In the judgement of Hitler biographer Ian Kershaw, this German 'Night of St Bartholomew' forged the SS into the 'sharpest weapon in the arsenal of the Hitler state'. Germany now became aware of the instruments which in the years to follow would define the terror of the SS: the seemingly all-powerful network of secret police and informers, the concentration camp system, and the deployment of totally committed elite troops, personally loyal to Hitler.

> To us the SS were small beer, only there to protect the top people. Right up to 1938 I never had any worries about the influence of the SS.
>
> *Paul Tollmann, communist and prisoner of the SA in 1933*
>
> I used to see the SS in those days and there weren't many of them. But you always had the impression that the SS was better organised than the SA, that they were a disciplined force. The SA on the other hand was more a kind of unruly mob.
>
> *Josef Zander, then living in Bad Godesberg*

The history of the SS had begun eleven years earlier in the bowling-alley of a smoke-laden Munich beer-house. The men in the back room kept on ordering more rounds. They waited until the barmaids had left the room, then they raised their glasses to the man whose picture now adorned quite a number of restaurants and bars in Munich: Adolf Hitler. They dedicated to him the one thing which, after the war, they believed they still possessed: 'We swear to you our loyalty unto death.' That bibulous night in May 1923 saw the birth of the *Stosstrupp Hitler*. Having grown out of a recently founded bodyguard force known as the *Stabswache* (Staff Guard), those founding members had no idea that they would form the nucleus of the 'Black Order' who, like the legendary

Nibelungs, would be faithful to the bitter end. As late as 1942 the Führer gushed with exaggerated romanticism about the 'men who were ready for revolutionary deeds and knew that one day the chips would be down'.

Die Nationalstrolchisten	The National 'So-shallow-ists'

A satirical poem by the Berlin journalist Hardy Worm, 1932

Anjetreten! Held markieren!	Fall in, lads! Act the hero!
Und Proleten massakrieren!	And massacre all the proles!
Saal umstellen! Blut muss fliessen!	Trash the hall, 'cos blood must flow!
Janze Blase niederschiessen!	Shoot down the whole damn crew!
Jeist ist Dreck, mit Dolch und Knüppel	Brains are crap, use blades and cudgels
Arjument der Geisteskrüppel,	to argue with mental cripples.
Haun sie ein auf jeden Mann	Lay into each and every one,
Wenn er sich nicht wehren kann.	If he cannot hold his own.
Phrasen dreschen, Mord ausbrüten	Wallop the wordsmiths, cultivate slaughter
Wie die wilde Tiere wüten!	Rant and rage like wild beasts oughta!
Das, nur das kann diese Horde,	That's about all this rabble can offer,
Stets bereit zum Meuchlmorde!	Always up for a cowardly murder!
Wenn's bezahlt jibt und die Pässe	When it's time to pay up or show your pass
Haun sie jeden vor die Fresse	They kick every one of us up the arse.
Jeld her! Die Kanone kracht!	Give us yer cash! Bang goes the gun!
Nachher ham se nischt jemacht.	In the end they've got nothing done.

By contrast the reality was rather bizarre. A stationer named Josef Berchtold, whose diminutive size scarcely matched the ideal image of the gigantic SS man, joined forces with the deputy cashier of the Nazi Party, Julius Schreck, and together they assembled a total of twenty men. One of them was Emil Maurice, an 'old campaigner' who later saw the light. He was a watch-maker with a previous conviction for embezzlement. Then there was Christian Weber, a horse-dealer, and the butcher and amateur wrestler Ulrich Graf. They made up a secretive club of First World War veterans, unwilling to allow outsiders any knowledge of the inner workings of the bodyguard force. Even then, their obedience was un-questioning; they only accepted orders from Hitler himself. Their sole task was to protect his life; wherever he appeared in public his new bodyguard was on hand. They followed him like a shadow on his tours of Munich's beer-cellars. Soon the group grew to over 150 men. The only recruits accepted were ones who had 'proved' themselves in the meeting-hall brawls of post-revolutionary Munich. Their simple motto was 'Might is Right', and they 'convinced' their opponents with 'erasers' and 'lighters', as they jokingly named their rubber cudgels and pistols. Their uniform was adorned with a special symbol: 'On our black caps we wear the skull as a warning to our enemies and to show the Führer that we dedicate our lives to his ideal', a later SS organiser, Alois Rosenwink, explained.

The death's-head symbol had been borrowed from elite units of the regular army. For centuries it had been considered a sign of particular loyalty to the unit commander. The 'Black' Hussars of Prussia's soldier-king wore the skull on their caps, as did the 1st Guard Reserve Pioneer Regiment in the First World War. They had operated far in advance of the infantry with a new type of weapon, the use of which demanded courage – and the killer instinct. The flame-thrower became one of the most feared weapons in that war. Death in the trenches and the large-scale annihilation of the enemy were idealised by the veterans as a purifying 'storm of steel', which gave a meaning and direction to their own existence. On 28 June 1916 Crown Prince Wilhelm of Prussia, as commander of an army group, ceremonially conferred on the unit the right to wear the white death's head on their sleeve – the highest award in his gift. In congratulating them he said: 'In the toughest situations officers and men have always put their weapon to effective use and in a short time succeeded in becoming the Frenchman's most feared opponent in close combat. I am quite sure that the outward emblem of this young force will always remain an exhortation to continue its development in the spirit of death-defying relish for battle.'

'Death-defying relish for battle' under the sign of the skull: it was with this attitude from the trenches of the First World War that the shock troopers proposed to topple the hated republic. 'These were simple men. Deep down they had remained soldiers', says the former SS man Robert Krötz, who met the members of the *Stosstrupp* in Munich. 'Some of the *Stosstrupp* men were brutal psychopaths, though you would not guess it to look at them; others were relatively moderate', recalls Munich lawyer Otto Gritschneder. 'But they were all totally dependent on Hitler.' Like so many, they too believed the Treaty of Versailles was a 'shameful peace', concluded by the 'November criminals' who had attacked Germany from behind. In Munich a number of people had got together, united by their loathing of the new republic. The chaos of the short-lived 'Soviet republic' in Bavaria had further fuelled hatred among the right-wing revolutionaries for the new form of government, and they eagerly absorbed the promises of this seductive new orator. In 1923, when inflation took hold, a litre of beer in the SS's favourite hostelry, the Torbräu, cost several *billion* marks. The money they had earned in the morning was, by that evening, worth nothing. As they saw it, the job of guarding Hitler lifted these men from the bowling-alley, from a humdrum existence, to the rank of an elite, a kind of combat force. They attributed this to what the First World War had taught them: loyalty, obedience and the cheapness of life.

In Munich from 1921 to 1923 political tension was running very high.

Karl Füss, then living in Munich

The mood in the hall was far from enthusiastic; it was more one of alarm. Or perhaps people just didn't know what these men actually wanted.

Günther Grassmann, eye-witness of the Munich putsch

We demand the abolition of the mercenary force and the creation of a people's army.

From the 25-point programme of the NSDAP, 1920

Scarcely six months had elapsed since the oath of loyalty was sworn at the Torbräu, when Hitler mounted his first attempt to overthrow the hated government. The exchange-rate for $1 had now reached 420 billion German marks. People's patience was exhausted, and the situation appeared to favour a 'national revolution'.

On the evening of 8 November, Bavaria's ruling triumvirate, von Kahr, von Lossow and von Seisser, had called a public meeting in Munich's Bürgerbräu beer-hall. Hitler intended to use this occasion to launch a coup d'état, by breaking up the meeting and then, as Mussolini had done in Italy the previous year, forcing politicians and army officers to join a 'march on red Berlin'. The former infantryman knew he had a star of the right wing on his side; the authority of the former Quartermaster-General of the imperial army, Erich von Ludendorff, would be Hitler's best argument against Kahr.

On the morning of 8 November a heavy grey sky hung over the Bavarian capital, when Hitler mobilised his shock troops – 'the vanguard of Germany's awakening', as he called them. In the Torbräu Josef Berchtold briefed his men on the plans for the putsch: 'Comrades, the moment we have all been longing for has arrived. Hitler and Herr von Kahr have reached agreement; this very evening the government will be overthrown and a new Hitler–Ludendorff–Kahr government will be formed. The action to be carried out by us will be the initial impetus for these new events. But before I go, I want to ask anyone who has any reservations at all about our cause to leave now.' No-one made a move.

From a secret armoury in Balanstrasse the men equipped themselves with machine-guns, carbines and hand-grenades, and then moved off in the direction of Rosenheimer Strasse. When they reached the Bürgerbräu the heavily armed storm-troopers jumped down from their trucks and blocked the street. Berchtold heaved a machine-gun from the back of the truck and dragged it up to the entrance of the beer-hall. From the running-board of an open car jumped an SA officer named Hermann Göring. With a steel helmet on his head and brandishing a sabre, he ran up the steps of the tradesmen's entrance. This bizarre picture was typical of the entire beer-hall putsch, which was doomed never to extend beyond the city centre of Munich.

So then of course I went to the Bürgerbräu and there I saw these people suddenly appear. They had swastika armbands and carried guns. They were in civilian clothes, but most of them were already forming up in groups with their rifles.

Karl Füss, then living in Munich

Inside the Bürgerbräu Hitler was waiting outside the door of the hall, preparing to make his entrance. His pocket-watch showed 8.30 p.m. He snapped it shut, took a last swig of beer and, in a theatrical gesture, threw the glass against the wall. Then he pulled a Browning revolver from his trouser pocket, flung open the swing-doors and stormed in with his retinue. Posted around him, as well as Göring, was the SA student leader Rudolf Hess, flanked by *Stosstrupp* men. Hitler jumped on to a chair and fired a shot into the ceiling, then clambered over a table and on to the stage. 'The national revolution has broken out!' he shouted. In a voice cracking with emotion, he continued: 'The building is occupied by 600 heavily armed men. No-one may leave this hall. The Bavarian government has been deposed, and a provisional government is being formed.'

At the same time another 'national revolutionary' had called a public meeting in the Löwenbräu beer-cellar. Ernst Röhm, an army captain in the First World War, greeted comrades in his paramilitary force, the *Reichskriegsflagge*, with a solemn promise: 'This evening's meeting', he said cryptically, 'will go beyond the limits of a normal old comrades' get-together.' He was inveighing in customary style against the 'November criminals' and the 'Jews' republic', when the news from the Bürgerbräu reached him. 'Successful birth' was the coded message. Röhm was in on the plot. Without hesitation he despatched his men in the direction of the regional HQ of the regular army. His job was to occupy the building and set up a 'headquarters' there for General Ludendorff.

Ernst Röhm was one of those men who found his destiny in war. His autobiography, *History of a Traitor*, began with the sentence: 'On 23 July 1906 I became a soldier.' Before that date

The impression he made was hardly trustworthy. A thoroughly brutish bully-boy type, like someone on the police's 'wanted' list.

Description of Röhm by Raban von Canstein, Wehrmacht officer

The leading figures came from the imperial German army and the Reichswehr. But the men in the ranks were recruited from the working class – unemployed people, who were given boots and clothing.

Paul Tollmann, communist, about the SA

he seemed not to have had a life at all. 'I view the world from my standpoint as a soldier. Consciously one-sided. A soldier knows no compromise.' He despised civilians; and being homosexual he loathed the bourgeoisie and their taboos. He romanticised the all-male community of the storm-troopers in the First World War as the ideal form of existence. Later he even saw it as the nucleus of a vague kind of 'socialism of the trenches'. The battle-hardened Röhm had a reputation for toughness. When fighting on the Meuse in the autumn of 1914 a shell-fragment had left him with a scar from nose to chin, which marked him for the rest of his life. In addition to this, his nose was misshapen as the result of a facial operation. All this combined to give him the appearance of a seventeenth-century *Landsknecht*, one of the mercenaries who fought in the Thirty Years War.

In postwar Bavaria he quickly found his feet as armourer of the Freikorps Epp, a force of irregulars that went into action against the reviled *Räterepublik*, the communist-inspired government which briefly ruled Bavaria in 1919. Later he supplied arms to extremist movements all over Germany, and thus united many strands of the anti-democratic right. He belonged to a number of associations of ex-imperial army officers, including the nationalist club known as 'Iron Fist', which he co-founded. It was here, in the autumn of 1919, that he met Adolf Hitler for the first time. From this meeting a complex relationship soon developed. Though they were on first-name terms, the seeds of mutual distrust took root at an early stage.

In June 1921, about two years before the founding of the *Stosstrupp*, Hitler, as the new chairman of the NSDAP, called for a force of toughs who would initially be there to protect him at public meetings. Röhm's militant war veterans seemed made for the job. Given the task of enforcing order, the unit was named the *Sturmabteilung* (Assault Section), or SA for short. Röhm and his associates recruited a rapidly growing band of raw-boned young men, mostly between the ages of seventeen and twenty-four, and led by officers who had fought in the First World War. In its founding declaration on 3 August 1921, the SA undertook 'to serve the Nazi Party as an organisation of iron resolve and gladly show obedience to the Führer'. The men soon earned an unpleasant reputation. Anyone heard raising objections to Hitler at meetings or in the street was bludgeoned to the ground without mercy. Outwardly Hitler and the SA seemed as one.

At the same time, however, a deeply rooted conflict underlay the relationship between the SA and its shadowy strongman on one hand, and Hitler and the Nazi Party on the other. It was not long before Hitler began to suspect Röhm of excessive political ambition. For his part, Röhm regarded the Nazi Party as nothing more than a recruiting organisation for his SA, which in the future he planned to deploy as a full-scale militia. He saw Hitler chiefly as an effective publicist, drumming up mass support for his private army. In 1922 Röhm said of Hitler: 'We must exploit his undoubtedly powerful impact. But he is a lightweight, and his vision does not extend beyond the borders of Germany. When the time comes we will put him aside.' Whereas Hitler regarded himself exclusively as a politician, Röhm thought of himself as a political soldier: 'I demand the soldier's primacy over the politician', he later wrote in his autobiography. The seeds of conflict were sown; thirteen years later it was to burst forth.

Although Hitler installed 'his man', Hermann Göring, as 'commandant' of the SA, Röhm remained the driving force. The men of the SA were not subject to Hitler's direct orders, and so his position was vulnerable. It was his realisation of this that gave Hitler the idea of forming the *Stosstrupp*, a bodyguard answerable to no-one but himself, to whom it would owe exclusive loyalty. The bloody end to the putsch of November 1923 would also give birth to the legend surrounding the *Stosstrupp*, from which the myth of the SS would grow.

Hitler's coup was planned on naïve assumptions. State Commissioner von Kahr was able to leave the Bürgerbräu without hindrance. He had no further interest in starting discussions with Hitler. Nor did the Reichswehr have any intention of making common cause with the rebels – quite the reverse. The following morning, 9 November, large detachments of Reichswehr troops and provincial police assembled outside the old War Ministry. It was only a question of time before Röhm's soldiery would be forced to surrender. A photo exists showing how the occupiers now became the besieged. It is the first appearance on the political stage of a pale-faced man with wire-rimmed glasses, though it seemed he was only to have a walk-on part. The young Heinrich Himmler, then employed as a fertiliser salesman, had joined the ranks of the *Reichskriegsflagge*, and was an ardent admirer of Ernst Röhm. Eleven years later, as Reichsführer-SS, he would organise the execution of the SA leadership and the slaying of his former mentor.

The euphoria of the 'revolutionaries' in the Bürgerbräu evaporated in the cold light of the following morning. In a final burst of enthusiasm General Ludendorff gave the order: 'Forward march!' By marching through the city they would attract attention, win the support of the masses and succeed in liberating Röhm and his men. '*Stosstrupp* assemble in the garden', Berchtold ordered his men. He swore them in once more. Then the procession formed up.

On Odeonsplatz, near the Feldherrnhalle military memorial, a company of Bavarian state police had already taken up positions. In a surprise move the marchers overran the first line of policemen, who tried to defend themselves with rubber truncheons, carbines and rifles. When the procession ignored the order to halt, a second police unit intervened. One Ulrich Graf, wearing the death's-head badge of Hitler's bodyguard, leaped between the two lines and shouted: 'Don't shoot, His Excellency Ludendorff and Hitler are coming.' His appeal was drowned out in the general clamour. A shot rang out across Odeonsplatz, and a man in uniform, Police Constable Fink, fell to the ground. Then rifle salvoes echoed through the streets in an exchange of fire that lasted for about a minute. A friend of Hitler's, Max Erwin von Scheubner-Richter, was mortally wounded by a bullet. As he fell he pulled Hitler with him, dislocating his arm. Graf was also wounded and collapsed on the ground beside his leader. From this incident the legend grew up later that Graf had thrown his body in front of Hitler and received the bullet that would otherwise have killed his leader. Of the sixteen insurgents killed that day, no fewer than five were members of Hitler's *Stosstrupp*.

The miserable end of this 'revolution' marked the birth of a myth. On the Odeonsplatz a bloodstained swastika flag was left behind. The 'Banner of Blood', as the Nazis later called it, at first disappeared into the vaults of the Munich police headquarters. Later on, the amateurish attempt to overthrow the government would be romantically transformed into the self-sacrifice of the 'old campaigners'. From 1933 onward the SS mounted a 'Guard of Honour' at the Feldherrnhalle. It was there, on 30 April 1945, that the last SS men were captured by American soldiers.

In that year, 1923, the swastikas, the storm-troopers and the name of Adolf Hitler almost disappeared into oblivion once more. No-one thought of him any longer as a potential factor in the struggle for power.

Stefan Zweig in Yesterday's World

After the failed putsch of 1923 the NSDAP broke up. It was five years before the party was back on its feet again.

Emil Carlebach, then a member of the German Communist Party

Hitler had several previous convictions. And if the court had not been so stupid as to release him early, he would have sat in jail until at least '29 or '30. By then it would all have been over anyway.

Otto Gritschneder, Munich lawyer

Calm did not return to the Bavarian capital. While Hitler sat out his sentence in the considerable comfort of Landsberg Castle, the restless Ernst Röhm was busy in Munich once more building up an effective paramilitary force. Both the Nazi Party and the SA were outlawed, and so he formed a new organisation, disguised as an athletic association and named the *Frontbann*. Under his strict command, Röhm gathered together the forces sympathetic to National Socialism. His brigade grew with a speed that can only be described as explosive. Whereas in November 1923 the SA could claim 2,000 members, by December 1924 when his awkward friend Hitler was released from Landsberg, Röhm could proudly report that the *Frontbann* numbered 30,000 men.

Röhm wanted to go on in the same old way, with himself as leader of the paramilitary troops. In future Hitler was simply to play the part of the 'drummer'. But his old friend seemed to have learnt the lesson of the early years. Hitler certainly did not want to be exposed once more to the vagaries of a party army whose unruly behaviour was beyond any control. And without the support of the party, Röhm was forced to knuckle under. On 30 April 1925, shortly after the lifting of the ban on the NSDAP and the SA, he had no choice but to say to Hitler: 'In memory of the wonderful times and the hard times we have lived through together, [I want] to thank you heartily for your comradeship, and to ask you not to deny me your personal friendship.'

A month later Röhm found the reason for Hitler's decision lying on his desk in black and white. It was a memo from his friend's office informing him that 'Herr Hitler is not planning to raise a new armed movement. If he did so in the past, it was only at the instigation of the gentlemen who later abandoned him. Today he merely requires protection at public meetings, as was the case before 1923.' It was a straightforward snub. After that Röhm tried with little success to make a career in civilian life. In 1928 he exiled himself to Bolivia, where he provided training for the Bolivian army.

With characteristic awareness of a dangerous competitor, Hitler manoeuvred his supposed friend out of the picture for the first time. During Hitler's spell in prison Röhm had built up the *Frontbann* massively. By the time the 'Führer' made his come-back, Röhm's *Frontbann* was many times more powerful than the Nazi Party. The militia had succeeded in doing what the party still had to achieve: to gain significance beyond the borders of Bavaria. Once again the NSDAP was in danger of being overshadowed by the SA. But now Hitler had robbed the SA of its charismatic focal point. The organisation still existed, of course, but lacked any central leadership. What remained was a geographically fragmented party army, incapable of cohesive action. For the time being it was sidelined as a factor in power politics. Now Hitler could get on with asserting his claim on leadership virtually unchallenged. He only placed his trust in those he sought out himself.

> The SA is the line infantry, the SS is the regiment of guards. There have always been palace guards: the Persians had them, the Greeks had them, so did Caesar, Napoleon, and the Prussian kings, right up to the Great War. And the guards of the new Germany will be the SS.
>
> *Heinrich Himmler*

> The word 'elite' was never mentioned, but for us it was a distinction just to be in the *Schutzstaffel Adolf Hitler*. I pictured myself among those in the very front rank.
>
> *Bruno Hähnel, former SS man*

> No SA officer is entitled to issue orders to the SS.
>
> *Adolf Hitler, 1930*

Years later Hitler explained the decision he reached in April 1925: 'I said to myself at the time that I would need a bodyguard which, though small, would be unquestioningly dedicated to me and would even go into action against their own brothers. Better to have just 20 man from a single city – provided they could be relied upon absolutely – rather than an unreliable mass.' He gave orders to the old shock trooper, Julius Schreck, to establish a new bodyguard. Schreck did as he was told and knew where to begin his search. In Munich's Torbräu beer-hall he gathered the 'old comrades' around him. The name which the troop adopted in September fitted the Führer's requirements at the time: *Schutzstaffel*, 'Protection Squadron', or SS for short.

Like the *Stosstrupp*, the SS saw itself from the outset as an 'elite', owing unquestioning allegiance to the Führer. The recruitment criteria were certainly reminiscent of Germany's rigorous and nationalistic *Turnvereine* (gymnastic associations) of the early nineteenth century. 'Chronic drinkers, busybodies and those afflicted with other vices will not be considered', the initial SS guidelines stated. In contrast to the SA, which continued to accept more or less anybody, applicants for the SS always had to submit to a selection procedure. They had to be aged between twenty-three and thirty-five, be able to provide two personal guarantors, be registered residents in the same area for five years, and be 'healthy and powerfully built'. SS formations were created in other cities as well as Munich. The SS was not intended to be a mass movement like the SA, but simply a small elite force, with units of ten men under one officer. Only in Berlin were the units twenty-strong, under two officers. The SS was formally attached to the SA, and wore the same brown shirt. Its only outward distinction was the cap and the armband with a black-bordered swastika. At first the small number of SS men seemed like a silent escort to the brown-shirted columns. Their rules of conduct were more reminiscent of a monastic order than a military unit. An order issued by the Reichsführer-SS, Erhard Heiden, in 1927 reads: 'The SS never participates in discussions at members' meetings. For the duration of the lecture no SS man shall smoke and none is allowed to leave the building. The purpose of these evenings is political education. The SS man must remain silent and never become involved in a matter that does not concern him' (a reference to the SA and local political leadership).

The SS seldom attracted any public attention, even when it took part in brawling, as it did in Dresden, where SS men at a party meeting beat off an attack by fifty communists. Rosenwink, the local SS leader, boasted that no leftist would dare to disturb them, 'ever since . . . the combined *Schutzstaffel* of Dresden, Plauen, Zwickau and Chemnitz not only gave the communists a frightful beating, but also threw some of them out of the window'. In 1929 the Munich police noted approvingly the discipline 'that is demanded of SS men. Even the slightest infringement of orders, according to current SS regulations, is threatened with cash fines, the withdrawal of the armband for a specified period, or dismissal from the service. Particular emphasis is placed on the conduct and dress of the individual SS man.' Every time a check was made, SS men were found to be carrying a Nazi Party card, an SS identity card – and a songbook. In 1929 no leading upholder of Weimar democracy would have objected to these lines from an SS song:

> When all are becoming disloyal
> We ourselves stay true
> So that for ever on this soil
> A flag will fly for you.

At an early stage Hitler cultivated the myth surrounding his *Schutzstaffel*. At the national rally of the Nazi Party at Weimar in 1926 he ceremoniously placed the 'Banner of Blood', since returned to the party, 'in the loyal hands' of the SS. From then on, SS *Truppführer* Jakob Grimminger could be seen carrying the banner behind Hitler at crass initiation rituals. The SS was now officially the elite guard of the brownshirt movement. Meanwhile, following Röhm's departure, the SA was plunged into its first major crisis. Small local units often acted independently. Not until the middle of 1926, when the party made new political gains, did Hitler see that the time had come to act more decisively.

With the help of the black-clad guards great things were to be achieved later on, but in order to get to that point he also needed the massed brown-shirt battalions, They proved to be indispensable in the overwhelming propaganda assault.

Hitler made his bid to centralise and control the SA on 27 July 1926. He recruited a popular Freikorps veteran for the job. Goebbels noted succinctly in his diary: 'To see the boss at

Lied der SS	Song of the SS
SS marschiert, die Strasse frei!	March on, SS, the road is clear!
Die Sturmkolonnen stehen!	The storm-troop ranks stand firm!
Sie werden aus der Tyrannei	Freed from the grip of tyranny
Den Weg der Freiheit gehen.	They'll tread the path to liberty.
Drum auf, bereit zum letzten Stoss!	So up and ready for the final thrust,
Wie's unsere Väter waren!	Just as our fathers were.
Der Tod sei unser Kampfgenoss'	Let death be our comrade-in-arms,
Wir sind die schwarzen Scharen!	We are the black-clad hordes!

noon. Our first discussion. Pfeffer is to be Reich leader of the SA.' Franz Pfeffer von Salomon knew the potential of his troops. Admittedly he fought shy of creating a militia on the Röhm model, but neither did he accept the need to subordinate the SA slavishly to the Nazi Party. The troops of the *Sturmabteilung* were admittedly under Hitler's authority, yet Pfeffer developed an independent stance in a way that Hitler could not have intended. The party and the SA were still at odds. The conflict simmered on; it was only the common struggle for political power that for the moment prevented open warfare from breaking out. The SA was now a large-scale organisation. Regardless of the leadership crisis, the economic slump of 1929 brought it new recruits in droves. Wherever an open space could be found, the Nazi Party's army staged parades and other events. Everywhere the 'brown battalions' were on the march. Their military demeanour and omnipresence made an impression on the population, especially in those parts of Germany where hitherto politicians had seldom strayed. Politics was something that happened in big cities, and an event there reached significantly more people than a tour through country villages. But it was in rural areas that the SA raised its colours – with success. Goebbels noted in his diary: 'People began to talk about us. No longer could they walk past us in stony silence or with a look of icy contempt. They were forced, unwillingly and inwardly seething, to mention us by name.'

It was especially their political opponents in the big cities who were 'inwardly seething' at having to speak the name of the Nazi Party. Here naked terror reigned. As they had done before 1923, the SA broke up their opponents' meetings, beat up communists and Social Democrats and cleared the way for the NSDAP. As they did so they invoked noble aims: 'The SA is marching . . . for Goethe, for Schiller, for Kant, for Bach, for Cologne Cathedral. . . . Now we must work for Goethe with beer-mugs and chair-legs. And when we have won, well, then we will stretch out our arms once more and press our cultural heritage to our hearts.' It was phrases like these that Wilfried Bade, a poet of the 'movement', placed in the mouth of his 'hero', Horst Wessel.

Police reports about acts of violence by members of the SA became more numerous. One example took place at the 1929 national party congress in Nuremberg: 'We slept on straw and couldn't afford a beer between us. But that didn't matter; we were excited to be there', an SA man named Krötz still recalls with enthusiasm today. The truth is that they went on the rampage and beat people up. In military order an SA troop marched towards the field where the rally was being held, and blocked the tramcar lines. When a tram-driver ordered the troop to let his vehicle through, the SA thugs stormed on to the car and beat up the driver and several passengers. On the fringes of the rally the SA terrorised the city of Nuremberg with a series of acts of violence. A bar was demolished because it was flying the black, red and gold flag of the hated republic, another was subjected to a bombardment of beer-bottles because it was accommodating labour unionists. When a policeman tried to protect a man from being pursued by SA men, one of the gang wrenched his sabre from his hand and stabbed him in the back with it three times. Any accusations of unwarranted brutality were dismissed by Hitler in one sentence: 'The SA is not a moral institution for the education of well-bred young ladies, but a force of tough fighters.'

It was in Berlin more than anywhere that furious brawling between extremists on the left and right were a feature of street life. The brown-shirted hordes deliberately forced their way into communist neighbourhoods in order to cause trouble. In the 'red' district of Charlottenburg, they installed a *Sturm* in the midst of a dense network of communist vigilante groups, tenants' associations and meeting-rooms. Another hot-spot was the 'Red island' in the Schöneberg district. As if following a script, spurious disputes were sparked off time and again. The SA drove through the streets in trucks, shouting slogans and throwing stones at communist establishments. Communist Paul Tollmann describes how his people fought back: 'We had a definite tactic. First let the Nazis in, then close off the streets. And as far as possible prevent them from getting out again. If we'd only shouted insults at them they would certainly have come back again.' When the Nazis seized power in 1933 Tollmann was one of the SA's first torture victims.

The SA's job was to spread fear. The Social Democrats and communists had to get used to the idea that SA thugs would always turn up at their meetings.
Otto Gritschneder, Munich lawyer, about the SA before 1933

It was the unemployed who joined the SA, because there were handouts, they could get food and drink. That's how the SA recruited its members.
Paul Tollmann, communist and prisoner of the SA in 1933

It was chiefly after the Crash of 1929 that the urban working class joined the SA in large numbers. Many donned the brown uniform to escape from penury and family crises. In the regular haunts of the SA the myth grew up of the 'brown battalions' which, more than anything, offered a refuge to the rootless. A 21-year-old SA man wrote to a friend from prison: '*Please* don't keep sending my mother here. She always cries and that gets me going too. If she asks you, tell her I can only have visitors every four weeks, or something like that. I can't wait to see you and all my mates.' SA hostels and hangouts known as *Sturmlokale*, were the focus of an intense brown-shirt subculture in the big cities. In bars like the Bornholmer Hütte, in a down-at-heel part of central Berlin, a swastika flag hung in the gloomy tap-room. Bicycle patrols kept watch in the district; and the bar itself could quickly be barricaded from the inside. In no time, strangers became enemies, and a hiding-place was often provided in an adjoining room or in the bowling-alley, where a pistol could be hurriedly made to disappear 'if the cops turn up unexpectedly', as one contemporary report put it.

Alcohol was important in fuelling this all-male buddy culture. A claim for compensation made by a Berlin bar-owner, Robert Reissig, tells us a lot: when the Prussian Ministry of the Interior banned the SA in 1932, Reissig demanded payment for 152.5 *tons* of beer – consumed in just three months. Meanwhile the SS, supposedly their comrades, observed this behaviour and muttered behind their backs about the 'Lumpenproletariat' of the Nazi Party. 'They had no discipline', says Otto Kumm, from Hamburg, who joined the SS in 1931.

In Berlin especially, the boundaries between the SA and the underworld became blurred. Numerous petty criminals were given membership cards. In the working-class district of Wedding the *Räubersturm* (Robbers' Assault Force) attacked both the law and the communists. The *Official History of the Berlin SA* even paraded the notoriety of its thugs in the Neu-Kölln district. 'Over 3,000 red activists against barely 70 men of *Sturm* 25. But it is a *Sturm* of which 80 per cent are workers and roughnecks, hard men who know every trick in the book. The Berliners call them the "pimps' brigade".' In the Charlottenburg district the SA's notorious *Sturm* 33 held sway. Popularly known as the 'Murder Squad', members of this unit killed or severely wounded several people in a short time around the turn of the year 1930/1. It was on 22 November 1930 that members of the communist 'Falcon' hiking club were dancing at the Eden Palace ballroom, when twenty SA men burst in. With a battle-cry of 'Beat the dogs to death', they bludgeoned the dancers to the floor and fired indiscriminately into the crowd. Three workers were hit; they collapsed and lay in their own blood.

Shortly before the Nazis seized power, some SA men in Beuthen literally kicked a communist to death. There was a jury trial and the SA men received death sentences. When Hitler came to power, they were immediately pardoned because they were now classed as courageous fighters for the National Socialist cause.

Otto Gritschneder, Munich lawyer

This time the brown-shirted thugs ended up in court. The charges were attempted murder, breach of the peace and causing grievous bodily harm. A young attorney, Dr Hans Litten, handled the prosecution of four of the SS men – and achieved a minor sensation. On 8 May 1931 he summoned Adolf Hitler to the witness-stand in the criminal court of Berlin's Moabit district. As Litten himself claimed, he wanted to tear the mask from the face of National Socialism, and expose the terrorism at the heart of the Nazi ideology. He attempted to prove not only that the Nazi Party tolerated violence, but that terror was in fact the central element in party policy. The examination of the witness lasted two hours. At first Hitler remained calm; he repeated like a mantra: 'The SA is under the strictest orders to desist from attacks on people with different views.' Litten confronted Hitler with countless statements by the Gauleiter of Berlin, Joseph Goebbels, to the effect that opponents should be 'kicked to a pulp'. The longer the questioning went on, the more impatient Hitler grew. Finally he blew his top. Jumping up, he roared, red in the face: 'How do you make out, Mr Attorney, that this is an incitement to break the law? There is no evidence whatever for that statement!' Litten nonetheless secured a conviction against all the accused. At that moment he did not suspect that he was signing his own death-warrant. In 1933 Litten was one of the first to be taken into 'protective custody'. On 5 February 1938, after years of severe maltreatment and an endless journey from one concentration camp to another, the courageous lawyer took his own life in Dachau.

That violence really was the SA's most important method of propaganda can be deduced from the statistics of the SA insurance scheme. The name of its manager was Martin Bormann, the man who rose to become Hitler's secretary. He reported a drastic rise in the number of SA men 'wounded in the course of duty', from 110 in 1927 to 2,506 in 1930. The police reports show a similar picture. In 1929 the Prussian authorities registered 580 major disturbances, but that had risen to 2,500 in 1930 and as many as 5,300 in 1932. In the first half of 1932, 86 people died in the bloody election campaign, and 72 of these deaths occurred in the six weeks immediately prior to the elections.

> Two farm-workers from Oranienburg had boxed the ears of a
> Hitler Youth boy. They burst his eardrum and he had to run
> to central Berlin for treatment. The SA men made the two
> farm-workers run round outside the camp the same distance
> as the boy had to run to Berlin. When we came back from
> work to the camp in the evening, they were still running. We
> saw that the ground where they'd been running was covered
> in blood. The skin was hanging in shreds from their feet.
>
> *Arno Hausmann, imprisoned in Oranienburg*
> *concentration camp in 1933*

The strategy of violence was successful. The membership of the SA
kept on rising – despite deaths and injuries on their side as well.
Yet did this self-sacrifice on the party's behalf bring any reward to
the swelling ranks of the SA?

The enemy was now not just on the left. More and more SA
men saw opposition within the party and its leadership. They
spoke out against the 'party bigwigs' and the policy of legitimacy
they had adopted. 'Among the SA especially, there was hope of
change in a socialist direction. National Socialism – that meant
something to me. Everyone had to be nationalist in those days,
and "socialist" somehow had a ring of justice about it', Berliner
Herbert Crüger recalls, of the time when, as an adolescent, he
joined the SA front organisation, *Frontbann*. Sometimes they
even sought advice and information from communists about the
planned economy; the ranks of the red and the brown organised a
combined strike in protest against fare increases on Berlin's public
transport. Various SA formations were dubbed 'Beefsteaks': brown
on the outside, red on the inside. Vague ideas about 'Socialism'
were even expressed to their own party. As early as 1929 a slogan
began to appear in the *Sturmlokalen*: 'Adolf is betraying us
proletarians', and SA revolutionaries distributed leaflets attacking
the 'treachery of the party clique headed by Hitler'. The Führer
himself was the target of these clumsy verses:

Entschlossen, seinen Geldgebern dankbar zu sein,
stellt er seinen 'Kampf' gegen das Finanzkapital ein.
Was kümmern ihn des Volkes Sorgen
Was kümmert ihn, was wohl sein mag morgen?

(Determined to be grateful to his benefactors, he ceases his 'struggle' against financial capital. What does he care for the people's woes? What does he care what tomorrow may bring?)

Specific demands were made: 'Preserve the old ideals, do not tolerate the betrayal of socialism by self-interested lobby politicians, for whom the Party is only there to serve their own ends!' There was a torrent of ribaldry when Hitler acquired an expensive Mercedes as his new official car. 'We proletarian elements in the Party are really happy about it. We just love shovelling steam-coal, so that our dear leaders can live like princes on their monthly incomes of 2,000 to 5,000 marks. We were also highly delighted when we heard that our own Adolf Hitler went to the Berlin Motor Show and bought himself a big new Mercedes for 40,000 marks.'

In the end the SA demanded a reward for their cracked skulls and broken bones. The leader of the Berlin SA, Walter Stennes, though a deputy to Pfeffer von Salomon, went to Munich several times to demand the allocation of parliamentary seats to the SA. When the party leadership drew up the candidate list for the 1930 Reichstag elections, and once more failed to include Stennes, there was a furious outburst: the SA went on strike against the party. At a meeting in Berlin's Palace of Sport, the principal speaker, Gauleiter Goebbels, was rendered speechless when the SA refused to provide security in the hall and left him to get on with the meeting himself. Goebbels was the target of a demonstration by the party foot-soldiers, who headed for Wittenbergplatz. The SA openly threatened to 'break up the whole Goebbels circus with their bare fists'. Goebbels reacted swiftly. He called for assistance from the people who could be relied on; and the local SS, led by Kurt Daluege, took on the job of keeping order in the Palace of Sport. It was the first time that the party had openly deployed its own appointed guards against the 'comrades' of the SA. Revenge was not long in coming. Two days later, on 30 August, SA men attacked the SS mounting guard at the party headquarters in Berlin.

Hitler hurriedly travelled to Berlin and made a tour of the *Sturmlokale* in the capital. What he offered would go a substantial way towards meeting Stennes' demands. By 1 September the dispute appeared to be over for the moment. But once again Hitler had become acutely aware of the threat posed by the anarchic brown-shirts. Once again he attempted to discipline the troops and began searching for a successor to the retiring SA commander-in-chief, Pfeffer von Salomon. That was when an old colleague made a comeback that no-one had expected. Hitler's personal friend Ernst Röhm returned from Bolivia at the end of 1930. By putting him back in charge of the SA, Hitler believed he was making a clever move. Röhm still had an excellent reputation within the SA but seemed to have distanced himself from all the in-fighting. What Hitler did not know was that even from far away in South America, Röhm had been stirring things up against him. 'Dolf is an ass', he wrote in a schoolboyish postcard to a friend in 1928.

The SA man basically has nothing to do with politics. So he never has to deal with questions of day-to-day policy.
August Schneidhuber, SA-Obergruppenführer, November 1930

The SS has a conservative attitude; it protects reactionaries and the petty bourgeoisie. Its subordination to the army and traditional bureaucracy is too great.
Röhm to Himmler, 1934

Revolution is not a permanent condition, and must not be regarded as such. We must divert the free-flowing current of revolution into the secure river-bed of evolution.
Adolf Hitler in a speech to NSDAP officials, July 1933

Yet even Röhm was unable to rein in the SA as quickly as was hoped. The disgruntled rebels were not going to knuckle under so easily. A year after the uproar over Stennes, leaflets began circulating again: 'National Socialists of Berlin! The Gauleiter of Berlin, Dr Joseph Goebbels, has been relieved of his post due to a breach of trust.' It was essential to 'prevent the party from betraying the SA and National Socialism. The SA is on the march, Stennes is taking command.' The leader of the Berlin SA, Walter Stennes, had once again demanded parliamentary seats for SA members. And once again the party turned him down. So Stennes issued a threat: 'In the long run nobody can rule with impunity against the opinions of the great majority of the people – in this case against the mood of the SA.'

Political opponents watched in astonishment as the Nazi Party appeared to be breaking up in a grotesque factional wrangle. Stennes won the support of almost all the SA commanders in the north and east of Germany for a coup against the party leadership in Munich. Hitler anticipated this and dismissed Stennes on 31 March 1931. But the dissident brownshirt did not give up. The SA took over the party, which for its part excluded the SA rebels. However, as the war-chest of the chronically hard-up SA emptied, the revolt slowly ran into the sand. The SA was swept clean of Stennes supporters and their structure was smashed. When the Nazis came to power Stennes was arrested by the SS, and only released on Göring's insistence. Later he made a new career as head of the bodyguard of the Chinese head of state, General Chiang Kai-Shek.

I always found the SS arrogant. They were our enemies. In 1940 I was ordered to join the *Waffen*-SS. I didn't like that at all, being an old SA type. But then I realised they were of a different calibre, everything was much stricter, much more disciplined. Naturally, I was impressed.

Robert Krötz, in the SA 1930–40, member of the Leibstandarte Adolf Hitler, 1940–5.

The young always look for novelty, whether on the right or left, just as long as it is something exciting. Nowadays one would say: where the action is. We were fascinated by the idea of race. The early SS was an elite, which was geared not just to racial purity but to purity as a way of life.

Luise Rinser, author

After the Stennes putsch the standing of the SS continued to rise. It was said that they stood behind Hitler to a man. And as the official historian of the SS, Heinz Höhne, wrote, Hitler only had 'the watchfulness of his *Schutzstaffel*' to thank for his victory over Stennes. From now on the SS adopted the motto which Himmler had given them after the dramatic events of 1932: 'SS-man, loyalty is thine honour.'

As the Reichsführer-SS gloated at a meeting: 'We aren't popular everywhere. After certain things we may have to do, we'll be sent to stand in the corner; we can expect no thanks. But our Führer knows what he has in the SS. We're his favourite and most valued organisation, because we've never disappointed him yet.' Many in the party underestimated the small, sallow man with rather large pince-nez; he was scarcely known to the general public. In newsreels he was seen in the third row behind Hitler and Röhm. Yet Heinrich Himmler, who on 9 November 1923 had carried a banner for Röhm, was no respecter of friendship when it came to career and power. Hardly anyone suspected that behind the amiable if schoolmasterly Bavarian exterior, behind the man whom war veterans tended to laugh at as an 'anti-soldier', there lurked a skilled tactician who played a long game in his quest for power. At every opportunity, he now pointed the way forward: 'The SA are the line infantry, the SS are the guards.'

Himmler's promotion became the turning-point in the history of the SS. From the day he took up his post in 1929 recruitment soared. At the beginning of that year the SS had 280 members; by the end of the following year its strength had increased tenfold. By 1931 close on 15,000 men wore the death's-head badge on their cap. Himmler further refined the already strict selection criteria and for the first time laid down regulations in an ideological form. 'The SS is a unit of German men of Nordic type, selected according to particular characteristics', we read in the 'Duties of the SS man regarding engagement and marriage', issued on 31 December 1931. It goes on: 'Every SS man who plans to marry must obtain an authorisation of matrimony from the Reichsführer.' Selective breeding was the only way to maintain 'good blood'. The regulations ended with the phrase, 'the future belongs to us'.

Now, however, the 'Black Order' was not merely attracting lower middle-class war veterans, but increasingly people whom the ramshackle democracy had filled with a kind of cultural disgust; men who, though too young to have fought in the trenches, felt drawn by the harshness and romanticism of combat experience. 'I saw only one hope for a prostrated Germany', says Otto Kumm from Hamburg, 'and that was Hitler. First I joined the SA; that was the obvious thing to do. But that was too soft for me, too inadequate. The SS only took specially selected men.' In Goethe's home city of Weimar, Horst Mauersberger was thrilled with the idea of the SS, even as a schoolboy. Later Mauersberger carried Goethe's *Faust* in his uniform pocket: to this day his son Volker owns his father's much-thumbed and heavily annotated edition. 'All my life', he says, 'I have wrestled with the question: how could it be that a man from such a respectable home, with those humanist ideals, with those visions and aspirations, ended up in the SS.' He blames the 'bourgeois elite of Weimar' for turning the young man into a dreamer and an extremist – and for making it possible for the Ettersberg hill, outside Weimar, where Goethe liked to go and seek inspiration, to became known to history under a very different name: Buchenwald. For a few years later the notorious concentration camp became the 'workplace' for Horst Mauersberger, who by then held the SS rank of *Scharführer*.

Quite a number of applicants to the SS thought like the Swiss doctor, Franz Riedweg. He was an early supporter of Nazi Germany, because he believed that it would provide a 'bulwark against communism'. 'Himmler's idea of breeding an elite made a lot of sense', he still maintains today. 'Dedication to a grand ideal – that was what attracted us. It was like a monarchy, where leading figures provide role-models.' Later, when Germany invaded the Soviet Union, Riedweg would recruit foreign volunteers for the *Waffen*-SS.

But there was something even more important: behind the mask of ideology, Himmler went on rehearsing for the final round in the struggle for power. He reshaped the SS from Hitler's bodyguard into an omnipresent party police force. In the early days there were few occasions when he was so frank about his intentions as on a train journey in the spring of 1929, which Albert Krebs, the Gauleiter of Hamburg, later recalled. In politics, what matters are the hidden details, Himmler said. How, for example, did the SA leader Conn come by his odd name, reminiscent of the Jewish 'Cohn', and what made the Gauleiter Lohse, a former banker, become dependent on Jewish capital? Krebs was treated to 'a strange mixture of martial bombast, small-town saloon-bar prattle, and the prophetic zeal of a nonconformist preacher'. What he failed to appreciate, like so many others, was the enormous staying-power and total lack of scruple with which Himmler pursued his objectives.

In the summer of 1931, Himmler took on to his staff the dishonourably discharged naval intelligence officer, Reinhard Heydrich. Before long, the rather random collecting of reports from within the party, which the SS had engaged in since its creation, developed into an elaborate network of informers. In the Brown House, the party headquarters in Munich, information was gathered for the newly founded '1c service', intended to unmask 'hostile spies' in the party. Here, old loyalties counted for little. The SS now marched completely to Hitler's tune, even 'against their own brothers', who had shown themselves to be so unreliable.

Not even the additional measures taken by Ernst Röhm were sufficient to calm the situation. The revolutionary mood of the SA continued to smoulder, and the dissension was further fuelled by the personal predilections of the SA's new chief-of-staff. Röhm made no secret of his homosexuality, and the sexual proclivities of his closest colleagues had also been public knowledge for a long time. In letters to a Berlin doctor named Heimsoth, Röhm expressed himself in unambiguous terms: 'I am engaged in an intense dispute with Herr Alfred Rosenberg, the muddle-headed champion of morality. His articles are aimed at me more than anyone, since I make no secret of my orientation. You may judge from this that where I am concerned "people" in Nazi circles have had to get used to my criminal nature.'

An affaire that Röhm had with a Berlin gigolo named Hermann Siegesmund came to the notice of the law, when the SA leader reported the rent-boy for the theft of his suitcase. In the record of a district court in Berlin we read: 'On 13 January 1925 Röhm offered to buy Siegesmund a glass of beer in the Marienkasino in Berlin, and then proposed the kind of activity that normally follows a pick-up of that kind.' Siegesmund gave evidence as follows: 'While we were sitting in the hotel bedroom, still fully dressed, Herr Röhm took a packet of cigarettes from his pocket. As he did so, I noticed a piece of paper drop to the floor and picked it up. After about half an hour I left the hotel room, because Herr Röhm asked me to perform a disgusting sex-act, which I could not agree to. It was not until I was out in the street again that I noticed that the slip of paper I had taken from the room was Herr Röhm's left-luggage ticket.'

The lower ranks of the SA often had a good laugh about their boss's homosexuality. One leaflet recommended to the party leadership that in winter Röhm should be used to 'warm up' the Brown House. ['Warm' is a German slang term for homosexual. *Tr.*] As for the new uniform being designed for Röhm's bodyguards, the anonymous authors called for riding-breeches 'with a fully functioning zip-fastener and an inside leg of 175 (an allusion to Clause 175 of the law on homosexuality)'. Gradually, friends of Röhm were put into some of the posts left vacant after the Stennes revolt. These men shared not only the political views of their chief-of-staff but also his homoerotic leanings. Rumours abounded about organised sex-rings and orgies in Munich and Berlin. Yet Hitler persisted in rejecting 'in the strongest terms, as pure speculation', all complaints about the dissolute lifestyle of the SA leadership. He still needed Röhm.

Then in April 1932 an obscure murder plot against Röhm and his friends emerged from within the party and made headlines. Its originator was the party's chief internal arbitrator and 'moral guardian', Walter Buch. Fearing for their lives, senior SS officers had spilled the beans to the police about the threat from Nazi 'comrades'. To Himmler, the SS chief, who would have preferred to keep the whole business under wraps as an internal party matter, this was an 'unpardonable breach of trust'. It ended with the instigators being put on trial, when further unsavoury details came to light. This was as much as the party moralists could stomach. Buch's son-in-law, Martin Bormann, complained in a letter to Rudolf Hess: 'This has completely knocked the bottom out of everything. One of the most prominent people in the party ticks off the equally prominent leader of his chief opponents . . . and refers to his own party colleagues, who are also senior officers, as *Schweinehunde*.' On the other hand, as Bormann wrote in reference to the Praetorian Guard in the Brown House: 'Take a look at the SS, you know Himmler and you know Himmler's capabilities.' The more unruly appeared the behaviour of the SA, from the rank-and-file right up to the leadership, the more clearly apparent was the *esprit de corps* of Himmler's more tightly run force. When and on whom the fatal blow would be struck in the power struggle between the SA and the SS was now only a matter of time.

The euphoria surrounding Hitler's appointment as Chancellor on 30 January 1933 disguised the deep rifts between the party rivals. Röhm's men, whom the street-fighting of the last few years had elevated to be a visible symbol of the new power, marched in a torchlight procession past the windows of the Reich Chancellery. Yet the effect of their theatrical propaganda bore no relationship to Hitler's tactic of an apparently legal assumption of power, and his temporary alliance with the forces of conservatism on whom he was still dependent. For the SA this day was like a safety-valve, the opening of which they had long awaited. They no longer considered themselves bound by the laws of civil society. Drunken SA men stopped and beat up passers-by at random. The brown-shirted gangs demanded '24 hours off duty', which meant no less than exacting revenge against their political opponents. They bawled slogans outside Jewish shops and businesses, collected money for the party or extorted it for themselves. Orgies of hate-filled revenge were a daily routine. In the first few months of Nazi rule approximately 100,000 people disappeared into the cellars, garages and other hideouts of the SA. 'Unofficial' concentration camps were set up everywhere, and sometimes the *Sturmlokale* themselves were converted into torture-chambers.

As early as March 1933 a camp was opened on the site of an old brewery in Oranienburg, north of Berlin, in which arrested opponents of the regime were to be 'concentrated'. Arno Hausmann, one of the last survivors of this early camp, remembers: 'A vagrant had just arrived in the camp, and the guards gave him such a working-over with brushes that the skin was hanging off him in shreds. A day later he was dead.' The SA called this 'protective custody'. They were in charge of this camp, situated in the middle of a residential suburb close to restaurants and cinemas.

This undisguised terrorising of the populace reached a climax in Berlin's Köpenick district. The SA's notorious *Sturm* 15 had set up its headquarters in, of all places, the local law courts. From there it organised a pogrom-like hunt for political opponents and for anyone they somehow 'didn't like the look of'. The SA crammed as many as twenty people into cells only a few feet square. When a gang of brownshirts forced their way into the parental home of the young Social Democrat, Anton Schmaus, he panicked and shot three of them. The SA took a hideous revenge. Schmaus' father was lynched on the spot, hanged in his own house. Anton managed to escape at first but was arrested a short time later and died when the SA shot him in the back. In a very short period, some 500 communists and Social Democrats were dragged off to Köpenick's *Sturmlokale* or to the cells of the police court, and brutally tortured. One eye-witness gave this account: 'When news came in of the shooting of the three SA men, we prisoners were subjected to a terrible bloodbath. They beat us up with chairs, whips and pistols. In the church hall about thirty-five working men were left soaked in their own blood. The clothes had been torn off them. The SA men trampled around on them in their boots. Blood and bits of flesh were swept up and carried out in buckets.' To this day it is not certain how many victims were claimed by that week of bloodletting. We know the names of twenty-three of them, but the true figure is probably nearer a hundred.

Should any proof be needed that there was no place in the new state for the brown battalions, now that Hitler wanted to win over the conservative elite – then it was provided by the SA's unrestrained terrorism following the Nazis' takeover of power. The SA chief brought the festering conflict to a head. In the summer of 1933 Röhm demanded that the nationalist revolution should now be followed by a National Socialist one. With the overblown romanticism of the shock trooper, he had dreamed of staging a revolution with field-guns and rifles, a revolution that would forcibly bring about the collapse of the old order, in a 'Night of the Long Knives'. None of this had happened, and Röhm was deeply disappointed by Hitler's alliance with the former powers. He was all the more bitter, since the rank and file of the SA were still awaiting their reward for the much-vaunted 'sacrifices of the fighting years'. The SA membership still included a large number of unemployed; their presence did nothing for its reputation. However, in Röhm's view, the SA should occupy a central position in the state. On 22 May 1933 he wrote in a letter to the party leadership: 'The Party must cease treating the SA like a stepchild.' In order to lend weight to their demands and put on a show of strength, the SA staged three mass demonstrations, culminating in a gathering of 80,000 in Breslau.

We have to produce something new, if you see what I mean. A new discipline. A new principle of organisation. The generals are old bunglers. They never have any new ideas.

Ernst Röhm

To everyone he was always just 'der Ernstl' [our little Ernst].
Rita Stephan, niece of Röhm's adjutant, Hans Schweighardt

The SA leaders were nationalistic officers, who'd had the epaulettes torn from their shoulders when they returned from the First World War. My uncle Hans came from a group known as the 'lynchers'.

Rita Stephan

Ernst Röhm had a very special dream: he saw the SA as the nucleus of a new German 'People's Army', which would simply absorb the small regular army, the Reichswehr. He himself would of course be in command. Röhm had already modelled his *Sturmabteilung* on an army in every detail. The service regulations were like those of a regular army, and the SA banners bore the numbers of old royal Prussian regiments. Röhm, the First World War army captain, nursed a hatred of the officer corps of the Reichswehr, whose representatives sometimes even refused to shake his hand at official events. It was they, he believed, who were partly responsible for the defeat of 1918. If the generals were 'old bunglers', then he liked to boast that he was the 'Scharnhorst of the new army', referring to Prussia's great military reformer. Röhm backed the power of the masses; he saw a People's Army as the army of the future. Sections of the *Stahlhelm* ('Steel Helmet'), the ultra-conservative First World War veterans' league, were already being absorbed into the SA. Ultimately four and a half million men took their orders from Röhm, who proclaimed his demands quite openly. In addition he claimed that he should be in charge of the border guards on the eastern frontier and have control of armouries in eastern Germany.

Yet the ungovernable SA was a threat to Hitler, who feared for the survival of his fragile alliance with the regular army and big business. He exchanged his brown uniform for a morning-coat and top hat, and in a cynically contrived public appearance in Potsdam, stood alongside the ageing president, Field-Marshal von Hindenburg, to demonstrate his supposed loyalty to the Weimar constitution. He still had to pay attention to the wishes of those who had the ear of the venerable head of state. There was still a possibility that he could lose everything he had gained. In the event of a serious worsening of the domestic political situation, Hindenburg could declare a state of emergency at any moment, transfer executive powers to the Reichswehr and thus sideline Hitler as Reich Chancellor. As long as Hindenburg was alive, Hitler had to watch him carefully.

The Reich Minister of the Interior, Wilhelm Frick, reacted to the brutal excesses of the SA by circulating a memorandum to the civil

In late January 1934 I heard Röhm make a speech. He shouted:
'I'd rather make revolution than celebrate revolutions – the
revolution is not yet at an end!'

Otto Gritschneder, Munich lawyer

Who has the power – the SA or the SS? We saw that this was
why they shot Röhm and replaced him with a yes-man like
Lutze.

Rita Stephan, niece of Röhm's adjutant

service and business companies: from now on posts becoming vacant
in the civil service should as far as possible be filled by political
officers of the Nazi Party, who would know more about the job
than office-hungry SA men. True, Röhm was given a government
appointment, but as Reich Minister without Portfolio, he – and
therefore the SA as a whole – were mere window-dressing. The
only post he was really interested in, that of Reich Minister for the
Army, remained firmly in the hands of a conservative military man.
Though the outward tone was one of comradely cooperation, by the
end of 1933 the tension was close to breaking-point. Hitler wrote a
letter to his 'dear chief-of-staff', expressing his 'heartfelt friendship
and grateful appreciation', and outlining a lukewarm compromise:
'While it is for the army to guarantee the nation's external security,
it is the task of the SA to ensure the victory of the National Socialist
revolution, and the continued existence of the National Socialist state
and of our ethnic community on the domestic front.' Hitler assured
the man whose murder he ordered only six months later: 'How
thankful I am to Destiny, that I may count such men as you [here
Hitler uses the intimate pronoun *Du*] as my friends and comrades-
in-arms.' At the same time he ordered the head of the state secret
police department, Rudolf Diels, to gather evidence against Röhm
and the rest of the SA leadership. 'It is the most important thing you
will ever do', Hitler told him.

Scarcely two months later he got the SA chief-of-staff to endorse
the supposed settlement with the military. On 28 February 1934

Hitler summoned the leaders of the SA and the Reichswehr to the marble-panelled treaty room of the Reichswehr ministry and exhorted the disputants finally to make peace and keep it. Röhm and the army minister, Blomberg, were obliged to confirm their agreement on a new formula, by which the Reichswehr would have sole responsibility for the preparations for national defence, mobilisation and the conduct of war, while the SA would provide pre- and post-service military training – albeit under the guidelines of the defence ministry. At a champagne breakfast in the Berlin headquarters of the SA the adversaries celebrated what appeared to be a reconciliation. Yet no sooner had the officers left the reception room than Röhm gave full vent to his fury: 'That man Hitler! If only we could free ourselves from him. . . . Nothing that ludicrous non-com says applies to us . . . Hitler is not to be trusted. He needs to take a long holiday, at the very least.'

Röhm thought he was safe among his SA officers. In an atmosphere fuelled by alcohol he talked himself into a rage: 'If we don't do the business *with* Hitler, we'll do it without him.' However, Röhm's fit of anger did not remain a secret. Disturbed by this outburst, an SA *Obergruppenführer*, Viktor Lutze, reported his chief-of-staff's tirade first to Hess, and then to Hitler. The response that Lutze's disloyalty provoked was brief: 'We must let this thing develop', Hitler replied. Hesitating to act – as he so often did at crucial moments in his political career – Hitler bided his time until the noose was skilfully and fatally knotted, ready to strangle his old comrade-in-arms and the rebellious SA. He would exploit this opportunity to play off the only two independent power groups within the state, Reichswehr and SA, one against the other. The regular army would give him their backing, while the SA would be sacrificed. The supposed threat of Ernst Röhm's 'treason' became the pretext for a bloody 'cleansing', and those who would carry it out were standing ready.

At this time Heinrich Himmler was giving his SS an outwardly conciliatory face. In Munich he invited industrialists, army officers and academics to a lecture. Accustomed to being denounced in the shrill tones of the street-fighters as 'bourgeois', 'decadent' and 'slaves to Jewry', the guests came fearing the worst. They could hardly believe their ears. No attacks came. Instead the Reichsführer-SS appealed to his audience to become part of a new elite. He asked those present for their cooperation 'in making possible a confluence of different currents of tradition in the SS'. Every state, he maintained, needed an elite, and in the National Socialist state that elite was the SS. The SS must, he said, combine in itself 'the tradition of genuine soldiery, the high-minded attitude, conduct and good upbringing of the German aristocracy, and the creative energy of the industrialist, on a foundation of racial selection, to meet the social challenges of the age'.

Himmler's masseur, Felix Kersten, later recalled that nearly everyone attending the event joined the SS. As the author Heinz Höhne says, the episode proved 'with what skill Himmler . . . was able to present his *Schutzstaffel*'. The so-called 'friends of the Reichsführer-SS' included leading industrialists like Flick and Oetker, the heads of the Dresdner Bank and the electrical giant, Siemens-Schuckert – in fact precisely those people who had been repelled by the terrorism of the working-class brownshirts, and their cries for revolution and expropriation. But for Himmler's SS they pulled out their cheque-books.

With great shrewdness the SS chief recruited the representatives of old and influential forces in society: for example, he used country riding-clubs as an entrée for the SS into hitherto closed landowning and agricultural circles. In the rural strongholds of East Prussia, Holstein, Westphalia, Oldenburg and Hanover, many riding-clubs joined the Black Order *en bloc*. The pact with the Kyffhäuser brought to Himmler the old soldiers who until then had leant more towards the First World War nostalgia of the SA. Even ex-army officers, loyal to the Kaiser, and conservative nationalists in the diplomatic corps, now donned the black uniform and the death's-head insignia – a fact which gave rise to open protest in the SS itself. For beneath their new uniforms many of these 'honorary officers' retained their old attitudes. Young lawyers and academics were systematically recruited, especially for the SS's new 'security service', the SD. This was a breeding-ground for the archetype of the cold, apparently non-political SS technocrat – 'clever, without illusions, subscribing to no ideology but that of power', as Höhne puts it. They were the 'operators' of the years to come.

In those early years was it already possible to see where the path of the new black guard would eventually lead? 'Everyone knew about Dachau', says Renate Weisskopf, daughter of the Munich music critic Willi Schmid, who was later murdered by the SS. 'Dachau was in the newspapers. But we accepted it, because we were told that the only people who went there, according to the SS, weren't human at all, but were "pests on the nation" as they called them.'

In the words of the former SA man, Herbert Crüger, the SS brought 'a fearsome efficiency to terror. What the SA did was appalling enough, but from now on the SS adopted a systematic approach to terror, humiliation and murder.'

From 22 March 1933 onward, the name of Dachau represented the new character of the SS. It was on that day that the first 'pests on the nation' entered its gates on open trucks, their route lined by 'numerous spectators who had been gathering for several hours at the entrance of the former powder-mill', to quote a newspaper report in the *Münchner Neueste Nachrichten*. The population were fully informed. The opening of a camp with a capacity of 5,000 had been announced by Himmler at a press conference two days earlier. Twelve years later, when US soldiers liberated the concentration camp, 67,000 prisoners were languishing in its barrack-huts. During the years of the Third Reich a total of 206,200 had been incarcerated there. The deaths of 31,951 inmates had been officially registered. How many actually died at the hands of the SS, how many would fail to survive human experiments by camp doctors, how many lost their lives on the final death-march in the winter of 1944–5 – none of this does the documentary record tell us.

On 13 March 1933 Adolf Wagner, commissioner for Bavaria at the Ministry of the Interior, set the guidelines: 'Should the prisons at the disposal of judicial authorities prove inadequate, I recommend the application of the same methods that were used against the large numbers of jailed members of the National Socialist German Workers' Party. It is well known that they were locked up in some disused ruin or other, and no-one cared whether or not they were exposed to the vagaries of wind and weather.' The term 'concentration camp' for the place where enemies of the state were confined was invented by the SD chief, Reinhard Heydrich; more than anything else it symbolises the SS reign of terror.

If we are to believe the report in the *Münchner Neueste Nachrichten*, the concentration camp at Dachau was more a kind of boy-scout hostel inspired by ideas of benefiting society as a whole: 'The plan is to divide the political prisoners into work-teams . . . to be employed in cultivation on Dachau Heath. . . . In their free time they will be given lectures on local history and religious topics. It is an attempt to make the internees susceptible once again to patriotic ideals through work, meals of an appropriate quality, and justice towards the individual.' Those operating in the background thought differently. Twelve miles away in Munich two men were working to gain control of the camp. Heinrich Himmler and Reinhard Heydrich wanted to remove it from the supervision of the provincial police and judiciary and place it directly under the SS. Dachau was to become a place for organised execution.

In the early days of the camp the intentions of the SS were only a vague rumour – yet they caused great anxiety in Dachau. Prisoners asked one of the police guards whether in future their function would be taken over by the SS. 'The SS? They'd be useless as prison guards. They don't even know how to pick up a rifle. All they do is boast about their heroic deeds', retorted a senior guard, who told them in no uncertain terms what he thought of Himmler's men: 'They're not even human; they're wild animals! No, no. Things haven't yet gone so far that you'd be left to *their* tender mercies.' The reassuring effect of his words did not last for long.

Himmler's rise to power sealed the fate of the camp's inmates. On 2 April, as the new commandant of Bavaria's political police, he placed the camp under his direct authority. Surreptitiously, control slid from the police to the SS. One night the prisoners were woken in terror by the bellowing of SS-Oberführer von Malsen-Ponickau: 'Comrades of the SS, you all know what the Führer has called upon us to do. We haven't come here to show humanity to those bastards inside. We don't regard them as people like we are, but as second-class human beings. For years they've been allowed to carry on their criminality. If those sods had got into power, they'd have cut all our heads off. That's why we won't give way to any befuddled sentimentality. Any comrade here who can't stand the sight of blood isn't one of us, and ought to drop out. The more of these sons-of-bitches we beat the hell out of, the fewer we'll have to feed.'

> I saw a Jewish lawyer being beaten up so severely during an interrogation that he died before my eyes.
>
> *Paul Tollmann, communist*
>
> With a few exceptions, the SS men were normal people who, thanks to a criminal super-ego, had turned into normal criminals.
>
> *Elie Cohen, prisoner in Auschwitz*

As early as the evening of 12 April, one day after they had taken over guard duty, the SS men showed that they could do more than mouth slogans. After being tortured for a whole day, four Jewish prisoners – Arthur Kahn, Dr Rudolf Benario, Ernst Goldmann and Erwin Kahn – were separated from the other prisoners in the evening. 'Come with me, you four', ordered SS-Scharführer Steinbrenner. They were led towards the rifle-range and then into the woods. 'A few moments later we heard shots and screams', an eye-witness reported. 'Shot while escaping', the SS informed the other prisoners curtly the next day. The truth was quite different: the SS men let their victims walk a short distance towards their doom. Then with no prior warning they opened fire on the four with their pistols.

At first the prisoners were subjected to arbitrary violence by their guards. It was not until Theodor Eicke took command of the camp at the end of June that the terror was cast in a regulated form. The guards called him 'Papa Eicke', and the maltreated inmates of the camp called their tormentors 'Eicke's boys'. In Dachau a large family of murderers grew up.

Theodor Eicke brought with him the notorious 'Disciplinary and penal rules for the prison-camp' and the 'Service regulations for escort staff and prison guards'. They specified that any person 'who engages in political incitement or conspires with others for that purpose, or who spreads hostile atrocity propaganda or the like, shall, under revolutionary law, be hanged as an agitator; that any person who physically assaults a guard, refuses to obey orders . . . or engages in any form of mutiny, shall be shot on the spot or hanged subsequently.' Eicke also envisaged 'milder' punishments: 'The following lesser penalties may be considered: compulsory exercise, punishment beatings, withholding of mail, withholding of food, confinement under severe conditions, tying to a post, reprimand or caution.'

At the same time Eicke injected his guards with that callous and cold-blooded sense of superiority that was to become the guiding principle of the concentration camps. All scruples and human instincts against brutality were, as Eicke put it, 'to be educated out' of them. He impressed upon his men that 'tolerance means weakness', and went on to lecture them: 'When you realise this, you will ruthlessly intervene wherever it seems necessary in the interests of the Fatherland. . . . You can say to the political agitators and subversive intellectuals: watch out you don't get caught, because if you do, you'll be grabbed by the throat and silenced according to your own recipe.' Little more than a year later the Dachau SS would prove just how biddable they were. Eicke's men would 'silence' their own former comrades.

In the spring of 1934 Ernst Röhm had little cause to be happy. It is true that he continued to express himself forcefully, loudly proclaiming that in his SA he could call on the might of thirty divisions. Yet this verbal muscle-flexing, which culminated in his treasonable statements in front of the SA leaders, some ostentatious arms purchasing, and ever more plans for military training, was followed by periods of profound despair.

At these times he would muse aloud about returning to Bolivia. His relationship with Hitler had reached rock bottom. But he was still no nearer to staging a coup d'état. On 20 April 1934, when the SA presented Hitler with a birthday gift of six aircraft, the chief-of-staff was not even there. The last occasion at which the two men had been seen together in public was three days earlier, ironically enough at a spring concert given by the SS in Berlin's Palace of Sport.

Nonetheless, rumours were seething behind the scenes about an imminent revolt by the SA. In conditions of the utmost secrecy Reinhard Heydrich was promoted to chief string-puller in a plot of unparalleled ruthlessness which, though attributed to Röhm, should have been named after the new head of the SD. There are admittedly no documents available that relate to it, yet we know from numerous statements made after the war by those involved that by the end of April 1934, if not earlier, Heydrich had begun to assemble incriminating evidence against Röhm. What emerged was an evil concoction of rumours, massaged evidence and false clues, which were intended to convince potential partners about the SA's intentions to mount a putsch. Röhm, who could only suspect who was intriguing against him, found himself the target of an out-and-out witch-hunt. Suddenly everything was going against him. Even the judicial authorities began investigating members of the SA, and

When joining one of the wings of the party, the so-called 'upper crust' chose the SS.
Walter Schellenberg, head of the foreign intelligence service of the SS, in his memoirs

No nation can afford to tolerate continual rebellion from below, if it is to survive as a factor in history. Nothing can be achieved by constant upheaval. Germany must not wander off into the wide blue yonder. . . . Sooner or later the movement must come to end, sooner or later a solid social structure must emerge, held together by an impartial administration of justice and an un-disputed state authority.
Franz von Papen, then Vice-Chancellor, in a speech on 17 June 1934

there was nothing he could do about it. For Röhm's enemies it was convenient that he had ruined his chances on all sides: unpopular with the public, feared by the Reichswehr, hated by Goebbels, Bormann and Göring, kept at arm's length by Hitler, the SA chief seemed an easy prey for his adversaries.

Heinrich Himmler, head of the SS, was late in joining the anti-Röhm cabal that had gradually been forming. After some hesitation, the man who had once been Röhm's standard-bearer sensed the new shift in power and abandoned his old loyalties. Even on Röhm's birthday, 28 November 1933, Himmler wished him 'as a soldier and a friend, that which can be promised in true allegiance. . . . That was and is our great pride in being among those most loyal to you.' It is probable that in early March, and again in April 1934, two secret meetings were held at Rathenow, near Berlin, between Röhm and Himmler, at which the chief-of-staff give the silent SS leader a thorough dressing-down: 'The SS has a conservative attitude, it protects reactionaries and the petty bourgeoisie, it is too strongly subordinated to the army and traditional bureaucracy.'

According to a statement by Himmler's adjutant, Karl Wolff, Himmler warned the SA chief against further homosexual excesses, which might come to the attention of the public. Röhm seemed to take this on board, but the following morning reports of yet another orgy were brought to Himmler. In the next few weeks Himmler visited SS units all over Germany in order to prepare carefully for what was to come.

Meanwhile Heydrich activated the few spies and informers he had at his disposal. The results were meagre in the extreme. True, there were reports of secret arms-stores in Munich, Berlin and in Silesia. True, Röhm had been to see the former Reich Chancellor, General Kurt von Schleicher, who at the time was definitely looking to make contact with groups hostile to Hitler within the Nazi Party, as his daughter Lonny remembers today. True, Röhm was even in touch with the French ambassador, François-Poncet. However, as the diplomat recalled, nothing more came of it than a tedious dinner. All the evidence put together could not even show the beginnings of a threatened coup. The 'Röhm Putsch' was no more nor less than a putsch against Röhm.

A press report gave further weight to the story abroad. The AP news agency mentioned discord in the upper echelons of the party hierarchy. Ironically, it was Edgar Jung, a confidant of Vice-Chancellor von Papen, who tirelessly spread a new rumour: Röhm had apparently allied himself with ex-Chancellor von Schleicher against von Papen, and cabinet lists had been circulated. Röhm was being discussed as a possible army minister, and Gregor Strasser as economics minister, but Hitler was to remain as Reich Chancellor.

Hitler himself, however, played down the matter publicly. In an interview with the American journalist Louis P. Lochner, he said: 'I have certainly not surrounded myself with nonentities, but with real men. Nonentities are zeroes, and being round, they roll away when things go badly. The men around me are four-square and straight-edged. Each one of them is a personality, each one is filled with ambition. . . . But never yet has one of the men around me attempted to impose his will upon me. Quite the contrary; they comply fully with my wishes.'

Where evidence was insufficient to prove the reverse, forgery and manipulation helped things along. Heydrich was so adroit in feeding the Reichswehr high command with supposed SA orders for general mobilisation that they were only too ready to believe that a coup was imminent. He also attempted to convince doubters with the help of forged documents. Thus, the CO of the SS *Leibstandarte Adolf Hitler*, Sepp Dietrich, presented the army ministry with what purported to be the SA's 'hit-list', from which it appeared that Röhm intended to have the top echelon of Reichswehr officers murdered.

If I'd refused at the time to carry out Hitler's orders, I would with absolute certainty have been shot on Hitler's orders myself.
Sepp Dietrich during an interrogation in 1953

A plain, upstanding man, who always remained true to himself and was like a father to the members of the *Leibstandarte*.
Hans Fischach, of the SS Leibstandarte Adolf Hitler,
about Sepp Dietrich

> Leader of a gang of murderers.
> *Otto Gritschneder, Munich lawyer, about Sepp Dietrich*

The carousel of conspiracy spun with ever-gathering speed. Between SS and SD, between Göring, Goebbels and Himmler, different death lists circulated containing a variety of names. The protagonists conducted cynical negotiations in secret over the fate of individual assassination targets, such as the senior SA officer and Munich police chief, August Schneidhuber, whom Heydrich personally placed on the list. It was a stroke of Göring's pen that rescued the former head of the Gestapo, Rudolf Diels, who had once been secretly ordered by Hitler to do some research on Röhm. The day was approaching when a great many old scores would be settled. For some time now the lists had contained many more names than those of the SA commanders. One of the men who compiled the death lists, an *Obersturmführer* in the SD named Ilges, is claimed to have said: 'Do you know the meaning of blood-lust? I feel I'm being allowed to wallow in blood.'

Early in June 1934 the noose was prepared for the SA. The perpetrators swung into action. Theodor Eicke, commandant of the Dachau camp, rehearsed the strike against the SA. His death's-head units simulated a march on Munich and the small Bavarian towns of Lechfeld and Bad Wiessee. SS units in Munich received orders to hold themselves in readiness for Day X.

The only person who did not seem to be playing along was Röhm himself. On 7 June, when the death lists had already been drawn up and the conspirators were waiting to go into action, Röhm sent the SA on leave. He himself went off to a health spa on the shores of the idyllic Tegernsee lake. His farewell message was: 'In order to avoid from the outset any misinterpretation that might be attached to this, the chief-of-staff wishes to state that once he has recovered his health he will continue to exercise his authority to the fullest extent.' And a day later: 'If the enemies of the SA are nurturing the hope that the SA will not return from their leave, or that only some of them will, then let us give them the pleasure of that brief hope for a while. At the due time and in the manner that appears necessary, they will receive a fitting answer. The SA is and remains the destiny of Germany.'

Yet this holiday would not save Röhm or the SA. The conspirators were certainly under pressure of time, but the verdict had been reached. A new turn of events now broke down Hitler's private misgivings. In a public speech, his Vice-Chancellor, Franz von Papen, inveighed against the SA and its demand for influence in government and the military. An ever more menacing scenario now began to emerge, which would suddenly have left Hitler completely stripped of power. Supposing the forces of conservatism around von Papen, supported by the Reichswehr, were to exploit the short time left to the ageing Reich President Hindenburg, and with his help were to overthrow Hitler and establish a military dictatorship? On 21 June, when Hitler went to pay his respects to Hindenburg at his country estate, Neudeck, the Reichswehr minister, von Blomberg, urgently requested him to bring the SA to heel permanently and restore internal order in Germany. On 23 June *Oberst* Fritz Fromm, head of the General Army Office, instructed his officers to issue weapons to the SS, should they request them. The SS, he said, were on the side of the Reichswehr.

Hitler saw that he was being forced into striking a blow against the SA, yet he hesitated in the choice of method. Did he try one last time to talk it out with his old friend? On 25 June, that is to say five days before the 'Night of the Long Knives', eye-witnesses in Bad Wiessee saw Hitler being brought across by motor-launch from St Quirin and landing outside the Pension Hanselbauer at 5.30 p.m. It seems he tried without success to have a conversation with Röhm, but as the weather was so beautiful, the SA chief had gone off on an excursion. Hitler then apparently talked to the hotel staff and asked to be shown the bedrooms. After waiting in vain for about 20 minutes, he left the hotel, as he had to return to Berlin the same evening.

Three days later, while Hitler was acting as a witness at the wedding of Josef Terboven, the Gauleiter of Essen, he received a call from Himmler, to say that a meeting between Papen and Hindenburg had been arranged for 30 June. Hindenburg, so Himmler claimed, was to be persuaded to hand over government powers to the Reichswehr and to remove Hitler from office. Back at his hotel, the Kaiserhof, Hitler received a second message from Himmler: an immediate putsch by the SA could no longer be ruled out. Incandescent with rage, Hitler ordered a meeting of the SA commanders – in Bad Wiessee, at 9 a.m on Saturday 30 June. Even so, the death sentence had not yet been pronounced. Could there not be a solution to the apparently unresolvable conflict with Röhm?

On the following day, 29 June, Hitler travelled to the Hotel Dreesen in Bad Godesberg, on the Rhine near Bonn. That evening more news reached him from Berlin. The situation was tense. The Munich SA had already been put on full alert status. This deliberately false information came from Himmler. It now caused Hitler to reach a swift and drastic decision which, as so often with him, would bring to an end a long period of hesitation. In this the head of his bodyguard played a crucial role.

I was studying in Berlin and had to go along to the big SS alert in Lichterfelde. We had no idea what was actually going on. An SS unit came marching out of the barracks gate. Until then I hadn't realised that in addition to our 'general SS', as it was called, there was also a barracks-based, militarily trained *Waffen*-SS, with white buckles and black steel helmets. Behind them came a line of open-topped personnel-carriers. On each of these, under heavy guard, sat a shaven-headed man in prison uniform. I didn't recognise any of them, but the local Berliners nearly always knew who they were and said: 'Hey, 'e's the Obergruppenführer of Silesia! That 'un's the Obergruppenführer of Pomerania!' and so on. All of them were shot.

Hans Lautenbach, army doctor

At 10 p.m. Hitler received the CO of the *Leibstandarte*, Sepp Dietrich. 'You'll take a plane to Munich. As soon as you arrive, phone me here in Bad Godesberg.' Meanwhile, two companies of the SS *Leibstandarte* were boarding a special aircraft – also bound for Munich.

Himmler called from Berlin to say that the SA's preparations in Berlin were complete, and that the following day, 30 June at 4 p.m., they planned to occupy the government buildings. Hitler did not know that at that point in time most of the SA men in Berlin were already on leave. At the same time, the Gauleiter of Bavaria, Adolf Wagner, reported that in Munich the SA were on the streets, noisily protesting against the Führer and the Reichswehr – a deliberate and gross exaggeration.

> On 29 June at 13.10 hours we were put on alert. It was clear that something would probably happen, but exactly what, we didn't know. We were even issued with live ammunition. Some soldiers were told to belt up the old machine-guns. And one of the men, a thoroughly idle type who would skive off anything, sat and did the job with incredible care. I asked why he was giving it more attention than he'd ever done before. He looked at me very seriously and said: '*Herr Oberleutnant*, tomorrow there mustn't be any hitches.'
>
> *Count Johan Adolf von Kielmansegg, then in the Reichswehr*

That night, Josef Zander, who lived next door to the Hotel Dreesen, noticed the lights suddenly go on in the hotel and a short time later saw a column of cars leaving the grounds.

At 1.50 a.m. Hitler boarded a Junkers 52 aircraft at Bonn's Hangelar airfield, and was then flown direct to Oberwiesenfeld, near Munich. With him on board was the turncoat SA Obergruppen-führer, Viktor Lutze, who noted in his diary:

> *Morgenrot, Morgenrot*
> *Leuchtest uns zu frühem Tod.*
> *Gestern noch auf hohen Rossen,*
> *Heute durch die Brust geschossen.*

(O dawn, you light our way to an early death. Yesterday we still rode our proud horses; today we are shot through the chest.)

Awaiting Hitler at the Bavarian airfield were the Gauleiter, Adolf Wagner, two Reichswehr officers and probably a few of his old

Stosstrupp comrades like Berchtold, Maurice and Weber. They told him that the Munich SA had marched under arms to the Feldherrnhalle. Hitler sent for the supposedly responsible SA Gruppenführer, Wilhelm Schmidt, and tore the insignia of rank from his sleeves. "You're a traitor. You'll be shot', the Führer shouted. Escorted by several SS men, he drove hurriedly to Bad Wiessee. Though it was only 6 in the morning, half the town was up and about. In the Königslinde bakery the ovens had been on for hours, preparing the banquet for the big meeting. The manager of the Pension Hanselbauer had just brought some boots to be polished.

> I was in the *Pimpfen* [junior Hitler Youth]. We were supposed to cordon off the Hotel Hanselbauer for the SA meeting. But that meeting never happened. At 5 a.m. two SS men suddenly appeared in my parents' guest-house nearby, and asked to see the register. They wanted to find out if any SA men were still staying with us.
>
> *Hannes Kuntze-Fechner, nine years old at the time*

Quietly the SS men surrounded the hotel. Wearing a black leather overcoat, Hitler went into the building. He apologised to the woman owner for the disturbance, and then the troop stormed up the stairs. An official of the criminal police knocked on the door of room 21. It was opened by Röhm himself, wearing only a vest. The door was flung back. Hitler burst in and berated Röhm. 'You're a traitor. You're going to be shot!' he bellowed. SA *Führer* Heines came out from an adjoining room; behind him could be discerned the shape of his sleeping bed-companion. Altogether seven men were arrested and carted off in a hastily commandeered bus to the Stadelheim jail in Munich.

In Munich Sepp Dietrich was handed a list on which Hitler had put green ticks against the names of six top SA men. In the courtyard of Stadelheim prison Dietrich had them lined up and shot. They were August Schneidhuber, SA *Obergruppenführer* and Munich police chief, Wilhelm Schmidt, a Munich SA *Gruppenführer*, Hans

Hayn, SA *Gruppenführer* in Dresden, Count Hans Joachim von Spreti-Weilbach, SA *Standartenführer* in Munich; Edmund Heines, SA *Obergruppenführer* and police chief in Breslau; and Hans-Peter von Heydebreck, SA *Gruppenführer* in Stettin.

I live for my Führer. Thinking about him is the only thing that sustains me. If I could no longer believe in my Führer then I would rather die.

Hans-Peter von Heydebreck, executed on 30 June 1934

People were blind or they didn't want to see. The fact that Hitler was a brutal criminal must have been obvious to anyone at least on 30 June 1934, with the so-called Röhm putsch, if not before.

Frieda Becker, living at the time in Frankfurt-am-Main

Some of the men cursed as they died, others gave the Nazi salute and shouted 'Heil Hitler' – still respecting the man who had pronounced their death sentence and who from now on would be both judge and executioner. Schneidhuber pleaded at the top of his voice: 'Sepp, old comrade! What's going on? We're innocent!' But Dietrich heeded nothing but his orders.

There was one tick missing on the list: as yet Röhm was spared. Hitler was heard to say that he would be shown mercy on account of the great service he had rendered.

Goebbels, who had been on hand to witness the drama in Wiessee, telephoned Göring in Berlin, and gave him the pre-arranged codeword: '*Kolibri* (humming-bird).' Now a wave of terror swept over the whole of Germany. In every part of the Reich SS and police officers opened sealed envelopes; in Berlin Heydrich issued the orders in person. The moment had come for the murderers to begin their work.

At 12.30 p.m. a car carrying two SS men stopped outside a villa in Potsdam; no. 4 Griebnitzstrasse was the home of the former Chancellor, General von Schleicher. The door was opened hesitantly by the cook, who was brutally pushed aside. One man stayed with her and the other headed for the study.

'Are you General von Schleicher?'
'Yes, I am General von Schleicher.'

At the same moment shots rang out. The general, and his wife who was also in the room, died immediately. By the time the Schleichers' fifteen-year-old adopted daughter, Lonny, came home from school, on the last day before her holidays, her foster-parents' home was already sealed off. The local police let her through. An aunt told her what had happened. 'It was the most terrible day of my life', Lonny von Schleicher says today. 'Mother dead, Father dead. My home gone.' The official story was that von Schleicher had pulled a gun to defend himself, but even at the time no-one gave any credence to that. 'He did own a gun, but it was kept in the safe. He couldn't possibly have got hold of it at that moment. They murdered him in cold blood.'

Meanwhile in the outer office of the Gestapo chief, Reinhard Heydrich, in Berlin's Prinz-Albrecht-Strasse, other SS men were awaiting their murder assignments. One by one Heydrich called in the leaders of the death-squads. He told SS *Hauptsturmführer* Kurt Gildisch: 'You'll take on the Klausener case. He's to be shot by you personally. Go over right away to his office in the Reich Ministry of Transport.' Gildisch did not know the man, but he did not hesitate for a moment. When the deed was done, he reported in by telephone and was given the order to make it look like suicide. The same day he fetched an SA officer named Ernst from Bremen to Berlin, followed by the adjutant of SA *Obergruppenführer* Heines and a medical *Standartenführer* by the name of Villain. Gildisch took the arrested men to the *Leibstandarte* barracks in the suburb of Lichterfelde, where they were immediately shot. Although the late editions were already reporting his death, Ernst thought it was a crude joke on the part of his fellow-officers. Incredulous to the end, he died with the cry of 'Shoot straight, chaps!' on his lips.

My father looked at us, didn't say much more and went upstairs; he packed a few things and within ten minutes they drove him away; all he said was: 'Don't worry, I'll be back soon.' But of course, we couldn't sleep. . . . Anyway, we waited and heard nothing more except that father was in prison in Potsdam. Then after three or four days he suddenly came back. What he told us was that he'd been taken off to prison and on the way, when the car stopped in a wood, he thought they would shoot him. But in the end they just took him to the prison and interrogated him, but of course he'd had nothing to do with the putsch.

Paul Adenauer, on the arrest of his father
Konrad Adenauer, postwar German Chancellor

Meanwhile Hitler was to be seen at a garden party for party notables and members of the cabinet – even spouses and children were invited. Yet this was the same Hitler who only the day before had been foaming at the mouth and vehemently denouncing 'the greatest act of disloyalty in world history', very much as though he had wanted to convince himself of it. While the salvoes of the firing-squads were still echoing around Lichterfelde, and the families of officers living nearby were fleeing from the area in a panic, Hitler mingled with his guests in an expansive mood, chatting, drinking tea and patting the children. As Hitler's biographer, Joachim Fest, writes: 'There is great psychological interest in that scene; it is not hard to see the countenance of one of those Shakespearean anti-heroes, who are no match for their own evil.' It seems that Hitler, from the safety of this pseudo-reality, gave the order that afternoon – the order that Himmler and Göring had repeatedly pressed him to issue and which ultimately he could not evade, since Ernst Röhm was no second-rank opponent, but a people's spokesman, who had to be silenced.

The task was not given to the Deputy Führer, Rudolf Hess, who the day before had shouted excitedly: 'Mein Führer, it's *my* job to shoot Röhm!' – but instead to two dependable killers in black

According to reports received, the operation planned by Röhm was to begin on Saturday 30 June, at 4 a.m. It was necessary to act immediately in order to prevent a catastrophe, since we were informed that Röhm's tactic was to win over the SA men by telling them that Hitler no longer supported them.

Hitler addressing a ministerial meeting on 3 July 1934

uniform. At about 6 p.m. the commandant of Dachau, Theodor Eicke, and SS-*Sturmbannführer* Michael Lippert, entered Röhm's cell in Stadelheim. A third man, the prison governor, Lechler, was obliged to present his star prisoner with the latest edition of the official Nazi newspaper, *Völkischer Beobachter*, which reported the events with banner headlines. Wrapped in the paper was a pistol loaded with just one bullet. Then the men left the cell.

Röhm did not act on this blatant order to commit suicide. No shot was heard. Once more the SS men opened the cell door – cautiously this time, since they expected their victim to be in a desperate mood. Slowly Eicke and Lippert aimed their pistols at Röhm, who stood to attention. 'Take it very slowly', hissed Eicke to his trembling accomplice. Two shots brought Ernst Röhm's life to an end.

We heard that Röhm had staged a coup and been shot. A friend came to see me and brought his toy soldiers with him. He even had an 'Adolf Hitler' who could actually move his arms, and a 'Röhm'. We beheaded 'Röhm' on the garden table and threw him away. To us, that was the Röhm putsch. We simply had no idea what was really going on.

Heinrich Kling, then a schoolboy

After the murder of Röhm and von Schleicher, the death of Hindenburg and the combining of the Reich Presidency and Reich Chancellorship, I was convinced that Hitler could never now be deposed.

Theodor Eschenburg, journalist

> To say that the Reichswehr had been alerted far in advance of 30 June 1934 is not correct.
> *Count Johann Adolf von Kielmansegg, Wehrmacht officer*

Meanwhile the wave of lynching rolled on across the country. It seemed just too good an opportunity to settle scores with actual or presumed enemies of the regime. *Generalmajor* Ferdinand von Bredow was arrested in his Berlin appartment. A Gestapo squad killed him near Lichtenberg. For the 71-year-old conservative, Gustav von Kahr, his opposition to Hitler's Munich putsch of 1923 spelled his doom. He was tortured in Dachau and shot on Eicke's orders in the detention quarters of the camp. His body was later found on Dachau Heath, hacked to pieces. Gregor Strasser, once a serious rival to Hitler, who had contemptuously nicknamed Himmler *'der Anhimmler'* ('the idoliser'), died in a Gestapo cellar in Berlin. In Silesia the SS commander Udo von Woyrsch lost control of the murder campaign he was in charge of. His killers pursued an SA officer named Engels into a forest and blasted him to death with shotguns. A former SS staff officer was murdered by one of Woyrsch's men, who was then himself shot. The SS *Oberabschnitts-führer* Erich von dem Bach-Zelewski set two SS men on to his rival, SS *Reiterführer* Baron Anton von Hohberg-Buchwald. The landowner was shot from behind in his own drawing-room. When the victim's seventeen-year-old son rushed into the room, one of the killers calmly remarked: 'We've just shot your father.'

It was an order from Hitler on 2 July that ended the first mass murder in the history of the Third Reich. In Berlin and Munich most of the documents were destroyed. Not until after the war, when Sepp Dietrich, Michael Lippert, Kurt Gildisch and Udo von Woyrsch were put on trial, could the events be reconstructed and the number of dead counted. Today there is documentary proof that eighty-five people were murdered, but this is no more than a vague indication of the actual number who died.

> After the Röhm putsch the SA was very subdued; it no longer had much of a presence on the streets. It wasn't used again until *Kristallnacht* in 1938.
>
> *Paul Tollmann, communist prisoner of the SA*

> The entire Reich cabinet agreed that the Röhm affair was indeed a national emergency.
>
> *Hans-Heinrich Lammers, head of the Chancellor's office, 1934*

A sepulchral calm now reigned. The press reproduced the justification offered by Hitler, who – flanked by steel-helmeted SS men – declared to the Reichstag temporarily accommodated in the Kroll Opera House: 'At that hour I was Germany's supreme judicial authority.' The statute which retrospectively legalised the murders consisted of just one sentence: 'The measures taken on 30 June and 1 and 2 July to crush the treasonable attacks on our nation are a legal act of self-defence by the state.' The SS was declared an independent organisation and the perpetrators were promoted. Their murders were rewarded with a dagger of honour, since they had given ample proof of what they called their loyalty.

> A pity they didn't wipe out the lot, root and branch. It was done with far too much restraint.
>
> *Robert Schulz, member of the SD, 17 August 1934*

> Woe betide any man who breaks his trust, in the belief that by rebelling he can serve the revolution! Adolf Hitler is the supreme revolutionary strategist. Woe betide the man who tramples clumsily on the fine texture of his strategic plans, with the deluded idea that he can make everything happen faster. That man is an enemy of revolution.
>
> *Broadcast speech by Rudolf Hess, 25 June 1934*

> In view of the great services rendered by the SS, especially in connection with the events of 30 June 1934, I am raising it to the status of an independent organisation within the NSDAP.
>
> *Decree of Hitler, 20 July 1934*

A few days after the unexplained killing of the music critic Willi Schmid, a coffin was delivered to his family. They were not allowed to open it. No relatives of the victims of 30 June were ever permitted to see their loved ones again. Most of the corpses were burned – the ashes that remained concealed the cruelty of death at the hands of the SS. Rudolf Hess expressed his regret that Willi Schmid had been confused with an SA officer of the same name, adding gratuitously that Schmid had died 'for a great cause'.

How could the confusion have arisen?

A few days before his death, as if driven by some premonition, Schmid had written a doleful letter: 'And life runs on; it trickles and pours away, hour by hour, night after night. . . . Well, that's the way it is. Nothing one can do. It is an iron and implacable law. And because it is so implacable, we have become frightened. I know I am. Don't tell me I'm a coward or too fond of living. It is just the urgent need for a few hours more of happiness.'

No-one could imagine the fear of death that Schmid felt as he faced the gun-barrels of his murderers in Dachau. 'He was so exactly the opposite of what those men in black uniforms embodied', says his daughter Renate Weisskopf today. 'To him life was sacred. *They* despised it. It didn't matter to them that he couldn't possibly have been the person they thought he was. It didn't interest them. The life of a human being was of no interest to them.'

Heinrich Himmler's SS had now displayed its true nature. It was not only the victor in a battle for power but on that day it laid the foundation-stone of the black regime of terror. Yet outwardly the SS continued for years to show what was considered the 'decent, better face' of the Third Reich.

I saw my father take his hat and wave goodbye to us. In those days of course no man ever went out without a hat. My mother tried desperately to show the SS men his passport. But they pulled their pistols on her. They couldn't have cared less who they'd got hold of. He was shot in Dachau straight away. When the coffin arrived we weren't allowed to open it.

> *Renate Weisskopf, daughter of the music critic*
> *Willi Schmid, who on 30 June 1934 was*
> *mistaken for an SA officer of the same name*

As I saw it the SS was an organisation dedicated to death and destruction, and to living for Hitler and his ideology – an organisation that was prepared to commit any murder and any injustice.

> *Josef Zander, then living in Bad Godesberg*

The 'masquerade of evil' was how the anti-Nazi pastor Dietrich Bonhoeffer saw it. He recognised the SS as the essential under-pinning of Nazi rule. In the early years it showed itself to be a master of camouflage. 'They used to go to concerts and were moved to tears by Beethoven's Ninth', recalls Wolfgang Held. He was one of the citizens of Weimar, mostly members of the Nazi Party, who at the end of the war were forced by the American Army to visit the recently liberated concentration camp at nearby Buchenwald. Only at that late stage did Held see the SS for what it was. 'They were predators. They looked very elegant and handsome. But they could inflict death at any moment. It came completely naturally to them.'

'What do our individual lives count for, compared to the millions of murders that came later?' asks Renate Weisskopf, who tries to quell her own grief with modesty. The answer might be that the murders of 1934, no less than the epochal genocide of later years, resulted from the perverse ethic of the SS, a construct of 'loyalty', 'performance of duty' and 'unquestioning obedience'. In his notorious 1943 speech in Poznan, Poland, Himmler himself drew the same parallel: 'To do your duty as ordered, and to put defaulters against the wall and shoot them . . . these things make everyone shudder, and yet everyone knew quite well he would do the same thing the next time, if ordered to and if it was necessary. I am referring now to the evacuation of the Jews and the extermination of the Jewish people.'

Seen in this way, the fate of Willi Schmid and the other victims of 30 June 1934 was in fact a prologue to what was to come.

CHAPTER TWO

HIMMLER'S MANIA

The Reichsführer was a busy man. His office diary for 13 October 1941 shows how crowded his schedule was, and how varied his areas of activity. After dealing with his mail and with some instructions regarding his mother's will – Hilde Himmler having died in early September – at 12.30 p.m. the Reichsführer told his Berlin secretary, Erika Lorenz, to send some flowers to a certain August Meine. This man had been on Himmler's personal staff before going off to fight in the Russian campaign, where he was wounded. The previous day, Meine had become a father. At 12.40 Himmler made a phone call to enquire about the health of the Reich Foreign Minister, Joachim von Ribbentrop, who had been rather poorly of late. Among Hitler's closest henchmen, Ribbentrop was almost the only one with whom Himmler had a tolerably good relationship. A year earlier the unsoldierly diplomat had been appointed to the honorary SS rank of *Obergruppenführer*. At 2.30 p.m. he put through another call to his secretary in Berlin; this time it was Erika Lorenz herself who was the lucky recipient of flowers from her boss – along with a Germanic-style statuette of an elk for her apartment. An hour later there followed a phone conversation with his daughter Gudrun, and then one with Reinhard Heydrich, his most powerful and most important subordinate, who now held the post of 'Reich Protector' of the Czech lands. The two most feared men in the Reich arranged to meet at the earliest opportunity.

At 4 p.m. a call came through from the 'Wolf's Lair', Hitler's military HQ in East Prussia. At that moment Himmler himself was on his special train, the *Heinrich*, and in fact only thirty minutes' drive away. Yet he never went to see his Führer unless summoned. On the line was Karl Wolff, after Heydrich the number three man in Himmler's hierarchy. Unlike his chief, Wolff was reasonably close to the Nordic ideal of the SS. His job was to maintain contact with Hitler and to provide the SS chief with key information from the daily situation meetings. The news that day sounded particularly gratifying. Army Group Centre, which for the past week had been advancing towards Moscow, was making such progress that the Soviets were apparently preparing to evacuate the government. Himmler seems to have been in the best of spirits. The chronic stomach-ache that had plagued him since youth was hardly noticeable that autumn. At 6 p.m. he called the last recorded staff meeting of that day. Two important subordinates had arrived from occupied Poland. One was *Obergruppenführer* Friedrich Wilhelm Krüger, former director of Berlin's waste-disposal services and now 'Senior SS and Police Officer', Cracow; the other was Odilo Globocnik, nicknamed 'Globus', the SS officer in charge of the Lublin district. The two SS 'governors' from Poland wanted to discuss the planned 'resettlement measures' for their districts. Ostensibly, this was the proposed settlement of entire tracts of Poland with German farmers, but behind it was actually the 'gradual cleansing of the *Generalgouvernement* [German-administered Poland]', to use the typical euphemism of the perpetrators, that is found in Globocnik's preparatory memorandum. When the three men were alone Himmler dropped all pretence and ordered 'Globus' to equip a special camp at Belzec for this 'cleansing'. This was the instruction for the building of the first death camp. By the end of 1942 a total of 600,000 people would be murdered in Belzec.

This man, Hitler's evil genius, cold, calculating and power-hungry, was probably the most ambitious and unscrupulous figure in the Third Reich.

Friedrich Hossbach, general in the Wehrmacht

To me Himmler seemed colourless, I had no deeper impression of him. He was always friendly when we saw him. He seemed like a friendly and kind person.

Martin Bormann Jr

> I wasn't at all impressed by Himmler. The man made me feel uncomfortable.
>
> *Ernst-Günther Schenck, SS doctor*

Sending flowers by day – planning death factories in the evening. The abrupt changes of pace that went with his job do not seem to have disturbed Himmler's equanimity. Posterity can only shake its head in disbelief. How does a human being become capable of such behaviour? What kind of monsters inhabited his mind? How can it be that Himmler's daughter Gudrun has memories of a 'particularly lovable father' – and that the same man was at the same time responsible for mass murder without parallel?

Even for his contemporaries the phenomenon of Heinrich Himmler was difficult to comprehend. The Swiss academic, Carl Jacob Burckhardt, sensed something 'unnatural' about him, 'a blinkered conscientiousness, a methodical inhumanity with an element of the automaton'. Albert Speer, as armaments minister, negotiated with him over the employment of tens of thousands of concentration camp inmates on the V2 rocket construction programme. He memorably described Himmler as 'half schoolmaster, half crackpot – a completely insignificant personality who, in some inexplicable way, had reached a prominent position'. Many who came across him were disappointed by his outward appearance. 'A rather minor functionary' was the verdict of Count Bernadotte, the Swedish diplomat who, shortly before the final curtain fell on Nazi Germany in 1945, conducted completely futile negotiations with the head of the SS about a separate peace with the western Allies. Even Himmler's long-serving Finnish masseur, Felix Kersten, who had perhaps the best opportunity to get to know the Grand Inquisitor of the Third Reich, though able to describe him after the war, could scarcely explain him: 'The real person never seemed to reveal himself. There was never any hint of openness. Himmler didn't fight, he plotted. The only way he defended his so-called ideas was with guile and deception. His methods were those of a snake – cowardly, weak, treacherous and infinitely cruel. Himmler's thinking didn't belong in the twentieth century. His character was medieval, feudal, machiavellian, evil.'

The life history of Heinrich Himmler seems to frighten people off. To this day there has been no comprehensive biography of him that meets the criteria of scholarship. Some corners of the shadowy world he ruled over have been illuminated by researchers – but many remain still largely in darkness. Yet the documentary record is good. Because Himmler was a pedant, who wrote almost everything down and also conducted extensive correspondence, veritable mountains of paper have survived to tell of his criminal activities. In addition, most of his numerous and often interminable speeches have come down to us. Yet interest in the Reichsführer SS remains remarkably small. The reason for this is perhaps that, outwardly at least, the pale, bespectacled Himmler lagged far behind the glittering potentates of the Nazi state – in comparison with men like the splendidly attired Göring, or Goebbels the brilliant orator, rabble rouser and skirt-chaser. It may also be due to the vast collection of posts and responsibilities he had assembled by the end of the war, which meant that any biography would inevitably become a mammoth tome. The lack of demand for information may be explained by the fact that engaging with Himmler's past can lead to uncomfortable conclusions. For, once the demonising that his accomplices have contributed to in order to minimise their own guilt, has been put to one side, what remains is a vacillating individual who above all was the product of his age. British and American historians in particular have attempted to explain Himmler's actions as the expression of severe mental illness with schizoid characteristics. But such an approach is misleading. Himmler's personality traits – the rigid application of minor virtues, a pronounced tendency to romanticise history, and a fatal lack of moral direction – these traits are those of an entire generation who were united by their collective perception of Germany's defeat in the First World War as a catastrophe. The only special thing about Himmler was the fact that the makings of the next catastrophe were present in him to an exaggerated degree and that he gained power in order to put his crass ideas into practice – ideas that were fed by the blend of *völkisch* and pseudo-scientific humbug that was circulating at the time. Concern with Himmler's form of insanity therefore entails concern with the disastrous trends in the society of that time. A German sickness or a German career-path? The story of the SS, of Himmler's fatal road, has something of each.

> Himmler was of course the son of a Bavarian schoolmaster, who had also been tutor to a prince. He was very influenced by the parental household. There was always something pedantic and schoolmasterish about him: cold, distant, disparaging. And he didn't have an ounce of kindness. His chief method of education was always punishment.
>
> *Ernst-Günther Scheck, SS doctor*
>
> Went with Father to church at 8 o'clock and took communion. Then did some learning. After lunch to prayers. Today there was a military exercise. I'd really like to join them. . . .
>
> *Heinrich Himmler, diary, 11 October 1914*

At the outset we find a thoroughly amiable lad. 'The gentlest lamb you could imagine.' That is how George Hallgarten, a historian who emigrated to the USA in 1933, remembers his schoolmate. Their teacher at Munich's Wilhelm High School praised Himmler as 'a very good-natured boy who, with tireless application, burning ambition and the liveliest participation in lessons, has achieved the best results in the class'. Young Heinrich certainly did not lack friends in his class; he was anything but a loner. From his early diaries we are amazed to learn that he was a regular churchgoer and even capable of remarkable compassion. In the Christmas holidays he read aloud to a blind academic, gave presents of bread and cakes to an impoverished old woman, regretted the brutal treatment of French prisoners-of-war he had watched on Landshut station in 1914, and organised charity events to raise funds for orphaned children. His relationship with his parents was a loving one. His father, Gebhard Himmler, was a conservative nationalist, a high school teacher who was conscious of his position in society. Even before the birth of his three sons, Gebhard Jr, Heinrich and Ernst, he had gained social standing as the tutor to Prince Heinrich of Bavaria. The name he gave to his second son commemorated the honour of having worked for the Bavarian royal family. Though some psychologically minded biographers have tried to prove that Heinrich suffered from having an excessively strict father, there is no hint of this in the sources. On the contrary, the schoolmasterly manner of the man who later headed the SS, and especially his weakness for Germanic pre-history and early history, points rather to the strong influence that the father, a passionate amateur archaeologist, had on his son. Certainly none of this suggests the early 'roots of evil'. Heinrich Himmler's childhood was secure and normal, if not particularly happy. In his youth we do not even find any evidence of the murderous anti-Semitism that later became the monstrous driving force of the entire SS. His father, Gebhard, was a loyal monarchist, a Catholic and a conservative nationalist – but he was not an anti-Semite.

There is only one aspect of Heinrich Himmler's early life that seems to have caused serious problems. 'Heinrich has been ill a great deal. Absent on 160 occasions . . .', we read in Gebhard's notes about his son's years in elementary school. Heinrich was smaller than his schoolmates, sickly, short-sighted and far from athletic. George Hallgarten tells us that sports sessions with a certain Herr Haggenmüller were pure torture for Himmler. Once, according to Hallgarten, Himmler tried to swing up over the horizontal bar, failed half-way and hung head-down in front of the assembled class, where Haggenmüller left him dangling. The sports teacher apparently then went up to the bar, tore the boy's glasses from his nose, and swung him back and forth until his knees turned black and blue. For the young lad who, like most of his schoolmates, wanted more than anything to become an army officer, such humiliations must have been a particular torment. Throughout his life his lack of physical prowess would remain the source of an inferiority complex. Not even rigorous training over many years was able to make an athlete of the unsporty and undersized man. By contrast, his SS men had to meet the highest physical requirements. Endless forced marches, high-risk tests of courage and the demand for 'absolute toughness' that was constantly hammered into them may actually have been a distant echo of those sports sessions with Herr Haggenmüller.

It was the advent of war that turned the life of young Heinrich Himmler upside down, as it did for so many of his generation. When the First World War broke out he was fourteen years old. Influenced by the 'patriotic' instruction in the royal high school and by what he heard at his father's table, there was nothing he wished for more fervently than finally to be allowed to serve his country – he would have preferred the navy, but they did not accept anyone who wore glasses. He spent hours playing war-games with his friend Falk Zipperer. 'I look forward to battle, when I shall wear the King's tunic', he wrote in his diary. Yet it was not until January 1918, as the war was drawing to a close, that '*miles* Heinrich' as he proudly signed himself in Latin when writing to his parents, finally entered an army barracks. He remained there until the armistice, without ever having seen the front line. Far from rejoicing in his personal good fortune, the young cadet saw it as an ignominious failure. At Christmas 1918, having achieved nothing, he returned to his parents' home in Landshut. His physical malaise was now compounded by the taint of not being one of the 'front-line fighters'. In the all-male coterie that would soon gather round the ex-corporal, Adolf Hitler, this would prove a thorn in Himmler's flesh, which he could only remove when he held the levers of power. In a speech he gave on 22 May 1936 to members of the Hitler Youth, we find for the first time a doctored version of his early career. Talking about 'racial ideas' he used the phrase, 'we, as soldiers, as fighters in the front line' and later, 'we who took part in the war'. Wishful thinking triumphed over reality – and later he even put this on paper. The 1943 edition of the *Manual for the Greater German Reichstag* fudged Himmler's CV shamelessly, claiming that the Reichsführer had served aged seventeen in the 11th Bavarian Regiment of Infantry and taken part in the 'battles of the Great War'. This was just one of the lifelong lies about the man who by then was already the second most powerful figure in Germany. Himmler did not engage in actual warfare until late 1944 and early 1945, as chief of the *Waffen*-SS and commander of two army groups, on the Upper Rhine and Vistula rivers – and even then he was never at the front.

Unlike his lord and master Hitler, he had never experienced at first hand the horror of industrialised slaughter. To the end, his romantic visions of heroic combat remained unsullied by bloody reality.

> Now I am once more in a state of inner conflict. If only I had dangers to withstand, if I could fight and put my life at risk, it would be of great benefit to me.
>
> *Heinrich Himmler, diary, November 1919*

The defeat of 1918 had an extremely damaging effect on the prospects of the schoolmaster's son. For the time being new officers were no longer needed. The secure upper middle-class background from which he came was gone for ever. After passing his school-leaving examination he decided – to his parents' surprise – on a career in farming. In autumn 1919 Himmler applied to the Faculty of Agriculture at Munich University. It was at this time that he began to take the wrong track. Within a few years a typical offspring of the educated middle class became a political extremist. His diary entries betray some of the reasons for this transformation. Some reflect the doubts and problems of a young man with an uncertain future, in search of guidance and an explanation for why he had been robbed of what he assumed were brilliant prospects. For example, on 4 January 1919 he noted: 'This evening we were talking in the back room. I was terribly serious and gloomy. I think momentous times are coming.' At other times the entries suggest that the student was increasingly coming under the influence of racist literature.

A book list, in which he meticulously catalogued everything he was reading at the time, provides precise information about the intellectual seedbed of his burgeoning fanaticism. We suddenly find anti-Semitic writings on his bedside table. On the anti-Jewish bestseller, *Race and Nation*, by the English-born Germanophile, Houston Stewart Chamberlain, Himmler commented: 'A truth of which one becomes convinced: it is objective and not filled with anti-Semitic hatred. For that reason its effect is all the greater.

That ghastly Jewry.' He devoured such tracts as *The Sin against the Blood*, *Manual of the Jewish Question* and *The False God* – all of them thoroughly unpleasant products of the *völkisch* mire that was spreading through the Bavarian capital at that time. Judged by today's standards almost all those exclusive clubs within the *völkisch* movement and the writings they purveyed were guilty on several counts under the Criminal Code, yet in the Weimar Republic conspiracies that threatened to undermine the foundations of democracy went unpunished. Within a few years, under the influence of the *völkisch* movement, Himmler formed his new and fateful vision of the world. Jews, Bolsheviks, freemasons and increasingly even the Roman Catholic Church were now responsible in his mind for the supposed 'destruction' of Germany. These were the same scapegoats which a hitherto unknown ex-corporal named Hitler believed at the same time he had exposed. It was the same pattern of hatred – based not on reason but on chimaeras in a fog of irrationality. But so far the seductive advocate and the cold-blooded executioner had not met.

Heinrich Himmler was not content merely to identify his enemies. While still studying he devoted himself extensively to the idealised world that would replace the misery to which he felt subjected. The search for 'redemption' and 'illumination' was a common phenomenon in the *völkisch* underworld; and Himmler found what he was looking for in antiquity. The 'Germanic hero', still untarnished by Roman decadence and the yoke of the Christian Church – this was the stuff of daydreams for the myopic student of agriculture. His chief source was *Germania*, by the Roman historian Tacitus, already a favourite hobbyhorse of his classically educated father. Himmler revered the 'magnificent depiction of how exalted, awe-inspiring and morally pure our ancestors were'. When brooding on this one evening he wrote: 'That is how we ought to be once again.' The truth about the Germanic tribes living east of the Rhine, beyond the frontier of the Roman empire, was that they were miserable, brutish and remarkably primitive. But Himmler was not to know that. The idealised account given by Tacitus had been written to set an example to Rome's youth, who in his view had become too soft. However, in those days it was still accepted as an accurate source, especially among German historians. Yet even if Himmler *had* known the historical truth, his deluded perceptions would scarcely have altered. Later he would frequently show his great readiness to bend history to suit his prejudices.

The conclusions he drew from this pernicious literature clearly point the way towards the most terrible crimes of the twentieth century. Among his reading matter was a pamphlet issued by an ethnic-Germanic group called the *Schutz- und Trutzbund* (League for Protection and Shelter) entitled: *An unintentional desecration of blood, the destruction of Germany. Natural laws of ethnicity.* In 1924 Himmler annotated it as follows: 'A marvellous little book. Especially the last section. The description of how it is possible to improve the race again is magnificent and morally uplifting.' The eugenic breeding of human beings, the extirpation of inferior specimens, the cultivation of an elite – in fact the whole crude and inhuman programme carried out by the SS, with racial selectivity, child abduction and mass murder, has been etched into the history of mankind. All of it was foreshadowed in Germany's *völkisch* subculture of the early 1920s. The only question that remains is whether the initiators were ever capable of imagining that their crackpot fantasies would be put into practice on a Europe-wide scale. Even for Himmler, who was still set on a career in farming, such radical schemes were at that time still only 'idealised concepts'. Two decades later, in the heady state of possessing almost unlimited power, he would appoint numerous *völkisch* pioneers from his Munich days to senior ranks in the SS.

As a student, Himmler led a rather desolate personal life. He was a member of at least ten societies and eagerly cultivated the acquaintance of his colleagues, yet he was disappointed with the little recognition he received. The exclusive Apollo Club had more than once declared him 'unable to give satisfaction' due to his lack of stamina with the beer-mug. For the sensitive Himmler this was a disastrous blow. It was only when he presented a doctor's certificate stating he had 'irritable bowels', that he was given a 'beer dispensation'. It is safe to assume that the bespectacled oddball with his half-baked notions was more an object of amusement than admiration among the beer-drinking Apollonians. Women showed even less interest in the studious nonentity. None of the rare social encounters with the opposite sex that are recorded in his diary even merit the description of 'flirtation'. There is considerable evidence that Heinrich Himmler did not have his first sexual experience until he was twenty-eight – after getting married to his wife Marga. 'And about time too', commented a Nazi official, Otto Strasser, at the time.

To judge from Himmler's reading list and his own writings, he found an escape from the failures of his daily life by increasingly taking refuge in the strange, make-believe world of his books. In ancient Hindu epics he discovered a troop of fearless warlords, who impressed him greatly. They were the Kshatriya caste, the landowning aristocracy of ancient Indian society. 'That is what we must be. That is our salvation', he claimed in 1925. Elsewhere we find admiring comments about the Japanese samurai or Rome's Praetorian Guard. To belong to an elite like that would be the solution to all his problems – Heinrich Himmler, a member, or better still, the leader of a caste of carefully selected and totally dedicated warrior heroes. His dreams turned into an obsession, a self-administered cure for his painful inferiority complex. The naïve aspirations of a young man who had problems with entering adulthood became the blueprint for the SS.

He found kindred spirits in the 'Artamanen League', one the many conspiratorial societies in the *völkisch* milieu. 'Artamanen' was a name concocted from Middle High German: 'art' meaning 'farming', and 'manen' meaning 'men'. They saw themselves as a chivalric order, whose aim was the German colonisation of eastern Europe. At their evening meetings these would-be settlers argued over the introduction of labour service for young people or a programme to stem the flight from the land. From the very beginning, conquest by force, dispossession and enslavement of the Slav population were key elements in the plans of the Artamanen, though they numbered scarcely 2,000. In his diary Himmler described how the settlements of the 'Germanic paradise' should look. Between the fortified villages of the people of 'Nordic blood' there would be camps 'of labour-slaves who would be forced, with no regard to their welfare, to build our towns, villages and farms'. Among the Artamanen the obsessive notion of the master-race was growing with a vengeance. It was here that the ground for Hitler's war of annihilation in the east was prepared. A membership list from the 1920s includes, along with Himmler, the nucleus of the 'blood-and-soil' fanatics who were later part of Hitler's inner circle. They included Walther Darré, who became head of the SS Central Office for Race and Settlement, Alfred Rosenberg, Reich Minister for the Occupied Eastern Territories from 1941 onwards, and Rudolf Höss, the notorious commandant of Auschwitz.

He who settles in eastern lands is no colonist but a hereditary follower of our forefathers, who had only for a time been forced to abandon this soil, because the need for land or a wanderlust drove them, and no Reich could protect them with the sword.

SS manual, June 1941

History is not a one-way street. Being infected by the *völkisch* virus or daydreaming about ancient Indian warrior castes do not compel anyone to become one of the greatest criminals of the twentieth century. Many members of the Artamanen League were never heard of again. Even in Himmler's case, it is possible to point to a moment when everything could have taken a very different course. During his studies he seriously considered the idea of putting his plans for colonising the east into actual practice. He took a course in Russian and enquired about emigration formalities. On 23 November 1921 he confided to his diary: 'Today I cut an article out of the newspaper about emigration to Peru. Where will I end up? Spain, Turkey, the Baltic states, Russia, Peru? I often think about it. In two years time I'll no longer be here.' At the Soviet embassy in Berlin Himmler asked if he could go to the Ukraine as an estate manager. The man who, two decades later, would despatch his units in the Ukraine to terrorise the rural population, wanted then to provide development aid as a peace-loving farmer. Had the Soviets granted his request Himmler, as a Ukrainian farmer, would have seen the German invasion from a quite different perspective.

When Himmler joined the NSDAP, the Nazi Party, in 1923, it was the logical end to an erratic search for recognition and political guidance. The party member, no. 42404, was initially no more than small fry in the wake of the then Reichswehr captain, Ernst Röhm. Later on, as chief of the SA, Röhm and his brown-shirted militia would bludgeon a path clear for Hitler to seize power. But then, like Himmler, he frequented the *völkisch* back rooms of Munich. He quickly took a liking to the zealous and devoted academic with the wire-rimmed glasses. On 9 November 1923, while Hitler was marching to the Feldherrnhalle, Röhm and his men occupied the former Bavarian ministry of war. A photograph of this *coup de main* shows Himmler carrying the banner of the *Reichkriegsflagge*. It was a defining moment in his life. Finally he 'belonged'. Despite the fact that the putsch was a miserable failure and the leaders sent to prison, Himmler had found his destiny – the political struggle for the 'cause'. He burned all his bridges. After a brief spell of employment as a fertiliser salesman in Schleissheim, his career in the agricultural sector ended for ever. This caused a serious rift between him and his beloved parents. Gebhard Himmler, the strict schoolmaster, disapproved of the 'political' ambitions of his second son, who in the summer of 1924 had been hired by Gregor Strasser, a member of the Bavarian provincial parliament, as his secretary at the modest salary of 120 Reichsmarks a month. During this period the Nazi Party was banned, and Strasser managed the substitute organisation, which went by the fairly transparent name of 'National Socialist Freedom Movement'. Another factor in the family dispute was Heinrich's private rejection of the Roman Catholic Church. For a while he had actually tried to reconcile himself with the Church through the absurd theory that Jesus was not in fact a Jew but an Aryan, fathered by a Roman centurion. But it was no use; Christianity and *völkisch* attitudes just did not go together, and Himmler became a militant opponent of the Church. Later he would have tens of thousands of priests thrown into concentration camps.

He's devoted to me and I use him as a secretary. He's very ambitious, but I won't be taking him north with me. He'll never set the world on fire.

Gregor Strasser on Himmler

At Strasser's side, Himmler began to make progress in the party. He roared on his motorbike from one Bavarian village to the next, holding 'political meetings' to drum up hatred against the Jews and capitalism – which was fully in line with Strasser's socialist leanings. After one such speech by Himmler in a small village, a visiting Jewish businessman was beaten up, and the young agitator related the story to his boss. Gregor Strasser and his younger brother Otto were, despite their left-wing tendencies, established figures in the 'Movement' in Bavaria at that time. They recognised both the energy and extremism in the young party secretary. In 1925 Himmler proposed making a list of all Jews resident in Lower Bavaria and publishing it – something which, even in the not over-scrupulous Weimar republic, would have been a monstrous thing to do. Gregor Strasser was apparently amused by this, but the laughter soon froze on his lips. Otto Strasser recorded that Himmler had told him he would even 'shoot his own mother' if Hitler ordered him to, and he would actually be 'proud of the trust' that such an order evinced. 'Heinrich, you scare me' – Strasser's riposte reflects the limitless fanaticism with which Himmler went about his work, even in those days. Men like that would be valuable to Hitler who, after the ban on the NSDAP was lifted in 1925, wanted to build an effective power-base. Himmler was first appointed manager of a *Gau*, or regional party organisation, then in 1926 deputy Gauleiter as well as deputy national head of propaganda and finally, in 1927, deputy Reichsführer-SS. At that point the *Schutzstaffel* was only 200-strong, and as a subdivision of the SA was no more than a superior bodyguard for Hitler. Its rise – to become the all-embracing state within the state, the incarnation of terror and violence, the synonym for the most disastrous perversion in the history of Germany – was closely bound up with the personality of its new representative.

It was on a lecture tour to Bad Reichenhall in 1926 that Himmler met Margarete Siegroth, who was eight years his senior. Himmler's brother Gebhard described her as 'everyone's idea of the Nordic woman', with strikingly lovely blonde hair and blue eyes. Later pictures of her show a rather 'well-built' person. The relationship

A woman is loved by a good man in three ways. As an object of love, whom he protects and cherishes but perhaps has to scold and punish if she misbehaves. Then as a spouse and a loyal and understanding companion, who struggles through life with her husband, and remains loyally by his side, without hampering his creative spirit or keeping him in chains. And as a partner, whose feet he must kiss, who gives him strength through her feminine tenderness and childishly pure holiness, so that he never tires in the hardest battles, and who gives him the most divine gift in the perfect moments of the soul.

Heinrich Himmler, diary, 1922

between the two does not seem to have matched the stereotyped gender roles of that period. Henrietta von Schirach, wife of the Hitler Youth leader, and a notorious gossip in Nazi circles, gained the astonishing impression that, at home, the ruler of the SS empire was very much under his wife's thumb. Marga was certainly a self-confident and determined lady, who passed on to Heinrich her deep knowledge of natural remedies and homeopathy. What is more, thanks to her father's generosity, she brought quite a substantial dowry with her which, after their wedding in 1928, the couple invested in a chicken farm in the Munich suburb of Waldtrudering. However, the image that is often conjured up, of Himmler the poultry-breeder who later simply applied his genetic rules to human beings, is not accurate. The truth is that Marga supervised the chicken-runs while her husband was away for most of the time on political missions. In 1929 the couple's only child was born, a daughter they named Gudrun. If the sources are to be relied on, Himmler made every effort to be a good husband and father, despite his frequent absences. The pages of his desk diary record almost daily phone calls to his wife and daughter – even at a time when he had long been busy fathering a second family with his mistress.

One would expect that a young man of twenty-nine, who had just become a father and was enjoying a certain professional success, would begin to show signs of maturity and an adult attitude to life.

You could say that he organised the SS according to the principles of the Jesuit order. It was founded on the precepts and spiritual exercises of Ignatius Loyola.

Walter Schellenberg, head of the foreign intelligence service of the SS, in his memoirs

With the SS I believe I have planted a tree whose roots are so deep that it will withstand any storm.

Himmler to his masseur, Felix Kersten

The men had no emotional relationship with their commanding officer. They saw him as a bureaucrat who was running the organisation.

Franz Riedweg, in the 'Germanic Office' of the SS

He was a man of quiet, unemotional gestures. A man without nerves.

Generalmajor Walter Dornberger about Himmler

Yet to outsiders Himmler appeared as restless as ever. In the spring of 1929, the party's Gauleiter in Hamburg, Albert Krebs, had an opportunity to study his character on a six-hour train journey from Elberfeld in the Ruhr, to Hamburg. 'Himmler was a man with any attractive or striking qualities whatever', Krebs recalled after the war. 'In that way he differed completely from Hitler and Goebbels who, when the occasion demanded, could be thoroughly likeable and charming. Himmler, on the other hand, behaved with a deliberate coarseness, very much parading his barrack-room manners and anti-middle-class attitudes, although it was obvious that he only did so to cover up his innate insecurity and gaucheness. Yet that in itself would have been tolerable. But what made his company on that journey almost unbearable was the idiotic and basically meaningless chatter that he forced on me without interruption. Even today I think I can say without exaggeration that I have never since been presented with so much political nonsense in such a concentrated form from a well-educated man. Himmler's pontificating was a remarkable mixture of militaristic bombast, small-town pub gossip and the prophetic zeal of a nonconformist preacher.' In essence this conglomeration would remain unchanged. Immature, ill-digested and far-fetched – Himmler's edifice of delusions would always be a cock-eyed affair.

How was it that, despite all this, he achieved one of the steepest career rises in the Third Reich? It was because Hitler looked for just such people and drew them along with him to power. The party boss did not need awkwardly independent men, such as the Strasser brothers, but dedicated, loyal, highly efficient figures who, as far as possible, had no independent views. Given this required profile, Himmler was the prototypical totalitarian executive. On 6 January 1929 Hitler appointed him Reichsführer-SS. By the end of that year he had more than quadrupled the strength of the death's-head troops to a good thousand. Himmler established guidelines for accepting applicants and thus endowed his *Schutzstaffel* with the attraction of a supposed elite force. Samurai, praetorian guards, the *kshatriya* caste – the new head of the SS put all his energy into turning the dream of his youth into reality. Applicants had to be 'of good blood', at least 1.7 metres (5 feet 7 inches) tall and had to meet a specific category of racial criteria: 'pure Nordic', 'predominantly Nordic or Falic', or 'with slight alpine, Dinaric or Mediterranean additions'. Anyone whom the assessors in the SS recruitment offices classified as a cross-breed 'of predominantly Baltic or alpine origin', or worse, 'of non-European origin', stood no chance of being accepted – unless Himmler, who personally examined a photo of every applicant, decided that for some other reason the SS should take him on. Incidentally, Himmler himself would have been turned down, if only because of his lack of height.

Thus the principle of 'selection' was there at the very beginning of the SS story. The gruesome procedure on the unloading ramps of Auschwitz, where SS doctors sorted the newly arrived Jews into those suitable for forced labour or doomed to immediate 'special treatment', was in fact the sadistic counterpart of the original selection process for the Black Order. Biological selection was the real and barbaric principle underlying the perverted doctrine of the SS. It was even applied to the brides of SS men. Himmler's orders on engagement and marriage, dated 31 December 1931, required that a prior biological check-up be carried out by the Racial Office of the SS on all women who were going to marry SS men. Only if the intended bride was 'healthy, genetically sound and racially at least equal' to her suitor did the Reichsführer-SS issue a marriage licence. Even after saying 'I do', the SS couple remained under supervision. It was their duty to procreate. Childless SS husbands had part of their salary docked, as a hidden premium on fatherhood. Later on, Himmler proposed in all seriousness to order SS men to divorce if, after five years, their marriage produced no offspring. He wanted to practise 'human stock-breeding' and, as he declared again and again in his speeches, to 'breed out the impurities in the Germanic race'. He told an audience of naval officers: 'I have set myself the practical task of raising a new Germanic stock. I shall eradicate the weak and unfit through selection by physical appearance, through constant exertion and through selectivity, applied brutally and without human sentimentality.' Individual desires, love, personal happiness – the essence of human dignity and civilisation – had no part to play in this, but were deemed 'sentimental' or 'decadent'. Himmler's insane obsession was aimed exclusively at maintaining and improving the 'race'. Why hundreds of thousands of people followed this crudely Darwinist doctrine can ultimately be explained only by the irrational longings of that era.

To outside observers the rise of the Black Order seemed both silent and relentless. In 1931, during a revolt against the party leadership by elements of the SA in Berlin, local units of the SS remained loyal, and Hitler presented them with daggers of honour engraved with the motto: 'SS man, loyalty is thine honour.' This phrase became the oath of the entire SS – a fatal formula that led to abuse and corruption. There could no longer be any criticism, any alternative view, any conscience. Hitler, too, recognised ever more clearly the value to him of the men in black uniform. For a long time it had looked as though Hitler was not altogether serious about the man whom Röhm had mockingly

A man of alien race, who seduces a German girl or woman, shall die by hanging. German men and women who consort with those of alien race, and alien women who consort with Germans, shall be sent to concentration camps.

Note by Himmler, 24 June 1940

My father and Himmler both held the view that racially 'valuable' German men should actually be allowed two or more wives after the war, so that the terrible loss of the nation's blood could be replenished more quickly – yet neither my father nor Himmler had the fair-haired, blue-eyed, glowing Germanic look at all.

Martin Bormann Jr

I give the ring to you and in doing so I not only wish you a love without end, but I wish you something more – namely that your line shall be without end.

Heinrich Himmler at an SS wedding, 4 March 1937

called *Anhimmler*, the 'idoliser', the man who lacked battlefield experience and the revolutionary 'smell of the stables'. Yet the serious impending crisis in the 'Movement' would alter this dramatically, and both Röhm, Himmler's old patron and friend, and Strasser, his other early mentor, would fall victim to this sudden change in Hitler's mood. The cold precision of the SS killings that left the SA leaderless in the summer of 1934 enabled Himmler to climb to the top rank of Hitler's henchmen. The real winners in the Nazis' 'Night of St Bartholomew' were not the Reichswehr, who had incited the strike against Röhm's militia, but the men with the death's-head insignia. The murders they committed were amply rewarded. Hitler released the SS from subordination to the SA and made it an independent wing of the party. Himmler was on his way to becoming the second most powerful man in the Reich.

Himmler appointed head of the German police. That's a good thing. He is clever, energetic and uncompromising.

Joseph Goebbels, diary entry for 19 June 1936

I know there are some who feel sick when they see this black tunic. We can understand that and do not expect too many people to love us.

Heinrich Himmler, 1936

After the Nazis seized power on 30 January 1933, Himmler had manoeuvred himself, in perfect coordination with his henchman Reinhard Heydrich, into the key positions in the new state. Starting in Bavaria, the two men gradually took over all the levers of executive power in the Reich. In police stations and in the newly established concentration camps, SS men gave the orders. The essential instruments of dictatorial power were concentrated in Himmler's hands. Arbitrary violence and the intimidation of ordinary citizens fell within his sphere of authority. In 1936 this process temporarily came to an end. The Reichsführer-SS became the sole head of all German police forces. It is true that he adopted the handy and reassuring slogan of the Weimar years: 'The police, your friend and helper' – but his own management style was very different. 'Whether or not our actions conflict with a particular article or sub-section is a matter of complete indifference to me', he blustered to his audience in, of all places, the Academy of German Law. 'To carry out my duty I fundamentally do that for which I can answer to my conscience in my work for Führer and nation, and which equates with healthy common sense. Whether or not the others whined about a breach of the law was of no concern to me. In truth, through our work we were laying the foundations for a new code of rights, the German people's right to live.' What Himmler dressed up as 'healthy common sense' was nothing more than brutality and terror.

Anyone who had the misfortune to come into his organisation's sights disappeared in a maelstrom of violence. Communists,

Jews, homosexuals and gypsies were systematically humiliated, maltreated and murdered in Himmler's dungeons and camps. The blind hatred against everyone who did not appear to fit the template of the supposed master race was being unleashed with dire effect even in the 'peacetime' years of the regime. Himmler personally drew up detailed rules for the day-to-day running of concentration camps – with the declared aim of avoiding arbitrary and excessive violence by the staff. Yet the reality looked very different. Despite the precise regulations, the camps became places where sadism had a free rein. Murders committed there could not be subject to state prosecution. In cases of doubt the Reichsführer-SS always ruled in favour of his guards. There is no record of a single case of Himmler punishing his camp guards for excessive violence. There are several accounts of the cynical way he dealt with prisoners. For example, in 1938 he greeted a column of new arrivals at Dachau with the words: 'You know you're in protective custody here. That means that we intend to do all we can to guarantee your safety.' Raucous laughter from the guards drowned the rest of his remarks.

> There was only one occasion when I remember Hitler bringing the conversation at dinner round to the subject of Himmler and concentration camps. We got the impression that they were labour camps. Hitler mentioned that Himmler used a very clever system in them. For example, a notorious arsonist was put in charge of fire-watching. Then, said Himmler, 'you can be sure, *mein Führer*, that no fires will break out'. We felt that these were well-organised labour camps, managed with skilful psychology. That was in fact the only time Hitler talked about Himmler. There was a note of respect and admiration in his voice for Himmler's organisational talent.
>
> *Traudl Junge, Hitler's secretary*

Despite the steady growth in his responsibilities, Himmler continued to work on his crude ideological edifice. On 2 July 1936 he arranged for a strange ceremony to be enacted by the Black Order in Quedlinburg Cathedral. SS men with helmets and rifles stood on silent guard, the crypt was decorated with 'green wreaths of German oak', and wax candles bathed the scene in a mystic half-light. Ancient Teutonic wind instruments called lurs, copied from archaeological finds, added 'uplifting' melodies. The occasion being celebrated was the thousandth anniversary of the death of the German king, Heinrich I. If we are to believe Felix Kersten, Himmler saw himself as nothing less than the reincarnation of that medieval monarch, and claimed to receive advice from him in his dreams. For 'historical reasons', that first king of the Ottonian dynasty was crucially important to the SS chief. With his colonisation of the east and his supposed resistance against the bishops of the Holy Roman Empire, Heinrich I had pointed the way for a 'Germanic rebirth' which now, a thousand years later, was at last coming to pass. The effect of this consecration, with its elaborate ceremonial, was not lost on those present. Within the ancient cathedral walls they found an outlet for their pent-up longing for a secular form of religious experience. A senior SS officer wrote about the 'devout hearts' and 'true German piety' that were displayed in this 'sacred place'. Common sense was befogged by an overwhelming collective emotion. We may assume that Himmler too, who had been to church hundreds of times in his youth, wallowed in the feeling of attending a solemn High Mass. 'Thus we have formed ranks and are marching according to immutable laws, as a National Socialist and soldierly order of exclusively Nordic men and as a sworn clan brotherhood, along the path to a distant future.' It was a typical speech by him, evoking a vague and hazy future, and setting no clear goals. From excavations of primitive Bronze Age settlements, he got archaeologists to construct a proto-Germanic culture that would justify Germany's claim to dominate the modern world; he commissioned sepulchres for SS men killed in action, based on prehistoric Germanic designs. But his visions of the future were always interpretations of a misunderstood past, a backward look at the graven images of his ancestors. A year later Himmler repeated the Quedlinburg ceremony, when the bones of King Heinrich I were 'laid to rest'. It was discovered after the war that the mortal remains found in the ground near the cathedral were certainly not those of the king himself – it was just that servile archaeologists had wanted to give the SS boss a special treat.

Rosenberg, Himmler and Darré must drop their nonsense about cults. . . . We . . . have to throw out all that occult Germanic rubbish. It simply puts weapons in the hands of saboteurs.

Joseph Goebbels, diary entry for 21 August 1935

It was there that I witnessed one of the occult fads that the head of the SS himself was occupied with. During the prosecution of [General Werner] von Fritsch [C-in-C of the army] he had sent twelve of his most trusted SS officers into a room next to the courtroom and ordered them to use mental concentration to exert an influence on the accused general. Himmler was convinced that Fritsch was bound to tell the truth under this influence . . .

Walter Schellenberg, head of the foreign intelligence service of the SS, in his memoirs

It is an indication of the power of mass suggestion in those days that Himmler's blasphemous substitute religion found so much support. Liturgical elements of Christian worship were shamelessly adapted and dressed up in 'Germanic' form. For example, among the papers Himmler left behind, there is a version of the Lord's Prayer, rewritten in the language of ancient Saxon nature-worshippers: '*Vatar unsar der Du bist der Aithar*,' it runs. '*Gibor ist Hagal des Aithars und der Irda!*' ('Our father, who art the sky, the great god, the spiritual protector of sky and earth.') One can imagine Himmler reverently murmuring this new 'prayer' at his desk for the first time. Pedantic as ever, he involved himself in the most minute ceremonial details of his new cult. According to these rules thousands of children underwent an SS name-giving ritual instead of a Christian baptism. In the centre of the hallowed area stood a swastika-decked altar with a portrait of Hitler as the 'new Christ'. Behind the altar three SS men in battledress stood on guard, flanked by bowls of flame and 'trees of life'. While the infant lay directly in front of the Hitler altar, with the ceremony being conducted over him, the congregation recited passages from

Mein Kampf in spoken unison. Nowhere was the total claim over body and soul expressed with more powerful symbolism than in this SS ritual. His favourite spot for celebrating the summer solstice was a group of ancient megaliths near Paderborn in Westphalia, but whether there, or at SS weddings and funerals, or Hitler's birthday, or the Yule festival that was to replace Christmas, Himmler relied on the powerful spiritual effect of cult ceremonies to hold his troop together. He used concentration camp labour to convert Wewelsburg Castle, in eastern Westphalia, into a cult centre, with a crypt for fallen SS officers and a marble-panelled ceremonial hall. The war prevented it from being put into service, but building plans and models show that, after the 'final victory', Himmler intended to make it into the spiritual focus of his Black Order. Around the fairly small fortress, a gigantic circular complex was to be constructed – a kind of SS Vatican, that would be the sacred and administrative centre of a 'new morality'.

Its central message was drummed into Himmler's men at every opportunity. With speeches, pamphlets and lectures the SS worked continuously on the 'ideology' of its members. The heart of the 'new thinking' was not the individual and his aspirations, but the good of the *Volk*, the race. Every member of the SS was meant to see himself merely as a link in the chain between ancestors and descendants. 'We bow in reverence before our forefathers', we read in Himmler's guidelines for yuletide speeches in December, 'whose blood flows as a mission and an obligation in our veins.' All those present then responded with the intercession: 'Their light shall shine forth.' The address was then continued: 'The bond of blood obliges the man to preserve his heritage. The purpose of his existence is to enable his heritage to bear fruit.' – 'Their light shall shine forth.' – 'We ourselves will one day be ancestors. Our children are witnesses to our breeding and our nature. And our grand-children will be heralds of our greatness.' – 'Their light shall shine forth'. The crux of this totalitarian message was the surrender of all individuality, all personal freedom. 'You are nothing, your *Volk* is everything.' The willingness of far too many to submit to this collectivisation under the sign of the swastika formed the remarkably durable cement of Hitler's dictatorship. It was also the prerequisite for recruiting personnel for mass murder. If in his speeches the Reichsführer-SS masked the

Holocaust as 'the most arduous service to *Volk* and Fatherland', this reflected the gruesomely distorted perspective of the SS. Murder as a 'service' to the race: the self-delusion of the perpetrators was the perverse consequence of Himmler's misguided teaching.

Any occasional doubts or signs of compassion were countered by the Reichsführer-SS with a demand for 'toughness' above all things. The number of times Himmler calls in his speeches and letters for the 'greatest harshness' or 'unyielding ruthlessness', is legion. For example, in his notorious Poznan speech of 4 October 1943 he sums up as follows: 'Blood, selection, toughness. The law of nature is simply this: whatever is tough is good, whatever is strong is good, that which prevails in the struggle for life, physically, spiritually and through effort of will, is the Good.' In the training of new SS recruits this principle led to frequent fatalities, when, for example, on Himmler's orders, live ammunition was used on exercises. The SS chief then boasted to the other paladins that the dead were 'deeply moral victims', because when war came they would prevent 'rivers of blood'. Kersten, the masseur, described a conversation with Göring in which the latter made fun of Himmler's 'thing about toughness'. When discussing the SS's use of live ammunition, the *Reichs-marschall* declared with 'a deadly serious face': 'Himmler, old man, I'm planning the same thing for my Luftwaffe. My "test-of-courage" order is ready for me to sign.' When Himmler enquired what the order contained, Göring replied: 'Very simple, a slight alteration to parachute-drill; twice with parachute, the third time without.' Whether Himmler saw the joke is not recorded.

Extreme and unquestioning conviction enveloped him like armour, which allowed no glimpse into his innermost self. It was only the constant flaring-up of his stomach pains that gave outward expression to his inner disturbance. Unpleasant demonstrations of particular 'toughness' seem to have helped him to don this camouflage. Himmler was notorious for making extraordinarily harsh examples of people within his Black Order. When sentences from SS courts crossed his desk he almost always increased their severity. In the spring of 1939 his own driver suffered under his excessive rigour. He was on an official trip when he collided with a motorcyclist. No-one was seriously hurt and no blame could be attributed, yet Himmler had his driver locked up for six weeks without a hearing. The poor man was not even allowed to send a message to his family. In the end, as the diplomat Ulrich von Hassell discovered, he was sworn to secrecy and released. It appears that at moments like this, despite all claims to the contrary, Himmler could be intoxicated by his own enormous power. A particularly striking example of this is the death sentence passed on his own nephew, SS *Obersturmführer* Hans Himmler. In a drunken moment, the man had blurted out official SS secrets, was condemned to death and then pardoned and sent to the front to prove himself as a paratrooper. However, he was arrested again for making 'derogatory remarks' and finally, in 1941, shot as a homosexual in Dachau, on Himmler's personal orders. Presumably the Reichsführer wanted to demonstrate his sense of 'decency' and incorruptibility – no special treatment for members of his family, no nepotism. It is quite probable that he really would have shot his own mother if Hitler had ordered him to.

Himmler was always sending people to hunt for the strangest herbs, and even worked with an alchemist, who had been given every possible facility. Afterwards, when no gold appeared, Himmler had him hanged, just like in the Middle Ages.

Reinhard Spitzy, then on the staff of the Foreign Minister, Ribbentrop

Himmler was a diet freak. Basically he was much closer to the so-called orientals than the 'effete' westerners. His hope was that after the war – he must have known it wouldn't work during the war – he could make all his troops into vegetarians, as well as non-drinkers and non-smokers. That was his vision of the future and he believed it was the best way to improve the breeding of the German race.

Ernst-Günther Schenck, SS doctor

We cannot think of this desk-bound dealer in death without a shudder. His ruthlessness sprang from his blind conviction that he was pursuing a mission on behalf of the *Volk* and the 'race'. Thus it was to him perfectly logical that moments after signing a death warrant he could immerse himself with equal seriousness in his absurd fads. A particular hobbyhorse of his was sending off numerous expeditions to remote places. Himmler sent researchers to Tibet, to uncover traces of the proto-Aryans; in the Black Forest he had rock formations examined to see whether they might be huge, prehistoric fortifications; he sent people to hunt in ruined castles for the elusive Holy Grail. The Reichsführer-SS always wanted to be kept informed in precise detail about the preparations for and results of these expeditions. Needless to say, very little of scientific value came out of them. Most importantly, there was nothing tangible to support his abstruse historical theories. Yet the SS scientists, as a rule, did not dare to reveal the futility of their missions. So they busily falsified, fiddled and distorted their findings in order to mollify their mighty patron. The organiser of terror was surrounded by a dense ring of charlatans and pseudo-scholars who were willing to sacrifice the objectivity of their research to the ideological mission. A particularly lunatic example of this is the so-called 'world ice theory' of an Austrian engineer named Hanns Hörbiger, whose offspring Paul and Attila achieved some fame as actors. In the face of all empirical evidence, Hörbiger held the view that a huge quantity of ice was present in space, which could be found in permanent rings with 'glowing suns'. The hail that falls on the earth, he claimed, came directly from space and was conclusive proof of the validity of his theory. Serious German scientists of course dismissed Hörbiger's thesis out of hand. A Berlin professor said it was 'for the standing of Germany a deeply regrettable lapse' into a 'primitive stage' of scientific research. However, Himmler vehemently defended the nonsense. In a letter with a threatening undertone, he pointed out that Hitler, too, had 'for many years' been 'a convinced supporter' of the 'world ice theory'. A member of his headquarters staff, who had done no more than ask leading astronomers to send him their critical comments on Hörbiger's 'theory', was dismissed by Himmler and 'banned from wearing the uniform and civil decorations' of the SS. In the frenzy of unlimited power common sense was left standing.

The Reichsführer never gave up trying to find scientific justification for his strange view of the world. As early as 1935 he founded an association called *Ahnenerbe* ('Ancestral Heritage'), which was to conduct research into the 'territory, mentality, deeds and heritage of the racially Nordic Indo-Germanic civilisation' – as a 'living forge of weapons' against those powers that were a threat to Germanity. With Himmler as its chairman, *Ahnenerbe* became a clearing-house for all sorts of obscure pseudo-sciences. By the end of the war, the association had more than forty departments. Criminal experiments on concentration camp inmates were as much a part of its activity as was relatively harmless 'ethnic research' in the South Tirol. A man who became the key figure in Himmler's crackpot historical fantasies was a mysterious former officer in the Austro-Hungarian army. It was Karl Maria Wiligut who, more than anyone fed Himmler's yearning for all things utopian, romantic and occult. The ill-assorted pair were first introduced to each other in 1933. Wiligut was then already sixty-seven – twice Himmler's age – and had, as it later transpired, spent nearly three years in a psychiatric hospital in Salzburg. He told the SS chief about his apparent gift of 'ancestral memory', which gave him access to the knowledge of generations long dead. He claimed to be the last offspring of a long line of Germanic wise men of the 'Uligoth' clan. His recollections confirmed, he said, that the Bible was actually written in Germany and that Germanic prehistory stretched back to around 228,000 years before Christ. At that time 'three suns' had stood in the firmament, and the earth was inhabited by 'giants and dwarfs'. Anyone else listening to him, whether, like Himmler, they had a university degree or not, would long since have sent him politely on his way, or else called for a doctor, yet the SS boss was absolutely afire with excitement. He immediately installed Wiligut as a section head in his 'Central Office for Race and Settlement' in Munich. This spontaneous enthusiasm for Wiligut's fantasies throws a revealing light on the two faces of Heinrich Himmler. Sober, meticulous and efficient at his desk, he could suddenly go off in pursuit of totally irrational, weirdly eccentric ideas, as if he were an immature schoolboy dreaming up a world of his own.

Wiligut, who was known to the SS by the pseudonym of Karl Maria Weisthor, become Himmler's very own Rasputin. He was allowed into the boss's office at any time, to reveal his latest 'ancestral memory'. He busied himself with the study of runes, the ancient Nordic script, wrote treatises for his patron on cosmology and mythological poetry, and penned the 'Our Father' that was found in Himmler's papers after his death. He was allowed to go on expeditions in search of the ancient centres of what he called the 'Irministic' religion, which he had concocted from the Saxon tradition of the great ash-tree of the world, known as *Irminsul*. Wiligut also planned the Wewelsburg complex, which he claimed to have recognised in a 'prophetic' revelation as a historic bulwark, upon which the 'Hunnish onslaught' from the east had foundered: historically speaking, this was sheer nonsense. However, Himmler was besotted by Wiligut/Weisthor and commissioned him to design a 'ring of honour' for the SS. Wiligut clearly completed the task to Himmler's complete satisfaction, for he gave the ring his blessing. The design combined the runic double 's', like two shafts of lightning, with the swastika and death's head, as well as a group of runes, which were apparently a tradition in the Weisthor family. Himmler decreed that rings taken from fallen SS men were to be kept in a chest in Wewelsburg castle – as an 'eternal memorial'. At the end of the war the chest was probably taken by Allied soldiers and shipped home.

We live in an age of the final conflict with Christianity. It is the mission of the *Schutzstaffel* in the next half century to give the German people the unique, non-Christian ideological foundation for leading and shaping their lives.

Himmler, in a plan to rediscover the Germanic heritage, 1937

Unfortunately Himmler's theories were never contested; Adolf Hitler believed they would be their own undoing.

Albert Speer, under American interrogation, May 1945

The demystification of the guru began in November 1938, when Himmler's adjutant, Karl Wolff, went to Salzburg to meet Wiligut's wife Malwine. She told the emissary how her spouse once threatened to murder her and was immediately transferred to a secure mental institution. Himmler noted the hitherto undeclared past of his 'seer', but took no action. Once again Wiligut's importance as a spiritualist silenced all doubts. However, a massive problem with alcohol and other shortcomings, some of a delicate nature, had been undermining his position for some time. A young and attractive female acquaintance of the Reichsführer, named Gabriele Dechend, had been told by Wiligut that Himmler wanted him to have children – and she was to be the mother! This was, said Wiligut, a matter of great importance and an honour for the young woman to be chosen for this role. However, Gabriele refused to let the old man have his way with her, and went to Himmler to complain about him. The SS chief was flabbergasted. He had never issued an order to his 'seer' to procreate. On 23 August 1939, three days before the invasion of Poland, the Wiligut era ended with his dismissal from the SS. Himmler requested the return of his death's-head ring, dagger and sword, which he personally took for safe keeping, as a sign of his attachment.

With the outbreak of war Himmler's areas of responsibility grew apace. Hitler, who had always made fun of his romantic and occult tendencies, now needed his efficient enforcer more than ever. The dark vision of *Lebensraum* in the east, which was first to be depopulated and then 'Germanised', finally seemed to be taking on a practical form. Himmler's staff began drafting plans for pushing the German 'ethnic frontier' as far to the east as possible. The end result was the 'General Plan East' of 1942, under which 30 million people from Poland and the western Soviet Union were to be deliberately starved to death. They would be replaced by armies of German settlers, who would secure the new Teutonic frontiers with fortified villages. With the first onslaught on Poland Himmler and Heydrich had launched operations for decimating the 'peoples of the east'. Behind the front line, in an unsystematic way at first, their *Einsatzkommandos* had hunted down Polish intellectuals and Jews. The hierarchy of command for this was always the same. In a personal discussion with the SS chief, Hitler laid down general directives, which Himmler then turned into specific orders to his men.

The relationship between the two principal perpetrators, however, was far from being the convivial rapport that the newsreels repeatedly led people to believe. For Himmler, the moments when he had to come face to face with his Führer were trials that were fraught with fear. Kersten, his masseur, and Wolff, the head of his personal staff, both agree in their description of how Himmler dreaded having to meet Hitler. 'No-one who didn't see it for themselves would believe that a man with Himmler's authority would be afraid when Hitler sent for him', Kersten told his interrogators, 'and he was as pleased as if he'd passed an exam, whenever things went well or he had actually received some praise.' It was a relationship of almost psychotic dependency. When Himmler told his subordinates that 'the Führer is always right', to him that was nothing short of a metaphysical truth – even if he, as the best-informed man in the Reich, must of course have known that Hitler had already taken all manner of spectacularly erroneous decisions. Yet in the deluded mind of the enforcer, the dictator really did play the role of saviour of the nation. 'He came to us in the hour of direst need', Himmler said of Hitler in 1940. 'He is one of those great guiding lights who always emerge in Germanic history just when the nation has sunk to its lowest point, physically, mentally and emotionally. Goethe was such a figure in the intellectual sphere, Bismarck on the political front. The Führer is our leader in every field. What is more, he is predestined by the karma of Germanic civilisation to lead the struggle against the east and to save Germanity for the world.' From Himmler such maudlin hymns of praise were no mere lip-service. For the man who took Wiligut's fairy-tales seriously, who believed in 'three suns' and an 'ice-world' in space, it cannot have posed an intellectual problem to exalt Hitler as a godlike being. Furthermore, this boundless adoration even calmed his deep-rooted need for a fixed point of reference and security, which some observers noted in the early years with his significantly older wife. His self-identification with the figure of Hitler went so far that subordinates like SS *Brigadeführer* Walter Schellenberg observed in Himmler a growing similarity with Hitler's phraseology and speech patterns.

Himmler was derisively known as 'Reichsheini'. People knew he'd never been a soldier yet was now one of the most senior army commanders. The jokes about Himmler were all in fact contemptuous and derogatory. The front-line soldiers rather looked down on the man, even though he now had the power to give them orders.

Ernst-Günther Schenck, SS doctor

Himmler walked through our field-hospital where we had sick and wounded – he first went through the wards of the wounded. Then he wanted to get away as quickly as possible, and as the senior doctor in the internal department, that annoyed me. I asked the Reichsführer if he didn't want to visit the sick wards. And he said: 'Why should I? I'll only catch something! Whatever will the Führer say if he has a sick Himmler?' That also annoyed me. I spontaneously dug into the pocket of my white coat, where I had a little tube of Pyramidon. I pulled out two tablets, handed them to him and said: 'Reichsführer, if you take these, you won't pick up any infection.' As he was now surrounded by his staff and had to save face, he took the pills and went through the wards with me at a gallop. He didn't talk much, except to say hello occasionally.

Ernst-Günther Schenck

In late September 1939 – when fighting was still going on around Warsaw – Himmler made a tour of inspection through occupied Poland, during which he visited several Jewish settlements. At that time Poland, with 3.3 million Jews in a total population of 35 million, had proportionately the largest Jewish community in the world. Himmler the inveterate anti-Semite saw a problem here, the 'solution' of which could only be placed in the hands of his SS. The decision to commit millionfold murder had not yet been taken – but Hitler and Himmler had long ago agreed that, in comparison with the ostracism and tormenting of the Jews in Germany, the already extreme harshness of German conduct in

Poland must be ratcheted up even further. In fact the SS chief, while on his tour, made no attempt to conceal his hate-driven determination. When some 'criminal types' were 'presented' to him, as a member of his escort noticed, he pointed with his baton at trembling old men, laughed at their unkempt locks and accused them of being parasites. By this time his SS men had already shot nearly 20,000 people. For years Himmler had been preparing the ground for the 'battle' that was now beginning. At the centre of his racial obsession was the division of living creatures into three categories: humans, 'sub-humans' (*Untermenschen*) and animals. At every opportunity he drummed into his SS men that Jews were 'sub-humans,' or at other times, 'human animals'. His speeches were larded with deliberate vilification of Jews, whom he verbally robbed of their dignity by calling them 'spongers', 'blood-suckers', 'parasites' or 'traitors'. Step by step, in speech after speech and pamphlet after pamphlet, their humanity was denied them, and thus the consciences of the perpetrators were eased even before the deed was done. In the end came the infamous equating of Jews with insects, which was quite openly put into words by Himmler. 'Removing lice is not a question of ideology', he ranted in Charkov in 1943. 'It is purely a matter of public sanitation.'

Whole battalions of scholars have debated over precisely when the decision on the Holocaust was taken – and who took it. Documentary sources do not give a clear answer, because the Nazi leaders preferred to deal with this most sensitive of all questions by word of mouth, so as to leave no record behind. Furthermore, much of what was written about the 'Jewish Question' was cloaked in a linguistic camouflage. 'Final solution,' 'special treatment', 'evacuation' – the perpetrators never called mass murder by its name. The only thing that is certain about the decision to proceed was that Himmler was right at the centre of the process. We also know that once the *Einsatzgruppen* unleashed their fury in the wake of the assault on the Soviet Union in the summer of 1941, the killing took on that new, unimaginable dimension that made the Holocaust unprecedented in its criminality. There is no argument over the approximate time of the decision; it was in the late summer of 1941. At the beginning of that year plans for the mass evacuation of Jews to Madagascar were still floating around the Central Office of Reich

Security, yet by the year's end hundreds of thousands of people, mainly Jews, had already been liquidated by the *Einsatzgruppen* in the conquered regions of the Soviet Union, and orders for setting up the first extermination camp had been issued.

Academics have argued fruitlessly over whether Hitler, in the countless meetings held that year, urged his henchmen on to ever more extreme measures, or whether they for their part 'did Hitler's work for him' by pursuing their own proposals further and further. For among everyone who was in on the secret there was complete agreement about the way forward. For the past eight years murder had been committed with impunity in German concentration camps; since 1939 the mass murder, sometimes by gassing, of mentally and physically disabled people had been carried on under the codename 'T4'; and SS and SD units had been cutting swathes of death through Poland and, from 1941, the Balkans as well. Long before the date assigned by historians to the beginning of the Holocaust, the number of people murdered by the regime had reached hundreds of thousands. For the principal perpetrators the step to the 'annihilation of the Jewish race', which Hitler had publicly proclaimed as early as 1939, was therefore only a question of time.

Himmler had never left his subordinates in any doubt that it was Hitler who made the final decision. After the war, the commandant of Auschwitz, Rudolf Höss, told his interrogators about a conversation in the summer of 1941. 'The Führer has ordered the final solution of the Jewish question,' Himmler told him. 'And we, the SS, have to carry out this order.' Three years later, on 5 May 1944, he was able to announce to the SS training college at Sonthofen that the 'Jewish question in general' had been 'uncompromisingly resolved' by his SS, and he added with maudlin emotion: 'You may well appreciate how hard it was for me to act on the order I was given as a soldier, but which I accepted and carried out with obedience and with complete conviction'. Elsewhere he complained about the 'hardest order' the Führer had ever issued to him. These are words of unparalleled cynicism. The murderers' commanding officer complains about the onerous nature of the deed. After the war his masseur Kersten even claimed to recall his patient revealing to him that he had 'never wanted to annihilate' the Jews at all, but had had 'quite different ideas'. Against that, however, are the countless vituperative speeches and the amoral efficiency with which he went about his work on the 'Final Solution'. A man like him cannot claim he was acting on strict orders from above. He was acting out of total conviction. It was his organising energy that made the dreadful scope of the operation possible in the first place. His penchant for intrigue and deception was precisely what gave the death camps their ghoulish character. The cruel deception with which the victims were told they were going for a 'shower' or for 'de-lousing', when about to be asphyxiated, can be traced to the malicious nature of the SS chief.

Yet what appears to posterity as the height of barbarity is the almost total lack of a sense of guilt. The chief perpetrators did not consider themselves to be criminals. Himmler was so caught up in his obsession that he was able, in all seriousness, to present the Holocaust to his men as a meritorious achievement. The most notorious example of this is the speech he gave to a gathering of SS *Gruppenführer* on 4 October 1943. In a calm, controlled voice, he explained to his audience in the grand hall of Poznan Castle. 'I want to talk to you here today about a very difficult matter. Among ourselves this must now be discussed quite openly, though we will never speak about it in public. I am referring to the evacuation of the Jews, the eradication of the Jewish people. It is one of those things that is easy to put into words – "Eradicating the Jewish people", any party member can say, "Fine, it's in our programme; removal of the Jews, eradication – we'll do it." Then along come all the 80 million good German souls, and every one of them knows one decent Jew. Of all the people who talk like that, not one has watched, not one has been through it. Most of you, though, know what it means when a hundred corpses are lying side by side, or five hundred are lying there, or a thousand. To have gone through this and at the same time – apart from some isolated cases of human weakness – to have remained decent people, has made us tough.' It is passages like that which represent the negation of everything that makes someone human. Himmler's 'decency' was in truth nothing more than a cloak for immense destructive energy. The master of the Black Order was blinded by the delusion that his 'ideology' was the only way to a better, *völkisch* world. Instead it led only into the abyss.

In August 1941, while on a tour of inspection in Minsk, the SS chief called in on the commander of *Einsatzgruppe* B, *Brigadeführer* Arthur Nebe. When Nebe had reported on the mass shootings recently carried out by his men, Himmler ordered the shooting of a further 100 alleged 'partisans', which he wanted to attend in person. According to a statement by Karl Wolff, up to that day the SS chief had never witnessed an execution with his own eyes. The following morning members of *Einsatzkommando* 8 and police battalion 9 escorted 100 prisoners, including two women, to a freshly dug pit. The victims were forced to clamber down into it in groups, and lie face downwards. Then the execution squad fired a salvo from above. Among the waiting prisoners Himmler spotted a strikingly fair-haired young man with blue eyes, aged about twenty, and had him sent over. An eyewitness, SS General Erich von dem Bach-Zelewski, described the exchange between them. 'Are you a Jew?' the SS chief asked. 'Yes.' 'Are both your parents Jews?' 'Yes.' 'Have you any forebears who weren't Jewish?' 'No.' 'Then I really can't help you.' The man was shot. As the executions continued to fill the pit, Himmler became visibly more uncomfortable. His nerve failed him and he had to vomit. Von dem Bach-Zelewski used the opportunity to point out how 'shattered' his men were after duties like that. Thereupon Himmler made a short speech in which he appealed to all perpetrators, telling them that 'as soldiers' they must obey all orders without question, and that furthermore it was not they but he and Hitler who alone bore the 'responsibility'.

Himmler was present when the first gas chambers were put into service. He looked through the peep-hole and it made him physically sick. Then he went behind the gas chambers and vomited. Two SS men saw him and were immediately sent to the battlefront. The great Heinrich Himmler does *not* throw up when Jews are being killed.

Hans Frankenthal, then a concentration camp inmate

From now on he paid special attention to the 'morale' of his murder squads. He discussed with subordinates 'more humane' methods of killing, and arranged trials with explosives, poison gas and the exhaust fumes from the engines of heavy trucks. He asked for the latest information and issued detailed new guidelines for annihilation. The culmination was the industrialised killing complex of Auschwitz-Birkenau with its containers of Zyklon B, the contents of which were thrown into the gas chambers. On several occasions Himmler saw for himself the mechanisation of the Final Solution – unlike Hitler, who never even set foot in a concentration camp. Thus, on 17 July 1942 the SS chief observed with interest the arrival and gassing of a transport of 449 Dutch Jews, in Bunker 2. This was followed, so commandant Höss reported, by a convivial evening at which the red wine flowed. Himmler concerned himself closely with the rules of conduct for *Einsatzgruppen* and death's-head units, in order to keep 'unnecessary roughness' and 'moral degeneration' under control. In a circular he recommended only moderate consumption of alcohol, good food and 'German music' to take the men's mind off the horror when off duty. He opposed with particular energy any personal enrichment on the part of the perpetrators. As he explained to his SS commanding officers: 'We had the moral right, and we had the duty towards our own nation, to kill that race which wanted to kill us. But we do not have the right to enrich ourselves even by a fur coat, a wristwatch, or even one mark or a cigarette or anything else.' Anyone who did take something for himself, Himmler went on, was 'as good as dead'. However, among the *Einsatzgruppen* and the camp guards the reality looked very different. In truth Himmler governed an empire in which every imaginable form of abuse, corruption and self-enrichment took place. And the supposed moral guardian at the head of the SS knew that perfectly well. When he made examples of people, it was only to impress the outside world. Internally Himmler regularly had to satisfy the greed of his accomplices with promotions, gifts and generous subsidies often disguised as loans; and he had tacitly to accept the fact that his camp commandants lived in luxury on the goods stolen from their victims. Incidentally, money for the endowments with which the murderers were rewarded flowed freely from the so-called 'Friends of the Reichsführer-SS', who included many of the greatest names in German industry – from Siemens to Deutsche Bank.

> He had absolutely no ethical inhibitions. He was prepared to commit any crime.
>
> *Franz Riedweg, SS 'Germanic Office'*
>
> Herr Kersten, how can you enjoy shooting poor creatures from your hide, while they're grazing at the edge of the forest! When you consider it carefully, it's pure murder.
>
> *Himmler discussing hunting with his masseur, Felix Kersten*

The accumulation of offices, which reached a new peak in 1943 with his appointment as Reich Minister of the Interior, and the almost endless multiplicity of responsibilities, seems to have led to a certain fraying of Himmler's personality. If we examine his decisions, which he frequently made while working at his desk until 2 in the morning, we gain the impression of dealing with several profoundly different people at the same time. Literally in the same breath, Himmler could express his emotional attachment to animals, which led him to abhor hunting and propose police powers for animal protection societies, and then immediately switch over to an office meeting about the 'evacuation' of a Jewish ghetto, which would result in tens of thousands of deaths. He might have just acted the loving and caring father in a phone call to his daughter, and then in a speech he would explain, apparently without emotion, why it was necessary to kill Jewish children. Between the two emotional states there was sometimes only a space of seconds. He once took his daughter Gudrun, whom he called 'Püppi' (Dolly), with him to Dachau concentration camp. That evening she wrote in her diary: 'We saw the herb-garden, the pear-trees and pictures that the prisoners had painted. Wonderful. Afterwards we had a lovely lunch.'

The same day her father had been busy with a lot of other things and had met one of his favourite medicos, the Luftwaffe staff doctor, Dr Sigmund Rascher, who worked at Dachau conducting experiments on prisoners. These almost always ended in their death. He carried out open-heart surgery without anaesthetic, locked prisoners in a low-pressure chamber, or froze them to death in tanks of icy water. He corresponded constantly with Himmler about how knowledge gained from such experiments could be applied to warfare. The Reichsführer-SS once proposed that experiments should be carried out on hypothermia victims, to see whether they could be resuscitated with 'animal warmth'. Rascher promptly conducted a trial with four women brought in specially from Ravensbrück concentration-camp. He forced the women to lie naked with their skin touching that of another prisoner who had been chilled to about minus 30° C. The outcome he reported on 12 February 1943 was that the provision of 'animal' warmth would 'unfortunately' not produce any better results than other methods. Later he suggested it would be better to conduct future experiments at Auschwitz, since the prisoners in Dachau were becoming too aware of them. 'Experimental subjects yell when they're freezing cold.' The SS chief, who watched films of Rascher's experiments at his headquarters and once even attended a 'low-pressure test' in person, supported the ghastly doctor with funds from his *Ahnenerbe* and also defended him vehemently against criticism from scientific colleagues. 'In those "Christian" medical circles', wrote Himmler, 'the view is held that of course a young German airman should risk his life, but on the other hand the life of a criminal is sacred and one should not be tarnished by taking it.' The Grand Master of the death's-head order was the driving force behind numerous human experiments carried out by German doctors in concentration camps and research centres – experiments which were as sadistic as they were pointless. They affected thousands of victims: human guinea-pigs who were forcibly sterilised by high doses of X-rays, deliberately infected with deadly pathogens or subjected to the notorious experiments on twins carried out by Dr Mengele in Auschwitz.

> This research . . . can be carried out by us with particular success, because I have personally assumed responsibility for making criminals and anti-social elements from concentration camps available for these experiments. Death is all they deserve.
>
> *Himmler in a letter of November 1942 about human experiments in Dachau*
>
> I was never aware that any research project requiring Himmler's approval was ever turned down.
>
> *Hans Münch, SS doctor in Auschwitz*

The murderous doctor, Sigmund Rascher, was in a macabre way both a perpetrator and a victim of his master's inhuman ideology. In 1941 he married a woman whom Himmler had known for many years, the Munich concert singer Karoline Diehl. At first Himmler refused to grant them permission to marry since the bride was already forty-eight, sixteen years older than Rascher and clearly too old to have children. Yet Karoline Diehl seems to have been blessed by a biological miracle. Within the space of a year she presented Sigmund with two strapping baby boys. Himmler gave the fertile couple his blessing. They were admitted to the Reichsführer's close circle of friends and frequently dined with him at his home. But then the whole deception was exposed. When Karoline became pregnant for the third time, suspicion began to grow in her husband's mind. How was it that none of the infants looked like him? The one-time spinster's edifice of lies finally collapsed. She confessed to having colluded with a female cousin to fake the pregnancies and births. The two women had been all over Munich, heavily veiled, bribing midwives, putting pressure on young mothers who had been bombed out of their homes, and had finally even stolen a baby from an orphanage. To make her third 'confinement' seem more realistic, Karoline had daubed her bed with red paint. Her husband had apparently been too preoccupied with his human experiments to spot the confidence trick. The couple ended up in prison. Shortly before the end of the war, they were both executed on Himmler's personal orders.

The example of Karoline Diehl demonstrates the dire effect of Himmler's fixation on maximising the birth-rate for the 'master race'. Once, when discussing marriage, Kersten assured Himmler that he knew many couples who were childless but happy; Himmler replied that he wasn't interested in whether 'Herr and Frau Müller are happy', the only thing that counted was the good of the *Volk*. Prolific national childbearing was simply a prerequisite for achieving the monstrous objectives of the regime. Only a rising birth-rate could compensate for the immense losses of the war and at the same time provide enough 'militarised farmers' to settle the vast regions in the east. To achieve this, virtually any means was acceptable to Himmler. He missed no opportunity to exhort his SS men to procreate – whether in wedlock or not. He decreed that homosexuals should be harshly persecuted, because they did nothing towards 'strengthening the body of the nation'. In the hostels of his *Lebensborn* ('Fount of Life') he enabled single women who met his 'racial' criteria to give birth to children in discreet surroundings. However, the purpose of these homes was certainly not to promote promiscuity, as salacious gossip often claimed after the war. Stories about muscular SS studs helping nubile German girls to make babies for the Führer are pure fantasy. The actual purpose of the homes was to prevent as many abortions as possible, when unwanted children were conceived. Healthy *Lebensborn* babies, whose mothers did not want to keep them, were put out for adoption by SS families, or else remained under the direct care of the SS. By 1945, 12,000 children had been born in the *Lebensborn* homes.

It was only when faced with the dramatically mounting losses after Stalingrad that the Reich's top human stock-breeder actually came up with the idea of organised procreation. Together with Martin Bormann, who was also interested in the subject, he considered the possibility of helping women who were widowed or could not find a husband, to realise the joys of motherhood. He even shared with Bormann the notion that polygamy should be introduced for 'worthy' men. In this Himmler probably had an eye to his own situation. In 1942 his mistress and former secretary,

Hedwig Potthast, known as Häschen, bore him an illegitimate son, who was christened Helge. In 1944 he was followed by a daughter, Nanette. The SS chief's relationship remained strictly hidden from the public under the Third Reich. Only the inner circle of Nazi leaders knew that for a long time Himmler had preferred to spend his few private hours with his new family, rather than with Marga and Püppi. It really seems to have been the great love of Heinrich Himmler's life – though it is hard to grasp such a notion in the private world of one of the vilest murderers of the twentieth century. Close to Hitler's Berghof, he furnished an attractive house for Häschen and their offspring, and the second Himmler family adapted well to the society of Hitler's Nazi entourage. Himmler even intended to divorce Marga, but she refused, chiefly for the sake of Püppi.

The contrast between these two rivals was great . . . both in appearance and character. While Bormann resembled a rampant wild boar in a potato-field, Himmler was more like a stork among the lettuces.

Walter Schellenberg, head of the SS foreign intelligence service,
in his memoirs

Himmler is constantly appalled by our unhealthy lifestyle. He says he has to be in bed by midnight, as a rule anyway. And we go on working until four in the morning, though we may lie in bed a bit longer.

Martin Bormann in a letter to his wife, 9 September 1944

So while, in his private life, Himmler was obliged to balance the interests of his own children, his SS kidnappers went in search of children in the occupied territories. They chiefly targeted orphanages, but also nurseries, schoolyards and playgrounds. Their principal victims were fair-haired, blue-eyed girls and boys. They were measured according to the rules of the 'SS Race Office', weighed and classified according to their physical appearance. If rated 'capable of Germanisation' they were then deported to the Reich. At a conference for SS and police officers, on 16 September 1942, Himmler summarised the objectives: 'We have to collect together whatever good blood, whatever Germanic blood, is available anywhere at all.' In a speech to his Gruppenführer he said: 'All good blood anywhere, all Germanic blood, that is not on the side of Germany, may one day be our destruction. That is why we are bringing back to Germany every Teuton with the best blood, to make him a German-conscious fighter, a fighter for us, and he'll be one less for the other side. I genuinely intend to collect Germanic blood from all over the world, to rob and steal it wherever I can.' It was this atavistic programme that gave rise to a particularly harrowing episode of the war. The number of children stolen by Himmler's baby-snatchers probably runs into hundreds of thousands. In most cases their parents were not even told. In the region around Zamosc in Poland alone, 30,000 children were dragged off; and at least 20,000 from the Ukraine and Byelorussia. In Germany they were given forged papers, and were adopted by loyal Nazi families. Quite a number of these children have never learned what really happened to them. They still live in Germany today as senior citizens; they have thoroughly German-sounding names and have no idea that they were once the victims of Himmler's racial obsession.

I consider it right and proper to obtain racially desirable infants from Polish families, with the intention of bringing them up in special (and not too large) kindergartens and children's homes.

Heinrich Himmler in a letter of June 1941

As a minimum number, four children are required from a good and healthy marriage.

Heinrich Himmler, Lebensborn order, 13 September 1936

By 1943, if not earlier, the Reichsführer-SS was considered by observers inside and outside Germany to be the unchallenged no. 2 man in the Nazi regime. It is no coincidence that his rise was possible in precisely the period when the tide of war finally began to turn against Germany. The setbacks on the battlefronts were met by the regime with increasing harshness – and that came into Himmler's sphere of authority. Battles lost gave a boost to his career. From 1943 onward he controlled not only all internal arms of the police and terror structure, but by now also the steadily growing *Waffen*-SS, a veritable military power-house. With the break-up of the Wehrmacht's own intelligence service, the *Abwehr*, under the inscrutable Admiral Canaris, all powers in the areas of espionage and counter-espionage also fell into Himmler's lap. Himmler had assembled a fearsome array of powers – yet he did not exploit them. When he went to see Hitler he remained the devoted vassal. As Kersten described it, the dictator could simply 'brush aside' any differing view from his SS chief with a sweep of the hand. We know of no matter, even of minor importance, in which Himmler's point of view prevailed. Sometimes Hitler even punished his 'faithful Heinrich' with deliberately hurtful words, because he knew how much his paladin would take them to heart. Thus, in 1942, Bormann wrote in a letter to his wife about outbursts from Hitler by which Himmler was 'deeply wounded' and 'clearly not just since yesterday'. The Reichsführer-SS had reached an impasse. Time and again he had sworn his black-clad legions to give unquestioning 'loyalty' to Hitler, and he was trapped by that oath himself. Hitler could rely on that, and it was in fact for this reason that he entrusted him with so much power. A putsch against him by Himmler was completely unthinkable. For he lacked the thing that next to terror provided the second important pillar of the regime – acclamation by the masses. Göring was always greeted with cheers, so was Goebbels, at least at the speaker's rostrum – but Himmler never was. When the Reichsführer-SS drove through the streets of a city no clusters of people stood on the kerbside shouting '*Heil!*' Himmler could never have become Führer – at best the head of a police state. Furthermore, a study of his official transactions shows how 'weak' his position remained right to the end, in the jungle of the Nazi hierarchy. The seemingly all-powerful SS boss had to clear even unimportant matters, down to the smallest detail, with party departments, the Wehrmacht or ministries, so that they could then be submitted to Hitler for his decision. Thus the long-running dispute about arming and supplying the *Waffen*-SS was a case where Himmler sometimes had to intervene on an almost daily basis – and not always successfully.

The only steps he took in defiance of Hitler's will were made in secret. It seems that at an early stage Himmler recognised, in moments of realism, that the war could never be won. Several times, from 1943 on, he put out feelers to the western Allies, which all had the same objective: coming to terms with the west, while continuing to fight in the east. As the war dragged on, Himmler clung ever more desperately – as indeed Hitler did – to the hope that a breach would open up in the alliance between the Soviet Union and the west. He despatched emissaries such as the Berlin lawyer Carl Langbehn and his own trusted lieutenant, Karl Wolff; he had meetings with representatives of neutral countries such as the Swedish diplomat, Count Bernadotte, and even sent a direct message to Churchill – the contents of which are unknown to this day. In July 1944 Churchill briefly noted the arrival of a radio message from Himmler as 'received and destroyed'.

To my great surprise he actually had extraordinary charm. He showed signs of humour, though he also betrayed a strong leaning towards the macabre.

Count Folke Bernadotte, about Himmler

Himmler, who in the past has been an extremist, now feels the true pulse of the country and wants a compromise peace settlement.

Count Galeazzo Ciano, Italian foreign minister,
diary entry in April 1942

Even today it is hard to fathom the Reichsführer's motives for these attempted contacts. Were the offers of talks a secret betrayal of his Führer? Was it simply part of the job of an intelligence chief to sound out all possible options? Or did Hitler actually know all about it? If Himmler did in fact toy with the idea of presenting himself as a serious partner in negotiations over a separate peace, then that would only be further proof of his progressive blindness to reality. The Allies had put his name right after Hitler's on their list of the most important war criminals. By now they had more than outline knowledge of the Holocaust that Himmler and his SS were carrying through. If the SS chief himself had no feeling of personal guilt, he should at least have seen that his adversaries had rightly identified him as the chief culprit.

Even Himmler's role in the imbroglio surrounding the attempt on Hitler's life, on 20 July 1944, remains largely obscure for want of any evidence either way. Contemporaries were certainly surprised that Himmler's comprehensive network of informers had picked up nothing about the conspiracy among senior Wehrmacht officers. Was it a coincidence that on 17 July the SS chief personally turned down a written request for permission to arrest two of the conspirators, Ludwig Beck and Carl Goerdeler? Was it also a coincidence that on the day of the failed assassination he did not even put Berlin's SS garrison on alert and that, the same evening, Kersten saw him burning papers at his headquarters? What is certain, on the other hand, is that the majority of the plotters around Stauffenberg would have been only too happy to remove the SS chief. Himmler was certainly no ally of the Men of 20 July. But did he wait, knowing or suspecting something, for the elimination of Hitler, so that he could then deploy his vast resources and take up the reins of power? That would probably have meant civil war – SS units against the Wehrmacht. On the outcome of that we can only speculate, as we also must about the extent of Himmler's knowledge on 20 July 1944.

All we know for a fact is that, when the coup against Hitler failed, Himmler was on the winning side. His SS was largely responsible for the bloody retribution against the conspirators and their families. In the process Himmler imposed the barbaric practice of *Sippenhaft*, the imprisonment, or worse, of the families of suspects. He had been applying this since 1943 against deserters – a further result of his cult of the past and his obsession with the 'customs of our ancestors'. On 3 August 1944 he had this to say about it at a conference of Gauleiters: 'You only have to read the old Germanic sagas. When they outlawed a family and banished them from the land, they said: this man has committed treason, the blood is bad, there is traitor's blood in those veins; it must be eradicated. And the blood vengeance wipes out the whole clan, down to the last member. The family of Count von Stauffenberg will be wiped out, to the last member.' In the event hundreds of relatives of the conspirators – wives, children, brothers, sisters, sometimes even parents and grand-children – were thrown into concentration camps. Stauffenberg's mother-in-law and one of his uncles lost their lives.

Faced with the imminent destruction of Germany, Himmler's reputation as a tough man of action seemed to single him out for military responsibilities as well. On 25 September he assumed military command of the *Volkssturm*. Made up of adolescent boys and old men, who had hitherto not been drafted, this formation was the regime's last desperate throw and was called upon to defend 'home soil' with the 'harshest fanaticism'. From the outset the SS chief knew perfectly well that these inadequately equipped and almost untrained units would suffer a high death-toll. Four days before the *Volkssturm* was called up, he told officers about an alleged custom of the 'Germanic seafarers', which he had evidently picked up from an old saga: 'When they crossed the sea on one of their voyages, in which the entire people took part, then if they were attacked and the ship began to leak, so that the load had to be lightened, the cry went up: boys overboard! Then the youngsters who weren't capable of fighting were thrown over the side and drowned. This was worked out quite logically in a *völkisch* way! The woman and girls, as mothers of the nation, had to be saved. Those fit for battle had to stay too.' In the end, he added, Germany too must be willing 'to send fifteen-year-olds to the front in order to preserve the nation'. Ultimately, Himmler almost inevitably became the prophet and the perpetrator of the collective sacrifice that Hitler had made his watchword. Behind the collapsing battlefronts SS commandos joined forces with the

Wehrmacht's 'drum-head courts-martial' in pursuit of deserters. Thousands ended up hanging from trees or lamp-posts, with a placard round their neck.

> Yesterday Heinrich H. drove to the Westwall. We're in daily contact by phone.
> He is tackling his job as C-in-C of the Reserve Army with splendid energy.
> *Martin Bormann in a letter to his wife, 3 September 1944*
>
> Even the SS has produced no particularly noteworthy strategist. Himmler has not really succeeded in finding such a man in his ranks. They make good daredevils, but don't have the greatest stature.
> *Joseph Goebbels, diary entry, 28 March 1945*

As commander-in-chief of two army groups, first on the Upper Rhine and then on the Vistula river, the SS boss was, at Hitler's behest, to put to the test in a military situation the extremism he had shown against 'internal enemies'. Yet the fulfilment of his dream of a soldier's life ended in disaster. His fronts collapsed just like those of the other commanders. Himmler was relieved of his command and withdrew to the Hohenlychen clinic near Berlin. Together with his mistress, Häschen, and their two children, he spent days there in deep depression. Everything was falling apart. His obsession now consisted of nothing more than hollow phrases. The elitist claims of his SS were scattered to the winds. Due to the shortage of cannon-fodder all 'racial' recruitment criteria had long since had to be abandoned. Slavic and even Moslem units had been formed under the runic and death's-head insignia – even though they were, in Himmler's perverted terminology, *Untermenschen*. Even his deepest convictions began to waver. He told Kersten he regretted having fought the churches, because ultimately they had 'proved themselves stronger'. The man who had claimed that after the 'final victory' he would deal 'mercilessly' with Christendom, now released twenty-seven clergymen from concentration camps on condition that they pray for him after the war.

On 20 April 1945 Himmler made his way to Berlin for the last time. Soviet troops were already at the edge of the city. The Führer's last birthday turned into a ghostly charade. Himmler took his leave of his lord and master, who was now only a shadow of his former self. Yet even in the face of the approaching end, the spell in which the SS chief felt trapped still held him. In the bunker beneath the Reich Chancellery he uttered no word of disagreement, no demand that the killing should finally be brought to an end. Instead Hitler launched into his usual tirades about a supposedly imminent turn of the tide – albeit with less conviction than in earlier days. The booming of Soviet artillery provided a dull acoustic backdrop to it all. It was only when Himmler was on his way back to Hohenlychen that he admitted with a sad shake of the head that 'those people in the bunker' had all 'lost their minds'.

The night after his last meeting with Hitler, he received an unusual visitor. Norbert Masur, a representative of the World Jewish Congress, had been smuggled in by plane through Allied-controlled airspace, in order to negotiate with the executioner of his people. Himmler greeted Masur with surprising warmth: 'Welcome to Germany, Herr Masur! It's time you Jews and we National Socialists buried the hatchet.' Masur replied sombrely: 'There is too much blood between us for that. But I hope that our meeting will save many people's lives.' Masur presented Himmler with a list of those who should, as a minimum, be released. They included 1,000 Jewish women from Ravensbrück concentration camp and the Dutch Jews in the 'showplace' camp of Theresienstadt. Himmler appeared accommodating: of course all the prisoners on the list would be released – and no, from now on there would be no more 'evacuation'.

That nocturnal rendezvous was the climax of Himmler's secret attempts to exploit the lives of the Jews still in his hands as a bargaining counter in his negotiations. The year before he had already offered an exchange of human lives for foreign currency and military supplies, under the cynical motto of 'blood for goods'. He still hoped for discussions with the West about a separate peace. It shows how incredibly remote from reality he was, that

Himmler actually appeared to believe that he of all people could be considered by the West as a suitable negotiating partner. Was he still trapped in the fog of his own crazy delusions? Had all those years of almost unlimited power robbed him of a simple sense of reality? Or was he driven by the fear of what would happen at the end of the war? It is a fact that his attempts at a dialogue with the West led to tens of thousands of Jews surviving the Holocaust – though hundreds of thousands more died on the death marches, when the camps in the east were brutally evacuated. However, his contacts with the West resulted in a complete break with Hitler, for on 28 April the BBC in London made public the SS chief's attempts to conclude a separate peace. In his bunker Hitler raged about the 'most shameless treason in world history' and dismissed the 'faithful Heinrich' from all his offices. Yet the verdict of his Führer did not reach Himmler's ears. While Hitler staged his own demise in his underground realm in Berlin, his enforcer had already decamped to northern Germany, where he vainly offered his services to the Dönitz government, in the hope of influencing the dying days of the Third Reich.

I will never forget my last meeting and leave-taking from the Reichsführer-SS. He was all smiles and in the best of spirits, even though the world – our world – was being destroyed. If he'd said: 'Well, gentlemen, it's all over now. You know what you have to do', that I would have understood – that would tally with what he had preached to the SS for years: self-sacrifice for the idea. But his final order was: 'Go to ground in the Wehrmacht!'

Rudolf Höss, former commandant of Auschwitz, on his last meeting with Himmler in 1945

As late as 19 March 1945 he had sworn that he and his SS would sooner die fighting to the last man, like the 'Ostrogoths on Vesuvius', than lay down their arms. Yet as the end actually approached, his heroic posture disintegrated. Rudolf Höss, one of the last of Himmler's loyal band, was left speechless when his Reichsführer announced that the best thing was to 'go to ground in the Wehrmacht'. It was the final collapse of the insane doctrine he had inculcated into the SS. The Grand Master of that death-mocking delirium was himself afraid of death. In the end he was nothing but a pitiful weakling.

> I am afraid of what is to come.
>
> *Heinrich Himmler, 22 April 1945*
>
>
> To the last, Himmler probably had the mistaken idea that he could get on with the Americans and that they would recognise him.
>
> *Ernst-Günther Schenk, SS doctor*

For many of his disciples the world was falling apart. Several dozen SS men committed suicide when they learned of Himmler's 'treason'. In Bohemia a group of SS officers lit a fire one night, stood and sang the SS vow, 'When all others are faithless . . .', and then together took their own lives. Meanwhile their one-time boss had shaved off his moustache, donned an eye-patch and slipped into the uniform of a sergeant in the Secret Field Police. With the identity papers of a certain 'Heinrich Hitzinger', a man who in fact had been sentenced to death by Roland Freisler in the People's Court, he set off on 20 May 1945, together with his adjutants, also in disguise, in an attempt to flee from his past. He was heading for southern Germany, where he intended to await the moment when the Western Powers would need him in the battle against communism. But he never got there, because the Allies were automatically taking prisoner all members of the Secret Field Police, a body that had been massively implicated in the war crimes in the east.

The three men were initially picked up by a patrol of Soviet soldiers, who were ex-PoWs under British command; a short time later they were handed over to the British military authorities. The Soviets had not realised whom they had netted, and Himmler found it

During the time that Himmler was under my supervision, his behaviour was completely correct. He gave me the impression that he recognised his fate and had come to terms with it.

Captain Tom Selvester, CO of the British Interrogation Camp no. 31

Even an insignificant man can of course, in an important post, become very important. The final phase of his life showed fully how insignificant he really was.

Albert Speer, under US interrogation, May 1945

preferable to come under the protection of a 'Germanic brother-race'. On 23 May he abandoned his alias and asked to be taken to the British officer commanding the Barnstedt prison-camp, south of Lüneberg. There he removed his eye-patch and said in a quiet voice, 'Heinrich Himmler'. Perhaps he was still toying with the idea that he could strike a political bargain. However, the victors did not treat him with the respect he had hoped for. Himmler was forced to undress completely and submit to a full medical examination. Finally, when the army doctor, C.J.Wells, tried to examine his mouth, the prisoner bit on a cyanide capsule which, according to his wife, he had always carried with him since the first day of the war. The British photographed and filmed the body, took a death-mask of him and cut a piece of brain from his skull, for research purposes. Then they wrapped the corpse of one of the century's greatest criminals in some camouflage netting and carted it off to Lüneberg Heath. Exactly where his bones lie is unknown to this day. In this respect at least, Himmler resembled the Saxon king, Heinrich I, whose reincarnation he believed himself to be.

He died, and when he was dead, we spread a blanket over him and left him lying there.

Sergeant-Major Edwin Austin, interrogation officer, 23 May 1945

CHAPTER THREE

HEYDRICH'S ASCENDANCY

It looked as if it would be a calm, sunny, spring day – as calm, at least, as any day under Heydrich's rule could be. Far away from the Gestapo's underground interrogation room in Prague, from the screams of the tortured victims, from the murderous business of the concentration camps, Reinhard Heydrich, the deputy 'Reich Protector of Bohemia and Moravia', was on his country estate, Panensky Brezany (then known by the Germans as Jungfern-Breschan), enjoying the sunnier aspect of his dark power. On that day, 27 May 1942, the man put in charge of the 'Final Solution', the organiser of the Holocaust, was in no particular hurry. In the spacious garden, framed by dense, shady woodland, Czech labourers were tending the magnificent setting. Outside the front door shafts of sunlight were reflected off the polished bodywork of the official Mercedes with the revealing number-plate: 'SS-3'.

The driver, SS *Oberscharführer* Klein, waited patiently while his boss said goodbye to his family: to Lina, his heavily pregnant wife, and his little daughter Silke, whom he lifted up once more and hugged. The kind of scene you see in any normal family. Daddy going off to work. A peck on the cheek, a smile. The same ritual as on every other morning. 'We hugged each other once more', Lina Heydrich recalled. 'I went with my husband to the porch. Reinhard climbed into the open-topped Mercedes, which immediately drove off. I waved. My husband waved back.' Back inside, the housemaid was touched. 'Oh, what a lovely goodbye!' she said to her mistress.

Heydrich was prepared for the fact that he would not see his family again for some time. The Junkers Ju 52, which was to fly him from Prague's military airfield to Hitler's headquarters at Rastenburg in East Prussia, was already waiting on the tarmac.

The next leap in his meteoric career was just around the corner. At the age of thirty-eight, SS *Obergruppenführer* Heydrich had come a long way. The all-powerful head of the security service (SD), of the State Secret Police (Gestapo), and of Germany's Criminal Police, the man with responsibility for the 'Final Solution of the Jewish Question', the 'man with the heart of iron', as Hitler admiringly called him, could also point to 'successes' in his post as Deputy Reich Protector of Bohemia and Moravia (today the Czech Republic). Over the land hung the silence of the grave. True, the anti-German resistance had not been broken, but it had clearly been seriously weakened. Conquered 'Czechia', as the Germans called it, the arms-forge of the Reich, had been subdued by Heydrich, or so he thought, with a mixture of carrot and stick, with drumhead courts and shootings, but also with concessions on social welfare. The first important objective had been achieved; Czech armaments production was continuing to supply weapons for Hitler's war.

Heydrich was the prototype of the 'new man' – of the kind of man National Socialism wanted. Heydrich was a leading representative of the absolutist generation: no longer was any form of inhumanity impossible.

Ralph Giordano, victim of the Gestapo

From his first day in the Protectorate, as everywhere else, Heydrich's name stood for terror. Shortly after taking up office, notices in red announced the names of those executed: more than 400 in the first few weeks alone. The writer Pavel Kohout who, like his father, was a member of the resistance, describes Heydrich's appearance in Prague as being like 'an entrance on stage, like a great star, with drums and trumpets. The red posters with the names of those executed showed us that this man was probably one of the most dangerous of all. And although the title "Deputy Reich Protector" didn't sound impressive, we had the feeling that the long arm of Hitler had appeared over Bohemia and Moravia.'

Heydrich did indeed see himself as being there to enforce the will of his superiors, Hitler and Himmler. 'The important thing is for the Czechs to stay calm, since we need this calm and quiet to achieve final domination of the region.' This was how Heydrich described his goal to his henchmen on arriving in Prague. The basic principle was 'that this region must simply become German and the Czechs in the region will in the end have no rightful claim to anything'.

At the end of May 1942 things had admittedly not gone that far, but Heydrich was firmly convinced that he had prepared the ground for Hitler's 'utopian' idea of making Bohemia and Moravia into a 'model' German state. Heydrich's talent for terror made him one of the great hopes of a 'greater Germanic Reich', which would subjugate 'auxiliary nations' as far eastward as the Urals, and would destroy millions of the 'racially inferior'. On 15 February 1942 Joseph Goebbels noted in his diary with genuine fascination: 'Heydrich is operating with success. He's playing cat-and-mouse with the Czechs, and they swallow whatever he feeds them. He has introduced a series of extraordinarily popular measures, including above all the almost complete suppression of the black market. He emphasises that the Slavs can't be educated in the way one educates Germanic nations; you have to break them or bend them with constant pressure. He is currently adopting the second method, with great success.'

Such 'experts' were rare and much in demand in the hot-spots of Hitler's rampantly expanding Reich: for example in occupied France, where acts of sabotage by the Resistance were increasing dramatically. Breaking down resistance was something Heydrich knew all about. He had already drafted a new occupation statute. It was to be expected that he would soon be able to add a further office to those he already held: Reich Protector for France and Belgium.

Only a few days previously, on 6 May 1942, Heydrich had inspected his new headquarters in Paris and declared off the cuff that in France a different policy would have to be followed from that in the east; the shooting of hostages was inappropriate. Yet the 'eastern policy', largely determined by Heydrich, consisted of much more than liquidating hostages. In somewhat more restricted circles the man in charge of the 'Final Solution' went into detail and spoke about 'buses earmarked for the transport of Jews from the station to the camp, from the camp to labour sites, and in which, during the journey, deadly gas is piped in'. However, this technique was apparently 'inadequate'. 'The buses are too small, the death-rates too low, and there are other annoying snags as well.' Heydrich promised bigger, more perfect, and numerically more 'productive' solutions, and ended with the words: 'The death sentence has been passed, not only on the Russian Jews in Kiev, but on the entirety of European Jewry. Even on the French Jews, whose deportation starts in the next few weeks.' Announcing death sentences was an everyday affair for the man who seemed to contemporaries like 'polished steel', and whom Hitler called 'my Duke of Alba'.*

Heydrich himself, lord of life and death, felt invulnerable. It never entered his head that he personally might become a target. He was convinced that 'his Czechs' would 'do nothing to me, and even if any of them wanted to, they wouldn't dare'. He attended concerts without a bodyguard and had himself driven around Prague in an open car. But for a long time foreign secret services had been keeping the SD chief in their sights, as one of the most dangerous Nazis of all. Evidence reached the German authorities that something was afoot – an operation of some kind or other against Heydrich or other top Nazis. When checking a train in March 1942 police found a musician carrying a specially designed rifle with telescopic sights and a silencer. The man, who was from Moscow, claimed he wanted to kill Heydrich. No-one believed him.

All over Bohemia and Moravia in the spring of 1942 Heydrich's security service recorded an increase in the number of acts of sabotage. The mood of the Czechs, according to a daily report by the Prague section of the SD on 26 May 1942, continued to be as anti-German as ever: 'In the night of 23/4 May in Ostrava-Vitkovice, Moravia, about 500 leaflets with communist slogans, of the kind already familiar, were distributed. These bore on one side the words "Long live the ČSSR, the Red Army and Stalin" and on the other side, in German, the rhyme: "*Sichel, Hammer, Hitlers Jammer. Die Armee rot, Hitlers Tod*" (Hammer and Sickle, trouble for Hitler. The Red Army, Hitler's death).'

* The Spanish Duke of Alba, governor of the Netherlands 1567–73, boasted that under his rule no less than 18,000 people had been hanged or beheaded.

'On 24.5 the front wheels of a locomotive were derailed at the junction of the Kladno-Prague line and the Kladno-Nučice line. It is assumed that the cause of the derailment was a loosened screw on the front bogie of the engine.'

'At about 23.00 on 23.5 passenger-train no. 816 from Čelakovice to Prague was blown up. The explosive, probably fitted with a time-fuse, detonated near the centre of the train and hurled some of the track in the air.'

Like a predatory animal, Heydrich sensed a mounting danger. 'I see and hear that foreign propaganda and a defeatist and anti-German whispering campaign are noticeably on the increase again in the region,' he warned journalists in Prague the day before his departure. 'You must know that, for all my patience, I will not hesitate to strike with unprecedented harshness, if I should get the feeling and the impression that the Reich is still considered weak, and that genuine helpfulness on my part is regarded as weakness.' That is how he really thought. He considered he was being helpful, and that his victims, the Czech population, should actually be grateful to him. He was gradually losing touch with reality.

> What was true of Heydrich was true of others too. Heydrich was like Himmler, like Höss, the commandant of Auschwitz, and other caring fathers. Their inhumanity was not obvious to the observer. Heydrich was known to be interested in things cultural. How does that fit? How does this disjunction, this schizophrenia, come about? It can be accounted for by what is correctly expressed in the phrase 'the absolutist generation'. They had given themselves over to evil, without describing it as such.
>
> *Ralph Giordano*

The 'Hangman of Prague', as he was known in the 'Protectorate' with a mixture of hate and fear, wanted to enjoy another concert in 'his' city. Prague, the capital of the SS's model state of Bohemia and Moravia, Heydrich's state, seemed to him more German than Nuremberg; Heydrich wanted to spend this last evening with his wife Lina at the Waldstein Palace in the elegant Mala Strana district. The main item on the programme, personally arranged by the Reich Protector, was an opera by his father, Bruno Heydrich, the founder and director of the Conservatorium in Halle. The work, entitled *Amen*, was thoroughly Wagnerian in style, and had been given its first performance in Cologne in 1895, nine years before Reinhard Heydrich was born. Like an evil prophecy, the title of the prologue is 'Reinhard's Crime'. It is about murder – how could it be otherwise?

While Heydrich was sitting in the front row listening with rapt attention to the music, in London the Czech government-in-exile waited with mounting anxiety for news from their homeland. The exiled Czechs, under President Eduard Beneš, had been unable to agree on what was the most sensible action to take against this Heydrich, and what was most likely to succeed. The previous year some had already called for an immediate and powerful strike against the German occupiers. Others warned against the Germans taking revenge on the civil population, against the inevitable harsh reprisals, should a man like Heydrich be targeted. The bolder ones won the day. They wanted to give a sign to the world that the Czech people had not given up. The assassination of such a high-ranking Nazi would give courage to all nations under the German yoke and would inflict a severe psychological blow to the hitherto victorious Nazis.

The ideal day chosen for mounting the assassination attempt was originally to be 28 October 1941, the anniversary of the founding of the Republic of Czechoslovakia. Two young men were to be parachuted in to carry out the dangerous assignment: Josef Gabčik, a locksmith from Slovakia, and a Czech named Karel Svoboda. All those involved knew very well what they were letting themselves in for – 'Operation Anthropoid', as it was codenamed, was a suicide mission.

The plan was strictly secret. Only the closest circle around Eduard Beneš knew for what purpose a small force of agents were being given weeks of instruction in British training areas. When Svoboda received an injury, Jan Kubis, a farmer's son from Moravia, took over as Gabčik's partner. The two had met in the Foreign Legion, had fought together against the Wehrmacht, were close friends and could anticipate each other's every move. So they made the perfect team for a risky undertaking of this kind. At 10 p.m. on 28 December 1941, after weeks of delay, a Halifax bomber took off with the two agents, from Tangmere airfield in Sussex. At 2.15 the next morning Jan Kubis and Josef Gabčik parachuted down about 5 miles south of Pilsen (Plzen) – a long way from the point that had been planned. The pilot had been hampered by fog. The aircraft had to fly low over the snow-covered landscape and it was feared that the loud noise of the engines would give them away. But Kubis and Gabčik were in luck. The first people they met, once they had landed on home soil, were not members of the Gestapo but a gamekeeper and a miller, both of whom were sympathisers of Beneš' government in exile. They fed the agents and kept them hidden. Kubis and Gabčik went underground, made contact with the Resistance, gathered information about Heydrich's habits and looked for the best way to kill him. The first idea was to blow up the Reich Protector with a bomb, while he was travelling by train to Berlin. However, there seemed more promise of success if they attacked him on his morning drive from Jungfern-Breschan to Prague.

On bicycles Kubis and Gabčik checked the route for a suitable spot for the assault. On their way into Prague they found the perfect place, on the northern edge of the city. On a street called V. Holešovičkách, a hairpin bend and a steep downhill slope forced Heydrich's driver to change into a lower gear. It was at that moment, before the car could accelerate again, that Kubis and Gabčik would strike. With a burst of fire from his collapsible Sten sub-machine-gun, Kubis was to kill Heydrich as he sat unprotected in his open car. Then, to make absolutely sure, Gabčik would throw a special hand-grenade whose high explosive charge would detonate on impact. The preparations dragged on for four months. Then information filtered through that Heydrich might leave the Czech lands earlier than first thought, on a trip to France. Kubis and Gabčik could lose no more time. On 20 May the Czech government-in-exile radioed to Prague giving their approval for the attack. Heydrich was to die in seven days time, on 27 May 1942.

The music that the audience was offered in Prague's Waldstein Palace on the evening of 26 May was no work of genius. *Amen*, the opera by Reinhard Heydrich's father, though certainly inspired by Richard Wagner, fell a long way short of its model. Yet Reinhard Heydrich, himself a gifted violinist and cellist, was not troubled by the composer's shortcomings. For him, *Amen* was a journey into his own past, to the boyhood in Halle of Reinhard Tristan Eugen Heydrich, who was to become known as one of the greatest criminals of the twentieth century.

> The strange thing is that he was fully conscious of his job as an executioner and was always ready with a positive justification for it. He saw his work as some kind of deed requiring great personal sacrifices, something he felt he had to bring to completion for the sake of the Cause.
>
> *Lina Heydrich, widow, in her memoirs*

It really should have turned out very differently. The omens were favourable. Reinhard Heydrich was the second of the three children of a family that was respected both socially and culturally in the Kingdom of Saxony. He was musically gifted and learned to play the violin and cello, but even as a schoolboy he was a friendless loner. He remained so throughout his life. Heydrich looked delicate and gangling, had a slight squint and a high-pitched voice, which earned him the nickname of 'nanny-goat'. Even at the peak of his career he was hesitant about speaking in public – worried that his high voice, so unbecoming to his athletic image, would once more make him a laughing-stock, as it had when he was a schoolboy. The young Heydrich was plagued by an inferiority complex, and he tried to protect himself by striving ambitiously to rise above his tormentors, to achieve more and be better in every field, especially sport. All his life he had to be the best, and often enough he succeeded in outrunning the rest. This did not make him any more popular with his contemporaries. Even as a youth, this limitless ambition gave Heydrich an aura of haughty arrogance. The elitist concept of the SS, the promise of a community of noble Teutons, seemed made for a man like Heydrich, who was all too often dismissed by those around him.

However, nothing hit the young Heydrich as hard as the claim that he had Jewish blood, that his grandfather was a Jew. During his time as a naval cadet, he was known as 'Blond Moses'. And when he sought refuge in music by playing the violin, his classmates called him 'Moses Haendel'. Even decades after the war, Heydrich's widow Lina was quite convinced that 'as far as his aptitude and abilities were concerned, Reinhard was always an artist. He could translate feelings into sound, and if things had not gone so terribly wrong, I would not today be the widow of a war-criminal, but without doubt the wife of a brilliant violinist.'

Once in the navy, Heydrich's world seemed reasonably under control. The 'White Moses', as he was also dubbed, won the respect of his colleagues by frequently beating them at fencing, swimming, sailing or riding. But even in the navy he made no friends. He remained an outsider, marred by affectation. He was his own worst enemy. This was to have disastrous results, for overnight Heydrich's world began to totter. His naval career was in the balance.

The whole affair was really a farce. As a young officer in 1931, Heydrich was forced to answer for himself before an honour court, because he had promised to marry the daughter of an influential naval architect, but then lost interest in her when, at a dance in Kiel, he met Lina von Osten, a village schoolmaster's daughter from Fehmarn, and was engaged to her only two days later. Heydrich cut the announcement of his betrothal from the local paper and sent it to the spurned girlfriend. The young lady promptly had a nervous breakdown. The scandal was complete. The father of the rejected bride complained to the naval high command. The accused, Reinhard Heydrich, on trial before the honour court, showed no feelings of guilt and appeared so self-satisfied that the honour council judged him to be of bad character and unfit to continue serving in the German navy. Heydrich was dishonourably dis-charged. He had lost his career, his reputation and a secure salary. His world fell about his ears.

What was he to do? Back in Halle, humiliated by failure, he is said to have cried like a child for days on end. There was no prospect of a job. Germany had plunged into a deep economic crisis. Reinhard Heydrich was now one of millions of unemployed, without hope of work. Finally, his mother turned to an old family friend, the head of the SA in Munich, Baron Karl von Eberstein, and asked him to help her son in his job search. Eberstein had access to Heinrich Himmler, who at that time was planning to create an SS intelligence service, in order to gather information on friends and enemies of the Nazi Party for himself and for the party leadership. As a trained intelligence officer Heydrich seemed to fit the bill. Eberstein arranged a visit to Himmler's chicken-farm at Waldtrudering, near Munich. Himmler was so impressed by Heydrich's towering Nordic stature, his manner and the plan he rapidly outlined for building up an SS secret service, that he hired the candidate on the spot. Once more Heydrich could don a uniform. 'At that time, the important thing for Reinhard', his widow recalls, 'was that he had an assignment that took him into the *völkisch* and nationalist environment, and was of a military nature.'

Heydrich was just twenty-seven years old when he took up his new post. Before the summer of 1931 he had had no contact with either the Nazi Party or the SS. All he knew about Hitler's party was what he had been told by his wife Lina, who had joined at the early age of eighteen. He did not think much of the SA's ranting hordes, but the elitist, quasi-chivalric demeanour of the SS exactly matched his own arrogant style. Thus began, in 1931, the fateful relationship between Himmler and Heydrich, which led to the SD security service and its murder squads, and determined the entire future course of the SS and police in the Nazi period. Heydrich had Himmler to thank for his career – and he repaid this with unquestioning loyalty and cold-blooded brutality in the implementation of SS policy. Himmler soon realised that Heydrich possessed capabilities that were indispensable in forging the SS and the police into 'a tool to carry out the Führer's will', and to create a culture of killing. Himmler's obsession with racial cleansing and Heydrich's ice-cold sense of the macabre formed a fatal combination. Often, when Himmler harped on about his dream of a Reich run by Teutonic noblemen, he would give way to Heydrich with the words: 'Oh, you and your damned logic! Whatever I suggest, you shoot down with your logic.' In fact, Heydrich tried as a rule to find a way of fulfilling Himmler's wishes, in order to be granted even more power in return. As Hermann Göring said: 'Himmler's brain is called Heydrich'. No other relationship in the history of the Third Reich had such dire consequences for millions of people as that between Himmler and Heydrich, two men with the same goals and the same determination to destroy. They complemented each other in a sinister way, without ever being friends. 'Reinhard had no friends. There isn't a man who can say he was Heydrich's friend', Lina Heydrich confirmed. 'He didn't want any friends. He didn't think he was allowed to form friendships.' They would only stand in his way when he carried out his bloody handiwork. Walter Schellenberg, later Heydrich's foreign intelligence chief, gained a similar impression of his superior officer. 'He could be unfair to the point of cruelty', says Schellenberg. 'Nonetheless, he liked to act the tender husband and paterfamilias during the regular musical evenings at his house – because his boss, Reichsführer-SS Himmler, placed great importance on a close family life.' The contradictions in the life of this great twentieth-century criminal are only superficial.

> My recollections of Heydrich are thoroughly positive. He was a good boss. I got to know him because I used to take him the press reports. I took the first edition to him personally in Prinz-Albrecht-Strasse. I had a good relationship with Heydrich. You could say it was like that between sportsmen. But I never received any official instructions or that sort of thing from him.
>
> *Karl-Heinz Hass, then in the press section of the*
> *Central Office of Reich Security*

The beginnings of Heydrich's SS secret service were modest, not to say impoverished. It lacked money, premises and staff. But Heydrich showed a talent for organisation and began eagerly building up a network of informers across the Reich. His 'qualities' became apparent at an early stage; his tremendous drive, his sheer, inexhaustible energy and the will to work hard all day long and through the night as well. At the peak of his career he kept his secretaries busy working shifts, and wore out adjutants by the dozen, unable to keep up with his pace. Heydrich developed into the archetypal modern manager, interested in only one thing: power. 'What mattered to him was not the power of the German Reich', says SS Obersturmbannführer Wilhelm Höttl about the SD chief, 'What he wanted was to have the sensual enjoyment of power for himself. That's all it was about.' He was never interested in pursuing political visions of his own. Heydrich remained essentially a man without principles. He had learnt his lesson when he was thrown out of the navy and recognised that a man only succeeds in a military organisation if he subordinates himself to it unconditionally. Heydrich carried out Himmler's wishes and never opposed him. He discovered early his fatal gift for predicting what Hitler or Himmler would do next. In this way he was able to make himself in-dispensable – as an amoral, all-purpose hit-man, who would stop at nothing.

For a long time, the only things that could threaten his dizzying rise were the shadows of his past and, even more dangerous for an SS man, the rumour of his alleged Jewish origins. 'In February 1932, only a few weeks after our wedding', Lina Heydrich recalls, 'we received some news that shocked us. When his shipmates found out that Reinhard Heydrich, having been discharged from the navy, had been given a job with the SS in Munich, they reported him to the Nazi Party Gauleiter in Halle and claimed that Reinhard's real surname was not Heydrich but Süss, and that he was a Jew.' The rumour had legs. On 6 June 1932 the Gauleiter of Halle-Merseburg, Rudolf Jordan, wrote to Gregor Strasser: 'It has come to my notice that in the party headquarters there is a party member named Heydrich, whose father is said to live in Halle. There is reason to suppose that the man in Halle identified as the father, Bruno Heydrich, is a Jew.' Attached to the letter was an extract from Hugo Riemann's *Dictionary of Music*. It might perhaps be appropriate, the Gauleiter wrote in conclusion, 'for the personnel department to look into this matter'. Years later the question was still being asked surreptitiously: did Heydrich hate Jews because he himself had Jewish antecedents?

According to Lina Heydrich, the rumour could be traced back to 1926, when Reinhard's brother Heinz failed to be accepted by a duelling fraternity in Dresden – allegedly because he was a Jew. Disappointed and dismayed, Heinz Heydrich then made his way 'on foot' from Dresden to Halle to confront his father Bruno about this. 'He found out that his father had gone on financially supporting his own mother (Reinhard's grandmother) even after her second marriage, to a master locksmith named Süss, and had sent her letters addressed to "Frau Heydrich-Süss".' Bruno Heydrich himself had been denounced by his violin teacher as 'Jew Süss', something which Heydrich Senior found rather amusing. (*Der Jud Süss* was a notoriously anti-Semitic novel, later filmed. *Tr.*)

However, for Reinhard Heydrich it was hardly a laughing matter. At the start of his SS career he was plagued by awkward questions, until on 22 June 1932 a 'Certificate of Racial Origin' appeared to clear the matter up. 'The attached list of forebears', the document stated, 'demonstrates that *Oberleutnant zur See* Reinhard Heydrich (Retd) is of German ancestry and free from coloured or Jewish blood.' Heydrich's grandmother, Ernestine Wilhelmine Heydrich, had taken a second husband, Gustav Robert Süss, but 'as the mother of several children from her first marriage often called herself Süss-Heydrich'. This formally did away with the rumour, but the suspicion remained. When the rumour was passed on to Himmler, he apparently wanted to dismiss it. Hitler, on the other hand, after a lengthy conversation with Heydrich, is said to have come to the conclusion that 'this man was highly gifted but also very dangerous, a man whose talents had to be retained for the Movement. Such people could only be allowed to operate if a firm hand was kept on them. His non-Aryan ancestry made him ideally suited for this work, for he would always be grateful to us for keeping him and not throwing him out, and would give us blind obedience.' That indeed proved to be the case, as Himmler confirmed: 'In his battle against the Jews, the Führer really couldn't have found a better man than Heydrich. He showed no mercy towards the Jews.'

When Hitler seized power in 1933, Heydrich and his security service seemed at first to gain very little from it. In the Nazi power structure the SS was still second rank. As chief of the political police in Bavaria, Heydrich was based in Munich's police headquarters. He was now Himmler's deputy and, like his mentor, he dreamed of incorporating the police into the SS throughout the Reich. By April 1934 Himmler had the political police under his control. The breakthrough came on 20 April 1934, when Hermann Göring handed over command of the Gestapo in the state of Prussia to Himmler, who in turn appointed Heydrich as its chief. From Berlin he would now extend the influence of the SS over the entire German police. Heydrich quickly demonstrated his ruthless amorality in the first massacre in his term of office.

Ironically, it was Ernst Röhm, head of the SA and the godfather of his first son, who had to be liquidated. Heydrich and Röhm were on first-name terms, but that made no difference when it came to the SS's claim on power. The pretext for the killings was the so-called 'Röhm putsch', and together with Himmler and Göring, Heydrich helped to draw up the death lists. Heydrich handled the bureaucratic side. To him the massacre of 30 June 1934 was just a 'measure', like the many other acts of terror that can be attributed to him, to 'his' security service, to the police which, from 1936, was reorganised on SS principles across the Reich, and especially to 'his' Gestapo.

The police must be everywhere, in order to deter any disturbance of law and order in the Reich, or to suppress it, even if no actual violation of the law has taken place – or not yet.

Dr Werner Best, deputy head of the Prussian secret state police

Our aim is to be as much feared by the criminal as we are regarded by the German citizen as a trusted friend and helper.

Himmler about the Gestapo in a radio talk on 'German Police Day', January 1937

Under Göring and its first president, Rudolf Diels, the Gestapo had already broken the law of the land, but it was only under Heydrich that the organisation was transformed into an 'ideological assault force', an apparatus of terror; for many of its victims it became synonymous with the Third Reich and differed fundamentally from the political police of other dictatorships. Heydrich's Gestapo saw itself as an 'ethnic police force', and regarded its adversaries as 'pests on the people', whom it had to combat 'biologically', in other words, eradicate. Like a doctor, the police had to preserve the 'national body' from diseases caused by 'germs'. Ralph Giordano had a total of six encounters with the Gestapo and came away with traumatic experiences, which even today often make him start from his sleep with terror. 'The Gestapo was everywhere', he says. 'It was short-hand for Hitler's Germany, for Nazi Germany, for terror, for our constant feeling that at any moment we could meet a violent death.'

The legend of the Gestapo conjures up an all-powerful, omnipresent, octopus-like surveillance system, whose very existence was meant to show everyone that resistance was pointless. Yet in terms of personnel, Heydrich's Gestapo was poorly equipped. For example, in Düsseldorf, a city of 500,000, there were only 126 Gestapo personnel operating in 1937. Essen, with a population of 650,000, only had 43, and Mönchen-Gladbach a mere 14. In most smaller towns there was only one Gestapo man, and quite often none at all. Nevertheless, the Gestapo appeared to see and hear everything. It was credited with almost mythical powers. As Heydrich claimed with satisfaction in 1941: 'The Gestapo and Security Service are woven around with all the secret mutterings and whisperings of a political thriller. In Germany people talk about them with a mixture of fear and horror, though their presence also gives them a certain feeling of security. But malicious circles abroad like to accuse our men of brutality in their work, of inhumanity and heartlessness verging on the sadistic.' Not surprisingly, said Heydrich, people in the Reich 'want to have relatively little to do with us'.

Only those interested in denouncing others turned to the Gestapo with confidence. And there were all too many of those. Without this army of slanderers the 'ethnic police' would have remained

> As soon as I saw S. for the first time, he immediately began talking politics. . . . Among other things he expressed himself in a derogatory tone. 'Germany wants to annex Belgium, Holland and all surrounding countries, and that's why action must be taken against Germany.'. . . I am convinced that S. is a thoroughly malicious opponent of the state, who . . . wants to influence all his customers.
>
> *Report against the hairdresser S. made by his tenant to the*
> *Wiesbaden Gestapo, 17 August 1938*

blind and deaf. As many as 85 per cent of their 'cases' began with a denunciation. Never before in German history had it been as easy as in the Nazi state to get rid of unpopular neighbours, rivals at work or others whom people wanted to harm. A single word could create huge difficulties for them, make them helpless victims of an arbitrary system, and deprive them of a livelihood and a future.

One of the legal foundations upon which Heydrich built his informer state was the so-called 'Law on Defamation' of 20 December 1934. Under this law it was punishable, among other things, to make 'openly spiteful statements, or statements manifesting a low cast of mind, about leading personalities in the NSDAP, such as are liable to undermine confidence in the political leadership'. This opened the doors wide to slander. A wave of malicious tale-telling swept the country. The traces of this deluge have survived in thousands of documents in state and provincial archives.

Here is a typical example, taken from an investigation report by the Gestapo office in Wiesbaden on 5 February 1940: 'It is relevant that on 31 January 1940 our friend Wulf made the following statement to us: "Yesterday, when the Führer was making a speech, I turned the radio off; I could not listen to all the shouting and the insults. Anyway, it did not interest me. Hitler is to blame for the war, and whether we win it or not, we ordinary people will still be poor."' Three of his 'friends' had just bad-mouthed the car mechanic to the Gestapo. 'Friend Wulf' was sentenced to four months' imprisonment. Three years later he would have been certain to receive the death sentence from Judge Freisler's 'People's Court'.

It is incomprehensible to me that, while German soldiers are loyally doing their duty, they can be stabbed in the back by agitators like this. I have known F. for quite some time and there has been no animosity between us. . . . However, since I cannot tolerate the way he continues to express such opinions publicly, I have voluntarily laid this evidence.

Denunciation to the Wiesbaden Gestapo by a German soldier on leave from the front, February 1942

In view of the war situation, F.'s manner of talking is . . . designed to undermine the fighting spirit of our troops and confidence on the home front. From the statements of the witness there is no doubt whatever that F. is an opponent of the Third Reich and stands outside the ethnic community. For this reason an exemplary punishment seems appropriate . . .

Final report on the same case by the Wiesbaden Gestapo, March 1942

In 1937 such 'malicious attacks' caused no less than 17,168 people to be reported. Ralph Giordano was among those denounced – by people he trusted. On 1 September 1939, the very first day of the war, he was arrested and interrogated for five whole days. What had happened? 'Playmates, two kids I had grown up with and played in the street with, had for several years copied down all the anti-government opinions I had expressed, and then via their parents or grandparents had passed them on to the *Blockwart* [neighbourhood Nazi watchdog], and he reported me to the Gestapo.' Details of who had been arrested when, how and for what, spread like the wind – reinforcing the legend of the all-knowing Gestapo, of the danger of being delivered up to the knife just because of an unguarded word. A climate of fear and distrust hung over the country. For in the worst cases the victims of denunciation did not just end up in prison, but in concentration camps, as a 'pest on the people', or else under the executioner's guillotine.

What went on behind the gates of a German concentration camp was something the Swiss academic, Carl Jacob Burckhardt, wanted to find out, when he came with a delegation from the International Committee of the Red Cross. As was only to be expected, Burckhardt's intentions met with resistance. The Germans wanted to work out the details of the programme and would only allow the delegates to talk to prisoners in the presence of the camp commandant and SS officers. Burckhardt refused to accept this, and threatened to return to Geneva and give an international snub to Germany. A dinner party with the Duke of Coburg was arranged, to clear the matter up. Burckhardt recorded his impressions of Heydrich that evening. His report gives us a unique insight into the psyche of a man who, some years later, was to become the architect of the Holocaust.

'Before he appeared, everyone was tense and expectant; even rather apprehensive; we spoke only in muted tones. Then the double doors flew open and Heydrich appeared in the first black uniform that I had seen at close quarters. He was slim and fair-haired. His Mongol-like eyes looked at us from a sharp, pale, asymmetrical face, the two halves of which appeared completely different. The famous executioner entered the Duke's drawing-room briskly, yet at the same time he seemed soft and sickly.'

At the dinner-table Heydrich sat on Burckhardt's immediate left. 'I was struck by his hands; lily-white, pre-Raphaelite hands, made for protracted strangulation.' The police chief began his conversation by talking about the nineteenth-century writer, Heinrich von Kleist, but he had reservations both about Kleist's story, *Michael Kolhaas*, and his play *The Prince of Homburg*. 'Then he changed the subject and tackled me head-on: "In your small country, the freemasons are the masters. That has to change, otherwise you too will be lost." "What sort of influence do you attribute to that society?" I asked him. "The freemasons", he retorted, "are the instrument of Jewish vengeance; at the very back of their temples stands a gallows in front of a black curtain, which conceals the Holy of Holies, to which only initiates of the highest degree have access. Behind the curtain is written just the one word, *Yahve*. The name alone says enough." Then warming to his theme, he went on: "Should the millennial task of the Führer not succeed, and we are destroyed, then everything will be revealed, then triumphs will be celebrated with orgies of cruelty, beside which the rigour of Adolf Hitler will appear very moderate."' A feeling crept over Burckhardt, that he was 'seeing a man plummeting down and grabbing at a wet, overhanging rock'.

After the table was cleared, Heydrich and Burckhardt sat down to talk privately in an adjoining room. 'Heydrich's eyes darted to right and left, and – out of habit – at the curtains. Only then did he look at me, for perhaps a second. But I felt two people were looking at me simultaneously, and this realisation was accompanied by a feeling of wanting to keep him at bay. That was the one time that Heydrich looked me in the face, for a fraction of a second.' Heydrich turned down Burckhardt's request to visit concentration camps of his own choosing. 'You must not forget that we're fighting, the Führer is fighting, against the international foe. It is not only a matter of getting Germany back to health again; we have to save the world from its intellectual and moral destruction. This is something you people haven't understood. So, it's not on. The answer from the Herr Reichsführer is negative. You will visit only those camps that we nominate.'

The 'conversation' ended inconclusively for the moment. 'We got up at the same time', Burckhardt recalled. 'Heydrich stood in front of me and while looking over my left shoulder, he said in a strained voice: "Abroad they call us bloodhounds, isn't that so? It is almost too tough for one individual, but we must be as hard as granite, otherwise the work of our Führer will come to nothing. Much later, people will thank us for what we have taken upon ourselves".' Then Heydrich left the party and Burckhardt felt he had encountered a 'young, evil god of death'. Two days later Heydrich summoned Burckhardt again and after consulting Himmler, he gave approval for the delegation to visit the concentration camps.

Burckhardt had encountered a man with a closed vision of the world. There was an unshakable certainty as to who the enemy was. For Heydrich there was never any doubt on this point. He was absolutely convinced he was doing the right thing. Someone who thought like that could issue death warrants from his desk during the day and after work be a fond and caring father of a family – a perpetrator who was clear in his own mind, and had his adversary constantly in view. In a series of articles for the SS magazine, *Das Schwarze Korps*, about 'The vicissitudes of our struggle', written in the autumn of 1935, Heydrich complained that 'even after two years of National Socialist revolution some of the German people are beginning to become indifferent to the Jews.' However, he said, the SS perceived 'on the part of the Jews, a tough, enduring and undeviating ambition to achieve their goal which is, and always has been, the domination of the world and destruction of the Nordic peoples.' In this ideological battle it was necessary to show ruthlessness. 'Because if we as National Socialists do not fulfil our historical mission, by being too objective and humane, we will not be allowed the excuse of mitigating circumstances. People will simply say: in the judgement of history they did not complete their task.' Therefore, he went on, there were no longer any 'enemies of the state', only 'enemies of the people', racial adversaries. As Heydrich put it in 1936: 'The driving forces of the opposition remain eternally the same: world Jewry, world freemasonry and a clergy that is largely political and which abuses confessional religion.' Heydrich considered the Jew as the 'deadly enemy of all Nordic and racially healthy peoples. His goal has been and remains the domination of the world through a more or less visible upper class. Every means and any form of organisation are permissible for this purpose, however stupid and ridiculous they may appear on the outside. The direction always remains the same.' As Heydrich's widow Lina attests, her husband was 'deeply convinced that the Jews ought to be separated from the Germans. In his eyes the Jews were rootless racketeers, who were out to gain advantage for themselves, and ultimately clung like leeches to the body of another nation.' In many conversations he apparently explained to her 'that anti-Semitism has nothing to do with politics, but is a "medical problem"'. As Lina Heydrich put it: 'Reinhard had no problem with the Jews politically or socially. But it was in the soul, in the psyche, that the Jews seemed intolerable, to him and to me.' A man who talks like that is a perpetrator by conviction.

Drawing on the writings of the historian Michael Wildt, Ralph Giordano describes Heydrich as 'the prototype of a new kind of man, the kind that National Socialism wanted. He was the leading protagonist of the absolutist generation. No extreme of inhumanity was ruled out any longer. Everything was possible, even the murder of millions of human beings.' Physically, too, the tall, fair-haired, athletic Heydrich looked like 'the embodiment of the new man, whom the Nazi racial doctrine worshipped as its ideal. Heydrich was the perfect example of what National Socialism pictured as its typical loyal follower.'

Everywhere in Heydrich's universe there were enemies that he believed obsessively he had to get rid of, in his role as the 'maid-of-all-work' or the 'rubbish-bin of the Reich', as he later called himself. The man who, in Hitler's eyes, was the 'ideal National Socialist', wanted to know everything about the 'crooked princes' as he sometimes called the Jewish 'pests'. 'The better I got to know this man', the SD's foreign intelligence chief, Walter Schellenberg, wrote of his boss, 'the more he seemed to me like a predator – always on his guard, always sensing danger, suspicious of everyone and everything. Along with that, he was smitten with the insatiable ambition always to know more than the others, to be in control everywhere. He subordinated everything else to this goal.' Admiral Canaris who, as head of the *Abwehr*, the Wehrmacht's intelligence service, was in competition with Heydrich's SD, saw him as 'the cleverest of beasts'.

When hunting, the 'predator' proceeded in a strictly bureaucratic manner. His SD set up a card-index, which contained the names of all the Jews in Germany, Jews who had emigrated from Germany and the most important foreign Jews. 'One of his particular gifts', says Schellenberg, 'seemed to be the ability to recognise immediately other people's personal, professional and also political weaknesses. He would file these away both in his phenomenal memory and in his card-index, and bring them out at the right moment.' For this purpose he had 250 officials in his central record office, collecting personal data, information and rumours about anyone whom he considered an enemy of the Reich or just a personal rival.

It is thought that Heydrich even kept files on Hitler and his top brass. What particularly interested him were Hitler's unexplained origins, traces of Jewish blood among Himmler's relatives, Goebbels' sexual affaires, and Göring's extravagance and tendency to corruption. A man who knew so much was feared, even by those who outranked him in Hitler's hierarchy. Filled with distrust of everyone, he spent days and nights behind mountains of papers, and studied files on Catholics, freemasons, Marxists and Jews. He was soon known as the 'Suspector-General', sniffing out revolutionary intrigues everywhere, and in his hunt for opponents he did not hesitate to use unconventional methods. Thus, as the SD's foreign chief, Walter Schellenberg, tells us in his memoirs, Heydrich made use of an up-market brothel called 'Salon Kitty', at Giesebrechtstrasse 11 in Berlin. Here prostitutes employed by the SD offered their services to senior men in the party, government, Wehrmacht and diplomatic corps, for an average fee of 200 Reichsmarks, and were expected to pick up all the information they could at the same time. The girls in Heydrich's bordello came from all over the Reich, including Austria and Poland. The lovelies were aged between twenty and thirty and spoke either French, Italian, Spanish, English, Russian or Polish, as well as German. Quite a few were fluent in three or more languages – and all had one thing in common: a murky episode in their past, which had driven them into the clutches of the SD. Among the girls who worked in the Salon Kitty were students who had dropped out, women who had had abortions, criminals and professional prostitutes, who were able to ply their trade in the service of the Nazi state without having to fear blackmail by the police. It is said that microphones were concealed all over their place of work. In the basement, Heydrich's experts recorded the conversations on disc. Only when the boss himself appeared for an 'inspection', did he 'give me express orders beforehand to make sure that all the sound equipment was switched off', as we are told by Walter Schellenberg, who probably originated the idea of exploiting moments of intimacy for the gathering of information.

Salon Kitty was patronised intensively. In 1940 alone over 100,000 men are said to have visited the Nazi brothel, an average of 30 a day, including many prominent figures, diplomats, generals, top Nazis, ministers, Gauleiters and entertainers. The circle of clients ranged from Sepp Dietrich to Joachim von Ribbentrop, from the Italian Foreign Minister, Count Ciano, to the head of the 'German Labour Front', Robert Ley, as well as leading film actors like Ferdinand Marian (famous for playing cads, womanisers and Englishmen) and the highly respected Hans Albers. The only people who remained unsatisfied were those trying to obtain information. As a rule Heydrich's whores failed to elicit any state secrets from their punters.

Action against Jews, especially against synagogues, will shortly take place throughout the Reich. This is not to be obstructed. However, liaison is to be established with the local police forces in order to ensure that looting and other excesses are avoided. . . . Preparations are to be made for the arrest of 20,000 to 30,000 Jews throughout the Reich. The well-off are to be specially targeted. Detailed instructions will follow in the course of the night.

Secret instructions from Inspector Heinrich Müller to regional police headquarters before the Kristallnacht *pogrom on 9 November 1938*

With a merciless and undeviating perfectionism, Heydrich carried through to completion every task he tackled. If he was going to have an informer state, he wanted 100 per cent coverage. When it came to persecution, no-one would be spared. And if 'the Jew' was considered an enemy of the people, then in his view every last one of them must be got rid of – never mind how. Heydrich had no time for the rabble-rousing anti-Semitism of a man like Julius Streicher, for the pornographic tirades in his smear-sheet, *Der Stürmer*, nor for unplanned pogroms. He wanted a radical solution of the 'problem', which at first did not expressly mean mass murder, but rather the centrally controlled expulsion of all Jews from Germany, if possible to Palestine. For Heydrich was convinced that 'either we overcome the opposition once and for all, or we are done for'. The 'Aryan legislation' on its own was not enough for him. It did not banish the 'threat of Jewry' from Germany. The Jewish organisations with all their international links were, as he saw it, still working towards 'the destruction of our nation and all its values'. But how did Heydrich intend to 'remove' the Jews? As a provisional objective, SS *Untersturmführer* Herbert Hagen drafted a note for Heydrich's file: 'First: suppression of Jewish influence in all areas of public life (including business). Secondly: encouragement of Jewish emigration.' From Heydrich's viewpoint there was only one way of solving the 'Jewish Problem': all Jews must be compelled to leave for Palestine. 'Being a National Socialist', he said cynically, 'makes me a Zionist.'

The first great test of this concept came with the *Anschluss*, the annexation of Austria into the Reich in 1938. In order to expel more Jews, even faster, Heydrich's henchman in Vienna, Adolf Eichmann, set up a 'Central Office for Jewish Emigration' in the former Rothschild mansion in Prinz-Eugen-Strasse. Those who wanted to leave the country could certainly obtain all the necessary papers there within a week, but it cost a fortune. Owners had their property confiscated; in order to demonstrate solvency, the emigrants were forced to acquire foreign currency at astronomical and totally fictitious rates of exchange. Heydrich and his accomplices made millions from the expulsions. A Jewish official from Berlin, invited to Vienna to visit the 'Central Office', noted the conveyor-belt efficiency of the operation: 'In at one end comes a Jew who still has some property, a shop or a factory or a bank account. He now goes through the whole building, from counter to counter, from office to office, and when he comes out at the other end, he has been robbed of all his rights; he doesn't possess a *pfennig*, but he does have a passport which says: "You must leave the country within 14 days, otherwise you will be sent to a concentration camp."' However, the men whom Heydrich and his enforcer Eichmann employed to commit this organised robbery were not, as one might imagine, from the SS or SD. Behind the long tables, noisily stamping forms, sat staff from the Jewish community. Thus victims became accomplices – a duplicitous system that bore the unmistakable handwriting of Heydrich.

> Heydrich was always rather abrupt, nervous, not without personal vanity, an excellent colleague to those of his staff who contributed in some way to strengthening his position.
> *Adolf Eichmann, 1959*
>
> I was of course 'the tool of Heydrich'; I was his subordinate.
> *Adolf Eichmann, 1959*

The Central Office in Vienna was to become the model for expulsion throughout the Reich. By contrast, Heydrich strongly disapproved of the nationwide pogrom on 9 November 1938, which became known as *Kristallnacht*, because of the quantities of broken glass. He called it a 'disgusting mess', a throwback to the time when drunken, howling mobs of SA went looting and bludgeoning their way through the streets. The pogrom, he said, was 'the severest blow to the state and the party since 1934'. Needless to say, Heydrich was not expressing sympathy for the victims. He simply condemned these brutal assaults as irrational. Like his superior, Himmler, he preferred a noiseless, bureaucratic form of terror, murder by rubber-stamp and signature, centrally controlled, and as smoothly impersonal as a conveyor-belt.

Three days later Hermann Göring summoned all the officials concerned, including Heydrich – over 100 in all – to a conference at the Ministry of Aviation, in order to discuss the economic consequences of *Kristallnacht* and measures for removing Jews from the German business world. The conclusion they reached certainly met with Heydrich's approval. Germany's Jews were to pay a 'fine' of 1 billion Reichsmarks; the Aryanisation of German business was to be pushed through, and Joseph Goebbels demanded greater discrimination against Jews in Germany; they would no longer be admitted to theatres, cinemas, circuses, public baths and swimming-pools, or even 'the German forests'. Finally Heydrich got up to speak and stressed the major concern for himself and the SD: 'Even if we remove the Jews from business life, we are still left with the basic problem of getting the Jews out of Germany. . . . On the instructions of the Reich Commissioner we have set up a Jewish emigration centre in Vienna, through which we have already removed 50,000 Jews from Austria, whereas in the Old Reich [Germany] only 19,000 Jews were expelled in the same period.' Heydrich proposed that a similar emigration centre be established in the 'Old Reich', that Jews be compelled to live in ghettos and to wear a distinguishing mark. This met with the unanimous approval of those present. The Minister of Finance, Schwerin von Krosigk, emphasised that the Jewish 'social proletariat' could not be retained in Germany. 'Consequently, our objective must be as Heydrich has said: to get rid of everyone who can be got rid of!'

The details of how Heydrich envisaged the 'solution to the problem' were revealed in the SS news-sheet *Schwarzes Korps*, edited by Gunter d'Alquen, a member of Heydrich's SD. An article published in late November 1938 filled out the scenario that Heydrich had sketched at the meeting on 12 November: 'The Jews must therefore be chased out of our apartment-houses and residential districts and accommodated in terraces or blocks, where they can be together and have as little contact as possible with Germans. . . . This parasitic race, restricted in every respect to its own kind, will then decline into isolated poverty, being neither willing nor able to work for themselves. . . . But let no-one imagine that we can then calmly watch this happening. The German people does not have the slightest desire to tolerate hundreds of thousands of criminals within its borders, who not only make their living by crime, but also intend to wreak vengeance! . . . Least of all do we wish to see these hundreds of thousands of poverty-stricken Jews become a breeding-ground for Bolshevism and a recruitment organisation for politically criminal sub-humanity. . . . When things reached that stage we would be faced with the harsh necessity of eradicating the Jewish underworld in precisely the same way that we customarily eradicate criminals in our strictly governed state: with fire and the sword. The result would be the real and final end of Jewry in Germany. It would be annihilated without trace.' From 1939 onward, Heydrich was given powers to coordinate all ministries and departments that were working on the 'solution of the problem' and were anxious to accelerate emigration. Pressure on the German Jews was increasing.

Berlin's Jews were compelled to submit a daily list of seventy families willing to emigrate. The Reich central office was soon able to chalk up a 'record': the figures for emigration from the 'Old Reich' almost doubled, from 40,000 in 1938 to 78,000 in 1939. Eichmann, now in Prague, got about 30,000 more Jews 'out of the door'. Heydrich even negotiated with the Jewish rebel army in Palestine, the Haganah, in order to increase the pace of the mass exodus.

Yet all the dreams of expulsion faded into the background on the night of 31 August 1939, when at 10 p.m. German radio interrupted its programme to make a historic announcement: 'At about 8 p.m. the Gleiwitz radio-station was attacked and temporarily occupied by Polish insurgents. The Poles forced their way into the transmission studio. They succeeded in reading out an appeal in Polish and some of it in German, but after a few minutes the intruders were overpowered by police.' The news was part of an operation planned a long time earlier and organised by Reinhard Heydrich, who told SS *Sturmbannführer* Naujocks quite openly: 'For the foreign press and for German propaganda we need actual proof of Polish incursions.' An SS commando was to dress in Polish uniforms and stage an attack on a German radio station, thus providing Hitler with a pretext for his invasion of Poland. Hitler's henchman, Heydrich, had no compunction about taking prisoners from Sachsenhausen concentration camp, putting them into Polish uniforms and having them shot at the site of the alleged assault. As planned, German propaganda made a great to-do about the 'provocative act' that Heydrich had arranged. 'Unprecedented attack by bandits on Gleiwitz radio station' ran the headline in the *Völkischer Beobachter*. The German Wehrmacht crossed the frontier into Poland. The war had begun without ever being declared. Now Heydrich did not just have the German Jews in his sights. The fate of three million Polish Jews was in the balance.

Four hours before the war started, Heydrich wrote a farewell letter to his wife, in which he named her his sole heir, should anything happen to him; he ended with the words: 'Bring up our children to believe in the Führer and in Germany, to be loyal to the idea of our Movement, to be tough in abiding by the basic laws of the *Schutzstaffel*, to be tough on themselves, to be magnanimous towards people of our own race and harsh towards all enemies at home and abroad.' Always those words 'tough' and 'harsh' – they were Heydrich's creed. The harshness advocated by Heydrich against enemies of the Reich was put into practice by the *Einsatzgruppen* of his SD in Poland. Even in the first three days of the war Heydrich's men reported numerous arrests to their headquarters in Berlin. However, when on 3 September ethnic German inhabitants were killed by Poles in the so-called 'Bloody Sunday of Bromberg', the *Einsatzgruppen* intensified their activities in Poland. Orders were now issued for a 'ruthless suppression of the Polish rebellion that is flaring up' and executions were sanctioned. Two days later on 5 September, some 50 Poles were shot in the town hall of Bromberg. On 7 September the first hostage shootings took place, with a death-toll of 400. When the Wehrmacht complained about arbitrary shootings, Heydrich reacted by remarking that, for him, it was 'all going much too slowly'. He said that 200 executions a day were 'insufficient'. 'We won't harm the ordinary people, but the aristocrats, the clerics and the Jews must be killed.' The war was to serve as a cover for the murder operations. 'The ruling class in Polish society is to be virtually neutralised', Heydrich is recorded as telling his department heads in the Gestapo headquarters in Berlin. 'The lower levels of the population that remain will receive no specialised education and will be kept down in various other ways.' The upper classes were to be sent to German concentration camps. Jews were to be concentrated in urban ghettos, so that they could be kept under better control and later deported. Heydrich seemed to be in his element. He was now lord over life and death.

On the ground in Poland Heydrich got a first-hand picture of the murderous work of his *Einsatzgruppen*, and of the 'ethnic reallocation of land' that Hitler had called for in Poland – the expulsion of all Jews and the Germanisation of the country. Hitler had pointed the general way forward. Himmler and Heydrich implemented the details. On a weekly basis Heydrich arrived in Berlin from Poland, made his report, urged ever higher numbers of executions and kept his departmental chiefs informed about the massive expulsion programme that was planned for that country. For the moment, Jews from the former western regions of Poland were to be driven as fast as possible into the 'Polish rump state', and concentrated in ghettos in a few accessibly located cities, until the strictly secret 'planned overall measures (i.e. the final objective)' could be set in motion. All over the Polish rump state, which was soon renamed the *Generalgouvernement*, ghettos were created. *Einsatzgruppen* and units of the security police and SD began the expulsions. But in the reception areas neither shelter nor food was provided.

Since the beginning of the war, Heydrich's terror tactics had been controlled by a new super-authority, the Central Office of Reich Security (RSHA) with its offices in Berlin, at 8 Prinz-Albrecht-Strasse. Heydrich's creation brought the secret police (Gestapo), criminal police (Kripo) and the official Nazi security service (SD) together in a single institution, combined their powers and exploited the effects of synergy, in order to make surveillance and prosecution even more effective. Most of all, it was Department IV, in which Eichmann's 'Jewish section' was housed, that earned a terrifying reputation as the 'headquarters of terror', the abode of desk-bound dealers in death. During the war, Heydrich, the most senior bureaucrat of extermination, was hardly ever seen in his office. The boss of the RSHA wanted to get involved in the action himself, and in the Polish campaign he flew missions as an air-gunner and later even as a fighter-pilot. Next to fencing, flying was his greatest passion. Ever since the police had been placed under Himmler's central control in 1936, and Heydrich's authority extended over the whole Reich, a four-seater aircraft had been put at his disposal for official trips. Every day before starting work he took flying lessons from his pilot in a biplane, and learned stunts like rolls and looping the loop. Even at the joystick, Heydrich was a daredevil who pushed things to the limit. When he outgrew the training aircraft, he practised secretly on larger planes at the Staaken military airfield near Berlin. 'And one day', Lina Heydrich recalled, 'he landed at a fighter-base called Werneuchen. Increasingly anxious to keep his activities a secret, he had all his papers carted over there and held meetings in primitive conditions.' His family watched him pursue his risky hobby with mounting anxiety. Himmler also became even more concerned, after one of Hitler's adjutants was killed in a flying accident. In May 1937 Himmler sent Heydrich a written injunction 'not to pilot an aircraft while on active duty.' For 'flying requires constant practice, which is not, however, to hand when flying after long intervals.' The ban must have hit Heydrich hard, but it did not stop him from continuing to fly and even passing his pilot's examination for the Luftwaffe.

Heydrich the bureaucrat was seeking direct contact with the enemy in the skies over the front line. During the invasion of Norway he piloted an ME 109. At the same time as Hitler's deputy, Rudolf Hess, undertook his mysterious mission to Britain in May 1941, Heydrich was taking part in reconnaissance flights over that country. While France was being invaded, he crossed swords with Royal Air Force pilots over Belgium and Holland. Dicing with death, Heydrich considered himself invulnerable in the cockpit. 'Believe me, it'll take a lot to put *me* out of action!' he wrote on a postcard to Himmler on 5 May 1940, and signed it 'Your loyal and grateful Heydrich'.

Reichsführer! I wish to report that I am entering service with my forward troops. Naturally, I still need a little more flying-time, but in a week I hope that I will perform in my role as a 'rookie' to the satisfaction of my superiors.
  Reinhard Heydrich in a postcard to Himmler, 5 May 1940

Time and again the mighty chief of the security service and the Gestapo flung himself into highly risky flying escapades, always in search of self-affirmation through being decorated as a successful fighter-pilot. Military awards were highly valued in SS wartime society. Himmler's masseur, Felix Kersten, explains Heydrich's behaviour by saying, 'he sat continuously at his desk, while the others were out there fighting'. He had to make 'decisions about life and death', and therefore needed to 'look death in the eye and prove his courage'. Heydrich never wanted to be a mere desk-man. He saw himself as a fighter in the very front line and, like Hitler, he seems to have loved the feeling of looking into an abyss and gambling for the highest stakes. Again, with the invasion of Russia, he was seized by a burning desire to be at the Front. On the ground his *Einsatzgruppen* were murdering countless thousands every day; in the sky above them Heydrich was hurling himself at enemy aircraft. However, on one occasion he seems to have pushed his luck too far. His plane was hit, somewhere east of Berezina, and he had to make an emergency landing. Heydrich was missing for two whole days. Had Himmler's closest associate fallen into the hands of the Red Army? Reinhard Heydrich as a prisoner of the Soviets – 'what a coup that would have been for the Russians', wrote his wife Lina.

Heydrich is believed to have hidden in a cave and waited until an assault-troop from his security service got him out. After this adventure Hitler also put a stop to his flying. Heydrich was needed for other assignments. Murder on the largest scale imaginable had only just begun.

At two of those receptions [given by Hitler] we went as a couple. The first one was in the Reich Chancellery. Hitler was standing in the entrance-hall. We went up to him. He stretched out both hands to us and said spontaneously: 'What a handsome couple. I'm most impressed!' Reinhard smiled to himself. Then we were left on our own.

Lina Heydrich, in her memoirs

As early as September 1939, Heydrich had realised that for Hitler the military conquest of the east and the annihilation of the Jews were inseparable goals. From then on he saw it as his task to show Hitler and Himmler ways to achieve them. He recognised at an early stage where the persecution of the Jews was bound to lead. In January 1941, when planning for an invasion of the Soviet Union was at a decisive stage, Heydrich knew that murder on a new scale was imminent. A 'special assignment' had to be carried out. The officers in charge of the *Sonderkommandos*, who were to do the killing behind the front line as the Wehrmacht stormed ahead, were only fed information by Heydrich a little at a time, as regards the orders he had received from Hitler. In April 1941 he called together the heads of departments in the RSHA to discuss the matter, but only talked about a 'tough assignment'. Their job was to 'secure and pacify' western Russia. After the SD chief had made things somewhat clearer, not a single senior SS officer, not even the notorious Gestapo boss, Heinrich Müller, volunteered for this bloody mission. Only under pressure from Heydrich did the leading ranks of the death squads form up. It was scarcely less difficult to recruit manpower for the *Einsatzgruppen*. One form of bait that was always attractive was money. Wilhelm Höttl, then working in Section IV of the RSHA, recalls that when recruiting these troops there was no mention of murder. 'People talked about "taking out" the Jews, which turned out to mean physical annihilation. We were invited to volunteer for this mission, and since far too few people did so, every section of the SD, Gestapo and Criminal Police, had to put up a certain quota, and groups were even seconded from the *Ordnungspolizei* [paramilitary police force].' At that time, says Höttl, the German economy was not in particularly good shape. 'For that reason the high daily pay that you could earn with an *Einsatzkommando* was a definite attraction. People said to each other, you only have to show up, you go to Bialystok or some such place and collect your money. And for a low earner those few Reichsmarks were a lot in those days.' It soon became apparent to whom and for what the men recruited in this way had sold themselves. However, money was certainly not the only motive for joining a murder squad. Many were convinced it was the right thing to do – not least for their career.

Using a combination of pressure and cash, Heydrich assembled his troops. By May 1941 3,000 men stood at the ready. Four *Einsatzgruppen* were formed, made up from Gestapo officials, Kripo crime-busters, men from the SD and the civil police, soldiers from the *Waffen*-SS and non-German police auxiliaries. *Einsatzgruppe* A, under Dr Franz Walter Stahlecker, was to follow

The intellectual, metropolitan Jews have to a large extent succeeded in escaping eastward ahead of the German armies . . . consequently it is hardly possible at present to keep the liquidation figures at the previous high level, precisely because the Jewish element is absent to a significant degree.

SS Brigadeführer *Arthur Nebe, commander of* Einsatzgruppe B, *in a report to the Central Office of Reich Security, 4 September 1941*

The solution of the Jewish question has been tackled energetically by the *Einsatzgruppen*, especially in the area east of the river Dniepr.

Report no. 6 of the Einsatzgruppen *for the period 1 to 31 October 1941*

Army Group North up to Leningrad, *Einsatzgruppe* B led by the chief of Criminal Police, Arthur Nebe, would follow Army Group Centre to just short of Moscow. *Einsatzgruppen* C and D, commanded by SS *Brigadeführer* Dr Otto Rasch and *Standartenführer* Otto Ohlendorf respectively, were to fan out across the vast area covered by Army Group South, from the Pripet Marshes to the Black Sea.

Heydrich gave only verbal instructions to the group commanders about their odious mission. Walter Blume, head of *Sonderkommando* 7a, recalled that Heydrich had described the extermination of eastern Jewry as 'orders from the highest level of government'. 'These orders were issued in such an unambiguous way', said Blume, 'that there could be no doubt as to what was awaiting us in Russia.'

How specific was Heydrich when addressing the leaders of the murder squads? 'All I can remember', said the former leader of *Einsatzkommando* 3, Karl Jäger, after the war, 'is that Heydrich stated in a speech that in the event of a war with Russia the Jews in the east would all have to be shot . . . I can still recall a police officer asking in these very words: "You mean we have to shoot the Jews?", to which Heydrich replied, "Surely that's obvious", or something of the sort.'

'I regarded those statements by Heydrich', Jäger admitted, 'as binding orders to the effect that, when taking up my activity in the east, the Jews had to be shot. For that reason I did nothing to prevent those shootings.'

In the first weeks of deployment, Heydrich's instructions were still open to interpretation. The murder mission was directed against Jews in communist party or government positions. This chiefly applied to men of military age. The more precise definition of these target groups was left to the discretion of individual squads. No blanket order for slaughtering the entire Jewish population of the Soviet Union had been issued – yet.

> At first I was unable to fathom why anyone could be so deranged as to deliberately bluff their way into that most repulsive of all repulsive 'professions', which Reinhard practised; but then I found out how crucially important that activity was. And for the first time I understood Reinhard's confession: 'I have to do it. Anyone else might pursue selfish interests or abuse the system.'
>
> *Lina Heydrich in her memoirs*
>
> Anyone who works their way up in the SD has to have a twisted personality, otherwise, in my view, they simply couldn't survive.
>
> *Albert Speer, under interrogation by the Americans, May 1945*

The army which, on 22 June 1941, launched itself upon the Soviet Union, was the largest armed force in history assembled for a single campaign: close on 3.2 million soldiers, divided into seven armies, and four armoured groups, with 3,580 tanks, 7,184 artillery pieces, and three *Luftflotten* totalling over 2,000 aircraft. Within a few days Hitler's Wehrmacht had swept over the western edge of the vast Red empire. Countless people were suddenly faced with a German occupation, which they could not yet assess, but whose worst aspects they would soon come to know. The war that began on that 22 June was the war Hitler had always wanted – a war of annihilation in the east for long-cherished goals: the seizure of *Lebensraum*, the eradication of Communism and the extinction of Jewry. Back in early March he had stressed to the commanders-in-chief of the three armed services and other senior officers: 'A war such as that against Russia cannot be conducted in a chivalrous manner. It is a struggle between ideologies and racial opposites and has therefore to be waged with unprecedented and merciless harshness.'

The tasks of the *Einsatzgruppen* were clearly defined: 'The combating of all elements hostile to Germany and the Reich to the rear of our fighting troops.' In practical terms this meant that they had to advance in the slipstream of the Wehrmacht, systematically comb the already occupied areas for ideological and racial enemies of Hitler's Reich and murder them. Gypsies and other 'anti-social elements' were also to be executed.

That, then, was the war that Hitler intended to wage in the Soviet Union: one that was unfettered by any civilised instincts. In this war – his war – no rules which would guarantee even the smallest degree of humanity should apply.

The systematic cleansing work in the eastern territories included, as required in our basic orders, the virtually complete elimination of the Jewish element. With the exception of the district of White Ruthenia, this objective has essentially been achieved through the execution of Jews totalling 229,052 to date.

Secret activity report by Einsatzgruppe *A for the period 16 October 1941 to 31 January 1942*

From the first day of the Russian campaign, the *Einsatzgruppen* murdered communists, intellectuals and, on Heydrich's orders, above all 'Jews in party or government posts', since they were potential 'trouble-makers'. The fact that boundaries between categories of victim were fluid and deliberately blurred, is perfectly exemplified by the first murders carried out by *Einsatzkommandos*

in the Latvian town of Liepaja, then known by the Germans as
Libau. As early as July 1941, the shooting of hostages was
a daily occurrence there. Since 29 June the port with its naval
dockyard had been in German hands – after the invasion of
Russia, the defenders of the town, Soviet sailors and militarised
dockyard workers had held out for a week before surrendering.
But there were still isolated skirmishes between the German
occupiers and pockets of defenders: reason enough for the men
of *Einsatzkommando* 2 to 'pacify' the town of Libau 'with the
most ruthless of measures', to quote their orders. They had been
called in by the town commandant, a *Korvettenkapitän* in the
German navy. He it was who announced draconian reprisals: 'For
each individual attempted assault, act of sabotage or looting, ten
hostages held by the Germans are to be shot.' The first 'hostages'
were shot in the dunes near Liepaja on 4 July with the help of the
SS section of *Einsatzgruppe* 2 – they were forty-seven Jews and five
Latvian communists. Three days later the town commandant raised
to one hundred the number of hostages to be shot in reprisal for
one wounded German soldier. The German death squads – Hitler's
willing executioners in the struggle against the 'international
Jewish-bolshevist enemy' – knew exactly who were to be selected
as hostages: the Jews in the town that had just been occupied. The
victims were still Jewish men 'of military age' – those were their
orders. Women, children and old people were spared.

I can confirm today that the objective of solving the Jewish
problem in Lithuania has been achieved by *Einsatzkommando*
3. There are no Jews left in Lithuania, except for forced-
labour Jews plus their families.
Report by the commander of the Security Police and SD,
Einsatzkommando 3, 1 December 1941

Press-gangs combed the houses in search of hostages, and young
Jewish men were picked up on the streets without warning. They
were easy prey for their pursuers, because after 5 July, on the
orders of the town commandant, they had to wear yellow patches
on their chest and back. It was during this period that the sixteen-

year-old high-school girl, Fanny Segal, lost her father. He guessed that there was trouble in store for the Libau Jews. 'One day he came home and told my mother that they were digging graves near the shore. "I think those graves are for us", he said.' On 8 July his fears were realised, Fanny Segal remembers: 'We were working in an army camp outside Libau. At 5 o'clock the Germans took us back to town and we had to go and apply for work-permits. We went to the town centre. There was a large hall in a big building. There were several hundred of us, and suddenly the order came: "All the men outside!" My father began to cry. He kissed me and gave me his watch. He knew it was the end.' In the first month of German occupation of Libau a total of 1,000 Jewish men were executed by *Einsatzgruppen* and the Latvian 'home guard'.

In Riga there is general discussion of the mass shooting of Jews formerly occupying the ghetto. The great majority of the population of Riga talk about it with satisfaction and are hoping for a total removal of the Jews, so that the ghetto can be released for residential purposes.
Report by the head of SS and civil police in Latvia,
23 December 1942

The decision to clear a district systematically of Jews required thorough preparation of each individual step and reconnaissance of the local situation. The Jews had to be concentrated in one or more places and, depending on their number, an area found and a pit dug.
SS Standartenführer *Karl Jäger, commander of the* Einsatzgruppen *and SD in Latvia, in a written report of late* *December 1941*

There were many Libaus behind the German front line in that summer of 1941. Yet there were factors that enabled Hitler, in his propaganda, to blame the Soviets for the brutalisation of the war for which he himself was responsible. In the first weeks of the war in Russia, mass murders – whether systematic or in a fit of blood-lust – did not take place on the German side alone. Stalin's secret police, the NKVD, did their own bloody work, with the aim of eliminating all opposition forces, such as politicians, intellectuals, civil servants, teachers and Ukrainian and Polish nationalists. In the first few weeks, in towns like Chortkov, Tarnopol, Riga and Zloczow, German soldiers came across evidence of gruesome massacres. Before the Germans entered Lvov, in the Ukraine, 5,000 people were imprisoned in the city's three gaols. Soon after the German invasion of Russia began, between 24 and 28 June, atrocities were committed there too. Stalin's political police were equally systematic in their killing – the head of the Soviet secret service, Lavrenti Beria, had given orders that all 'class enemies' and 'counter-revolutionary elements' were to be shot. Thousands of prisoners were killed in their cells by a bullet in the neck; others had their skulls smashed with a sledge-hammer. In the pandemonium before the Germans arrived, the surviving inmates attempted a mass escape. They were machine-gunned down by the Soviet warders, who then threw grenades into the still overcrowded cells.

It was on 29 June that German troops reached Lvov, and the Soviets withdrew from the city. The citizens began searching for relatives and friends among the piles of rotting corpses left behind by the Soviets. They were out for revenge. Since the real culprits had fled, they soon found scapegoats. The hastily formed Ukrainian militia began rounding up Jews all over the city. The German soldiers had no intention of stopping them – especially not the *Einsatzgruppen* who were on hand. It was part of their job to incite pogroms as 'inconspicuously' as possible. A Polish woman, Jaroslawa Woloszanska, who was twenty-two at the time, saw what happened in Lvov, where almost one-third of the population of 340,000 was Jewish. 'There was a terrible pogrom. They came at dawn and dragged Jews out of their houses. And the most dreadful thing was that they even killed children. The whole thing was quite horrible! The entire city stank of death and rotting flesh.'

Members of the *Einsatzgruppen* watched the mayhem going on, and quite a number joined in. It all fitted their distorted picture of the world. SS *Hauptscharführer* Felix Landau readily followed Heydrich's orders not to stand in the way of 'efforts by anti-Jewish circles to clean up their own back-yard'. In his diary he described the events in Lvov: 'Hundreds of Jews run along the streets, their faces covered in blood, gashes in their heads, fingers broken and eyes hanging out. Some blood-spattered Jews carry others who have collapsed.' In the space of three days, 4,000 Jews were beaten to death on the open streets – by the local militia, by some of the German *Sonderkommandos,* and by the civilian population. And Lvov was not an isolated case. In the report by the head of *Einsatzgruppe* A, SS *Brigadeführer* Dr Franz Walter Stahlecker, dated October 1941, we read: 'In the very first hours after our arrival, local anti-Semitic forces were incited to pogroms against the Jews, albeit under considerable difficulties. In accordance with orders, the security police were determined to resolve the Jewish question with all means and with complete decisiveness. . . . It was necessary to show the outside world that the indigenous population had taken the first steps themselves, as a natural reaction against decades of oppression by the Jews and against the recent reign of terror by the communists.' The pogroms which, on Heydrich's instructions, the *Einsatzgruppen* were to trigger off 'without leaving evidence', were welcome if only because it was hoped that atrocities by the local inhabitants would lessen the qualms and resistance in the ranks of the SS and the Wehrmacht. Furthermore, pogroms carried out by the population provided the SS units with a welcome relativisation of their own brutal misdeeds.

Throughout July 1941 German newsreels reported on the massacres supposedly committed by the Jews and provided an ideological pretext: 'No mercy for the real instigators, the Jews.' In the Reich, the film sequences with suitable commentary served their purpose. The security service carried out surveys of public sentiment, and in a report dated 7 July we read that cinema-goers 'were in the main convinced that today it was precisely such images of the true nature of Bolshevism and of Jewry in their terrible reality that needed to be shown again and again'.

Propaganda like this gave ideological support to the killing-frenzy of the SS. From the middle of August onward, throughout the occupied regions of the east, the *Einsatzgruppen* overstepped the boundaries of selective terror, which up to that time had largely been directed against Jewish men of military age, and later against women. Now the whole Jewish population was being murdered indiscriminately. Even the children had to die. The Holocaust had begun.

> It is forbidden for Jews aged six years or over to show themselves in public without a Star of David. Anyone who infringes this ban, deliberately or through negligence, will be fined up to 153 Reichsmarks or imprisoned for up to six weeks.
> *Police decree on the identification of Jews, 1 September 1941*
>
> The Jewish communities in towns and cities are to be assembled in ghettos, to provide better control and the possibility of disposal later on.
> *Reinhard Heydrich addressing senior police and* Einsatzgruppen *personnel on 20 September 1939*

The name of one town came to symbolise the Holocaust: Byelaya Tserkov, about 40 miles south of Kiev. In was in the middle of August that men of the 295th Infantry Division moved into the town – to 'freshen up', they were told, since they had been through several weeks of heavy fighting. The exhausted infantrymen wanted only one thing: 'peace and quiet'. But there was no chance of that in Byelaya Tserkov. There were Jews living there and soon the soldiers heard shots. Franz Kohler, a divisional radio-operator, wanted to find out for himself what was going on in the nearby forest. When he reached the rifle-range of the local army barracks, he could not believe his eyes. 'There was a row of men there, all doing somersaults at the same time. What's going on, I thought. I went closer until I saw that they were all being shot. They all fell into a pit.' Part of *Sonderkommando* 4a, a platoon of *Waffen*-SS and the Ukrainian militia were in the act of murdering several hundred Jewish men and women. What Kohler saw appalled him: 'There was an elderly man and two women, who must have been his daughters. They were the last three. The old man held the women in his arms, then an SS man came along and shot them in the neck with a pistol.' When the horrified Kohler asked what would happen to the children of those people, one of the riflemen replied: 'That's not our business. We only shoot them from age fourteen up to granddads. We don't have anything to do with the children.'

The tragedy of Byelaya Tserkov was not yet over. A week later, trucks came and collected the children to be shot as well. Soldiers informed Wehrmacht chaplains. There was a protest and the operation was briefly halted. Ninety children were locked up in a building at the edge of town – without food or water. No-one could avoid hearing their crying and whimpering. Repeated protests could do nothing to save them. *Feldmarschall* von Reichenau, a Third Reich careerist, repeated the order he had issued previously, that the children were to be shot. 'I have decided as a matter of principle, that now the operation has begun, it has to be carried through in an appropriate manner.' So much for the morality of the *Feldmarschall*. The then commander-in-chief of the Sixth Army approved and ordered the killing of Jewish children – and thus made himself an accomplice in Heydrich's murders.

August Häfner, the SS *Obersturmführer* in charge of *Sonderkommando* 4a, described to the Nuremberg War Crimes Tribunal how at the time a dispute flared up about who should shoot the children. There was an exchange with his superior, the notoriously efficient SS *Standartenführer* Paul Blobel: 'He gave me the order to carry out the shooting of the children. I asked him: "Who has to do it?" He replied: "The *Waffen*-SS." I objected and said: "But they're all young men; how can we justify to them the killing of little children?" To which he (Blobel) said: "Take *your* men, then." I said once again: "Why should they have to do it? They've got young children themselves." This tug-of-war went on for about ten minutes . . . I suggested that the Field Commandant's Ukrainian militia should shoot the children. No-one raised any objection to this proposal.'

Leaving the killing to others increasingly became the preferred method of the SS and others involved. Indeed the *Einsatzgruppen* showed a growing tendency to hand over the 'dirty work', the shootings, to the auxiliary troops recruited among the local population. In those situations the Germans settled for the job of sealing off the area – and many actually deluded themselves into believing that in this way they would not be personally guilty of killing, but that all the guilt lay with their local collaborators. The number of 'foreign auxiliary personnel' rose rapidly; in the course of the war they would increase roughly tenfold, from about 30,000 to 300,000 men. They were a means not only to exonerate the German perpetrators but also to raise the efficiency of the murder machine. The collaborators became willing tools and were often all too keen to vent their anti-Semitic prejudices – which were wide-spread in the conquered areas – on innocent people.

A Jewish woman from Latvia, Rozèle Goldenstein, experienced the brutality of the firing-squads at first hand: 'They rounded us children up to shoot us. Some tried to escape. But they were shot on the spot.' Rozèle saw what she thought was the last moment of her life approaching; for her the walk to the pit was almost a relief after days and weeks of lonely and uncertain waiting. 'They had shot my mother; I wanted to be dead as well, and now it was finally going to happen. I knew I would see my mother again.' As if by a miracle Rozèle survived the slaughter. On hearing the first shots she dropped into the pit. Dead bodies fell on top of her and covered her as she lay motionless. Rozèle was sure her end had come. It was several minutes before she realised she was still alive. When she heard the murderers leaving the spot at the edge of the forest, 'drunk and singing loudly', she crawled out of the pit and went into hiding.

Many survivors report that during the shootings and especially afterwards, the riflemen were drunk. Issuing the executioners with alcohol had a point. Petras Zelionka, who was a Lithuanian police auxiliary in 1941, tells us: 'Every one of us knocked back as much as we could handle. They gave us all the drink we could possibly want. When the liquor took effect, we all felt brave enough to begin the operation.' On the same subject a policeman named Tögel, a member of *Einsatzkommando* 10a, had this to say: 'I well remember an execution where the SD men were drunk afterwards, so they must have been given a special issue of schnapps. Us gendarmes didn't get any, and I remember we were very annoyed about it.' It was not the killing that gave cause for complaint, but the lack of anything to numb the memory.

> Generally speaking, the Germans who came into the ghetto were very brutal. We were afraid of them all. You had to raise your hat to anyone in German uniform. But quite a few asked: 'Why are you raising your hat? I don't even know you.' Others hit you if you *didn't* raise your hat. Every Jew tried to avoid anyone in uniform. Even so, there were cases where uniformed Germans, if they were alone, behaved decently and sometimes gave Jews bits of bread. They would tell us they were from Hamburg, and were members of a union or of a left-wing party. They wanted to let us know that they didn't approve of it all. But that only happened when they were alone. If they saw another soldier approaching, they altered not just their tone of voice, but their whole behaviour.
>
> *Professor Israel Gutman, Polish Jew then living in the Warsaw*
> *ghetto*

The prime mover of all these events, Adolf Hitler, was kept fully informed about the mass-scale executions. From 1 August this order was in force: 'Reports on the work of the *Einsatzgruppen* in the east are to be submitted to the Führer on a continuing basis.' This instruction from the Gestapo boss, Heinrich Müller, was followed to the letter. It was an absurd undertaking, when one thinks about it, since these acts of barbarity demanded absolute secrecy, yet at the same time there was an absolute requirement to document the crime in minute detail.

In the Central Office of Reich Security, Heydrich was also kept constantly up to date. 'Incident reports' from his *Einsatzgruppen* flowed into his Berlin headquarters without interruption, as the death-squads pitilessly annihilated the Jews of Russia. Every day he read reports such as the one from *Einsatzgruppe* B on 19 December 1941. 'During checks carried out, in consultation with the civil police, on the roads leading out of Mogilev, a total of 135

persons, mainly Jews, were apprehended. 127 persons were shot.'
A nearby transit camp for Soviet prisoners-of-war, the report tells
us, was 'combed for Jews and [communist] officials. 126 persons
were handed over and shot.' Then in Paritchi, near Bobruisk, 'a
special operation' was mounted, 'in the course of which 1,103
Jews and Jewesses were shot'. The numbers mounted steadily,
running into hundreds of thousands, all meticulously entered in
the books of the Central Office of Reich Security.

Notwithstanding the mass murder to the rear of the eastern front,
it was now an official maxim of Nazi racial policy that the Jews
had to be removed from the whole of Europe, one way or another.
'The Jews are the scourge of humanity', Hitler told the Croatian
leader, Marshal Kvaternik, on 21 July 1941. Where they were sent,
be it Siberia or Madagascar, was of no importance. The details of
how such a 'Final Solution' was to be implemented were still vague.
Many possibilities were investigated. Yet with every day that passed,
a decision became more pressing. The situation in the ghettos of
Poland's *Generalgouvernement* was dramatically worsening. 'This
winter there is a risk that we may not be able to feed all the Jews',
wrote the head of the SD section in Poznan, Rolf-Heinz Höppner,
to Adolf Eichmann, the 'Jewish expert' at the Central Office of Reich
Security. He was referring to the Lodz ghetto, which by now lay
within Reich territory. 'We must seriously consider whether the most
humane solution might not be for those Jews who are no longer fit
for work to be finished off with some kind of fast-acting chemical.
At all events that would be pleasanter than letting them starve to
death.' The *Generalgouverneur*, Hans Frank, flatly refused to set
up new ghettos in Poland, 'since according to a clear statement
by the Führer on 19 June this year, the Jews would be removed
from the *Generalgouvernement* in the foreseeable future, and the
Generalgouvernement is to be no more than a kind of transit camp'
on the way to the imaginary 'reservation beyond the Urals'.

While the mass killings behind the front line were at their
height, Heydrich found the leisure time to indulge in sports. In
August 1941 he took part in the German fencing championships,
in the special Reich class of the top twelve, and in December
of that year, when the Wehrmacht were sitting out the Russian

winter outside Moscow, Heydrich fenced in an international match against Hungary – and scored the highest points on the German side. He used to train every morning between 4 and 6 a.m.

As early as the beginning of 1941, Heydrich was working on a comprehensive programme for deporting all of Europe's Jews to the east. Now that victory seemed imminent, the day was approaching when Hitler would usher in the most extreme phase of the 'Final Solution'. Heydrich wanted to be prepared for that moment when, in Hitler's words, 'the final solution of the Jewish question will undoubtedly come'. At the peak of a deceptive certainty of victory, Heydrich asked his subordinate, the 'Jewish expert' Adolf Eichmann, to draw up a document for him, which Hermann Göring signed on 31 July 1941. In 1938 Göring had been entrusted with 'the comprehensive solution of the Jewish question', and by signing the document he authorised Heydrich to 'make all necessary preparations for a comprehensive solution of the Jewish question in the German sphere of influence in Europe'. The Holocaust, which had started with the murders by the *Einsatzgruppen* in the east, was now to reach into western Europe and even French North Africa. By obtaining this 'authority' Heydrich secured his position. It 'promoted' him to the rank of senior 'Commissioner for Jews' throughout Europe – responsible for one of Hitler's central objectives. After the war, Lina Heydrich claimed that she had asked her husband 'again and again' to give up his 'profession'. But apparently all he said to her was: 'You don't understand. I have to do it. I'm the only one who can. The others can't do it.'

'Jewish expert' Adolf Eichmann was, on his own admission, informed by Heydrich in person about the far-reaching plans. As Eichmann told his Israeli interrogators in 1961, his superior looked unusually ill at ease, and seemed to be feeling thoroughly unwell. 'The Führer . . . well, you know . . . this emigration . . . ' Heydrich had begun hesitantly. 'The Führer has ordered the physical annihilation of the Jews.' 'And, as if he wanted to judge the impact of his words', Eichmann continued, 'he then paused for a long time, which was quite unlike him. For a moment I was unable to assess the implications, because he had chosen his words with such care. But then I got the message and said nothing in reply, because there was nothing more I *could* say to that.' Heydrich had told Eichmann, because it was he who would have to organise the transport. The executives of the Holocaust were only given as much information as they needed in order to know what their job was.

Reinhard Heydrich relied on ruthlessness to carry the 'Final Solution' through. On 20 January senior bureaucrats gathered under his chairmanship in a lakeside villa near Berlin, Grosser Wannsee 56/58. The only subject on the agenda was how the mass murder might be organised. The conference had originally been scheduled for 9 December 1941, but after the Japanese attack on Pearl Harbor and Germany's subsequent declaration of war against the United States, the meeting had to be postponed. Heydrich did not call the conference in order to reach fundamental decisions about the 'Final Solution'. The mass murder of Jews in the conquered regions of the Soviet Union had begun long ago, and new extermination camps were being readied. The important thing now was to involve the top ministerial bureaucracy in the planning.

> Jews were to be removed as rapidly as possible from *General-gouvernement* territory, because it was there especially that the Jew represents an obvious threat as a carrier of disease, and also, his black-market trading is continually upsetting the economic structure of the country. . . .
>
> In place of emigration, a further possible solution is the evacuation of the Jews to the east, after appropriate prior discussion with the Führer. . . . The number of Jews to be considered with regard to this final solution is around 11 million.
>
> *From the minutes of the Wannsee Conference of 20 January 1942*

The minutes of the meeting were taken by Eichmann. It was he who provided the facts and figures for Heydrich's opening address, in which he confirmed what Göring had empowered him to do. 'Within the scope of this Final Solution of the

Jewish question in Europe', Heydrich told his audience, 'there are some eleven million Jews to be considered.' They would be 'used as labour in the east', and in the process 'doubtless a large proportion will drop out through natural wastage'.

'What was meant by "natural wastage"?', asked the Israeli police captain Avner Less, when interrogating Eichmann twenty years later.

Eichmann: 'It meant death by completely normal causes. Let's say heart-failure or pneumonia. If I were to die at this moment, then that would be natural wastage.'

'"The residue that will inevitably be left at the end", Heydrich explained to the gentlemen at the conference-table, "will certainly be those with the most stamina, and representing a natural selection, they would, if released, form the nucleus of a Jewish regeneration. So they must be treated accordingly."'

Avner Less asked Eichmann: 'What did "treated accordingly" mean?'

Eichmann stuttered: 'It . . . it was . . . that stuff came from Himmler. Natural selection . . . it . . . it was one of his hobbyhorses.'

'OK, but what does it mean here?'

'Killed, killed! Certainly!'

Words like 'killed' do not appear in the minutes of the Wannsee Conference. In taking the minutes, Eichmann 'translated' what was openly expressed around the table into the coded language of the murderers. In the written record no indication is found that the participants had in fact, as Eichmann confirmed in court, 'discussed the matter in very blunt words. . . . They actually talked about killing, eliminating and exterminating.' Heydrich, together with the eight permanent secretaries, the six police and security experts and the ministerial department head, sitting at the table in that Wannsee villa, were speaking in plain language.

After the meeting Heydrich, Eichmann and the Gestapo chief, Heinrich Müller, foregathered round the open fire in the drawing-room of the villa. Stewards poured them glasses of brandy. The mood became buoyant. 'I had never seen Heydrich so relaxed', Eichmann recalled. The signals for mass murder were finally at 'go'. From March 1942 onward, transports arrived in the death camps from all over Europe. The man responsible for the central control of the deportations was Heydrich's sidekick, Eichmann.

What goes on in the mind of someone who is planning the murder of millions? To the outside world Heydrich looked – true to the clichéd image of the steely, emotionless SS man – cold and hard, his actions ruled by a merciless logic. Yet there are indications that he performed his duties with more self-loathing than pride. One of his department heads, named Streckenbach, believed that even giving killing assignments to the *Einsatzgruppen* was for Heydrich 'the worst job in his life'. The task he now had to discharge exceeded everything that had gone before.

> The operation approved by you in consultation with the head of the Central Office of Reich Security, SS *Obergruppenführer* Heydrich, that is to say the special treatment of some 100,000 Jews in my *Gau* territory, will be capable of completion in the next 2 to 3 months.
>
> *Arthur Greiser, Gauleiter of the Warthegau district of Poland, in a letter to Himmler of 1 May 1942*

Heydrich justified his work to himself by the 'duty to be harsh'. Lina Heydrich tells us that her husband always worked on the assumption 'that he had to perform every task down to the last logical requirement'. This did not alter the fact that he had increasingly 'negative' feelings about these 'tasks'. At least he does not seem to have had any inner need to behave with brutality. He was always restless at night, his widow said. 'He often rolled over uneasily from one side to the other and couldn't get to sleep. He never explained why.' Since the summer of 1941, since the *Einsatzgruppen* had been murdering in his name, he had been looking for a new sphere of activity, for a new opportunity to improve his status.

The chance came when the Czech resistance in the 'Reich Protectorate of Bohemia and Moravia' threatened to gain the upper hand and the 'Protector', Konstantin von Neurath, fell out of favour with Hitler. Mass demonstrations, strikes and acts of sabotage had assumed alarming proportions for the occupiers in the 'Protectorate', which was the beating heart of the armaments industry outside Germany itself. 'Things in Prague have pretty much reached crisis-point', Joseph Goebbels wrote in his diary for 24 September 1941, 'and the Führer has now decided to take energetic action. [He has] decided to detail Heydrich off to clean up the situation there. . . . In critical situations like this you need strong men at the oars. These strong men must possess a firm and unerring hand; they must not be diverted by sentiment from the real goal.' Neurath was stripped of any real power, and in Heydrich a man was installed at his side, who was to stifle all resistance with an iron fist. Heydrich was delighted with his new assignment. His wife initially resisted the relocation, but he told her: 'I can do a lot of good there. If you want to rule a country, you first of all have go about it with rigour and "defeat" all opposition. Then you can rule with a far lighter hand, which is more enjoyable.' At last, he said, he had a 'positive' task. 'Reinhard was convinced', Lina Heydrich tells us, 'that he had a "mission" to fulfil in Prague.'

At the end of September 1941, Lina Heydrich took her children, Klaus, Heider and Silke, and set off in the limousine on the journey from Berlin to Prague. The reception she was given there was worthy of a queen. 'From the central station we drive in a motorcade to Prague Castle. The side-roads are sealed off. Police line the route. I do not have time to think until I am standing at a window in the castle and looking down over the gleaming, golden yellow city. I am seized by sublime feelings: I feel that I am no longer an ordinary human being. I am a princess in a fairy-tale land. There is no war, there are no enemies, no distinctions. I am standing in the midst of God's garden and can experience, gaze at and enjoy it all. Then I think about the history of this city of destiny, in which I feel that all political, patriotic and emotional threads come together. To me Prague is simply Europe.'

Now Prague was one thing above all else: a stage for Heydrich's reign of terror. His term of office began with a drum-roll. On the very day of his arrival the new ruler in the Hradčany citadel announced a stage of emergency as from 10 p.m., imposed summary justice and a ban on assembly, as though there were

Then, with the arrival of Reinhard Heydrich, the situation changed in a big way. I can still remember today how shocked we all were by the red posters with the names of the first people to be executed, and also by the fact that the long list of these names was read out on local and national radio. As far as I know, more than 300 or 400 people died right after Heydrich took office. So we knew that everything was about to change . . .

Pavel Kohout, Czech author

rebellion within the walls. The number of death sentences passed in the first twenty days climbed to more than 400. His objective, he informed journalists in Prague, was 'that this region should fully realise its economic potential. Anything that hampers this objective, I will crush, regardless of what quarter it comes from.' In fact Heydrich wanted even more. 'He wondered', Lina Heydrich tells us, 'how he could well and truly integrate that country into Adolf Hitler's "world".' In practice, this meant 'wholesale Germanisation of the region and its people', 'giving a new nationality to racially suitable Czechs', 'outward resettlement of racially incompatible Czechs and of the anti-German intelligentsia'. For the first time Heydrich was ruling a country with unrestricted power. Here in Bohemia and Moravia, he intended to realise his vision of the SS state. The 'Protectorate' was to become the model for all countries under Nazi occupation. But first he must break down people's resistance. In Theresienstadt (today's Terezin), he had a 'model ghetto for old people' built, which was to become a transit camp for the death factories in the east. The deportations began soon after Heydrich's arrival.

In Prague's Czernin Palace, the seat of the 'Protectorate Administration', a small, hand-picked audience heard from the future tyrant, a few days after his arrival, about how he visualised his new empire. Everyone in the room was sworn to maintain strict secrecy. Yet word of what Hitler's man in Prague had in mind spread through the city like wildfire. The words Heydrich addressed to his executives amounted to a declaration of war. The 'immediate task' was 'on a war footing' and there was also an 'ultimate, long-range task'. Firstly, as long as the war continues, 'I need calm in the region, so that the workers, Czech workers, can devote their energies fully to the German war-effort. . . . This means that the Czech workers must be given as much to eat – if I can put it so bluntly – as they need to carry out their work.' In a speech filled with hate for the 'Czech riff-raff', Heydrich freely admitted that he did not really want to win the sympathy of the population. Anyway, he would not succeed, even if he tried. Nonetheless, he believed that the Czechs ought to appreciate his rule, which was at least bringing benefits to the labour force in the form of higher food rations. That flames of hatred were being fanned by his death sentences never entered his mind. Wherever he showed his face, the 'Hangman of Prague' felt safe and invulnerable. 'Why ever would my Czechs shoot at me?' he asked Albert Speer, who had expressed surprise at the careless way Heydrich drove around Prague in an open-topped car. He firmly believed he had 'pacified' the country with a mixture of carrot and stick. On 16 November 1941 he informed the Führer's 'secretary', Martin Bormann, about the situation in the 'Protectorate': 'Forces of resistance largely paralysed except for a few individuals who are being hunted down, as they are in a position to be instrumental in reorganising the smashed resistance network. The intelligentsia is incorrigibly hostile to the point of hatred, yet outwardly obsequious and excessively courteous. The youth, under the influence of the teaching profession, is completely imbued with nationalist ideas. The workers have remained non-political and independent, thanks to their good wages and standard of living. The government are timid, obsequious and yet anxious to avoid worse things happening, by being infinitely friendly and accommodating in every small matter, so that in the long run they can preserve enough of Czech nationality and culture for some form of independence to evolve again. In the same way there are attempts to curry favour at a social and personal level.'

> At no time did the Czechs side with Heydrich, but they were happy to let themselves be bought by him.
>
> *Pavel Kohout, Czech writer*

The golden, historic city of Prague that to Heydrich was 'even more German than Nuremberg', nourished his interest in the past. He was fascinated by the military leader Albrecht von Wallenstein (1583–1634), who bloodily crushed the rebellion in Bohemia with his cuirassiers. To Heydrich, Wallenstein seemed to symbolise the inseparable interweaving of Prague's history with Germany's. Any physical resemblance to Wallenstein was purely coincidental.

Heydrich believed in the 'natural attachment of Bohemia and Moravia to the Reich'. He turned the legendary King Wenceslas (AD 903–35) – like Wallenstein, he was murdered – into part of Reich tradition. With the arrogance of a Roman emperor he made the Czech president, Emil Hacha, hand over to him the seven keys to the crown jewels and the crown of St Wenceslas itself. In a ceremony in the Wenceslas Chapel of St Vitus' Cathedral, a place sacred to the Czech nation, Heydrich made the humiliating gesture of handing back three of the keys to the president for safe keeping. 'Regard this as a simultaneous symbol of trust and obligation', he said. He seriously believed that this action would earn him popularity. But on 27 May 1942 – on the hairpin bend in the Prague suburb of Liben – he was to learn otherwise.

On the spot the tension was unbearable. The assassins, Josef Gabčik and Jan Kubis, waited impatiently for Heydrich's car. He should have come round the bend at about 9.30 a.m. It was now 10 o'clock and there was still no sign of the dark-green official Mercedes. What had happened? The agents could not guess that on that day Heydrich had taken longer than usual to say goodbye to his family. Half an hour later, at 10.29, Josef Valcik, who was posted 200 yards up the hill, gave the long-awaited signal with a hand-mirror: Heydrich is coming.

Now every second counted. The car turned into the bend. Gabčik threw off the coat that was concealing his weapon, and pulled the trigger. Nothing happened. The sub-machine-gun had jammed. The driver, Klein, braked. Heydrich jumped up and was about to open fire. At that moment Jan Kubis threw the high-explosive grenade. It only hit the right rear wheel. But the force of the explosion was so great that splinters pierced the seat and hit Heydrich in the back.

Heydrich was taken to the Bulovka hospital, with severe injuries. The same day Professor Walter Dick sent a telegram to Himmler, summarising Heydrich's condition: 'Entry-wound to the left of the lumbar vertebral column without damage to the spinal cord. The projectile, a piece of sheet-metal, shattered the eleventh rib, opened the chest-cavity, penetrated the diaphragm and came to rest in the spleen. The passage of the wound contains numerous bristles and hairs, apparently upholstery material. Risk of sepsis of the costal pleura and of peritonitis. We operated to remove the spleen.' Hitler's and Himmler's personal doctors arrived from Berlin. Czech doctors, who had been the first to treat Heydrich, were no longer allowed near him. Even Professor Dick was denied access. He was only a Prague German, not a Reich German. The racial obsessions of the SS did not even stop at the operating theatre.

In Hitler's headquarters there was a profound sense of shock at the news from Prague. Hitler was beside himself with fury. He immediately fired off an instruction that a reward of one million Reichsmarks was to be offered for the capture of the assassins. 'Any persons who offer them any help whatever or know their whereabouts and do not report this to the police, are to be shot, along with their entire family', ran Hitler's personal order. It went on: 'As a reprisal, 10,000 Czech suspects, or the sort of people who have a police record, are to be arrested or, if they are already in custody, are to be shot in the concentration camps.'

A huge manhunt was launched. A state of emergency was declared throughout the 'Protectorate', and a curfew imposed from 9 p.m. to 6 a.m. Trains and other public transport ceased to run. Cinemas, theatres, restaurants and coffee-houses were closed. An eerie silence reigned in the city streets. Only armed police and Wehrmacht patrols were to be seen. Then, at about 10 p.m., began what was probably the biggest manhunt in European history.

Uniformed men combed the country, house by house, searching for the proverbial needle in a haystack – and found nothing.

For a whole week the severely injured Heydrich fought for his life. On 4 June 1942 the deputy 'Reich Protector', the head of the security police and of the SD, the man charged with the 'Final Solution', died from 'infected wounds' as stated in the hospital records. When Himmler visited him on his deathbed, Heydrich was ready with a verse from his father's opera, *The Hurdy-Gurdy Boy*: 'Ah well, the world is just a hurdy-gurdy, turned by the good Lord himself, and everyone must dance to whichever tune happens to be on the cylinder,' Even he was forced to accept that, despite all his power, he could not determine his own destiny. The lord over the life and death of hundreds of thousands, the man who all his life fought against 'pests on the people', was laid low by 'bacteria or poisons . . . which entered the body along with the splinters, took hold chiefly in the pleura, the peritoneum and in the spleen area, accumulated and were able to proliferate.'

I am deeply shocked to hear that Heydrich has died from his injuries. The loss of Heydrich is irreplaceable. . . . He was the most radical and successful fighter against enemies of the state. There is no doubt that those who laid him low have inflicted the severest damage on the National Socialist cause.

Joseph Goebbels, diary entry for 5 June 1942

Hitler called Heydrich's death a 'battle lost'. Eichmann heard of the death of his superior while playing skittles in Bratislava. On his own admission he was completely taken aback and stood there 'numbed'.

With a grandiose state funeral in Berlin, on 9 June 1942, Hitler's Reich paid tribute to a National Socialist who had been transformed into an idol. 'I have but few words to devote to our dear departed', said Hitler as the body lay in state. 'He was one of the best National Socialists, one of the strongest defenders of the idea of the Reich, one of the greatest adversaries of all enemies of this Reich. He died as a witness in blood to uphold and preserve the Reich.' Admiral Canaris, the head of military intelligence, spoke with a tremor in his voice about 'a friend' whom he had lost. By contrast, SS *Obergruppenführer* Sepp Dietrich, commander of the *Leibstandarte Adolf Hitler*, shed no tears over the death of the 'Senior Suspicion-Monger'. He spoke for all Heydrich's adversaries when he said: 'Thank God, now the bastard's snuffed it!'

What saddened me was the fact that the Czechs, of all people, removed Reinhard in the way they did. I could not understand it.

Lina Heydrich, his widow, in her memoirs

Hitler, still furious about Heydrich's death, initially toyed with the idea of appointing *Obergruppenführer* Erich von dem Bach-Zelewski to succeed him. Later on, as head of the German 'combat gangs' in Russia, this man earned himself the reputation of being a particularly ruthless executioner. Hitler believed that Bach-Zelewski could 'be guaranteed to act even more harshly and brutally than Heydrich and to wade through a sea of blood, without any compunction'. The Czechs would be made to see that 'when they shoot one of us, then someone much worse will come along every time.' But Hitler was also critical of Heydrich's behaviour: 'heroic gestures', such as driving around in an open, non-armour-plated car, or walking around the streets of Prague without security, were 'a nonsense', which were no help to the nation. If it was not absolutely necessary for 'a man as irreplaceable' as Heydrich to expose himself to danger, then he could only call it 'stupidity or sheer obstinacy'. Men of Heydrich's 'political stature' should realise that people were 'lying in wait for him, as if he were wild game'.

Now the 'predator' was laid low. But the terror continued – and was even further intensified. 'The period after the assassination was terrible', Pavel Machacek from Prague remembers. 'Every day, lists on red paper were published with the names of the people who had been summarily tried and were to be shot that

It was odd, the way my parents comforted me. They said: nothing can happen to you, Pavel; you won't be fourteen for another three months. And only those aged fourteen upwards are being shot. This was an indirect way of telling me that they were both in great danger.

Pavel Kohout, Czech author

The interrogation was very unpleasant. I was beaten on my buttocks. I counted 187 blows, because I had to concentrate on them so as not to scream. Then they dragged me to a bathroom next door. One of them got into the bath and I had to bend over again. One man had a bull-whip and a second had a stick. They took turns to beat me. Finally they stopped and sent me to their building in Charles Square. I arrived about 10 o'clock at night. There were eight of us in one cell, and the others asked me why I was there. I showed them my backside and they said they'd never seen anything like it.

Pavel Machacek, then living in Prague, arrested by the Gestapo after the attack on Heydrich

day. All it took was for someone to say it served Heydrich right. Anyone talking like that was immediately arrested, then sent to concentration camp or shot.' The revenge of the regime was terrible. Berlin wanted to make an example of the Czechs. Gabčik and Kubis were killed by the SS, together with 120 other members of the Czech resistance. In the 'Protectorate' as a whole, the occupiers executed 1,331 Czechs, including 201 women. One small village was to achieve tragic fame as a symbol of senseless reprisals against the innocent: its name was Lidice. Its inhabitants had given support to the assassins, or so it was alleged. They were told to go to the school-house for interrogation; nothing would happen to them. On their way to the school 172 men from the village were 'outsorted' and immediately shot. The 195 women of the village were dragged off by the SS to Ravensbrück concentration camp. Scarcely one of them survived. After the massacre their village was razed to the ground.

My uncle Frantisek used to listen secretly to western radio-stations. During the reprisals after the assassination of Heydrich, he was denounced. We still don't know by whom. He was arrested, taken to Pankrac, and then we heard nothing more from him. We found out through the public notices that he, like so many others, had been executed. He was forty-four years old.

Eva Nemcowa, a Czech woman

If Nazi rule had lasted longer, then Reinhard Heydrich would have been the coming man – no doubt about it. He was the prototype of what Hitler wished for. He was inhumanity personified.

Ralph Giordano

It was not until after the war that I heard for the first time what had happened to Lidice. That the village had been burnt down, that my father had been executed and my mother sent to a concentration camp. I had a brother who was two months past his fifteenth birthday. And it was precisely those two months that sealed his fate. He wasn't taken to Poland with the other children; he was shot. . . . For us children, it was the worst thing that could happen at that age. We had lost what was most dear to us: our homeland and our parents.

Marie Zupikova, abducted as a child from Lidice by the Gestapo

What would have happened if Heydrich had survived the attack on him? Heydrich was a foretaste, an inkling, of what Hitler's 'new Europe' would have become. Had the Third Reich been victorious, then, under the plans that had been laid, 90 million

Slavs would have come under Nazi domination. Of these, 14 million would have been used as slave-labour, some 30 million would have been killed, and the rest deported beyond the Urals to the steppes of Siberia. Reinhard Heydrich, as the man of the future, and probably in charge of the SS, would not have hesitated to make this vision of horror a reality. As the prototype of an absolutist generation, he was pre-destined for this.

At the Nuremberg war crimes tribunal, the 'Hangman of Prague' was missing from the dock. But there is no doubt that he would have been condemned to death.

CHAPTER FOUR

DEATH'S HEAD

It was March 1942 and for a group of young people at Darmstadt's Justus Liebig Technical School it was their big day. They strode through the venerable sandstone portals, past the bust of the pioneer of chemistry who gave his name to the school, and into their classroom. There they had to sit their school-leaving examination. Among the candidates, though older than the others, was twenty-year-old Hans Stark, the son of a police superintendent. Since December 1941 he had been given leave from military service, so that he could prepare for the examination. Stark was well briefed, since he had been given expert coaching in his free time by people at his place of work. One of the examination subjects was essay-writing. Stark selected a topic that echoed the spirit of the times: 'Adolf Hitler's liberation of Germany from the fetters of the Versailles Treaty.' The hackneyed phrases that flowed from his pen sounded so ready-made that they might have been based on model texts from the Ministry of Propaganda: 'Thanks to its brilliant head of state, Germany has regained its place in the world. Our nation is still engaged in a struggle for survival, whose out-come is in no doubt. . . . The Treaty of Versailles rendered the German people defenceless, but in doing so it was sowing dragons' teeth and will reap a bloody harvest.'

In appearance, too, Hans Stark was distinct from the other pupils. For the examination he wore the walking-out uniform of the SS *Totenkopf* brigade. In the concentration camps this unit served as guards, tormentors and murderers. Stark was one of them and was now taking the school certificate during his camp service. In swotting up his maths, history and German literature he had been helped by Jews in Auschwitz. 'How come you know about Goethe?' he had enquired in amazement of his emaciated teachers. One of them, a man named Kasimir Smolen, can remember the young Stark's look of wonder. He had obviously been completely taken in by the anti-Semitic propaganda about the 'sub-human' Jew. After passing his exams he would return to the camp and carry out his murderous handiwork for a while longer.

In 1962 he finally stood in the dock. One witness gave evidence on the behaviour of the school-leaver, Hans Stark, and on how his sadistic brutality drove him to commit acts that no regulations required of him. One appalling account weighed heavily in the verdict against him: 'During further gassing of Jews in May 1942 . . . Stark often pulled Jewish women aside. When the other Jewish victims were in the gas-chambers, he stood the women against the wall of the courtyard of the small crematorium. Then he shot one or two of the women in the chest and the feet. And when the other women trembled and fell on the knees . . . imploring Stark to let them live, he shouted at them: "C'mon, Sarah; on yer feet, Sarah!" Then he shot them all, one after the other.' The witness to these hideous acts had never been able to forget the face of the perpetrator. 'All my life, I've been seeing Stark. All my life, wherever I go, I see him. It's terrible.'

Hans Stark died in 1991. His brother, seven years younger, is still alive and living in Wiesbaden. Günther Stark, a professional photographer, has never been able to free himself from Hans's history. Time and again he has asked himself: 'How could he have turned into someone like that?' It seems that as a boy Hans was fairly unremarkable: 'a gentle, lovely kid; every day when he went off to school in the morning, his mother gave him a few pfennigs to buy a piece of *wurst*. The best thing in the world that could happen to him was to have a piece of *wurst* to eat.' He did have rather a need to be noticed, and sometimes he acted the clown. Occasionally he got such a terrible beating with a strap from his father that he was literally driven up the wall. But his mother took him to her heart all the more. Quite a number of young men had a similar start in life.

It was in 1937 that the career of Hans Stark took a decisive turn. He had really wanted to enlist as a volunteer with the Wehrmacht. But there they told him he was too young and that he ought to join the SS; they would be sure to take on someone like him. So it was that Hans Stark became a recruit in the *Totenkopf-Standarte* 'Brandenburg'. His father gave his consent. The police officer had always been a convinced National Socialist, even before the Nazis seized power. Like many of his contemporaries, he saw Hitler as the 'Saviour', who alone was capable of erasing the ignominy of Versailles. In 1933 Hans Stark's father joined the National Socialist Party. For the Führer's visit to Darmstadt Frau Stark dutifully sewed a swastika flag; sadly, the hooked cross was back to front, which infuriated her husband. Stark Senior was a depressive, who was later to take his own life.

In the SS barracks of Sachsenhausen camp Stark learned the usual drill of the *Totenkopf-Standarte*. You could call it toughness training: being schooled in uncompromising harshness, towards yourself and others; humiliation by your superiors, which was intended to make you compliant and willing to give unquestioning obedience. It was important to efface any 'weakness' – that was the big thing. A grim ritual on the parade-ground served to temper the recruits to steely hardness. Before their eyes, prisoners were beaten up until they streamed with blood. The trainees were not allowed even to pull a face. Then it was their turn to deliver a storm of blows.

Naturally, there had to be a 'sense' to their activities. For that they were fed the usual platitudes of Nazi delusion. The world was divided into black and white, friend and foe, into 'valued' and 'valueless' lives. Their entire existence was a permanent state of war, a struggle between nations and races. Enemies were lurking not only beyond the borders of the Reich, but at its very heart. And in the end, so the phrase went, either 'they' would die, or 'we' would. It was just as Himmler had declared in 1933: 'You men are the Black Corps, the most loyal instrument of the Führer and of the Movement, the most feared enemy of all our adversaries. We are soldiers, and as soldiers we know that the only opponent who can do us no harm is one who is dead, who has been destroyed.' The recruits were absolved of all responsibility for their acts. Most of them accepted this offer and this image of the enemy. Those you are bludgeoning and torturing, they were told, are not real human beings. After all, they were merely 'criminals, drop-outs, enemies of the state, layabouts, politically unreliable types, thieves and Jews'. Above all, it was the Jews who were labelled as 'pests', who had to be 'isolated' and 'exterminated'. That was why the Death's-Head units were so 'important', precisely because they had to deal with the worst enemies of nation and state. The language of the SS was infected with such deluded ideas, but the young recruits were meant to regard it all as quite natural and to act accordingly – after all, were they not the enforcers of the so-called 'will of the Führer'? 'I swear to thee, Adolf Hitler, obedience unto death': Hans Stark was one of many who took that oath.

However, the subservience demanded of the recruits had its own kind of reward. The very first time Stark stood in the watch-tower of a concentration camp, he tells us he experienced a feeling of absolute power. The camp survivor, Kasimir Smolen, confirms that Stark enjoyed 'having the right to mete out more violence' than he had ever been allowed to do in civilian life. Sometimes he acted like a headmaster, Smolen recounts. 'We had to write out 200 times: "I must be at work on time".'

According to Hans' brother Günther: 'After he joined the SS, Hans appeared much more self-confident.' He was no longer a loner. 'When he came back to Darmstadt in his smart uniform, I was very proud of him, and my school-friends asked: "Hey, who's that?" and I said, "That's my brother!"' Günther Stark never learned the whole truth. Once, when he asked: 'What's a concentration camp?', his brother gave him this answer 'You know Latin, don't you? They concentrate people together and put a fence round them; that's a concentration camp.'

It wasn't Hitler, Göring, Goebbels, Himmler or any of that lot who dragged me off and beat me up. No, it was the local shoemaker, the milkman, or a neighbour. As soon as they got a uniform, an arm-band and a steel helmet, suddenly they were the master race.

Karl Stojka, a gypsy from Vienna, deported to Auschwitz in 1943

We Jews were terrorised by the SS. The SS men were like robots. Every Jew watched out for the SS, because there wasn't a decent man among them.

Morris Venezia, Greek Jew, a prisoner in Auschwitz

Hans Stark rose rapidly through the ranks, typically of someone who adapted unquestioningly to the Death's-Head system. The stages in his career included many of those places of death which would earn themselves a gruesome reputation: Sachsenhausen, Buchenwald, Dachau – and later Auschwitz.

The lad from Darmstadt was one of many in the SS's realm of death. The system of concentration camps and later extermination camps required the deployment of large numbers of people. Several tens of thousands served in them, supported by auxiliaries from outside. How was it possible that so many took part in the murder of millions of human beings? How could a system have been created that would lead to that?

There have been many attempts to provide an explanation: life under a dictatorship, brutalisation by hardship and war, totalitarian indoctrination through monopolistic control of information, the promotion of hatred for the enemy, state-sanctioned violence, the obligation to obey military orders and the targeted recruitment of potential killers. But there was also careerism, blind obedience, an exaggerated respect for authority, compromise and racism. Many years earlier, Sigmund Freud had written that war in itself was enough to make people live out their basest and most unpleasant fantasies. Once the state has lifted the prohibition on killing, he said, 'the suppression of evil cravings also ceases, and people commit acts of cruelty, perversity, treachery and grossness, of a kind that one would imagine to be totally inconsistent with their cultural standards'. If we want to understand why hundreds of thousands behaved in this way, we must take a look at individuals – at their entire personal histories and personal responsibility.

Gentlemen, if a generation should ever come after us, that is too soft and feeble to understand our great undertaking, then the whole of National Socialism will indeed have been in vain. But I believe, on the contrary, that bronze plaques should be put up, recording the fact that we had the courage to carry through this great and necessary work.

Odilo Globocnik, head of SS and police in Lublin, occupied Poland

It'll be a good thing if terror precedes us – terror that we are going to exterminate the Jewish race.

Adolf Hitler speaking in his military headquarters, 25 October 1941

In an interview with us before his death, the Auschwitz survivor Hermann Langbein described the characteristics of the murder-machine, as he himself experienced it: how the regime created a climate of hostility, how it aroused the urge to destroy real or imaginary adversaries, how the 'Führer principle' took the place of personal conscience, how the pernicious notions of 'races of greater and lesser value' bore their evil fruit. Then how bureaucracy added a managerial dimension to the apparatus of murder, time-and-motion crime, impersonal slaughter – how all this contributed to the horrendous efficiency of the extermination camps.

It all began with the abandonment of personal conscience, the subjugation of one's individuality to the so-called 'Will of the Führer'. As Langbein puts it: 'It was the slogan "Führer, command! We will follow – Führer, command! We will follow blindly!" that led to Auschwitz.' And that was true even for the sort of people who did not seem pre-ordained for it. 'I knew some SS men who were far from happy about what they had to do. Orders were given, orders were carried out, and then there was a check on how they had been executed. Orders were orders. You had to say "*Jawohl!* Yessir!" And do what you were told without taking any responsibility for it. That was the prevailing climate in Auschwitz.'

Yet there were always perpetrators who did not need to be checked up on, who threw themselves into the work voluntarily and with great zeal: 'Nearly all of them were very young, even the SS officers, who just wanted to get on. You could rise very rapidly at Auschwitz. Anyone who wanted to, knew what was expected of him. He didn't need any orders; he used his own initiative. Oh yes, you could certainly make a career for yourself at Auschwitz, if you were eager, obedient and ahead of the game. Back then they talked about the "Thousand Year Reich", and it was fine if you were one of those on top. That wasn't true of everyone, but of many.'

The former SS camp doctor, Hans Münch, has this to say about the mental attitude of the camp personnel: 'Most of them were perfectly ordinary men. Sadists and former criminals were in the minority. But if there was one thing that distinguished them, it was chiefly that there were far more opportunists among them, than you find in everyday life. They said to themselves: if I join the party, I have certain advantages. If I join the SS, I have even more advantages. But if I join a very special mob within the SS, the ones to whom Himmler said: "You lads have the hardest job of all', then I'm a king, I'm right out in front. It was a situation where many felt like an elite, even though most of them knew that what they were doing was filthy work. But not one of them said so.'

These are battles which the generations that follow us will no longer have to fight.
Heinrich Himmler, during a visit to Auschwitz in 1942

Yet even those who were not promoted still wielded power over human beings, over life and death; and that was very alluring to many of them, Münch believes: 'You're one of the master-race, you can exploit that. You too can be a Führer, at least in a limited field. This had a big effect. It was something that led certain people to do what they did in Auschwitz, without necessarily having been born sadists or criminals.'

The SS camp system went a long way to turning men into a mechanism for criminal ends. Part of the system for controlling the camp was a strict hierarchy, with functions assigned to different groups often competing for status. Thus there were five sections, all reporting to the commandant's office, which was the highest authority in all camp and service matters. At the same time the commandant was the officer commanding all the SS personnel at the camp. Section I was the adjutant's office. Then came the notorious Section II, the camp Gestapo, which was able to act with relative independence. It decided on the admission and release, punishment or execution of inmates. Section III, known as 'Protective custody camp management', was the real centre of power and its senior officer also acted as deputy commandant. Reporting to him were the officers in charge of divisions, blocks and squads. These in turn were not only empowered to give orders to the prisoners but were also responsible for the forms that their terrorising would take from day to day: whether inside the camp or outside, on forced labour detachments. Section IV was responsible for administration. It made decisions about feeding and clothing the prisoners, and was thus jointly responsible for the living conditions of the inmates. It also handled the prisoners' confiscated property.

Section V was set up to control 'environmental health', and ran the sick-bay with its doctors and nurses. Its chief task was to fight epidemics and to get sick prisoners fit for work again. Yet what actually went on was so appalling that prisoners often regarded being sent to the sick-bay as a sentence of death. In later years, deadly injections of phenol and macabre human experiments were a matter of daily routine in many camps.

The carefully worked-out structure of hierarchy, competition and division of labour even extended to the inmates. The SS deliberately involved certain prisoners in the surveillance and management of the camps. Following the principle that 'absolute power is delegated power', an elaborate system based on collaboration was developed. It meant that victims, too, became perpetrators. Quite a number of the so-called 'operational prisoners' rivalled the SS thugs in their brutality; others attempted as far as possible to mitigate the horror and protect their fellow-inmates. At the summit of the prisoners' hierarchy was the *Lagerälteste*, the oldest and therefore senior prisoner in the camp.

Subordinate to him were the block-seniors and room-seniors. Alongside them were the *Oberkapos* and *Kapos*, who supervised the work detachments either in the quarries, on building-sites, in the stores, kitchens or workshops. The concentration camp survivor Eugen Kogon describes it like this: 'The camp system owed its stability not least to an auxiliary team of *Kapos*, who kept day-to-day life running and took a lot of the load off the SS personnel. This meant that absolute power was wielded everywhere. Without this delegation of power the system of discipline and surveillance would have rapidly broken down. In all this, the competition for jobs in surveillance, administration and catering simply gave the SS a welcome opportunity to play off the prisoners' cliques and elites against each other and to keep them in a state of dependency. However, the average prisoner was subject to a double burden of authority – the SS, who for much of the time were scarcely seen in the camps, and the operational prisoners who were there all the time.'

However, a crucial factor in the 'effectiveness' of the camps was, of course, the recruitment of SS personnel. At the very beginning, Hitler and Himmler had appointed to this job a man whose impact and importance has for a long time been underestimated. His name was Theodor Eicke, and he played a key part in laying the foundations of the murderous SS programme. He wanted to establish sites that would set a standard for the system of terror and extermination. He represents what has been called the 'Dachau School'. Eicke's Dachau was the model for all other concentration camps within and later outside the Reich.

He it was who created the 'elite' specifically for this purpose, and achieved this with horrifying success. He wanted to shape his 'Death's Head' men into an unquestioningly obedient executive arm of the system. Eicke not only recruited them himself, he drilled, indoctrinated and trained them – to wield violence without inhibition. He never visited Auschwitz himself. But his pupils later tyrannised the camps, striving to excel one another in ruthlessness.

Born in 1892, Eicke was the son of a stationmaster. Because of his poor grades he dropped out of school, in order to join the imperial army as a seventeen-year-old in 1909. Serving as a paymaster on the western front in the First World War, he reached senior non-commissioned rank. Like many ex-soldiers, the end of the war plunged him into a social abyss. In common with most of his contemporaries, he regarded the defeat of 1918 as a national humiliation and the Weimar Republic as the spawn of alien ideas, and responsible, more than anything, for his wretched personal circumstances. For a while he worked as a police informer, but was dismissed for expressing anti-government opinions. The regular career in the police that he aspired to was denied him. So he allied himself with people who shared his hate for the new dispensation. In 1928 he joined the Nazi Party. At the same time he was earning enough to maintain his family, working as a security officer with the chemical giant, I.G. Farben. Yet once again his career came to a sudden end. His excessive 'commitment' to political violence had not escaped the notice of his employers. In 1932 he joined the SS at a time when Himmler was looking for people to help him forge the *Schutzstaffel* into a willing instrument of Hitler's domination. He found the right man in Eicke, who proved his worth by building up the first battalions in record time, but was again marked out by his aggressive behaviour. In the same year Eicke was convicted for taking part in a series of political murders and for illegal possession of explosives. He was sentenced to two years' imprisonment – but at Himmler's behest he escaped to northern Italy. When Hitler came to power Eicke returned to Germany, only to wage a personal feud with a Nazi Gauleiter named Bürckel, a man far more powerful than himself. Bürckel had no great difficulty in getting Eicke confined to a psychiatric hospital in Würzburg, where his mental condition could be examined. Eicke's devious, sometimes uncontrolled and ruthless behaviour was exceptional, even by the standards of the SS.

However, that no longer mattered, since the Reichsführer had an awkward post to fill. In Dachau, one of the new Nazi regime's first SS camps for political prisoners, chaos reigned, out of sight of Hitler and his henchmen. Eicke, who was not known for his gentle touch, seemed to be the ideal man to restore order. He combined a number of qualities that recommended him for the job: total obedience to the leadership, a talent for organising, and the ability to enthuse people as well as to subordinate them.

Added to these were a fanatical devotion to Nazism and a violent hatred of everything that was 'un-German' or merely different – all indispensable prerequisites for the spirit of inhumanity.

After Eicke had demonstrated his loyalty and total lack of scruple, by shooting Ernst Röhm in his prison cell in 1 July 1934, his reward in the form of promotion followed only a few days later. He was given the newly created post of Inspector of Concentration Camps and head of the SS prison guard units. However, since scarcely more than 2,000 people were being held in camps at that time, this recognition was scarcely flattering to the man who had committed such an important murder in the name of the state.

In five years Eicke built Dachau up to be the centre of a web of camps, a system for grinding down and destroying the 'enemies of National Socialism' through forced labour, hunger, sickness, torture and murder. He designed the camp machinery – and he recruited the men to operate it.

As commanding officer of the Death's-Head units, he used his own discretion to select the SS officers and guards who were to serve in the camps. Any guard who gave a hint of compassion was considered a weakling, unfit for the work. Anyone who got too close to the prisoners should, according to Eicke, be thrown into a concentration camp himself. To witness punishment beatings, or to administer them, without batting an eyelid no matter how much the victim suffered, was what the Death's-Head chief demanded. He personally drafted draconian instructions for the brutal treatment of prisoners, and invented special forms of torture. The striped prison clothing, the tattooed identification marks, the daily maltreatment – all were products of his criminal imagination.

The survivor Eugen Kogon saw the SS guards as having been chosen as the very worst of those 'who lived by the bludgeon and the revolver, who had lost any foothold in society, failed truck-drivers, forestry labourers, hairdressers, shop assistants, students, prison warders'. Turning to the officers, he calls them 'the men who fought with the *Freikorps* in the Baltic countries [after 1918], who had failed to get promotion or had been forced to resign their commission for some other reason'.

This catalogue is a blend of the impressions that camp survivors gained at the time, with the information that began to appear after the war in biographies of the perpetrators. To this day, with the exception of a few basic studies, it is a subject that has not been sufficiently researched. True, the historian Karin Orth, in her study of concentration camp officers, demonstrates that, in terms of their background and achievements, they were a remarkably homogeneous group who certainly did not come from the fringes of society. The majority of this officer group came from the families of lower to middle-ranking managers and civil servants. They grew up in the *völkisch* milieu of the 1920s, an atmosphere in which political thinking was shaped by an amalgam of the 'stab-in-the-back' myth, disgust at the 'disgrace of Versailles' and intense xenophobia. In countless instances, the economic slump of the early 1930s spelled doom for many lower middle-class careers. The rise of National Socialism seemed to offer new prospects for skilled craftsmen and commercial wheeler-dealers. In most cases they rapidly clambered up the career-ladder within the party organisation. Positions in the SA were followed by entry in the general SS or, more often, a Death's-Head unit.

Eicke inspired those who wanted to be something more than they were, to believe that they belonged to the 'Order of the Very Best' – as 'men of action' with 'real character' and 'a clear set of values'. They had been chosen, he said, to be 'the pillars of the National Socialist revolution', they were to be the 'saviours of the German people'. He demanded toughness, but also gave them the feeling they belonged to a community of blood-brothers. 'Papa Eicke' radiated *esprit de corps*.

The 'Inspector of Camps' eagerly set about centralising the system. The concentration camps at Dachau, Buchenwald, Flossenbürg, Mauthausen (in Austria), Ravensbrück and Sachsenhausen were transformed into focal points of terror. Later other camps and sub-camps were added to the list. In public, the SS chief, Heinrich Himmler, tried to keep their real function a secret. What went on there, he claimed, was 'hard, reforming labour, and strict but just treatment. Our educational methods are designed to teach people how to work again and to acquire skills of a manual nature. The motto that is written above these camps, reads: There is but one road to freedom. Its milestones are obedience, industry, honesty, order, cleanliness, sobriety, truthfulness, self-sacrifice and love for the Fatherland.' Work and discipline, the Reichsführer insisted with breathtaking cynicism, were the means necessary to bring the nation's lost sons and daughters back into the National Socialist community.

The number of concentration camp personnel rose steadily. A list of camp staff dated 15 January 1945 showed, under the heading of SS guards: 37,674 men – and 3,058 women, a fact that was for a long time overlooked.

Concentration camp service was generally considered a male domain. Yet thousands of women also had many jobs to do there – associated to a greater or lesser extent with the crimes being committed. They worked as wardresses, doctors, laboratory assistants or shorthand typists – the range was wide, and only a proportion of them belonged to the SS. Whereas the female civilian employees, such as secretaries and telex operators, remained more or less spectators of the misery, the female warders in the SS contributed significantly to it. Some of them were in fact wives of SS men, as a letter dated 1 March 1943 from the Commandant's office at Lublin concentration camp indicates: 'On the orders of the head of the SS Economic Administration Office, the wives of SS members, if they have no children, are to be deployed as warders in a women's concentration camp.' However, it is not known how many wives answered this call.

After a thorough selection process, the young female recruits completed a 'Course for female SS warders'. This included subjects like 'Guidance on ideology and national policy', 'Job-knowledge and probationary duties', or 'Personal conduct and leadership'. Former prisoners tell us that, during their course, the SS's mostly young female trainees were required to act with unbridled ruthlessness and naked violence.

Between 1942 and 1945 more than 3,000 women were accepted into the SS and, as required by their Reichsführer, trained to be 'a genuinely dedicated female corps of the SS, imbued with National Socialist ideology and the spirit of the SS'. Here too, brutal behaviour was the key to promotion. Nanda Herbermann, a survivor of Ravensbrück, a women's camp, says: 'The "most reliable" were usually the most brutal among them.' Maria Mandel and Else Erich were examples of such 'career women'. The former served as a senior wardress in Auschwitz-Birkenau from October 1942 until the camp was evacuated in January 1945; the latter did the same job in the Lublin-Majdanek death camp, from October 1942 until its closure. After the war, both women were convicted of exceptional cruelty and executed. More than 50 years after the war, Hertha Bothe, the notorious SS wardress in Bergen-Belsen, replied in this way to the question of whether she believed she had made 'mistakes': 'Did *I* make a mistake? Nope. The mistake was having concentration camps in the first place. But I had to work there, otherwise I would have been put inside myself. That was my mistake.' Decades after the event, this self-deception was still exerting its influence.

In the concentration camps a self-contained economy grew up, characterised by slave-labour and theft, especially of Jewish property. The SS was instructed to run the camps on the basis of 'self-sufficiency'. Subsidies were only provided by the general SS when absolutely necessary.

With the labour supplied by the prisoners the SS could build up camp activities on a massive scale. In the course of the war, hundreds of satellite camps were set up. For example, the *Deutsche Erd- und Steinwerke GmbH* (DESt) was a quarry business wholly owned by the SS, which went on to develop into a highly diversified industrial empire. One of its fourteen production sites was the factory at Berlstedt making bricks, gravel and building materials. Prisoners from Buchenwald concentration camp were used as slave-labour there. In August 1943 alone they completed 46,200 man-hours.

Often the choice of location for a camp had an economic motive, as was the case with Flossenbürg, for instance. The DESt company was already operating profitably there. The material hewn from the granite quarry was sold to the German government. From late 1942 Flossenbürg prisoners were deployed in war production in factories run by Messerschmitt, the aircraft firm, as well as the Flick, Siemens, Osram and Junkers companies. The satellite camps were located all over Bavaria, Saxony and western

Czechoslovakia. Whereas in 1938 there were only a few SS men supervising the first prisoners building the Flossenbürg camp, by 1945 the guards there numbered more than 4,000 men and 500 women.

One company that become notorious for its collaboration with the SS was the vast chemical concern, I.G. Farben. This was not only because it produced the killing agent Zyklon B, but also because its pact with the SS sealed the fate of countless thousands of slave-labour victims. As early as 1941, I.G. Farben was one of the few privately owned German companies to obtain permission to employ concentration camp inmates in their workforce. The corporation decided to build a plant near the town of Monowitz in Upper Silesia (now Poland). With the help of prisoners, these production facilities, situated not far from the Auschwitz complex of camps, were to manufacture synthetic rubber, called 'Buna' and also synthetic motor fuel.

The basis of the 'pact of friendship' between the management of I.G. Farben and the SS officers at Auschwitz was a kind of barter: the representatives of I.G. Farben undertook to supply the commandant of Auschwitz, Rudolf Höss, with the building materials he urgently needed for the expansion of the camp. In return the Auschwitz SS said they were willing to make their prisoners available for the construction of the I.G Farben plant. During negotiations in March 1941 the productivity quota of the prisoners was fixed at 75 per cent of the output of a fit German worker. In summer the working day was to last ten or eleven hours and in winter around nine hours.

This cynical calculation did not work out in practice. The I.G. Farben managers and SS officers had got it wrong. As a result of the murderous working conditions, the productivity achieved was only 30 to 40 per cent of the German norm. The prisoners, completely exhausted before they started, had to march to work – a distance of nearly four miles – in all weathers. In January 1945, when Red Army soldiers reached Auschwitz, they found a new I.G. Farben factory, virtually ready to start production. Its construction alone had cost 25,000 human lives. Quite apart from this barbarity – even when the economic absurdity of the 'pact' became apparent, the SS and I.G. Farben refused to abandon it.

Such was the involvement of a major German corporation in the programme of 'extermination through labour'.

In other respects, too, the concentration camps were less hermetically sealed off from the world than was long assumed to be the case. This was true of the personnel, for example. The guards and their officers by no means formed an isolated unit. It is true that as early as 1934 Himmler had acceded to Eicke's request that the camp guards should be drawn from the general SS and placed under his direct authority, as 'Inspector of Concentration Camps'. However, Hitler's war-plans rapidly gave rise to new assignments, both inside and outside the barbed wire. In October 1939 the Führer, now also war leader, approved the establishment of field divisions of the SS (later to become the *Waffen*-SS). This also meant a widening of the scope of the Death's-Head units, which soon formed a division of their own. As early as the assault on Poland in September 1939 Eicke had formed three SS *Totenkopfstandarten*, who waged their own brutal war at the front and also operated behind the lines alongside other SS *Einsatzgruppen*, slaughtering Jews and members of Poland's intelligentsia. At the same time, older members of the SS were transferred to camp guard units.

In 1940 the military combat units of the SS, which had been deployed as part of the regular army, were combined under the name of *Waffen*-SS (armed SS). The *Totenkopf* (Death's Head) division was also integrated; by being assigned to SS headquarters, concentration camp personnel were now formally part of the *Waffen*-SS as well. The intention was not only that Eicke's division should reinforce the combat strength of the *Waffen*-SS; it was also important that the death camp guards should prove themselves 'outside' and become familiar with the new dimensions of violence, so that they could return – suitably 'trained' – to the 'internal' battle-front. As the writer Miroslav Kárny reveals, this led to a regular rotation of personnel between Death's-Head units and combat units of the SS, so that probably more than 60,000 members of the *Waffen*-SS served for a time in the death camps.

Furthermore, from the middle of 1944 onwards older or wounded members of the Wehrmacht were transferred to SS guard duties. The high casualty rate in Death's Head units, due both to lack of experience and particularly merciless combat activities, created staff shortages in the death camps, so that not only older members of the general SS, but even policemen and civil service employees had to be drafted in. To those were added ever more *Volksdeutsche*, ethnic Germans from occupied eastern Europe, and finally a steadily growing number of foreign volunteers and collaborators.

During the war, in addition to the concentration camps, in which the majority of prisoners died through malnutrition and sickness, forced labour, execution or lethal injection, the SS set up in occupied Poland what can only be called 'death factories'. The sole purpose of the camps at Belzec, Sobibor, Treblinka and Chelmno was murder on an industrial scale. The actual perpetrators were men who had previously taken part in the criminal euthanasia programme known as 'Operation T4' – and not all were paid-up members of the SS. Majdanek and Auschwitz functioned both as concentration camps and extermination centres, but remained the domain of the Death's Head SS. The latter two death factories drew their personnel from a core of 300 men in their camp commandants' departments. They were the true executioners. Unlike the SS guards this group was largely closed to external entrants. The 'industrial' liquidation of millions of human beings was to take place in secret. The camp known as Auschwitz-Birkenau became a synonym for the Holocaust.

I always had the shootings carried out by quite large firing-squads, as I refused to make use of 'bullet-in-the-neck' experts. Each squad went on shooting for about an hour and was then relieved.

Sworn statement by Paul Blobel, commander of a 'Special Squad', given at Nuremberg in 1945

Behind the battle-fronts of 'Operation Barbarossa', where the systematic shooting of civilians – the so-called 'unauthorised holocaust' – had begun, those responsible for the frenzy of bloodletting were by no means exclusively members of the SS. Himmler's 'Black Order' only accounted for a proportion of the *Einsatzgruppen* ('action squads') that were despatched to execute tens of thousands of people, mainly Jews. It seems that no recruitment drive for the 'elite' SS was necessary in order to find men prepared to commit mass murder. For these squads also included units markedly different from the SS. These were the battalions of so-called *Ordnungspolizei* (*Orpo*, or gendarmerie). In the early stages of the war there were only 500 *Orpo* men in the *Einsatzgruppen*, but after the invasion of the Soviet Union a further 5,500 were added. These rapid-reaction police units were housed in barracks and consisted in part of men who were too old to be drafted into the Wehrmacht. But they also included volunteers, who had joined the police in 1939 when war was looming, in order to evade military service. The officers and NCOs were experienced full-time members of the *Orpo*. Many of these policemen were 'perfectly ordinary men', as the American historian Christopher Browning calls them in his standard work called *Ordinary Men and Nazi Policy*. They had received no more than two months special training to prepare them for their new assignments in the Soviet Union. When they decided on a career in the police, none of them could have guessed that one day they would become the enforcers of a murderous occupation policy. Nonetheless, they adapted themselves to the planned and systematic liquidation of 'enemies of the state'.

> Leaders of the Jewish intelligentsia (especially teachers, lawyers and Soviet government and party officials) were liquidated.
> SS Brigadeführer *Arthur Nebe, in a report dated 5 July, 1941*

In order to coordinate the 'interplay' of SS and police units, Himmler and Heydrich had created the post of 'Senior SS and Police Officers' (*Höhere SS und Polizeiführer*, or HSSPF). Even the commanders of the *Einsatzgruppen* had to take orders from these 'top men'. One of them was the chief of Germany's crime police, Arthur Nebe. Though he had an SS rank, he was a policeman to his fingertips. One way and another, it was a strange assortment of exterminators, who assembled to take charge of the *Einsatzgruppen*: some had never joined the SS, many others had done so by devious routes. The list of their names reveals academics, quite a few with doctorates, senior civil servants, a Protestant clergyman and an opera singer.

Even in the Weimar years, Nebe, the dedicated policeman, had an obsession not only with combating crime but eradicating it completely. As a frustrated constable on the beat, he had little time for civil rights and the freedom of the individual. However, he was not really a Nazi in the ideological sense, though he was in agreement with some of the party's dogma. Where he went wrong was in deluding himself that crime could be 'removed biologically', that no criminal should be allowed to 'inject bad heredity into the nation by procreating criminals without restraint'. To Nebe's mind, putting an end to 'undesirable lives' was not only permissible but made good sense. As chief of the Reich Criminal Police Department he provided 'technical' assistance in the murder of mentally and physically disabled people. He supplied chemical agents for poisoning and gassing the victims.

Quite why Nebe volunteered to take command of *Einsatzgruppe* B is not documented. Was he hoping to impress Heydrich? He was well known for being 'pathologically ambitious'. In the four months that Nebe commanded *Einsatzgruppe* B, his force murdered more than 45,000 people.

After their money, valuables and some of their clothing had been taken from them, those persons who were to die were loaded into the gas-trucks. Each gas-truck could accommodate 50 to 60 people. The vehicle then drove to a place outside the town, where members of the detail had already dug a mass grave. I myself saw the corpses being unloaded; their faces were not distorted. The death of these people occurred without any symptoms of convulsion.

Sworn statement by Ernst Emil Heinrich Biberstein, head of Einsatzkommando 6, made at Nuremberg in 1945

Starting in August 1941, the 'activity and situation reports of the *Einsatzgruppen*' were radioed to Berlin every day without fail by their commanders. In what were known as 'incident reports', detailed accounts were submitted of the 'job performance' of the special squads and action squads.

According to one of these, by October 1941, *Einsatzgruppe* A had already killed 118,430 Jews and 3,387 'communists'. A further 5,500 Jews had died in Latvia and Lithuania, victims of the pogroms that had been deliberately incited there. Another report, submitted by SS *Standartenführer* Karl Jäger, was such a painstakingly accurate catalogue that it has gone down in the annals of the Holocaust as the 'Jäger Report'. In this document, dated 1 December 1941, he spoke of having liquidated 137,346 Jews. In August of that year the numbers had begun to rise dramatically. Even the number of children murdered in the various executions were now shown separately. Thus we read, for example, in his report for 19 August 1941: 'In Ukmerge: 298 Jewish males, 255 Jewish females, 88 Jewish children.' On 2 September: 'Janova: 112 Jewish males, 1,200 Jewish females, 244 J. children'; 9 October: 'Svenciany: 1,169 Jewish males, 1,840 Jewish females, 717 J. children.'

The list could go on endlessly, Jäger wrote. In conclusion he stated: 'I can confirm today that the objective of solving the Jewish problem in Lithuania has been achieved by EK [*Einsatzkommando*] 3. There are no longer any Jews in Lithuania, apart from Jews on forced labour, plus their families. I had intended to take out these labour-Jews and families as well. However, this provoked a sharp official reaction from the civil administration (the Reich Commissioner) and the Wehrmacht. . . .'

Reports from the death-squads flowed in from other regions too. Up to 31 October 1941, *Einsatzgruppe* B reported 45,467 shootings. In the area where *Einsatzgruppe* D was active a total of 54,696 people were killed, 90 per cent of whom were Jews. The leader of that unit could look back on a particularly 'exciting' career. His name was Otto Ohlendorf and once again, he was one of the long-serving SS men. After the war he was tried at Nuremberg, and left the judges with a more ambiguous impression than almost any other defendant. The terrifying thing about him, in the eyes of many observers, was how exceptionally 'normal' he appeared. As Jason Weber, one of those present, sums it up: they were struck by the way he 'embodied both the kindly human being and the cold-blooded commander, a man who acted without conscience yet believed he was innocent'. The prosecuting counsel, Benjamin Ferencz, recalls: 'He gave the impression of being ice-cold, but at the same time an honest, intelligent, well-educated, good-looking man, the father of five children. And then he openly admitted that on his orders 90,000, yes, 90,000 innocent men, women and children were murdered.' The verdict of the tribunal included the following words: 'If the philanthropist and death-squad leader merged into one person, one might assume that we are dealing with a character . . . who resembles "Dr Jekyll and Mr Hyde".'

Who was Otto Ohlendorf, this apparently 'quite normal man', who became a perpetrator of mass murder? He was acknowledged as being anything but an opportunist; he was not a confirmed anti-Semite, nor a psychopathic loner, who would violently direct his sudden and absolute power against his fellow-men. Otto Ohlendorf was a promising young academic and an economic expert. During the trial his defence counsel produced 500 pages of sworn affidavits asserting Ohlendorf's integrity. In court he was the only defendant who frankly admitted what he had done.

The unit selected for the assignment would arrive in a town or village and issue orders to the leading Jewish inhabitants to assemble all Jews for the purpose of resettlement. They were told to hand over their valuables to the unit's officers and also to give them their outer clothing shortly before the execution. The men, women and children were then led to the execution site, which was usually a deepened anti-tank ditch. Then they were shot, kneeling or standing, and the bodies were thrown into the pit.

Sworn statement made by Otto Ohlendorf, head of Einsatzgruppe *D, at Nuremberg in 1945*

Ohlendorf was brought up in a conservative, middle-class, Protestant household. In 1925, when still a schoolboy, he joined the NSDAP and the SA – which made him one of the earliest

Nazis. Only two years later he could count himself as one of the 'intellectuals' of the party, and the SA transferred him to the SS. Ohlendorf was committed, educated and intelligent. As was recommended practice for young academics, after completing his examinations in 1931 he went abroad for a year – to fascist Italy.

Like many of his contemporaries, Ohlendorf rejected Weimar democracy. Nazi ideology seemed alluring to him; he found plausibility in its view of life as a struggle. As the historian Ulrich Herbert tells us, Ohlendorf belonged to the 'pragmatic generation'. He seemed to represent the 'uncompromising member of the German master-race', as projected by Hitler and Himmler, which was indeed intended to be the model for young SS men.

As soon as Ohlendorf had taken command of *Einsatzgruppe* D in the Ukraine, in 1941, he started perfecting his murderous skills; the desk-bound perpetrator become an enforcer on the ground. He did not merely carry out orders with indifference, he was actually possessed by ambition to do the job particularly well. The suffering of his victims meant nothing to him; all that mattered was the welfare of the executioners. He wanted to minimise the psychological burden on the firing-squads, and so had two riflemen shoot at each victim. Not only did Ohlendorf appear to believe in the necessity of his task, he seemed to derive an inner satisfaction from carrying it out. In a letter to his wife he wrote that he was achieving more for National Socialism through his 'activity in the field of population policy' than he ever did in the *Reichsgruppe Handel*, the Office of Trade. It mattered to him that he should be just as effective in carrying out mass murder as he had been with necessary measures in economic policy.

When the German army marched into Russia I was commanding *Einsatzgruppe* D in the southern sector, and during the year in which I led *Einsatzgruppe* D, it liquidated approximately 90,000 men, women and children.

Sworn statement by Otto Ohlendorf at Nuremberg in 1945

> What they made us do – it was a thoroughly nasty business. But they gave us as much drink as we could possibly want. And later, when the schnapps began to work, we all had the nerve to take part in the operation. When the last of them were brought up, I fired at them too.
> *Petras Zelionka, former Lithuanian auxiliary policeman*

Ohlendorf was, of course, sentenced to death. Yet right up to his execution he displayed neither remorse nor any sense of guilt. 'On the contrary', says his Nuremberg prosecutor, Ferencz, 'all his arguments were an attempt to justify even the murder of children.' He recalls going to see the defendant after sentence had been passed: 'I asked him: "Herr Ohlendorf, is there anything more I can do for you? Shall I give a message to your family? Do you want to say or write anything? Is there any favour I can do for you?" He looked at me in amazement and said: "The Jews in America will suffer. You will see what you have done."' Even after the death sentence, he was incapable of understanding.

The number of Soviet Jews murdered by the *Einsatzgruppen* in the first five months of 'Operation Barbarossa' exceeded half a million. Private memoirs also provide shattering proof of the murderous frenzy that was rampant everywhere. In July 1941, for example, SS *Hauptscharführer* Felix Landau confided to his diary: 'Oddly enough, I feel nothing, no emotion at all. No sympathy. Nothing. It just gets done, and that's all there is to it.' Elsewhere he wrote: 'With some madly sexy music playing, I'm writing my first letter to my darling Trude. Even as I write, they're shouting: "Get your kit ready for action, steel helmet and carbine, 30 rounds of ammo." . . . We've just got back again. 500 Jews were lined up to be shot.'

We hear him saying that murder was a tiresome daily chore, performed with sultry background music; 'it just gets done', not nice, but necessary. What he describes in his diary cannot be explained by peer pressure, nor by the need to act on orders; it simply suggests a cynical routine.

> The women screamed and wept, and so did the men. Some
> tried to escape. The men rounding them up shouted just as
> loud. If the victims didn't do as they were told, they were
> beaten. I particularly remember a red-haired SS man who
> always carried a length of cable with him, and when the
> operation wasn't going as it should, he flogged people with it.
> *Richard Tögel, policeman and member of Einsatzkommando*
> *10a, in a court statement*

It hardly matters whether these crimes were committed by SS men or
by policemen on secondment – the acts were identical. And at times
the 'normal' horror turned into unspeakable atrocity. On 27 June
1941 Sergeant Pipo Schneider, a platoon commander in 3 Company,
Police Battalion 309, was in a motorised column rumbling towards
Bialystok. When he and some of his men discovered shops in the
town selling vodka, they did not wait to be invited; they looted
the stocks and helped themselves generously. Then, dutifully, they
applied themselves once more to the job in hand. That day the
battalion CO, Major Ernst Weis, gave orders for the town of 80,000
inhabitants to be combed, and all Jewish males to be rounded up
– he did not specify further, but left the rest to the initiative of his
company commanders. Pipo Schneider had a clear grasp of what he
had to do. Among his men he was well known as a fanatical racist,
who 'saw red at the mere mention of a Jew', so it was said. His
anti-Semitism, combined with the effect of alcohol, drove him into
a murderous rage. In his hunt through the town for Jewish men,
he shot at least five; other members of the battalion followed suit.
What began as a pogrom ended in systematic shootings. Groups of
Jews were taken into a park and gunned down; rifle salvoes echoed
through the streets late into the night. The survivors were driven by
policemen into Bialystok's main synagogue – people were forced in
with blows from rifle-butts until no more could be accommodated.
The terrified Jews began to sing and pray aloud. Then Pipo
Schneider initiated one of the most brutal massacres of those terrible
weeks: he posted guards all round the synagogue, now crammed
with 700 people, and bolted the doors. The building was set on fire

with petrol. Hand-grenades were flung through the windows to add to the conflagration. With their clothes already in flames, the few who tried to escape the inferno were mown down by machine-gun fire.

The Bialystok 'operation', in which some 700 Jews burned to death in the synagogue and a total of over 2,000 people lost their lives, was not the result of direct orders, but was carried out on their own initiative by a handful of fanatical armed police. The rest of the men in the battalion either allowed themselves to be carried along or else acted 'instinctively' in the manner that was expected of them. Their commanding officer was discovered drunk by horrified soldiers of the Wehrmacht's 221st support division. When questioned, he claimed he knew nothing about the events.

During the war, one could at least try to get transferred from an *Einsatzgruppe*. I myself tried it successfully. . . . When sent back to my unit, I was not demoted and suffered no disadvantage except that I was in personal dispute with Heydrich until his death. There were certainly cases where being transferred out of an *Einsatzgruppe* brought disadvantages. But I cannot remember any individual instances. At any rate, to my knowledge, no-one was shot. You also had a chance to volunteer for the front line, or to be released for other activities.

Franz Six, SS Oberführer, *Einsatzgruppe B, in a court statement*

The personnel of Police Battalion 309, who predominantly came from the eastern Rhineland, had, in their over-hasty obedience, turned into murderers. Not all were trigger-happy sadists or fanatical anti-Semites like Pipo Schneider. Many of the police acted, as did numerous SS members, under pressure from the group; to them, keeping the respect of their colleagues was more important than any feeling of solidarity with the victims. As they saw it, the Jews were outside the sphere in which they felt any obligation or responsibility towards their fellow human beings. This was true even of very mixed units such as Hamburg's Reserve

Police Battalion 101. Christopher Browning shows how few of the men made use of the opportunities offered in certain operations to absent themselves from the killing.

In the SS, the pressure to act in 'solidarity' with a unit sworn to allegiance was certainly even greater. Thus, SS *Scharführer* Schwenker could not bring himself to ask to be excused from a firing-squad, because 'the others would look on me as a wimp. I was worried that my future prospects could be damaged, if I was to appear too soft', and that 'others would get the impression that I wasn't as tough as an SS man ought to be'. So he attempted by other means to stay in the background during the killings.

In Kaunas, Jews were locked up in the Ninth Fort – three or four hundred of them. Holes were dug in the ground – graves – where they were needed. We were then taken to the Ninth Fort. There were a number of Germans there, SS troops. They had set up machine-guns and got us to escort the Jews, 20 or 30 at a time, to the graves. After a head-count, the order was given: 'Forward – move!' Straight into the graves. Then they had to lie down and the SS men shot them where they lay.

Petras Zelionka, former Lithuanian auxiliary gendarme

As the spells of 'action' against defenceless civilians grew longer, the soldiers often became habituated to it. As Christopher Browning writes: 'Ultimately the Holocaust occurred because, looked at simply, individual human beings over a lengthy period killed countless thousands of other human beings. The perpetrators who carried this out became "professional" murderers.' After spells of duty, many of them numbed their minds with alcohol. Only a few resisted the peer-pressure and refused to take a personal hand in the shootings. Though their 'comrades' may have scoffed at them, there is no proven case of such a refusal leading to serious disciplinary measures. Sometimes participation in shootings was actually made voluntary. SS *Sturmbannführer* Ernst Ehlers tells us himself how he reacted to the issuing of an order to commit murder: 'This revelation hit me like a hammer-blow; I could not grasp that an order like that could have been given. I was desperately anxious to avoid this duty and decided to request my superior officer, Nebe, to relieve me of my post as commander of *Einsatzkommando* 8. Nebe duly noted my request and straight away took me on to his group staff.' The argument that military orders had to be obeyed cannot be dismissed out of hand, and yet – as the one time Nuremberg prosecutor Benjamin Ferencz comments – many perpetrators carried out the murders so meticulously, and even hunted down escaping victims with such zeal, that in many cases this argument lacks all credibility.

What was the reaction to such events outside this narrow circle? What was the attitude of Wehrmacht soldiers to the killings? On frequent occasions they witnessed the violence against Jewish civilians, saw executions taking place outside villages, watched Germans in uniform murdering the innocent. However, it did not escape their notice that the perpetrators wore uniforms and insignia that were different from those of the Wehrmacht, the regular armed forces. As Peter von der Osten-Sacken, then a Wehrmacht officer, recalls: 'They weren't part of the Wehrmacht, but special units of the SS.' It was his first encounter with the death-squads. 'Shortly after a small town had been occupied by the Wehrmacht, Jews were rounded up and taken to the market square. It was a dreadful scene. And many of the ordinary soldiers who were watching, didn't understand. They said: "What's going on here? What do they think they're doing? We can't go along with *this*!" You noticed these objections even among the lowest infantrymen. But not all of them, of course. Many were pretty indifferent.' Karl-Heinz Drossel, then a lance-corporal in the 415th Infantry Regiment, was traumatised by the experience of watching an SS execution in Dagda, Lithuania. 'I saw a little boy there, maybe six years old; he kept reaching out to the man on his right. I assume he was the father. Then the SS man behind him took out his pistol, shot him in the neck and kicked him into the pit. That was the limit for me. I still see that little boy today.' Drossel did what he felt he had to: in Berlin he later rescued Jews from the clutches of the Gestapo.

In many places Wehrmacht soldiers were drawn into the mass shootings as 'auxiliary logistical personnel'. They were witnesses – and more – to the atrocities. Not all were guilty, but far too many were, especially in the larger towns and cities. Some reacted with horror, others with disgust. But very few protested. Scarcely anyone enquired into the reasons for it. Quite a number never found out about the crimes, being constantly concerned with their own survival. Then again there were others who applauded the murderous activities of the *Einsatzgruppen*, encouraged the perpetrators and humiliated the victims even in the moment of their death. Sometimes it was the regular soldiers who did the killing – often, though not always, acting on orders. In letters written home to relatives, there is comparatively little to be found about this first phase of the slaughter of the Jews. Yet when the soldiers went home on leave, they reported what they had seen, often under their breath. In this way, information about the mass shootings in the east gradually filtered through.

Meanwhile the killing by the *Einsatzgruppen* was taking on gigantic proportions. In the incident report of Army Group C we read: 'Several reprisal measures were carried out in the context of the major actions. The largest of these took place immediately after the capture of Kiev; it related exclusively to Jews and their entire families.' What is being glossed over here, in bureaucratic language, was a mass murder like no other. On 29 and 30 September 1941, 33,771 Jews were shot in the Babi Yar ravine, near Kiev, by *Einsatzkommando* 4a from *Einsatzgruppe* C.

On 29 September 1941, soon after German troops had occupied Kiev, a long human column snaked its way towards the ravine. Mothers with their babies, older men and women, teenagers and children – more than 30,000 people trailed out of the city in a seemingly endless procession. They were responding to a summons which the invaders had announced in a poster-campaign all over the city. Anyone who failed to comply they threatened to shoot on the spot. None of the Jews who had assembled at the appointed place, near a cemetery, knew what lay in wait for them. Could it be evacuation? Internment? If so, why did they have to leave their clothes behind? Terrible fears grew in their minds as they were forced to walk along an alleyway formed by two rows of policemen, who assailed them with truncheon blows. But that was just the beginning. Having suffered the agonising beatings, when they reached the ravine they were split into small groups and forced to lie on the ground in rows. Then the firing-squad went into action. A salvo of machine-gun fire, a few shovelfuls of earth, scarcely enough to cover the corpses, and then the next group was herded into the ravine. This hideous procedure was repeated over and over, hour after hour. Exhausted by the task of murdering so many thousands, the German death-squads worked in shifts – an hour's killing, an hour's break – and so it went on until darkness fell. Those Jews still left alive spent the night crammed into empty halls, many still believing they were to be 're-settled' – until the next morning when they were unresistingly slaughtered by the now refreshed 'special units'.

Huge numbers of Jews had gathered there and a place had been set up where they had to leave their clothing and luggage. After we'd walked about a kilometre, I saw a big natural ravine. The terrain was sandy. The ravine was about 10 metres [30 feet] deep and 400 metres long. At the top it was about 80 metres wide and at the bottom about 10 metres. As soon as I arrived at the execution area, I and some colleagues had to go down into this hollow. It wasn't long before the first Jews were brought up to the ravine. . . . I can still remember the horror on the faces of the Jews, as they looked over the edge of the pit and down on to the corpses . . .

Kurt Werner, member of Sonderkommando *4a, in a court statement about the massacre at Babi Yar on 29-30 September 1941*

As we passed the ravine after the shootings, the soil was rippling, like waves on a lake. Presumably not all the victims were dead yet. It was a sight I shall never forget.

Walter Gehrke, a Wehrmacht soldier at Babi Yar

One of the few who did survive, Ludmilla Sheila Polishchuk, remembers: 'Mother and I were herded into an assembly-area. I began to scream. Mother grabbed me by the hand and said: "Don't scream, little one, otherwise they'll kill us. If you keep quiet, we might just stay alive."

'Then a firing-squad formed up. Mother did not wait for the order to shoot but threw herself with me into the pit and fell on top of me. The special units began to cover us with corpses. After that they shot another group. Mother sensed I was suffocating underneath her and put her two fists under my throat, to stop me choking on blood. Then I heard soldiers coming to look for survivors. Luckily, one soldier stood right on top of my mother and bayoneted the bodies lying beside her. When they'd gone, Mother pulled me out unconscious and carried me away. In a suburb of Kiev called Podol, there was a brick-works. She took me into a cellar there, where we hid for four days and nights.'

The massacre lasted 36 hours. Then the SS men attempted to remove all traces of it; they dynamited the ravine. The murderers had been meticulous in their accounting: 33,771 dead; 150 men to do the shooting – from that moment on, throughout the Soviet Union, Babi Yar would stand as a symbol of German barbarity. It is estimated that in the Kiev region alone nearly 200,000 human beings were put to death: shot, beaten to death or gassed.

I believe it was in December 1944 that I first received definite information about the mass murder of the Jews. An officer back from the east, on secondment to the military administration, gave us detailed reports about the mass killing of Jews north of Kiev – in a place that later became notorious as Babi Yar.

Walter Bargatzky, former major in the Wehrmacht and lawyer with the military HQ in Paris

---

The man directly responsible for the massacre was *Einsatzgruppenleiter* Paul Blobel, who had also organised the shootings in Byelaya Tserkov. His father had been a small-time craftsman in the eastern Rhineland; he himself had been an apprentice bricklayer and joiner. His ambition and single-mindedness were such that, even without a school-leaving certificate, he was able to train as an architect; then, as a volunteer in the First World War, he was awarded the Iron Cross 1st Class. In 1920 he joined a highly respected architectural practice, then married a girl from a good family. By 1926, at the age of thirty-two, Paul Blobel had achieved everything he could wish for: he was an architect with his own practice, was married into the upper middle class and even had a home of his own.

Then in 1929 came the worldwide economic slump. No more commissions were coming in, he was on the dole and facing ruin. In October 1931, in search of political reassurance, he signed up with the SA – and, oddly, joined the German Social Democratic Party at the same time. Early in 1932 it seemed that he had found his true calling, and became one of the first members of the SD, the security service of the SS. This involved spying on Social Democrats as well as communists. For the ambitious Blobel it was the second chance he needed. A total lack of scruple and unquestioning adherence to Nazi racist ideology were the essential qualities required for advancement in the SD. However, Blobel brought with him other qualities as well, which qualified him for his subsequent killing assignments: he was intelligent, but not an intellectual. By the beginning of 1941 he was already a *Standarten-führer*, equivalent to a colonel in the regular army. Blobel seemed ideally suited for the 'special missions in the east', since he was judged to be an 'energetic personality', with 'excellent leadership qualities'.

Under his command, *Sonderkommando* 4a of *Einsatzgruppe* C murdered some 60,000 men, women and children. 'And he murdered out of conviction', said the man who later prosecuted him, Benjamin Ferencz: 'His constant invoking of superior orders became a farce.'

Early in 1942 Blobel was ordered back to the Reich – very probably on account of alcohol problems, because he seemed unable to cope with the killings any longer, either psychologically or physically. Yet only nine months later the Central Office of Reich Security (RSHA) sent him off on a new mission. 'Operation

The precise number of persons executed is something I can no longer recall. At a superficial estimate, the accuracy of which I cannot vouch for, I suppose that the number of people whose executions *Sonderkommando* 4a had a part in, lies somewhere between 10,000 and 15,000.

Sworn statement by Paul Blobel, leader of Sonderkommando
4a, Nuremberg, 1945

During my visit in August, I myself watched the burning of corpses in a mass grave near Kiev. This grave was approximately 55 metres long, 3 metres wide and 2½ metres deep. When the covering of earth had been removed, the bodies were soaked in fuel and set alight. It took about two days for the grave to burn out completely. . . . Then it was filled in again, and all traces were virtually obliterated.

Sworn statement by Paul Blobel, leader of a Sonderkommando,
Nuremberg 1945

105' was to remove all traces of the massacre. The SS man, now apparently 'stable' once more, performed this task with gusto. He had the mass graves reopened, the corpses burned on oil-soaked iron grids, and the remnants of bone ground up in specially designed mills.

After the war, when on trial at Nuremberg, Blobel displayed no remorse. He believed as strongly as ever in his superiority as a *Herrenmensch*, one of the master-race. Like his fellow SS killer, Otto Ohlendorf, he felt less sorry for the victims than for the perpetrators who, he claimed, 'suffered more nervous distress than those who had to be shot.' The last words of the man who was executed for crimes against humanity, were: 'As a soldier I remained disciplined and loyal. . . . Now discipline and loyalty have led me to the gallows. Even today I do not know how else I should have acted.' A greater perversion of the soldier's moral code is scarcely imaginable.

In Group D I never approved shooting by individuals, but gave orders that several men should fire simultaneously, in order to avoid any direct, personal responsibility.
Sworn statement by Otto Ohlendorf, head of Einsatzgruppe *D,*
Nuremberg, 1945

Blobel was one of those who murdered out of conviction, but bore the psychological scars. Many suffered from the crimes they had themselves committed. The results were nervous breakdowns, drunkenness, stomach complaints and other psychosomatic ailments. Yet others indulged in unbridled sadism, beat up their victims indiscriminately, murdered gratuitously. Gustav Fix, a member of *Sonderkommando* 6, later made this statement in the *Einsatzgruppe* trial: 'I would just like to add that due to the considerable psychological stress of such executions, there were numerous men who were no longer capable of carrying out the shootings and therefore had to be relieved. However, there were other persons who could not take part in them often enough and frequently volunteered for those executions.' In 1941 Boris von Drachenfels was in the *Ordnungspolizei*: 'Every day more than 30 men, sometimes as many as 50 or 60, came marching in wanting to report sick. But as a rule only a few of them were excused duties. They were given pills of some kind. I was told some men had nervous breakdowns. There were suicides and people were sent to mental asylums.' What is indicative is the way the perpetrators later described these phenomena at the Nuremberg trials: their sympathy was generally reserved for the killers, not their victims. One statement by Kurt Werner, a member of *Sonderkommando* 4a, is characteristic: 'A rifleman stood behind each of the Jews and killed them with a shot in the neck. . , . You just cannot imagine what nerve it took to do that filthy job. It was dreadful . . . I had to stay down in that ravine all morning and keep on shooting for quite a time. . . . '

The perpetrators were SS men, convinced Nazis and fanatical racists, but they were also members of police battalions, who hardly seemed destined to become mass murderers. Their officers

In close co-operation with SS Brigadeführer Zenner and the exceptionally able head of the SD, Dr Strauch, we have liquidated about 55,000 Jews in White Ruthenia in the last 10 weeks. In the province of Minsk the Jews have been completely exterminated. . . .

Wilhelm Kube, General Commissioner for White Ruthenia, in a report of 31 July 1942

demanded terrible things from them, a fact that their chief, the Reichsführer-SS Heinrich Himmler was well aware of. He worried about his enforcers. Thus, in an order dated 12 December 1941 to 'senior SS and police officers', he drew attention to their 'duty of care' towards the men under their command: 'It is the sacred duty of senior and commanding officers personally to ensure that none of our men, who have this difficult duty to perform, are brutalised or suffer damage to their character and disposition. This task will be completed through the severest discipline in service duties, and through comradely gatherings at the end of a day that has brought difficult assignments. However, such gatherings must never end in alcohol abuse. They should be evenings where – as far as circumstances allow – the men sit down in traditional style to a good German meal, and where the time is filled by music, lectures and the introduction of our men to the finer aspects of German intellectual and spiritual life.' What was intended would be a sinister crossover between 'normality' and mass murder.

Himmler was very anxious that the killing be done 'decently', that formalities be observed and that no 'base motives' should prevail, such as sadism or self-enrichment through the robbing of victims. In his perverted view of the world, this was reprehensible behaviour, though the slaughter of hundreds of thousands was not. Such morbid distinctions were not only found in the minds of the SS leadership. An SS man, Ernst Göbel, later reported on one of his junior NCOs: 'The way he killed the children – it was brutal. He grabbed several of them by the hair, hauled them up off the ground, shot them in the back of the head and then threw them in the pit. In the end I couldn't watch any more and made him stop . . . I told him to kill them in a more seemly way.'

Himmler tried unceasingly to make his men believe they were being called upon to perform a great, even an idealistic deed which, though harsh and cruel, would ultimately ensure the survival of their own nation. No-one in the SS or police hierarchy spoke out against the Reichsführer – least of all during that notorious speech he gave to officers of the SS and police at Poznan on 6 October 1943: 'Most of you will know what it means when 100 bodies are lying side by side, or 500 are lying there. To have come through this and – apart from some isolated instances of human weakness – to have remained decent, is what has made us tough. This is a distinguished page in our history, but one which has never been and is never to be written.'

From the outset Himmler concerned himself with the moral wellbeing of the murderers. On several occasions he went to witness their deeds as they were being committed in the field. The 'Senior SS and Police Officer' Erich von dem Bach-Zelewski was keen to show Himmler what effect the gruesome activities had on his men. 'Look in those men's eyes', he was heard to say. 'Their nerves will be ruined for the rest of their lives. We're breeding neurotics and wild animals here!'

Himmler showed some sympathy, but he lectured the riflemen on the necessity of their assignment, and how they should free themselves from moral concerns, since he and Hitler would bear the responsibility. Battles had to be fought, which future generations would be spared. Nonetheless, Himmler and his senior officers sought ways of making the killing less 'liable to hold-ups'. Simon Wiesenthal, who after the war not only assembled the evidence against the perpetrators, but also tried to explain the origins of the Holocaust, described it in simple terms: 'A number of the murderers killed themselves, because they could stand the murder no longer. A man who had three children at home and who himself killed other children, was no longer the same man. That is why more impersonal methods of killing were sought. And thus they hit upon gas.'

The people are to be asphyxiated with diesel exhaust-fumes. But the diesel engine won't work. Hauptmann Wirth comes along. You can see he's embarrassed that it should happen the very day *I'm* here. . . . The people are waiting in the gas-chambers. But nothing happens. We can hear them crying, sobbing. After 2 hours 49 minutes – all carefully timed by stop-watch – the diesel engine starts. Up to this moment 3,000 people were alive in these four chambers – 750 people in each 45 cubic metre space! Another 25 minutes pass. Right, many of them are now dead. We look through the little window, while an electric light illuminates the chamber for a moment. After 28 minutes only a few are still alive. Finally, after 32 minutes, the whole lot are dead!

Kurt Gerstein, SS 'Health Officer' in a report written while in prison

Large goods vans were converted into gassing vehicles, using the invisible poison of carbon monoxide. SS *Standartenführer* Walter Rauff later made this statement: 'I cannot say whether I had any doubts about using gassing trucks at the time. Uppermost in my mind was that the shooting put a lot of stress on the people who did it, and this stress was removed by the use of gassing trucks.' It was only the beginning. Soon it was not just a matter of relieving the perpetrators but also of adding a new dimension to the mass murder – it was now rigorous, mechanical, and with a capacity of millions.

The hour was now striking for Eicke's pupils. They were imbued not only with the Nazis' frenetic hatred of Jews but also with the strong-arm methods of camp discipline. Rudolf Höss became commandant of Auschwitz, Max Kögel that of Majdanek. Adolf Eichmann, who had served under Eicke at Dachau, was now in the Central Office of Reich Security where he was to be the organiser of the Holocaust.

When a concentration camp was set up at Auschwitz in 1940, not even the senior executioners yet had any concept of the extent of the crime that would very soon be committed there. When SS

Hauptsturmführer Rudolf Höss arrived there at the end of April 1941, he was, as he himself said, filled with an urge to get on with things. His job was to transform the existing artillery barracks into a 'proper concentration camp'.

As is well known, all SS personnel at Auschwitz are instructed, obliged and sworn on oath to maintain silence in respect of all installations and incidents that come to their knowledge in the course of their duties. There has been reason to point out once again that any violation of this sworn undertaking will be treated as treason.

Order No. 8/42 from the commandant's office,
Auschwitz concentration camp

In memory of the 'good old days', he had a sign bearing the cynical motto *Arbeit macht frei* ('Work liberates') put up over the gates of the camp – just as it was at Dachau. But apart from that the newly appointed commandant wanted nothing more to do with the old regime. As he put it later: 'From the very start I realised that we could only make something viable out of Auschwitz by hard and tireless work, from the commandant down to the last inmate. But in order to harness everyone for this task I had to break with all tradition, with all the customs that had grown up in concentration camps.' Eicke had regarded the prisoners above all as palpable enemies of the state and the people. Höss's definition of the opposition was new and eliminatory. The future of the German people, he said, depended on how effectively it rid itself of 'harmful elements'. Höss, being both ambitious and unscrupulous, was to prove just how effective he could be as commandant of Auschwitz.

As we drove through, I saw a large building. It was almost the size of a factory with a giant chimney, and Höss said to me: 'There's capacity for you! Ten thousand!'

Adolf Eichmann, in exile in Argentina, 1956

His early life history was typical of those times. As a child he was accustomed to the firm hand of his father, a businessman from Baden. Rudolf wanted to become a Catholic priest. But while he was at school his solidly based vision of the world fell apart when a priest betrayed his confessional secrets.

The First World War gave him a new perspective – as it did to so many young men who later joined the SS. From the start the war strengthened his hankering for things military, for uniforms and order. Although not yet sixteen years old, Höss managed to get accepted by the army. In the trenches of a pitiless war of attrition, the recruit, like many others, lost his fear of taking life. And like so many, he too found himself adrift at the end of the war. He joined a *Freikorps* unit of anti-communist irregulars, and was sentenced to ten years imprisonment for acts of political violence. Höss was impressed by the strict regime of prison life. He wanted to be a model prisoner; it gave him another solid structure he could fit into. His reward was release after less than six years of his sentence.

Höss fled from the intellectual turmoil of Germany's first republic into the romantically idealised and self-sufficient life of a farmer. But in 1934, when Heinrich Himmler launched a recruitment drive for the SS, Höss opted for the Black Order and was plunged into Eicke's toughening-up programme. He was a quick study; as he admitted later, unquestioning obedience and total discipline in the name of the cause were second nature to him. And what of decent, civic values? In his eyes, needless to say, they were only for people whom the state had branded as the enemy. His defining characteristic was keenness. When there was not enough barbed wire to enlarge the camp, he got someone to steal some more. The end justified all manner of means. And the end was determined by others – as he kept convincing himself. Höss was one of those people who always needed someone above him, telling him what to do. After the war he denied all responsibility for his actions: he had only been following orders, he said.

> Höss led an exemplary family life and was modesty personified; punctual and precise.
>
> *Adolf Eichmann*

The first prisoners to be transported to Auschwitz were 30 'trusties' from Sachsenhausen concentration camp. Their job was to act as *Kapos*, and as camp, block and room 'seniors', supervising the other inmates. They themselves did not have to do any physical work. They got better food, wore high leather boots and tailored prison garb. 'Divide and rule', was his motto, as Höss wrote arrogantly in his journal. The graded distribution of power assigned everyone a place in the camp hierarchy and made each one a part of the system. It also turned victims into perpetrators. It was the distinguishing feature of camp existence.

Three weeks after the *Kapos* arrived, the first Polish prisoners were herded into the old barracks, accompanied by kicks, blows and loud shouting. They were resistance fighters, politicians, representatives of the Polish intelligentsia, priests and Jews. Karl Fritsch, the 'Senior Protective Custody Officer' and right-hand man of the camp commandant, greeted the new arrivals with a speech that wiped out at a stroke all hope of ever leaving the place alive. 'You lot have not come to a health-farm. This is a German concentration camp, from which there is only one way out – up the chimney. Anyone who doesn't like it can go and throw himself on to the electrified wire. If there are any Jews in this shipment, they have no right to live longer than two weeks. Priests, if there are any, can live for a month; all the rest, three months.'

> They opened the doors of the railway wagons and beat us as we emerged, to make us get out faster. Left behind in the wagons were old people and children who had been crushed or had died in other ways.
>
> *Shlomo Dragon, Polish Jew*

After the invasion of the Soviet Union, the camp filled up with Russian prisoners-of-war. Under cover of the 'Commissar Order' issued several months earlier, the head of the Central Office of Reich Security, Reinhard Heydrich, ordered that all officials, especially 'professional revolutionaries and People's Commissars' were to be picked out and liquidated. Since there were to be no

At the corner stood a tough SS man who said to the poor wretches in a soothing voice: 'Nothing at all is going to happen to you. Inside the chambers you have to breathe deeply to expand the lungs. This inhalation is necessary because of illnesses and epidemics.'

Kurt Gerstein, SS 'Health Officer', in a report written while in prison

witnesses to this killing operation, the concentration camps were chosen as the scene of the crime.

It was on 5 September 1941 that the SS used the cyanide preparation, Zyklon B, for the first time to murder people in Auschwitz. The trial was 'successful', and the executioners were clearly satisfied. Nearly 600 Soviet prisoners-of-war and some 300 sick civilian detainees met their death in the cloud of lethal gas. The means of committing murder on a mass scale had been discovered. The 'advantage' of Zyklon B over the mass shootings that were already being carried out in the camp seemed obvious: not only did it kill faster and more cost-effectively, it was also 'more humane' – for the perpetrators, that is, not for the victims. The camp commandant Rudolf Höss later stated in evidence: 'I must be frank and say that, on me at least, the gassing had a reassuring affect, since in the foreseeable future a start would have to be made on the mass extermination of the Jews. I always dreaded the shootings. But now I was reassured that we would be spared all those blood-baths.'

When I think about it all again, I feel guilty because I did wrong then. The whole Jewish business was a crime. I am sorry about it and regret that I took part in it.

Karl Frenzel, SS Oberscharführer in Sobibor camp; condemned to life imprisonment in 1966 for complicity in the deaths of at least 150,000 people

He was a sadist and a brutal murderer. His spell at Sobibor was not limited to participation in mass gassings; he committed numerous murders and other crimes that he was not ordered to do.

Herschel Cuckierman, Polish survivor of Sobibor, about Karl Frenzel

Yet the prisoners were certainly not spared from horrific and personally administered violence. Punishment beatings were a daily occurrence. They came in an endless variety of forms, since the sadistic imagination of their tormentors knew no limits.

A particularly notorious technique used during interrogations was the 'swing'. The prisoner was made to pull up his knees and hold his hands in front of them. He was then handcuffed and his wrists locked across his legs. Finally, a solid iron pole was pushed between the victim's elbows and knees. The pole was placed on two wooden blocks so that prisoner hung head downwards. Guards then beat him with a bull-whip on his buttocks, genitals and the bare soles of his feet. The blows were so violent that the torture victim spun around the pole. When his screams grew too loud, a gas-mask was placed over his face. In Birkenau, many people died, not because they had been guilty of some trivial 'crime', but purely for the amusement of the camp personnel. Sometimes the tormentors picked their victims completely at random. They forced the unfortunate victim to stretch out on his stomach, then placed a truncheon on the back of his neck and jumped on it with all their strength, thus breaking his neck. A survivor of Auschwitz, Rudolf Vrba, conjures up apocalyptic images: 'Wild-eyed "kapos" carved a bloody swathe through the crowds of prisoners, while SS men, like cowboys on TV, who had wandered by mistake into a grotesque and unending horror-movie, were shooting from the hip.' The bodies of prisoners shot while trying to escape were propped up on the parade-ground as a deterrent. SS men hung placards round their necks that read '*Hurra, hurra, wir sind wieder da*' (Hooray, hooray, we're back again'). Escapers who had been recaptured alive were hanged in front of the other prisoners. To make life easier for the guards, the camp management made every effort to provide 'Rest and Recreation'. Most SS men in Auschwitz spent their free time in the sauna, at the football ground or in the brothel. At the Buchenwald concentration camp there was a falconry that had been specially installed for Hermann Göring, and a riding-arena built for the wife of the camp commandant.

As a rule, the senior SS ranks were accommodated with their families in detached or terraced houses. Each had its own small garden, and the housing was built in clusters around the various areas of the camp. A written order has survived, which shows the importance Rudolf Höss attributed to a well-tended environment: 'The newly laid out horticultural areas are an ornament to the camp. It goes without saying that every SS man must treat these areas with care and not damage the beds by walking on them.' Furthermore, the SS men were required by their commandant to work on their gardens themselves: 'Married SS officers, NCOs and men may only fence off as much garden space around their homes as they can cultivate themselves. Inmates cannot be put on to gardening work, since the guards are needed for more urgent duties': this was a reference to the supervision of forced labour in SS industries.

Höss was constantly concerned to promote togetherness among the camp guards. Whether in competitive sports or convivial evenings, what mattered was the *esprit de corps* of the SS. The wide variety of orders that were issued by the commandant's office give us an insight into the social life of the camp; for instance this invitation to a 'get-together' at Auschwitz: 'A comrades' evening for all SS members at Auschwitz concentration camp will be held on 16 August 1940 in the theatre building located beyond the detention camp. Start: 19.00. Everyone must be in their seats by 18.50. The head of the detention camp must ensure that the work-squads return punctually, so that the SS men can be free by 18.15. Wives and fiancées of SS men, who are currently staying at the camp, are invited to the comrades' evening.'

Sports events also provided a diversion. The very day before the invasion of the Soviet Union, the following order was issued in Auschwitz: 'On the occasion of the summer solstice of 21

June 1941 a light athletics competition will be held at the sports ground of the SS sports association. On that day, work-squads will only be sent out to vitally important factories, so that the companies will have the opportunity to take part in this sports event in large numbers. No leave will be granted on that day.' And only three weeks after Hitler had unleashed his war of extermination in the east, came this order: 'On Sunday 13 July 1941, three football and handball competitions will be held on the Auschwitz sports ground. The following matches will take place: 14.00 to 15.30: SS Death's Head football team versus Altberun Sports Club; 16.00 to 17.30: SS handball team versus Birkental Sports Association; 17.00 to 18.30: SS football team versus Birkental Sports Association. Entrance to the matches costs 10 Reichsmarks.'

At this time the final step in the epoch-making crime still lay just ahead. Only a few months after the first gassings, industrial-scale killing began at Auschwitz. However, Block 11, where the first group of victims had been murdered with Zyklon B, proved unsuitable for larger operations. Simply ventilating the chamber there took several days. That seemed too long for the 'effective' form of killing that was sought. Consequently, the second phase of gassing was soon moved to the crematorium, where the mortuary had equipment for removing and replacing the air. A number of holes were bored through the roof, through which the crystals of Zyklon B could be thrown – bringing death in the air itself. The engines of heavy trucks were started up to drown the cries of the dying. The first gas-chambers in Auschwitz had commenced operation – though not yet for Jews.

That required a further decision. And this was made against the background of Hitler's war of extermination, which had now ground to a halt. In the autumn of 1941 Hitler's conversation turned with increasing frequency to the 'Jewish question'. The dictator had seriously underestimated Stalin's empire, though of course he did not blame himself for this error. The war, he claimed, was the product of an international conspiracy. And those he presumed were pulling the strings behind the scenes would have to atone for it. The Jews were now to pay the price for the German blood spilled on the Russian front. What the dictator had decided in his deluded frenzy, the Auschwitz commandant, Rudolf Höss, was to hear from SS chief Himmler in person. The circumstances were enough to indicate that this was no ordinary meeting. For contrary to his usual custom the Reichsführer-SS received his guest alone, with no adjutant present. The Führer had ordered the 'final solution of the Jewish question', Himmler informed the camp commandant. As Höss remembered it, he was left in no doubt as to what was meant by 'final solution': 'The Jews are the eternal enemies of the German people and must be exterminated. Now, while the war is on, all the Jews we can get hold of are to be annihilated without exception. If we do not succeed in destroying the biological basis of Jewry, then one day the Jews will destroy the German people.' He had selected Auschwitz for this purpose, Himmler continued, because of its convenient transport links and isolated location. Höss was well aware of the monstrous nature of this order. Yet as a fanatical Nazi he was blindly obedient to his Führer. He also felt flattered that he, of all people, had been selected for the task of solving such a crucial problem. He wanted to show he was worthy of this trust: 'Only one thing mattered to me: to keep advancing, driving things forward . . . so as to be able to carry through the measures as ordered.' But for the time being, he still had to wait. Himmler had not given precise instructions about how this 'final solution' was to be implemented. All that was clear was the objective – the total annihilation of Europe's Jews.

During this period (as far as I am aware) a total of 5 or 6 transports, each with 5 to 7 wagons holding 30 to 40 people each, arrived at Belzec. The Jews from 2 of these transports were still being gassed in the small chamber, then Wirth had the gassing sheds torn down and put up a massive new building, with a considerably greater capacity. The Jews from the remaining transports were then gassed in the new facility.

Josef Oberhauser, SS Obersturmführer, *in a court statement*

The green light was given at the 'Wannsee Conference' on 20 January 1942. In this elegant lakeside mansion near Berlin, far removed from the daily horror of Auschwitz, the logistics of the greatest murder of the twentieth century were calmly signed off. As early as 26 March 1942 the first of the trains organised by Eichmann arrived at Auschwitz, laden with Jewish women from Slovakia. They were billeted in the former barracks for Russian PoWs. Of the 10,000 Soviet soldiers originally brought to the camp, no more than 1,000 were now still alive.

In September 1941, due to the lack of existing capacity, work had started on a new camp. Höss drove the construction work forward with merciless harshness. In the nearby village of Birkenau, Russian and Polish prisoners had to tear down the houses and erect primitive, stable-like huts in their place. Originally planned as a prisoner-of-war camp, Birkenau was destined to become the centre for mass murder – a death factory for the Jews of Europe.

> Even in the spring of 1942 there were rumours in the Warsaw ghetto that the Germans were experimenting with gas, with motor exhaust, that people were herded into some kind of shed, and gas was piped in, and that was how they were murdered. . . . At the time I was one of the many who didn't believe it.
>
> *Marcel Reich-Ranicki, then living in the Warsaw ghetto*

Outside the new camp perimeter, at the edge of a wood, stood two pretty and well-kept farmhouses. With their thatched roofs and surrounded by orchards, these houses seemed the perfect camouflage for what was to be enacted inside. They looked so harmless that the victims would be fooled until the last moment. On the doors the murderers had put up signs reading: 'To the disinfecting area' and 'To the wash-room'. Beside Bunkers I and II, as the houses were called from now on, three huts had been built for the prisoners to undress in. By the end of June 1942 both bunkers were 'ready for service'.

Globocnik said: 'This whole business is one of the most secret matters there is at the moment, if not *the* most secret. Anyone who talks about it will be shot immediately.' Only yesterday, two blabber-mouths had been shot, he said . . . 'Your main job is to carry out the disinfecting of the very considerable amount of textile materials. . . . You others have the far more important task of converting our gas-chambers, which currently work with diesel exhaust fumes, to some better and faster method. I'm thinking particularly of cyanide.'

Kurt Gerstein, SS 'Health Officer', in a report written in prison

When Himmler visited Auschwitz in July 1942, he told Höss: 'Eichmann's programme is under way and being stepped up month by month. See that you get ahead with the expansion of Birkenau. And be equally ruthless in getting rid of all Jews who are unfit for work.' That same evening the senior SS man sat down to a convivial round of drinks with his accomplices in murder. Himmler was 'in the best of moods, positively beaming', Höss recalled. 'He even drank a glass of red wine and smoked, something he didn't normally do.'

Close to the small two-platform station there was a little hut, known as the 'cloakroom', with a large counter for valuables. . . . Then a little avenue between birch-trees, fenced in on both sides with barbed wire, and with signs: 'To the inhalation and bathrooms!' Facing us was a kind of bath-house with geraniums, then a short staircase leading to 3 rooms on the right and 3 on the left, each measuring 5 x 5 metres [260 sq ft] and 1.9 metres [6ft 4 ins] high, with garage-type doors.[. . .] On the roof as a 'clever little joke' was a Star of David!

Kurt Gerstein, SS 'Health Officer', in a report written while in prison

Himmler's directive became murderous reality: six extermination camps were built – at Chelmno, Belzec, Sobibor, Treblinka, Majdanek and Auschwitz – in which Jews were systematically gassed. The machinery was already running at high speed. From his desk, Adolf Eichmann directed the trains death-wards with a merciless attention to detail. On 8 November 1942 Hitler announced to a selected audience in Munich's Löwenbräukeller: 'You will recall the session of the Reichstag, in which I declared that if the Jews somehow imagine they can bring about an international, global war that will destroy the races of Europe, then the result will not be the extermination of the European races, but the extermination of Jewry in Europe.'

In 1944 during the big transports from Hungary and Holland, the gassing went on every day, of course. But under normal running conditions, everything was shifted to night-time; gassing only took place at night.

Hans Wilhelm Münch, SS doctor at Auschwitz

Over the years I learned from experience which hooks I had to use for which fish.

Adolf Eichmann, on the deportation of Hungarian Jews in 1944

By now, the arrival of deportation trains had become routine in Auschwitz. Thousands of people from all over Europe trod the unloading-ramp every day. Driven from their homes and robbed of their possessions, they were crammed into trains and sent off on their final journey. Men, women and children, the sick and the aged were packed tightly into cattle-trucks. Many of the deportees died of thirst or exhaustion even before reaching their terrible destination. Those who survived the journey had no inkling of the horrors awaiting them.

At the end of the agonising trek, everything began to happen very fast: the doors were flung open and the exhausted victims dragged out, and hustled along with loud shouts and the barking of fierce SS dogs. Anyone who moved too slowly was kicked and beaten forward. The shambles was created deliberately – a perfect system for cowing the victims into submission. Disorientated and demoralised by the misery of the journey, they simply did as they were ordered. Once all the living had been removed from the trucks, their luggage was confiscated and the dead bodies of those who had not survived the hellish trip to Auschwitz thrown from the train. The prisoners had to do this themselves; the Death's-Head thugs did not want to get their hands dirty. The fate of each deportee was decided at the end of the platform. Mothers were separated from their children, husbands from their wives; families were torn apart in seconds. The SS men allowed no time for goodbyes. Thus, many of the survivors have traumatic memories of the moment of selection. When the new inmates had been sorted by age and sex, they were made to line up in rows of five. The camp doctor then walked past, gesturing to the right or left. Those 'fit for work' were sent to the right; the old, weak and sick, to the left. If the selection was taking too long, and the perpetrators got tired, the remaining victims only had one direction to go: to the left and to their death.

What went on in the minds of those doctors? A slight wave of the hand decided on life or death for thousands. Some drank or took stimulants to make it easier to play the part of judge. However, the most notorious Auschwitz doctor, Josef Mengele, apparently kept a clear head at all times. According to prisoners' accounts, he did his selecting in a calm and regular rhythm. To the right, to the left, to the right, to the left. Eye-witnesses tell us that he sometimes whistled to himself – waltzes or tunes from operetta – as his hand passed sentences of death.

> It is in the nature of a sadist to enjoy inflicting pain on his victim. With Mengele one had the feeling that he simply didn't notice the pain. It never occurred to him; to him the prisoners were guinea-pigs, laboratory rats, whose inner life and suffering was of absolutely no concern to him.
>
> *Dr Ella Lingens, prisoner and doctor in Auschwitz*

> He smiled, whistled or sang, even at the worst moments. In selecting from 2,000 people, he only chose about a hundred for temporary survival.
>
> *Camille Bentata, Auschwitz survivor, on a selection in which*
> *Josef Mengele was involved*

Even after the 'selection', the SS doctors betrayed their profession. Sick people, who would have recovered under normal circumstances, were 'outsorted' by the white-coated perpetrators. Those infected with typhus in particular were not usually given medication, but a 'flushing out'. This meant a fatal injection of phenol in the heart. The Viennese woman doctor, Ella Lingens, who as a prisoner had to work in the sick-bay, once challenged an SS doctor named Klein about how he could reconcile his murderous activities with the Hippocratic Oath. Klein replied: 'Because I have sworn the Hippocratic Oath, I remove the appendix from the body of a human being; and the Jews are the festering appendix in the body of the world, which is why they must be excised.' In the eyes of many doctors this inhuman attitude legitimised not only killings but also various pseudo-medical experiments. The SS camp doctor, Josef Mengele, usually selected his victims – preferably twins – as soon as they arrived on the unloading-ramp. As Yitzhak Traub recalls: 'My twin brother and I were on our way to the gas-chambers with our mother, and she suddenly said: "Children, run back to where they're looking for twins."' Yitzhak and his brother Zerah ended up in Dr Mengele's experimental laboratory. The doctor of death contemptuously referred to the children as 'my guinea-pigs'. He wanted to be immortalised in the medical textbooks for his theory on twins. In the name of 'research' he injected chemicals into the children's eyes, to see whether brown eyes could be turned permanently blue. He killed others with injections of Evipan or phenol and removed their organs. Today the name of Josef Mengele is synonymous with the inhuman medical experiments at Auschwitz. Yet this man from the small Bavarian town of Günzburg was by no means the only doctor to place himself unreservedly in the service of murderers.

> When we were tied down on Mengele's experimental table,
> we never knew what would be done to us next. We felt a cold
> hand on our backs, a stethoscope and then an injection that
> hurt terribly. We were dreadfully afraid.
> *Kalman Braun, a twin and victim of Mengele in Auschwitz*

Among the female SS, women doctors and nurses were also
notable for their unscrupulous conduct. The sick and wounded
were deprived of all care, unless it was to keep them fit for work.
In the first Ravensbrück trial, the prosecuting counsel stated that
'prisoners were often seen to die on their feet, or to collapse on
parade, because they refused to go to the sick-bay'. They knew
what was awaiting them there. Probably the most notorious Nazi
camp doctor was Dr Herta Oberheuser. At the trial of doctors at
Nuremberg, she was the only woman to be tried and convicted
for crimes against humanity. In 1935 she was a 'block leader' in
the BDM, the 'League of German Lasses'; after joining the Nazi
Party in 1937, she volunteered in 1940 to serve as an SS doctor
in Ravensbrück women's concentration camp. There she helped
to plan human experiments on Polish women prisoners. In passing
sentence, the judge remarked: 'Oberheuser was fully informed
about the nature and purpose of the experiments. She helped to
select subjects, examined them medically and also prepared them
in other ways for the operations. She was present at operations in
the operating-theatre and helped with them. At the end of each
operation she cooperated obediently with Gebhardt and Fischer,
making sure that the patients were deliberately neglected, so that
the wounds inflicted on the experimental subjects would become
as highly infected as possible.'

However, there were also some SS women who helped the
prisoners. One of the few was Maria Stromberger, from 1942
onward a nurse in the SS sick-bay at Auschwitz. One survivor tells
us about her work: 'One day something surprising happened. It
was evening, but we did not head back to the camp, because we
had been "detailed". There were just two of us in the kitchen,
Nurse Maria and me. I was washing up the dishes. Suddenly I

heard a loud bang in the camp, not far from the kitchen window. I knew just what it meant. In those days prisoners very often "went to the wire" and electrocuted themselves. At the same time I heard a soft cry behind me, where Nurse Maria was standing by the window. I turned round and saw that she had turned very pale and had sunk on to a chair in a faint. I was scared and called Nurse Margarete. After a few minutes everything was fine again, but Nurse Maria went straight home.' After this incident Maria Stromberger found out about the terrible things that went on in the Auschwitz camp. She learned of the gassings, the burning of corpses in the crematorium, of other arbitrary killings and of the daily tormenting of prisoners. From that moment on she dedicated herself to the fate of the inmates. She helped them in whatever ways she could. She got hold of food and medicines for them and finally joined the resistance movement in the camp, acting as a messenger for them. Towards the end of the war, when rumours about her help to prisoners began to spread, she was transferred by the camp's resident medical officer, Eduard Wirths, to a rehabilitation clinic for morphine-addicts. Immediately after the German surrender, Maria Stromberger was arrested and placed in Polish detention. In a letter from prison sent to some Auschwitz survivors, she wrote: 'At the moment I am in an internment camp! I am suspected of having treated inmates with phenol. Just imagine, here I am surrounded by Nazis, SS, and Gestapo! Me – their greatest enemy! And now I have to listen to complaints about the "injustice" of what people are doing to them. Then I think back to my experiences in Auschwitz! I see the glow of the burning pyres. I smell the stench of burnt flesh, I see the wretched columns of labour-squads returning and dragging the dead behind them, I feel the choking fear I had for you every morning, before I saw you before me, safe and sound; and now I feel like screaming in the faces of these men and lashing out blindly at them.' Thanks to the intervention of former concentration camp inmates, Maria Stromberger was released from Polish detention.

Yet in the world of the SS camps people like Maria were extremely rare. Members of a profession originally dedicated to saving life became the enforcers of murderous plans – often a gesture of the hand was all it took. The ones whom the doctors waved to the left, were destined for death and were immediately forced to go into the gas-chamber. Those who could no longer walk were transported there on trucks. It all had to happen quickly; the murderers wanted to waste no time. Up to the last moment, they tried to lull their victims into a sense of security: the trucks bore the comforting symbol of a red cross. Even in the rooms where they were made to undress before entering the gas-chamber the fatal deception was carried on. The unsuspecting victims were told they would be given a shower, then disinfected, but they must be quick: 'Hurry up, your food and coffee are getting cold', they were warned. As a rule this mollifying ruse worked. However, when there were occasional signs of unrest, the 'troublemakers' were unobtrusively taken out behind the building and shot with a small-calibre weapon. The others noticed nothing. Obediently they noted the number of the hook on which they had hung their clothes, 'so that you can find everything again quickly after being disinfected', the SS men informed them.

When I constructed the extermination building at Auschwitz, I used Zyklon B, crystallised cyanide, which we threw into the death-chambers through a small opening. Depending on the weather conditions, it took 3 to 15 minutes to kill the people in the death-chamber.

Rudolf Höss, commandant of Auschwitz, in a sworn statement at Nuremberg, 5 April 1946

The Zyklon B thrown in from outside initially produced its deadly fumes at floor-level. It only gradually penetrated the upper layers of air. For this reason the unfortunate victims trampled each other down, climbing on top of one another. The higher they were the longer it took for the gas to reach them. What a terrible struggle to prolong their lives by two minutes.

Miklos Nyiszli, Hungarian prisoner-doctor

The victims went naked into the gas-chamber. The room was clean and painted white. There were what looked like shower-heads hanging from the ceiling and connected to a water-pipe. Nothing out of the ordinary, all quite normal. But from behind more and more people were pressing into the supposed shower-room; group after group were shoved through the door by guards. In the confined space, the first screams could be heard; now those still outside also realised what was happening. But there was no longer any way out. Now the SS operatives, the 'trained disinfectors', as Höss called them, began their work. They were the executioners. From the 'Red Cross' vehicles they hastily fetched metal drums filled with the toxic bluish-green crystals. The Zyklon B was then tipped through holes into the chamber. A small viewing window allowed the murderers to observe their victims' death-throes.

'*Shema Israel!*' – 'Hear us, O Israel!' This Jewish supplication was often the last thing the handful of witnesses heard from those they had condemned to die. The SS men mocked the prayers of the dying and shouted: 'Keep chucking it in!' After about 20 minutes, when silence had returned, an SS doctor would announce: 'It's all over.' The people inside were dead, the work of the doctors and orderlies was done. The murderers climbed into the 'Red Cross' truck and left the scene of the crime.

> The dead stand upright, like basalt pillars, pressed tightly against each other in the chambers. There would have been no room for them to fall or even to tilt forward.
>
> *Kurt Gerstein, SS 'Health Officer'*

It was then that the real work of the so-called *Sonderkommandos*, or 'special squads', began. These were Jewish inmates who were forced to clear out the gas-chambers after the killing process. 'Sometimes, when we went into the gas-chambers we could still hear groaning, especially when we began to drag the bodies out by their arms. One time we found a tiny baby, wrapped in a pillow. Its head was actually inside the pillow-case. When we removed it, the baby opened its eyes. So it was still alive. We carried the bundle over to *Oberscharführer* Moll and told him the baby was alive. Moll laid it on the ground, trod on its neck and threw it into the fire. I saw him tread on the baby with my own eyes. It was waving its little arms about.' Scenes like this, described by Shlomo Dragon, a *Sonderkommando* member, leave one utterly stunned.

Children of a tender age were indiscriminately exterminated, since they were incapable of working, due to their youth.
Rudolf Höss, in a sworn statement at Nuremberg, 5 April 1946

The men who wore the Death's Head went home every evening and calmly spent their free time there. Many of them had wives and children. This, too, was part of the forward planning by the SS leadership. They deliberately made the families of SS men live within the concentration camps, or close to them. By allowing the perpetrators to have an apparently normal family life at the scene of the crime, the intention was to lend an air of normality to their professional 'activities'. For this reason, one of the principal duties of wives living in the camps was to 'cultivate social life'. After 'work', the SS families were expected to visit each other, have meals together, go out or organise other leisure activities. In her study of women in concentration camps, Gudrun Schwarz underlines this: 'The stable, domestic framework, providing a place where the SS man could reflect on his private self, and the involvement in social commitments, were intended to ensure the psychological equilibrium of the SS men and their career in the apparatus of annihilation.'

In Auschwitz, more than anywhere, the camp officers sought to make the executioners feel that their actions were taking place in a legal and orderly framework. While on duty they were not permitted to drink or smoke. At the same time, adherence to police working hours was meticulously observed. Höss demanded that his personnel maintain an immaculate appearance: 'I draw your attention to the fact that, for all SS men and police, but especially for those in their home country, shaving is part of service uniform. No superior officer may tolerate a sloppy or unkempt appearance.'

Deliberate rigour towards the SS personnel seemed a way of maintaining the deception, as though everything was proceeding along a regulated path. As Höss noted: 'The Reichsführer-SS sentenced an SS man to four weeks solitary confinement for driving a vehicle over the speed limit ordered by the Führer. What is more, the Reichsführer punished the officer responsible for the journey in question with three days confinement to barracks, because he had not been able to impose discipline on the driver.' Even inadequately equipped bicycles were a punishable matter: 'Every SS man who owns his own bicycle must make sure himself that it is equipped in the regulation manner (bell, front-wheel brake, red rear light etc); anyone failing to do so must expect the severest penalty.' A pedantic emphasis on trivialities was also part of the reality of everyday murder.

How I envy my comrades, who were allowed to die with honour as soldiers. I unwittingly became a wheel in the Third Reich's machinery of extermination. The machine has been smashed, the motor destroyed, and I must go with it. The world demands it.
Rudolf Höss, commandant of Auschwitz 1940–3, in his journal

After the war Commandant Höss wallowed in self-pity: 'In Auschwitz, once the mass extermination began, I was never happy again', he wrote in his journal. Whenever his misdeeds became too much for him, he mounted his horse 'and then galloped away from the horrific images'. When the murder-machinery of his death-camp was running at top speed, Höss handed over the day-to-day management to his deputy and took refuge in drawing up expansion plans. Not letting the horror get too close to them was the way many SS officers made their lives tolerable. That, too, was part of the Auschwitz system: 'As a rule, many SS officers avoided all contact with the prisoners. Höss, for example, just looked right through them. To him they weren't human beings', says Auschwitz survivor Hermann Langbein.

Quite a number got others to commit atrocities for them: 'A

lot of them never beat anyone, but they promoted junior men if they'd handed out a good beating. They got given special leave when they did what was expected of them. That's how the evil mechanism worked', Langbein explains.

Many of the perpetrators got along by treating the killing as something that only happened during duty hours and which did not impinge on them at other times. Morris Venezia, a Greek Jew from Salonika, has this memory: 'There was this one SS man. He was the best of the bunch. He never beat us. Sometimes he even gave us a cigarette; sometimes we gave him one. We talked and laughed together. . . . He was the best SS man we came across there. A really fine guy. But when they brought in the sick, often 200 or 300 of them, who had to be shot – it was a pleasure for him to go down to the cellar and pull the trigger.' Many prisoners, who had to wait on the senior officers and so gained more of an insight into their world, had similar experiences – finding that they changed their personalities with their clothes. A survivor named Helmuth Szprycer describes an SS *Untersturmführer* in this way: 'When I'd taken off Schwarzhuber's boots and jacket for him, to clean them, and he stood there in his vest, he looked like nothing at all. When they didn't have their uniforms on, they were all nobodies. But as soon as I'd dressed him in his jacket and boots again, suddenly he looked like a monster.'

When Hans Stark from Darmstadt put on the Death's-Head uniform, his feeling of self-worth also took a leap upward. He made a career at Auschwitz under Höss, first as a *Blockführer*, then from 1941 in a senior position in the 'Political Section'. He rose to be the youngest squad leader in the camp. Over his desk hung a sign reading 'Compassion is weakness'. The Auschwitz survivor Kasimir Smolen, who later served for many years as director of the Auschwitz memorial centre, remembers that Hans Stark did more than he was obliged to: 'He certainly did more than the normal SS man, because he belonged to the Political Section where the really bad things went on; executions, gassing, selection. He didn't *have* to beat the prisoners. But he beat them anyway.' Stark was a real Jew-hater, says Smolen: 'Whenever there was a Jew named Stark in the intake, he laid into him.'

Stark took part both in shootings and gassing. Six months after he had taken his school-leaving certificate, Jews from his home town of Darmstadt were being sent to Auschwitz. By this time his high school had become a collection-centre for the deportations. On one occasion Stark had to collaborate in a gassing: 'I was one of the people ordered to . . . pour Zyklon B through the aperture', he said in court after the war. 'This was another gassing of a transport of 200 to 500 Jews, and once again there were men, women and children. Since this Zyklon B was in granular form . . . it trickled on to the people when poured in. They began to scream horribly, because they now knew what was happening to them.'

Did he suffer any pangs of conscience afterwards? Clearly Stark was unable to suppress memories of the crime completely. After leaving the execution site, he washed his hands obsessively; a Jewish auxiliary was made to polish his shoes to a high shine, then Stark sat down at his desk and brooded for several hours. Later, he had violent nightmares, his brother tells us.

Twenty-one years after the crime, the judge asked Hans Stark: 'What emotions did you feel?' To which Stark replied: 'I thought: never again!' Judge: 'Why? Did you consider you had done wrong?' Defendant: 'No, not at all. When a person was shot, that was something quite different. But the use of gas was unmanly and cowardly.' He did in fact have the greatest distaste for the manner of the killing, but not for killing as such. It would never have occurred to Hans Stark to refuse to carry out an order. He admitted what he had done. But he never accepted that what he had done was a crime. Because he was under twenty-one at the time of his acts, in 1963 he was sentenced under the juvenile penal code to ten years imprisonment.

Most of the defendants at the Auschwitz trial in Frankfurt denied any part in the killing. Ralph Giordano witnessed the proceedings both as a victim and a journalist. 'The survivors had forgotten nothing, the perpetrators everything', he wrote. 'Men like the mass murderer Oswald Kaduk, like Robert Mulka and Karl Höcker, both adjutants to the camp commandant, Rudolf Höss, who was executed in Poland in 1947; men like Dr Capesius, who did the selecting on the unloading-ramp. None of them admitted guilt, none uttered a word of remorse or comprehension. They went on claiming to be the harmless private citizens they had appeared to be at the time of their arrest – fathers of families, employees, schoolteachers, doctors, pharmacists. At the clinic where Kaduk, the "Terror of Auschwitz", worked as a male nurse, the patients called him "Papa Kaduk!"'

In fact, most of the wearers of the Death's-Head insignia who survived the war slipped unobtrusively back into postwar German society – a society that wanted to look forward, not back. But that was not the only reason why numerous perpetrators were 'overlooked'. Not a few of them were inconspicuous men who knew how to adapt, to subordinate themselves, and to fit in with the new order as though nothing had happened.

The order was given for everyone to be sent off on the death march southwards. The SS went into the huts and tried to drive the people out at pistol-point. But the German and foreign prisoners who had been chosen for this, formed a circle round the SS men. The SS realised that the strength of the prisoners was so great that they couldn't get through, so they withdrew. In the last two days no transports were assembled.

Hans Gasparitch, German communist imprisoned in Buchenwald camp

---

Since then, the question of what drove the perpetrators to act as they did has become a vexed one. Were they specifically evil people who even under 'normal circumstances' would have committed those crimes? Two years after the Holocaust, Eugen Kogon could still characterise the men who served in the death camps as 'deeply frustrated losers . . . retards and under-achievers of all kinds, and mostly people who had failed in society'.

Today we know that this description is only true of a proportion of them. For the number of perpetrators who came from the 'core of society' is greater than was assumed. The notion long cherished by the public that the death camps and murder-squads had been manned mainly by sadists, criminals, anti-Semitic extremists and other scum of society – the deep-rooted hope that 'normal men' would be incapable of murdering innocent women and children themselves, or allowing them to be murdered by others – was exposed as an illusion.

At the time, I didn't know about the gas-ovens. But the fact that Jews were starving to death in concentration camps, that Jews and Poles were being killed – that I did know. I also knew about the euthanasia programme and that Germans were being killed. In short, I knew that the whole thing was criminal.

Baron Philipp von Boeselager, member of the 20 July 1944 plot to kill Hitler

The same afternoon the SS officers were executed. That night the other ranks met the same fate.

Arthur Haulot, Belgian concentration camp inmate, on the liberation of Dachau by the US Army

The theologian Richard L. Rubenstein has written: 'It is tempting to present the National Socialists as obsessed or perverted, for such a view preserves the illusion that we have about ourselves. If we regard the Nazis as more or less normal human beings, that does not mean that we excuse their deeds or minimise the danger that they pose. On the contrary – it means that we recognise how weak are the bonds of morality and decency, which protect a human community from total collapse.'

CHAPTER FIVE

THE *WAFFEN*-SS

6 June 1944 – the Allies land on the Normandy beaches, push open the gates of 'Fortress Europe' and take the first steps that will finally bring Hitler's Reich to its knees. British and Canadian troops swiftly overrun the German defences and advance inland. Soon they announce the fall of Caen – but prematurely. For in the confusing terrain of copses and hedgerows they come up against an implacable foe: fresh-faced young soldiers, not yet eighteen years old, fighting grimly for every foot of ground; they attack again and again as though possessed and even overrun the Canadian front line. Easily recognisable in their camouflage uniform, they are the boys of the SS Hitler Youth division. They halt the Allied advance on Caen and defend the town for six long weeks against massively superior forces. Led by *Waffen*-SS officers, veterans of the eastern front, and indoctrinated with Nazi slogans, they put up a bitter, often merciless resistance. Doug Barrie, who took part in the Normandy landings as an officer in the 3rd Canadian Infantry, remembers: 'Most of the prisoners we took were very young. Their officers and NCOs were seasoned soldiers who had mostly fought in Russia. The young lads had no combat experience – it was the first time they had been in action, just as it was the first major battlefield deployment for us. But they were fighters. Many of them fought to the bitter end; they just wouldn't give up.' For their part, the SS youths did not always take prisoners; there were cases where Canadian soldiers were surrounded by the Germans and then killed.

The fighting by the Hitler Youth division of the SS is characteristic of the whole *Waffen*-SS. Was it an elite force or a gang of criminals? Were its men soldiers like any others or a mob of well-

Handing out death and taking it – this phrase describes very well the conduct of the *Waffen*-SS. To kill and sooner or later to be killed oneself was a notion that they took for granted.

Baron Philipp von Boeselager, former Wehrmacht officer

drilled murderers? Opinions could not be more divided on this point. Since the Second World War, whenever discussion of these troops arises, the statements made about them are irreconcilable. Was the *Waffen*-SS the 'cream' of the Nazi ruffians and killers, young men who had been deliberately and carefully brutalised, so that they were willing and eager to strike down anyone and everyone? In other words, not really soldiers at all, but an armed police force, who fought with equal ferocity against both the internal and external enemies of the Nazi state? Or were they the epitome of military courage and aggressiveness? Was this, as some believe, a warrior-caste whose fighting prowess was unmatched and unsurpassed by any other unit?

These men are no ordinary soldiers; to be precise, they are not soldiers at all, although they may sometimes fight on the front. They are a heavily-armed police-force that is trained to protect the Nazi regime against rebellion amongst the civilian population – German or otherwise – or, if necessary, even against mutiny in the German Wehrmacht itself. They are the hard core of Nazism, the Praetorian Guard of this last lunatic empire.

J.B.Priestley, British novelist, playwright and broadcaster, 1943

The *Waffen*-SS presented an extremely heterogeneous picture – but more than anything it was a product of the final phase of the Nazi Reich. This perhaps explains why it holds such fascination for certain writers. By the end of 1944 its strength was over 900,000 men; in 1938 it had been just on 7,000. But its character can best be revealed by looking at its origins:

- the *Leibstandarte Adolf Hitler*, a bodyguard formed in 1933 as a Praetorian Guard, dedicated to Hitler's protection
- the SS-*Verfügungstruppe*, or rapid reaction force, which in 1934 grew out of the 'political units' of the upper echelons of the SS
- the SS-*Totenkopf* or Death's Head units, responsible for guarding concentration camps

In the autumn of 1939 all three units were merged to form the *Waffen*-SS, or armed SS; and it was at this point that the term '*Waffen*-SS' first appears in documentation. What was its assignment, in the eyes of its service chief, Heinrich Himmler? The Reichsführer-SS wanted to build up his *Schutzstaffel* into a comprehensive state protection corps. Its men would combat the enemies of the Nazi state in many different functions, so to speak, whether as secret service informers, in concentration camps or at the front. To this end there was a system of standardised 'officer training' at the elite SS schools in Bad Tölz, near Munich, and Braunschweig (Brunswick), east of Hanover. Here the young men were schooled militarily and ideologically and afterwards were not only sent to the front, but also to concentration camp duties, to the secret service or the administration branch of the SS. As part of the SS, the *Waffen*-SS was the armed wing of the National Socialist Party. It is impossible to see their role as restricted either to the military or the political domain. The members of the *Waffen*-SS were without doubt soldiers, but by no means were they 'soldiers like any others'. Himmler sharply rejected the notion of the *Waffen*-SS as 'straightforward military men, divisions of the army who merely happened to wear black uniforms'. They were to be the *political* soldiers of National Socialism who fought under the motto, 'Loyalty is my Honour', not against a clearly defined external enemy as the Wehrmacht did, but in a battle for a political movement and against internal and external adversaries, in which military functions were clearly of prime importance.

The rise of armed SS units to become an organisation in competition with the army could not have been predicted in 1933. The *Leibstandarte Adolf Hitler*, formed on Hitler's orders

I seriously intend to collect Teutonic blood from all over the world, to rob and steal it wherever I can. Not for nothing is the 'Germania' unit so named . . . I have set myself the target that within two years at the most the 'Germania' unit will consist of Teutonic men who are not German citizens.

Heinrich Himmler, November 1938

in March 1933, had just 100 men. It consisted mainly of former SA men, received its pay from the Prussian provincial police and its military training from the elite 9th Regiment of the Reichswehr, the army of the Weimar Republic. If only because of its small size, this cross-bred force, for which there was no precedent, could scarcely arouse any suspicion among the senior Reichswehr officers.

The SS *Verfügungstruppe* was also initially intended as a strike force for the Nazi party in domestic politics, and for the moment its military application remained in the background. As for the Death's Head units, under the definition of their commanding officer, Theodor Eicke, they had no military role.

However, Himmler was quite determined to turn his SS units little by little into fully-fledged military formations. In this he called on the support of the Reichswehr minister, Werner von Blomberg, who on 24 September 1934 gave his approval for the setting up of an SS rapid-reaction force; it was to have the strength of three regiments, together with an intelligence section. This meant that the Reichswehr's monopoly as the nation's only body bearing arms, was broken – not long after the SA had been eliminated as an unwelcome competitor in June 1934.

After this, the army command, who had not given their approval to Blomberg's measure, stiffened their resolve to oppose any further expansion of the armed SS and in particular to deny it access to any heavy weaponry. However, in 1938 the spine of the Reichswehr was broken. Hitler himself took over from Blomberg as Reichswehr minister and dismissed the commander-in-chief of the army; the chief of the general staff resigned. This 'seizure of military power' removed all hurdles. The Führer decree of 17 August 1938 laid down that from now on the SS would indeed be supplied with heavy armaments, and that the *Verfügungstruppe* was to be expanded to full divisional strength. Its deployment in the front line, which had long been planned behind closed doors in the event of war, was now official policy.

Consequently, on 19 August 1939, a mobilisation order was issued to the 18,000 men of the *Verfügungstruppe* and the more than 8,000 members of the Death's Head units. They were under the authority of the army high command and from 1 September onwards took part in the assault on Poland, though not yet as a large, self-contained formation. The various regiments of the SS *Verfügungstruppe* – including the *Leibstandarte* – were attached to different divisions of the army. The 'Oberbayern', 'Thüringen' and 'Brandenburg' Death's-Head units were deployed to the rear of the front line in so-called 'pacification' and 'mopping-up' operations.

The *Waffen*-SS is said to be the most extreme of our forces, one which takes absolutely no prisoners but wipes out every opponent to the last man.

From an SD report on German public opinion, 1942

The units ordered to the front were virtually submerged among the vast numbers of soldiers in the regular army. In the opinion of General Blaskowitz, the motorised regiment *Leibstandarte Adolf Hitler* was 'an average unit, still inexperienced, nothing out of the ordinary'. Another army general actually complained that the *Leibstandarte* soldiers fired aimlessly in all directions and during the advance 'routinely' set fire to Polish villages. The formation was under the command of Sepp Dietrich, one of the very first men to join the SS. He was the epitome of the *Landsknecht*, a rough, hard-bitten footsoldier. As a former sergeant in the First World War, he had never been through officer training, yet in the course of the Second he rose to the rank of full general in the *Waffen*-SS. To Hitler he represented the ideal SS officer – yet in the army Dietrich's minimal education, uncouth manners, and not least his brutality often made him the object of derision, even contempt. A Wehrmacht officer on Manstein's staff, Hubertus von

Humboldt, tells of a meeting with Dietrich: 'Manstein was sceptical because he knew that the leadership qualities of the SS people were not of a kind that exactly coincided with our own. We had a conference with Dietrich at headquarters. Manstein was amazed at Dietrich's attitude when he said: "My men'll do that."' But Dietrich was admired by his soldiers to the point of idolatry. 'We just called him "our Pop",' recalls Horst Krüger, then a soldier in the *Leibstandarte*. If a symbol of the Janus-headed nature of the regime is needed, then Sepp Dietrich embodied it, body and soul.

The fact that the *Verfügungstruppe* was capable of waging war at all was chiefly due to Paul Hausser. In 1932 Hausser had retired as a *Generalleutnant* in the Reichswehr, but joined the SS in 1934 in order to exploit the career opportunities it offered. As a military professional his task was to provide Himmler's men with a thorough training. There is no doubt that he did this with some success. Despite considerable resistance on the part of the regular army, by 1939 the military skills of the SS men had developed to the point where they could be sent into action with army divisions.

While the SS *Verfügungstruppe* was being deployed at the front in Poland, it was the task of the three Death's Head regiments to tackle the 'enemy' to the rear of the fighting troops. These units seemed especially 'suited' for this; since 1933 Theodor Eicke had developed Dachau as a 'model' concentration camp and had risen rapidly to become head of the entire concentration camp system. From the guards, the so-called 'Death's Head' units, he created a body of men totally loyal to himself. They were capable of any atrocity against presumed enemies of the state. Eicke had played a prominent part in the Röhm affair, when on the night of 1 July 1934 he used his own pistol to shoot the chief of the SA, Ernst Röhm.

In Poland the Death's Head units, together with non-military SS formations, set about killing all those whom Hitler had defined as 'enemies of the state' – chiefly Jews, but also members of the Polish intelligentsia. Thousands of people fell victim to Eicke's thugs. The atrocities reached such a scale that *Generaloberst* Blaskowitz stated in a letter of protest: 'The attitude of our troops towards the SS and police veers between repugnance and hatred. Every soldier feels disgusted and repelled by the crimes that are being committed in Poland.'

> The accumulating acts of violence in recent days show such an utterly incomprehensible lack of human and moral sensibility, that one can truly describe them as bestial.
> *General Wilhelm Ulex on the crimes of the Death's Head units*
> *in Poland, 2 February 1940*

Nonetheless, the Polish campaign was the signal for expanding the manpower of the *Waffen*-SS. Several tens of thousands of men from the general SS and reinforcements from the police were drafted in. By the end of 1939 the strength of the *Waffen*-SS, excluding the Death's Head units, was 56,000. The *Leibstandarte* was raised to a motorised infantry regiment, and the SS *Verfügungstruppe* expanded to a motorised infantry division. Members of the gendarmerie, the *Ordnungspolizei*, together with men seconded from the regular army, formed a separate SS police division. Some of the Death's Head units, which had now swollen to a total of 18,000 men, were combined by Eicke into another motorised infantry division, the command of which he assumed himself, even though he possessed no military training. The remaining Death's Head units were not incorporated into the structure of the *Waffen*-SS until April 1941, when they were deployed behind the front line within various SS formations.

> We don't carry weapons just to look like the army, but to use them if the Führer and the Movement are in danger.
> *Theodor Eicke, commander of the Death's Head units, 1936*

At the start of the invasion of France in May 1940 Himmler thus had at his disposal a respectable fighting force of three-and-a-half divisions, as well as a number of special formations which were not, however, deployable in the front line. True, these units did not carry much military weight compared to the 157 divisions of the regular army. Nonetheless – with the exception of the police division – they *were* motorised. Due to the serious shortage of motor vehicles at this time, the ordinary soldier still marched on foot, and field-guns were pulled by horses. Only 16 large formations were fully motorised – chiefly the 10 panzer (armoured) divisions, which were to play a decisive role in the whole western campaign. At that time the newest weapons, such as assault rifles, were not issued to the SS, only to the elite *Grossdeutschland* regiment of the regular army.

On the personnel side things looked very different. Himmler had established strict selection criteria for recruitment into the SS which, true to his concept of a 'chivalric' order, he defined first as the 'social' and later the 'Teutonic' elite of Europe. This also applied to the *Waffen*-SS. What the medical examination committees were chiefly looking for was 'racial quality'. In general the SS personnel department was expected to ensure that only tall, racially outstanding volunteers were accepted, preferably those at the height of their youthful powers. To guarantee this, the applicants had to submit themselves to a comprehensive medical examination, in which their 'racial quality' was evaluated on a five-point scale. Furthermore, applicants for the *Verfügungstruppe* were only accepted if they were under twenty-four years old, at least 1.74 metres (5 feet 8½ inches) tall and did not wear glasses. A 'certificate of Aryan ancestry' dating back to 1800 was required. The medical examination was followed by extensive tests of athleticism. However, educational attainment was of practically no importance. This was subject to nothing more than a twenty-minute 'intelligence test' with a three-line passage of dictation, a few comprehension questions and three fairly undemanding arithmetic problems. The principal requirement was unquestioning allegiance to the National Socialist state.

Many wanted to become soldiers, but at 17 only the SS would take you; you couldn't join the Reichswehr until the age of 18.

Baron Philipp von Boeselager, Wehrmacht officer

I personally didn't know of a single case where a young man who applied to join the *Waffen*-SS was turned down.

Alexander Dorneck, formerly with the 'Teutonic Office' of the SS

Such stringent physical selection criteria could not, as it turned out, be maintained for very long. Even at the end of 1938 Himmler decreed that 'in the next five years, for all sections of the SS, shortcomings that are not determined by heredity or race, should be subject to lower requirements'. In spite of this instruction, by the time of the invasion of France, the *Waffen*-SS was made up of soldiers whose physical performance, at least, was exceptionally high. In fact, after watching an exercise by the Death's Head division, *Generaloberst* Weichs declared himself 'highly satisfied with the outstanding physical stamina of the SS troops who, after three hours of strenuous action, showed absolutely no signs of fatigue.'

Admittedly there were considerable problems, particularly with the Death's Head division, in turning men with scarcely any previous military training into a unit fit for combat. This was especially true of the 6,500 concentration camp guards who were incorporated into the division. Theodor Eicke, having had no military training, lacked any understanding of complex military manoeuvres and believed that aggression and energy alone were enough to meet the demands they posed. What is more, he was extremely obstinate and allowed no-one else to have a say in the internal affairs of his division. 'The combat training of the NCOs and men is inadequate', wrote *Generaloberst* Bock after an inspection on 19 April 1940. 'This will cost a lot of blood. It's a great shame, for they are a magnificent body of men!'

Troops like the SS must pay a higher toll in blood than any-one else.

Adolf Hitler

There is no doubt that, as far as discipline and soldierly attitude are concerned, the *Totenkopf* division made a good impression. They always attacked with tremendous guts and proved their steadfastness in defence. But the force had above-average casualties, because they and their officers had to learn for the first time in battle what the regiments of the regular army had long since mastered.

Generalfeldmarschall Erich von Manstein

In the early hours of 10 May 1940 the Wehrmacht began its assault on the Benelux countries and France. In a daring operation, known as the *Sichelschnitt* or sickle-cut, German panzer formations crossed the thickly forested Ardennes mountains at various points, made a surprise thrust towards the Channel coast and ripped through the Allied defences. On 25 June the guns fell silent: within six weeks the Wehrmacht had succeeded in winning the greatest victory in Prusso-German military history.

Given their modest numbers, SS units did not play an outstanding role in these events. They were not involved in any clashes that were crucial to the success of the campaign. In the case of the Death's Head division, the serious lack of training soon became obvious, especially among its officers. For a while chaos reigned within the division, after a number of the few experienced officers were killed or wounded. The panzer commander, General Hoepner, clashed violently with Eicke over his amateurish leadership. When Eicke sought to justify himself by saying 'losses don't matter', Hoepner was so incensed that he called him a 'butcher'. This was truer than he could know at the time.

> The regiment is not in a position to recommend these personnel for a decoration, because they died in action.
> *From a battle report by Felix Steiner, May 1940*

In France some of the SS divisions suffered heavy losses. On the other hand, their war crimes were like nothing seen before. On 27 May 1940 about a hundred British soldiers surrendered to a unit of the Death's Head division, after their ammunition had run out. *Obersturmführer* Fritz Knöchlein lined them up against the wall of a barn and had them mown down by machine-gun fire. Knöchlein survived the war, was sentenced to death by a British military court and hanged. Only a day later, men of the *Leibstandarte* committed a similar crime outside Wormhoudt, not far from Dunkirk. 'It was a nightmare', says Charlie Daley, one of the survivors. A hundred British prisoners, including many wounded, were herded into a barn. When a British officer protested about their undignified treatment, one of the SS men shouted crudely back at him: 'There's room for everyone where you're going.' Another eye-witness, Richard Parry, recalls: 'Suddenly some hand-grenades came flying into the barn, five in all. Then I was flung out through a gap in the barn wall.' The surviving Britons were forced outside where the SS men opened fire on them. Over eighty British PoWs were murdered in cold blood.

> They locked us in a barn. Then they called five of our men out and shot them. They called out another five and they were shot too. When those of us inside started getting uneasy, I saw a German bend down, pull a stick-grenade from the top of his boot and throw it in at us.
>
> *Alfred Tombs, a British soldier who survived the*
> *Wormhoudt massacre*

Needless to say, Hitler expressed complete satisfaction with the 'achievements' of the SS units and made special mention of them in his speech at the victory parade. It was clear to him that the *Waffen*-SS had to be expanded further. However, he encountered reservations in the army about the military deployment of the *Waffen*-SS. In order to pacify the generals Hitler therefore issued a decree on 6 August 1940 in which he tried to make the future assignments of the *Waffen*-SS appear harmless, by limiting them to what he called 'internal matters'. 'The borders of the Greater German Reich, in its final form, will not', he said, 'exclusively enclose populations whose attitude to the Reich can be assumed to be benevolent.' It would therefore be necessary, he added, to maintain a state police force which, in any internal situation, was empowered to represent and impose the authority of the Reich. This 'state police' would only be able to wield the necessary authority if it was militarily equipped and had proved its worth at the front. Therefore a force must be created which would prevent a second 'November Revolution' (the replacement of the Kaiser by a Social Democrat government in 1918), but would also be capable of crushing by military means any revolts by non-German peoples in the future 'Greater German Reich'. Hitler went on to say that the force would always have to be an elite whose units would not exceed 5 or 10 per cent of the peacetime strength of the regular army.

> Through this war the German panzer corps has earned a place in world history; the men of the *Waffen*-SS have a share in that honour.
>
> *Speech by Hitler in the Reichstag, 19 July 1940*

This decree has often been taken at face value and its true import has not been recognised. If it had really only been a question of enabling a state police force to earn front-line combat honours, one or two prestige divisions would have been ample. The rest of the general SS could perfectly well have fought in the Wehrmacht. But Hitler wanted more. He wanted to see a strengthening and expansion of the military roles of the *Waffen*-SS and thus the promotion of a Nazi-orientated core force, which would represent a clear alternative to the regular army, though without replacing it.

Consequently, the *Waffen*-SS was further expanded. The *Leibstandarte* was given so many reinforcements that it was raised to divisional strength. In addition, a new SS division was established, which was initially named 'Germania'. At the end of 1940 it was renamed 'Wiking' (Viking). Back in November 1938 Himmler had announced that he would 'rob and steal' Teutonic blood from all over the world. So before the war he was already planning to recruit 'Teutonic' volunteers for the *Waffen*-SS as soon as possible. Following the occupation of northern and western Europe Himmler immediately tackled this task and formed a 'Nordland' regiment from Danish and Norwegian volunteers, and a 'Westland' regiment made up of men from the Netherlands and Flemish-speaking Belgium. This fitted in with Himmler's plans for Europe. After the war, Holland, Flanders, Denmark and Norway would be subsumed into the 'Greater German Reich', and it was from their ranks that the future 'state police' would be drawn. However, his ambitious hopes of men volunteering in substantial numbers would soon be dashed, since in their native countries they were often regarded as traitors. 'My father had very little time for my political views', wrote Leo Larsen, an SS volunteer from Norway. 'So little that when I tried to visit him on Christmas Eve – I was on leave and hadn't seen him for seven or eight months – he threw me out of the house.' At the start of Operation Barbarossa in late June 1941, there were precisely 1,143 foreigners in the Viking Division: 631 Dutch, 294 Norwegians, 216 Danes, and one each from the neutral countries of Sweden and Switzerland. Despite the division's name, it thus comprised 90 per cent Germans.

However, once the German assault on the Soviet Union was under way, recruitment for service in the *Waffen*-SS became significantly easier. The propaganda slogan of the 'Crusade against Bolshevism' succeeded in firing the enthusiasm of quite a number of young men in the occupied territories. By early July 1941, the Chief of the Army General Staff, Franz Halder, was able to write euphorically: 'Every country in Europe, even France, is sending its legions to the east. Europe is closing ranks against Asia and finding a unity, which is the historic purpose of this war.' However, such words bore little relation to reality. True, more men were volunteering, but even now there was certainly no huge rush to serve under the swastika. By the end of that year 12,000 'Teutonic volunteers of non-German nationality', as they were officially described, were fighting in the *Waffen*-SS, including 1,180 Finns, whose ethnicity was anything but Teutonic. At the same time about 24,000 Frenchmen, French-speaking Belgians, Croatians and Spaniards had been integrated into the Wehrmacht. As 'non-Teutons' Himmler did not want to have them in the SS – not for the moment anyway.

The vision of a 'pan-Germanic' army was certainly made somewhat harder to realise by the political aspirations of the fascist movements in the different countries. The SS leadership had initially hoped to 'gain the confidence of the nations concerned' by forming nationally homogeneous legions, which were not part of the SS. However, it soon emerged that these units became 'adopted' by the pro-Nazi movement in each country and thus took on a political function. Initially, due to considerable resistance, the units could not be integrated into the SS at all. This was because the volunteers were fighting for the role to be played by their own country in a postwar Europe dominated by Germany; certainly against Bolshevism as well, but not primarily *for* the Germans. Therefore they were largely out of sympathy with the ideas of the SS. Thus by 1943 this had led to a split among the European volunteers: one group, who had volunteered for service in the 'pan-Germanic' *Waffen*-SS, fought in the Viking Division, while the other, with a more nationalist agenda, were going into action with their own legions. Not until 1943 was this duality removed, when the 'Flanders', 'Norway' and 'Denmark' legions were transferred to multinational units of the *Waffen*-SS, though this provoked much resistance and many refusals to serve. By now Himmler had abandoned his objections to accepting the hitherto despised 'Latins' into his 'Teutonic' order. The 'Wallonia' legion of French-speaking Belgians also became part of the *Waffen*-SS, as did a unit from France. Henri-Joseph Fenet, one of those French volunteers, tells us: 'For many Frenchmen the defeat in 1940 had been a dreadful humiliation, and fighting on the eastern front in the ranks of an elite force was an opportunity for us to erase that humiliation.'

I felt much more comfortable with those young men than I did at home. The SS was the elite.

Ingemar Somberg, Swedish member of the SS

To me it wasn't a foreign uniform, because I had always felt a racial bond with Germany.

Remy Schhrijnen, Flemish SS volunteer

Although Himmler never really succeeded in putting into practice his notions of a 'pan-Germanic' army, the number of 'Germanic' volunteers in the *Waffen*-SS throughout the war was nonetheless considerable; it is estimated at between 123,000 and 166,000, though admittedly the bulk of these were not recruited until 1944, when a large number of collaborators attached themselves to the retreating German armies. At the same time, many volunteers from the early years had by now turned their backs on the Germans in bitter disappointment. For example, by September 1942 a quarter of all Dutch SS men had been discharged and, in the months that followed, the crisis in recruitment of 'Germanic volunteers' could not be resolved. It arose from the war situation, which since Stalingrad had swung against Hitler's Reich. By 30 June 1943 no fewer than 5,883 volunteers quit the SS – 21.5 per cent of all those recruited in Flanders, Holland, Norway and Denmark. 'In the Germanic countries we are now at a loss about what to do', wrote a frustrated SS *Brigadeführer*, Gottlob Berger. As well as being harassed by the German instructors, who often behaved with high-handed arrogance towards them, the 'volunteers' must have gradually realised that Hitler's propaganda in July 1941, about a 'war to liberate the whole of Europe', did not mean that Germany was waging war on Europe's behalf. The beneficiaries of the war were to be 'the Germans alone'.

In 1941 I had to go on a trip with Himmler. My personal impression of him was dreadful, but the impression among the men of the *Waffen*-SS, who knew him better, was even worse. He was probably the man the professional officers of the *Waffen*-SS hated most. Sepp Dietrich wouldn't even shake his hand. When Himmler announced he was going to visit the *Leibstandarte*, Dietrich made a point of being absent.

Robert Krötz, SS war reporter

Shortly before the invasion of the Soviet Union Himmler had amassed sufficient power to extend the concept of an 'armed SS' a good deal further. In April 1941 he made it clear that it should include not only SS troops fighting in the front line, but also a further *179* units and service departments. Since August 1940 it had already included the concentration camps and their guards. This meant that these men wore the same uniforms and carried the same pay-books as the front line troops, although in

1942 they were placed under the SS Central Office of Economic Administration, and were thus formally separate from the *Waffen-SS*. Himmler's concept of a state protection corps logically led to an expansion of the *Waffen*-SS beyond a purely front-line role. Although a division of assignments developed – front-line formations on the one hand and police formations on the other – it is still not possible to speak of two completely separate bodies. The training and ideological indoctrination were too uniform, and the interlinking of personnel too close for that to be true.

On 22 June 1941 Hitler's assault on the Soviet Union launched the war he had always wanted to wage – the war of annihilation in the east with the long-held aims of eradicating communism, extinguishing Jewry and gaining 'living-space' by conquest. Playing their part in this were the five SS divisions, all fully motorised, a feature which distinguished them from most of the other army formations. However as yet the *Waffen*-SS did not possess any tanks.

The five divisions fought in the front line with all three army groups, in the north around Novgorod and Leningrad, in the centre outside Moscow, and in the south at Rostov-on-Don. Now and again their lack of experience was still noticeable. In Finland, in September 1941, the still inadequately trained SS Battle Group North, made up of two Death's Head regiments, 'failed completely', as a Wehrmacht officer smugly noted, and ran away during a Soviet attack. Unlike the militarily professional units drawn from Hausser's *Verfügungstruppe*, the Death's Head formations saw themselves as pillars of the 'National Socialist revolution'; their attitude was anti-bourgeois and anti-military. Eicke had deliberately forbidden any exchange of personnel with the *Verfügungstruppe*. Thus the Death's Head division had to accept high casualties in Russia, and in the face of these the particular *esprit de corps* of Eicke's division gradually evaporated. The formation that at the end of June 1941 had marched into Russia with a good 17,000 men had, by March 1942, lost 12,000 of them, but had received only 5,000 replacements. It remained in action until October 1942 and was almost completely wiped out. The unit that was established as a new 'Death's Head' in France, in the summer of 1942, had scarcely anything in common with the one that had marched on Russia a year earlier. Most of the men of the concentration camp guard squads had lost their lives. True, there was still an active exchange of personnel between the Death's Head division and the concentration camp guard units, but the latter were also seconded to other divisions with the intention of maintaining a unified structure for the SS.

In general, the men of the *Waffen*-SS had numerous points of contact with the camps. In 1943 a man named Wolfgang Filor, who had been wounded, found himself in the recuperation company of the panzer section of the SS's *Das Reich* division, which was stationed in Buchenwald. 'One evening I was taking one of our detainees to the detention quarters, which was next to the concentration camp. I had just handed him over when two camp guards came out, dragging a prisoner; they dragged him along the ground on his knees. I was a front-line soldier, and when I saw that I said: "Hey, come on, pick the poor guy up. He can't walk like that." And one of the guards said to me: "You must be new around here. Move along! This one's going to the sick-bay. He gets an injection, then he's gone."'

Today, when someone from the SS says: 'If I hadn't done it, I'd have been shot', I say: that's not true, or else he had a superior officer with no humanity or comradeship. For example, in October 1942, in Stralsund, I was ordered to take part in the execution of an NCO in the SS. I went to my superior officer and said: 'I volunteered to fight at the front. I don't want to execute anyone.' He asked me: 'Are you refusing to obey an order?' But he let me go. Twenty others did volunteer because they got a bottle of wine and the next day they were given a pass to walk around Stralsund.

Wolfgang Filor, soldier in the Das Reich *division of the SS*

Looking simply at the military achievements of the *Waffen*-SS on the eastern front in 1941–2, the picture we get is very similar to that of the regular army; there were successful units and less successful ones. Sometimes the army divisions may have outclassed them, but this was not the general experience. Indeed, the SS units were considered particularly tough and aggressive. Thus General Mackensen wrote a letter to Himmler, full of praise for the *Leibstandarte*'s 'internal discipline, their refreshing audacity, their cheerful get-up-and-go and unshakeable steadfastness in a crisis'. Not all the SS units were possessed by the fanaticism that some authors claim was universal, though a number certainly were. Their losses did *not* differ significantly from those of the regular army, as has been shown by the most recent research.

> . . . a truly elite force, which I am proud and happy to have had under my command.
> *From General Eberhard von Mackensen's letter to Heinrich Himmler, 26 December 1941*
>
> There was a general respect for the courage and self-sacrifice of our *Waffen*-SS comrades. I never heard of any crimes against Jews or any civilians on the part of the *Waffen*-SS – they fought with iron determination in the very front line.
> *Count Clemens von Grafeneck, Wehrmacht officer*

Yet it is quite clear that the *Waffen*-SS became known for their exceptional brutality in Russia. There is ample evidence of serious war crimes. For example, in the Ukraine the 'Viking' division murdered 600 Galician Jews; in the Minsk area the *Das Reich* division 'assisted' *Einsatzgruppe* B in the murder of Jews; and in April 1942, according to unconfirmed reports, the *Leibstandarte Adolf Hitler* killed 4,000 Russian prisoners. The number of cases that became known after the event is small. However, the murky statistics of unknown atrocities may be far higher. Among the *Waffen*-SS the shooting of prisoners-of-war, and the ruthless onslaught against 'Slavic' civilian populations, were more the rule than the exception. The SS cavalry brigade commanded by Hermann Fegelein was guilty of particularly repulsive acts. In summer 1941 it was assigned to make a sweep through the almost impassable Pripet marshes. Reichsführer-SS Heinrich Himmler issued the men with 'guidelines for combing and patrolling the marsh areas': 'If the inhabitants are, from a nationalist standpoint, hostile and racially or humanly inferior or, as is very often the case in marshy areas, made up of criminals who have gone to ground, then everyone suspected of supporting the partisans is to be shot. The women and children are to be deported. Livestock and food are to be confiscated and taken to a secure location. The villages should then be burned to the ground.' On 27 July SS *Standartenführer* Fegelein passed on a crucial order from Himmler to his units: 'Jews are for the most part to be treated as looters.' The perpetrators had no hesitation in equating partisans with Jews – the combating of potential guerrilla fighters was to them the same as murdering the Jews they found in the villages.

> They were expressly asked if they wanted to be blindfolded. I was 16 at the time and was in the front row of the firing squad. The range was 10 metres and I was glad I didn't have to look the two men in the eye. The two *Unterscharführer* went up to the condemned men again and ripped the shirts from their chests, so that we riflemen knew where to aim and shoot.
>
> *Siegfried Schütze, trooper with the SS 'Florian Geyer' cavalry division*
>
> Where the partisan is, there is the Jew, and where the Jew is, there is the partisan.
>
> *Slogan from a training course on fighting partisans, late September 1941*

On 30 July at 7 in the morning, the mounted sections of the two SS cavalry regiments set off on their first mopping-up operation in the marshes. The following day, Himmler added a sinister edge to his orders in a personal conversation with the 'senior SS and police officer' in the region, Erich von dem Bach-Zelewski. A short while afterwards a radio message came through to the sections: 'Express orders from the RFSS. All male Jews must be shot. Jewish women are to be driven into the marshes.'

The SS cavalrymen acted with the most extreme violence – in the villages they passed through they killed not only Jewish men, but women and children as well. And they used machine-guns to mow the people down, rapidly and indiscriminately.

The 2nd Regiment restricted themselves to shooting men between the ages of eighteen and sixty. In compliance with orders, Jewish women and children were chased into the marshes. But Himmler's enforcers reported their disappointment: 'Driving women and children into the marshes was not as successful as it should have been, because the marshes were not deep enough for them to sink in. Below a depth of one metre they usually touched solid ground, so it was impossible to sink any further.' Nonetheless, by 13 August the two SS cavalry regiments had killed nearly 14,000 people.

On 7 August a decree was issued by the German military command. It said that Jews who were unemployed had to show up at the station on 8th August. And bring food for three days with them. On the day, about 1,000 people showed up. They were led out of the town towards Sagolevo and they were shot in a potato-field. A few survived; they came back and told us what had happened.

On 9 August another decree was issued, about labour duty. No-one went and a hunt began for Jewish men in the town. That day between 8,000 and 10,000 people were shot. The Germans broke into the houses, and took away one six-year-old boy. They forced their way into our apartment – I was sitting on the toilet in the yard, which is why I survived, but they took away my brothers David and Aron. They were shot the same day.

Piotr Ruvinovitch Rabzevitch, survivor of the massacre in the Pripet marshes

---

It must be said that 'normal' infantry and armoured divisions also killed countless Russian prisoners and murdered civilians. And many Wehrmacht units securing territory behind the front line acted with just as much brutality as the SS cavalry brigade. For example, within the space of a month in Byelorussia the 707th Infantry division shot more than 10,000 Russian civilians. The war of annihilation in the east knew no distinction between the different arms of the military. At best, those Wehrmacht units that became involved should have shown more restraint. They were not all guilty, but far, far too many of them were.

The SS men were all extremely young, very arrogant, and apparently proud of their dreadful exploits.
Erich Mirek, Wehrmacht soldier and eye-witness

There, essentially, the whole thing is a question of leadership. And this, in my view, is inadequate.
Erich von Manstein, on the officers of the SS panzer corps, 8 February 1943

In 1942 the *Leibstandarte*, *Das Reich*, Death's Head and Viking divisions were re-equipped as panzer (armoured) units, with the most up-to-date weaponry. They were now 'elite forces' within the *Waffen*-SS, giving it a characteristic face to the outside world. Alongside them were units that were deployed on secondary fronts (such as the 6th SS Mountain division *Nord*), or were chiefly engaged in the fight against partisans, as was the case with the 4th SS Police division, the 7th SS Mountain division and the 8th SS Cavalry division. A good example of this was the 7th SS Mountain division, 'Prinz Eugen'. Formed in 1942 from the 'Siebenbürgen' ethnic Saxons in Romania and ethnic Swabians from Banat in northern Serbia, this unit was for a long time considered the step-child of the *Waffen*-SS. The division was largely armed with captured weapons, and being transferred to it was often regarded as a punishment posting. The partisan war in Yugoslavia was marked by brutality and atrocities, and these were not the exclusive preserve of the Germans – the different ethnic groups spent more time massacring each other than fighting off the invaders. The Wehrmacht was involved here too; as early as 1941, when crushing the Serbian uprising in the autumn of that year, Wehrmacht units were guilty of appalling outrages, and in this period they murdered virtually all the Serbian Jews. Nevertheless, it must be said that right from the beginning the 'Prinz Eugen' division of the SS had a disproportionately greater tendency to commit war crimes. In December 1942 it was officially reprimanded for the second time and instructed to refrain in future from 'avoidable harshness' against the civil population, such as 'the shooting of women and children and the burning down of villages and homes'. This happened at a time when the division was not yet engaged in serious fighting against the partisans. When the officer commanding the division attempted to apologise to a Croatian minister by saying that a massacre by his unit was a 'mistake', SS *Oberführer* Werner Fromm retorted: 'Since you lot have been here, I'm afraid there's been one foul-up after another.' These 'foul-ups', as SS *Sturmbannführer* Reinholz noted, had 'begun to have a negative effect on German interests in this region'. The murder of 2,000 Croats on 24 March 1944, in the Knin area of Dalmatia, caused a greater outcry than any so far and led to violent protests by the Croatian government. In a similar way, the 4th SS Police division earned notoriety when it killed 223 civilians in the Greek town of Klissura on 5 April 1944, and a further 300 people in Distomo on 10 June.

How are these crimes to be judged? Were they merely acts carried out by individual units? Or are they representative of the entire *Waffen*-SS? The continual expansion and restructuring had mixed up the personnel of the divisions to such an extent that it was scarcely possible any longer to talk of individual units having a particular 'character'. In the fight against the partisans – or what were described as such – the *Waffen*-SS had a very widespread tendency to excessive violence, exceeding that of the regular army, in every theatre of war. This was not only the case in the Balkans, but also in France and Italy, where in August and September 1944 a unit of the 'Reichsführer-SS' division massacred hundreds of Italian civilians. This kind of furious bloodlust increased in intensity as the tide of war turned against the Nazi regime, following the catastrophic defeat at Stalingrad.

By now the 'core divisions' of the *Waffen*-SS had been re-equipped as panzer divisions. This provided the Army High Command with a welcome instrument with which to stabilise the eastern front, at a time when it was under the greatest pressure. Remember that in November 1942 the Soviets had bottled up the Sixth Army in Stalingrad and in December had switched to a major offensive along the entire front. The poorly equipped Italian, Hungarian and Romanian formations were as little able to withstand the onslaught as were the few remaining German divisions. Relentlessly the Red Army stormed westward; the whole southern wing of the front was about to crumble. Now the SS panzer divisions, *Leibstandarte Adolf Hitler*, *Das Reich* and Death's Head, were formed into a corps and went into battle under the command of Paul Hausser, to 'relieve' Stalingrad. Winrich Behr, then an officer in the Wehrmacht, recalls the Führer's assessment of the situation: 'What Hitler was saying about sending help to Stalingrad was so obviously unrealistic that even I as a 25-year-old panzer officer could tell that it plainly didn't add up. Hitler told us about the SS panzer army that was meant to relieve Stalingrad. I had heard from Field-Marshal Manstein that even as the army's tanks and equipment were being unloaded, they had been shot to pieces by Russian T34s. And here was the Führer trying to tell me that this panzer army was meant to go 400 kilometres through snowstorms to relieve Stalingrad! That was clearly total eyewash!' The rescue of the Sixth Army from the Stalingrad pocket did indeed fail to materialise, but even so the SS Panzer Corps played a significant part in the German counter-offensive in February and March 1943. This stabilised the front and led to the recapture of Charkov, the fourth largest city in the Soviet Union. Earlier Hausser had refused to defend the prestigious regional capital against hopeless odds and made the decision to withdraw, in direct defiance of the Führer's orders. At that moment the SS general was clearly not willing to make corpses the price of obedience. Later, he was.

In the last big German offensive on the eastern front, at Kursk, the 1st SS Panzer Corps was once again thrown into the centre of the battle, acting so to speak as a battering-ram. Although this operation ended in failure, the period from February to July 1943 nevertheless did much to substantiate the much-vaunted reputation of the *Waffen*-SS as the 'fire-fighters of the eastern front'. They were the key force on that front, it was said, always found fighting where the danger was greatest, and consistently at the head of every counter-attack. This is confirmed by Horst Krüger who, in spring 1943, was transferred from the Luftwaffe to the *Leibstandarte* division of the SS. 'We were a roving commando; we always had to go where things were getting hot. No-one stopped to ask questions.'

Like any myth this contains a grain of truth. Without the SS Panzer divisions the German spring offensive in 1943 could scarcely have been implemented. However, they did not come charging at the enemy from the middle of nowhere; they always acted in combination with units of the regular army. Even the much-cited exclusive equipment of the SS units was not much to write home about. The most modern types of tank, the Panther and the Elefant, were initially allocated to units of the regular army. For example, all new Panther tanks went to the *Grossdeutschland* division, which was even better equipped than Hausser's divisions. The latter were certainly given modern equipment – each division, for instance, had one company of highly effective Tiger tanks. However, there were also regular army units that operated on a similar level. In August 1943 the *Grossdeutschland* division was in fact reinforced with a whole battalion of Tigers.

At the turn of the years 1943 and 1944 the bulk of the 'old' SS divisions were fighting at the hot-spots on the eastern front. In February 1944 the SS Viking division and the SS assault brigade, 'Wallonia', had been encircled by the Red Army in Tcherkassy. These units led the German troops in a bloody and costly breakout, while the relief forces pushing in from outside were headed by the *Leibstandarte Adolf Hitler*. In April 1944 the Russians had bottled up an entire panzer army in Kamenz-Podolsk. The recently formed 2nd SS Panzer Corps, hastily brought in from France, smashed the ring of encircling troops and extricated the trapped army divisions and the *Leibstandarte Adolf Hitler*.

These were all military successes. Yet at the same time some 20 other panzer divisions of the army had been engaged in similar actions, had scored similar achievements and in some cases were also similarly equipped; some, as has already been mentioned, were even better equipped. On closer inspection, the reputed 'heroic deeds' of the *Waffen*-SS prove far less spectacular than they are repeatedly presented as being, and are to a considerable extent the product of popular literature (much of it in English), which to this day has fallen victim to a kind of mythologising that can only be explained in psychological terms.

The hiatus in the course of the war, which came in the winter of 1942–3 with the devastating defeat at Stalingrad, also marked a decisive turning-point in the history of the *Waffen*-SS. From December 1942 to January 1944 no less than twelve new SS divisions were established – an increase of 150 per cent! With this the transition to a full-scale army was finally complete. Whereas in mid-1940 the *Waffen*-SS comprised 100,000 men, by the end of 1941 it had already reached 220,000 men, in autumn 1942 240,000 (including 140,000 field troops), at the end of 1943 500,000 (including 240,0000 field troops) and at the end of 1944 no fewer than 910,000 men.

It is clear that with such a large expansion of personnel the character of the *Waffen*-SS had to change radically. It had long since ceased to be an elite order. It is true that the volunteer principle had never officially been breached, but from an early date there was no way that it could be maintained in practice. That is why, as early as 1940, members of the general SS were transferred into the *Waffen*-SS under varying degrees of coercion. From 1942 onward the pressure had to be extended to other areas. The personnel for the shortly to be established SS 'Hohenstaufen' and 'Frundsberg' panzer divisions was largely recruited compulsorily from the camps of the Reich Labour Service. These men had precious little in common with SS ideology. As a female colleague of the diplomat Ulrich von Hassel reported in 1943: 'The National Socialist spirit of the *Waffen*-SS is becoming more and more questionable. They identify completely with the fighting forces of the Wehrmacht.' It was increasingly common even for high-ranking SS officers to distance themselves from Hitler. One man in particular, Felix Steiner, was known for his acid criticism of the Reichsführer-SS. When he began saluting his soldiers simply with the word '*Heil*' instead of the regulation '*Heil Hitler*', it got too much for

Himmler, who had enquiries made into Steiner's reliability. But Himmler was unable to remove him from his position – Steiner was protected by high-ranking allies in the SS.

> We had a kind of inner hostility to the *Waffen*-SS; somehow we knew they did things you didn't want to have anything to do with. Not that we had any precise knowledge of the facts that later came to light – but we had an unpleasant subconscious feeling.
>
> *Günter Adrian, then in the Hitler Youth*

> At that time I wanted to join the *Waffen*-SS but my father was very angry about it. He said: You don't know what you're letting yourself in for.
>
> *Manfred Rommel (son of Field-Marshal Erwin Rommel), then a member of the HJ*

> We even 'adopted' front-line units, and when SS officers visited us, some of the girls may well have wished they could one day marry a dashing SS officer like that.
>
> *Herta von Bergh, then a pupil at a Nazi party boarding-school*

In their endless search for new reserves of manpower, the office of the SS command reached an agreement with the Reich Youth Office in February 1943, that members of the Hitler Youth born in 1925 and 1926 (i.e. those aged seventeen and eighteen) should be formed into a new SS division. One of those *Hitlerjungen* was Bernhard Heisig. He had actually applied for a regular armoured unit. But at the medical inspection he suddenly found himself facing an SS officer: 'He only had one arm – clearly a fact that much impressed me – and he said: "Don't you want to join *us*?" So I say: "I've just volunteered for the tank corps!" "Oh", he says, "Well, we've got lots of tanks. Or have you got something against us?" That was the catch-question. I had nothing against them. So I said: "OK, Why not?"'

Ulrich Krüger, a medical orderly with the Hitler Youth, tells of a health check-up in which the lads were tested for TB: 'After they'd been through the X-ray they went up to a table where they were given a form that said: "I hereby confirm that I have taken part in the screening" and so on. Date, place, signature. But below the line, in very small print was written: "I hereby declare that I wish to volunteer for the *Waffen*-SS." So I thought to myself: this can't really be true – that people can be simply made to do something willy-nilly, without having it explained to them.'

> They were handing out beer, and there were sausages to eat. Anything we wanted. As well as application forms for the *Waffen*-SS. Nothing wrong with that. Because anyone who didn't want to join was promised faithfully that they could go into the navy, or the cavalry, or an office job. They then crossed out '*Waffen*-SS' in pencil and wrote in the other choice. I'm convinced they only left it there for ten minutes, then they rubbed it out again.
>
> *Lothar Schmitz, then in the Hitler Youth*

The greatest problem proved to be the lack of trained officers and NCOs. They tried to get by with improvisation. Fifty officers from the regular army, most of whom were former members of the Hitler Youth, were seconded to the division, to ease the worst shortages. The bulk of the support personnel came from the *Leibstandarte Adolf Hitler*, which was considerably weakened by this haemorrhage. In June 1944, when the Hitler Youth (HJ) division went into action in Normandy, it was still 2,000 NCOs short – half its required strength.

The problem of obtaining sufficient manpower to feed the constant expansion of the *Waffen*-SS was in itself not new and had existed virtually since 1940. The Wehrmacht High Command had fixed a quota for the allocation of personnel to the *Waffen*-SS, but this certainly did not satisfy Himmler's far-reaching plans. Therefore, since the start of the war, the SS chief had also been trying to recruit in places where he would not be in competition with the Wehrmacht, that is to say, outside the Reich. The volunteers from western Europe have already been mentioned. Now, from 1940 onwards, additional recruitment was carried out among people of ethnic German origin – known as *Volksdeutsche* – in Hungary, Yugoslavia and especially Romania. After these men had travelled illegally to Germany, international treaties were signed with the governments in Budapest and Bucharest, under which the men were permitted to do their military service in the *Waffen-SS*. Thus, by the end of 1941, as many as 6,200 *Volksdeutsche* were serving in the SS Viking division and the *Nord* mountain division. Starting in the winter of 1943 these manpower sources were systematically tapped and all 'militarily suitable *Volksdeutsch* men' were simply drafted. In the end this meant that almost one *Waffen*-SS man in four was a *Volksdeutscher* from the Balkans, a total of over 200,000! In the years 1943 and 1944 almost all the newly established units were largely manned by *Volksdeutsche*. In the 'Hohenstaufen' and 'Frundsberg' panzer divisions mentioned earlier there were nearly 8,000 of them. Ironically, even in the SS's 'Nordland', there were more *Volksdeutsche* from Romania than Danish and Norwegian mercenaries. And many of these men had little enthusiasm for putting their lives at risk for Germany. Even a bruiser like Eicke, not exactly an intellectual himself, remarked: 'Among the *Volksdeutsche* there are quite a number who you could call mentally inferior. A lot of them can't read or write German. They don't understand army commands and have a tendency to disobedience and shirking.'

Now even the recruitment of 'non-German' soldiers went into top gear. Back in May 1942 Himmler had had great reservations about such recruitment: 'The establishment of units of the *Waffen*-SS made up of Estonians, Latvians or even Lithuanians, is certainly a tempting proposition; but it holds very great risks.' The Baltic German Alfred Rosenberg, Reich Minister for the Occupied Eastern Territories, put it more bluntly. The Lithuanians, he said, were 'in large part racially inferior', and the Latvians 'considerably infiltrated by a Russian migrant population'; the Estonians on the other hand were, in his view, 'the elite of the Baltic peoples'. After Finns had begun serving in the *Waffen*-SS, the attitude towards the ethnically

Many Hungarian-Germans, Polish-Germans and Romanian-Germans joined the SS, not because they had any idea about SS ideology, but so that they could do their military service in the German Wehrmacht. They didn't actually know the difference.

Baron Philipp von Boeselager, officer in the Wehrmacht

It makes you sick. I keep hearing about the SS spirit. Total rubbish. There's no sign of it.

An informant of the SS Central Office on the ideological attitude of the Waffen-SS, *October 1943*

related Estonians changed. In October 1942 Hitler approved the establishment of an Estonian SS legion; further units followed in 1943, and then in 1944 a whole Estonian SS division was created. In the case of the Latvians, too, the convoluted pseudo-racial arguments soon gave way to pragmatic ones. Ultimately *two* divisions of Latvian soldiers were established. The integration of the Baltic recruits into the SS was comparatively easy: they hoped, by fighting on the German side, to regain their national independence, and it was a desire that the Germans for their part deliberately encouraged. At the same time they were fairly skilful in concealing their own occupation plans. Added to this, in Latvia anti-Semitism was very widespread. Not a few Latvians – and also Lithuanians and Ukrainians – either took part in the shooting of Jews or were put on to guard duties in the death camps.

The battlefield value of the military units made up from eastern Europeans was extremely varied. Within the SS, those considered the worst were the Byelorussian units, who in combat situations sometimes killed their German officers or handed them over to the Soviets. There were also bad experiences with the Ukrainian division, which was said to have 'failed completely' the first time it went into action in July 1944. Estonians and Latvians, on the other hand, put up a grimly determined defence of their homelands against the advancing Red Army. Latvian SS units fought right up to the surrender in the Courland pocket. Then some of their members went underground and for years continued their resistance against the Soviets as partisans.

Following the wave of newly formed units in 1943, the front-line forces of the *Waffen*-SS now consisted of three parts: the divisions predominantly made up of Germans from the Reich, then the so-called volunteer divisions made up mainly of what in Nazi terms were 'Germanic' and *volksdeutsch* soldiers, and finally the 'non-Germanic' units, known as the *Waffen*-Grenadier divisions of the SS. The fighting capability of the units within these three groups was highly variable. Only a core of Reich German divisions could in any way be considered as 'elite'. But even with these, the heavy losses and the lack of trained officers and NCOs increasingly took their toll. Thus, in 1943–4 a growing number of Alsatians, ethnic Germans from Alsace in eastern France, were drafted into the *Das Reich* division. Many of them deserted when faced with the Allied invasion forces in Normandy.

A critical problem for the *Waffen*-SS was the professional military training of its officers. The two elite SS academies in Bad Tölz and Braunschweig could no longer train new young officers fast enough to keep pace with the heavy casualties and continuous establishment of new units. In the *Waffen*-SS there was absolutely no training of staff officers, and for this reason SS officers attended the relevant courses with the regular army. In order to fill the gaps that still remained unfilled, a number of officers from the army's general staff were seconded to the *Waffen*-SS. Hitler was at first sceptical about this procedure because he feared that his SS would be infiltrated. However, in view of the personnel crisis he was soon forced to put such anxieties behind him. But even this was no panacea, since initially these transfers could only take place with the consent of the officers concerned – and many simply did not want to go over to the *Waffen*-SS. Ultimately, the lack of staff officers remained a problem until the end of the war, though in most cases the particularly important position of Principal Staff-Officer Operations was successfully filled with appropriately trained personnel.

The lack of officers was even more critical in the non-German units. The bulk of the *Volksdeutsche* had been levied under duress, so they felt little inclination to become officers within the SS. Furthermore, it proved impossible to bring in a worthwhile number of senior officers from other branches of the army. This was as true in south-eastern as in western Europe. One notable exception was SS *Obergruppenführer* Arthur Phleps, a former officer in the imperial Austro-Hungarian army, and later a general commanding a division in the Romanian armed forces.

In his search for more and more new 'human material' Himmler displayed a zeal that stretched the SS ideology of the Germanic master-race to absurd lengths. Thus, in 1944 even a Byelorussian division was formed. Troops of Cossacks and a unit of Soviet Moslems were also put under the command of the *Waffen*-SS. As early as the spring of 1943 Himmler had, with Hitler's approval, made a start on one of his pet projects: he planned to establish an SS division from among the Moslem population of Bosnia. From a military standpoint the idea was not so outlandish. The former Austro-Hungarian province of Bosnia-Herzegovina had for centuries been riven by a feud between Christians and Moslems, which the Germans could now easily exploit to their own advantage. Zvonimir Bernwald, a soldier in the SS division that later became known as the *Handschar*, explains: 'The Bosnian Moslems joined the *Handschar* because they hoped to be given weapons with which to fight the Serbian "chetniks" in Bosnia. They couldn't have cared less about Nazi ideology.' In the middle of 1943 the recruits were sent to France for training. The division had been granted considerable privileges; for example they had freedom to practise their religion, each battalion had its own imam, and every regiment its own mullah. In spite of this, some of the units mutinied; they killed German personnel, stole the regimental cash and disappeared. The patron of the division, the Grand Mufti of Jerusalem, had to be brought in. Finally, however, the SS succeeded in putting together a militarily useful formation. An SS officer later gave his verdict on these troops: 'Fantastic material – unsuitable, of course, from a racial point of view, but nonetheless all vigorous young chaps.' From spring 1944 the SS *Handschar* division was transferred to northern Bosnia, where it fought against Tito's partisans. However, the Bosnians showed little enthusiasm for fighting outside their homeland. Most of them deserted when, in autumn 1944, the Wehrmacht withdrew from Bosnia. This made the whole expensive exercise seem of very doubtful value.

Even more pathetic were the attempts to create an SS division of Albanians, which was named 'Skanderbeg' after the Albanian national hero. Here the Germans failed even to get the men to fight the communist partisans.

At the end of 1942 we were told that only Reich Germans with German passports could join the Wehrmacht. We were then living in the independent state of Croatia and had Croatian passports. Then they said: volunteers can join the *Waffen*-SS. So we applied. They kept reminding us that as *Waffen*-SS we were a cut above the others.

Zvonimir Bernwald, SS Handschar *division*

They only kill with the knife. One of the men had been wounded. He had his arm bandaged up and with his left hand he finished off another 17 of the opposition. There are also cases where they cut an enemy's heart out.

Hermann Fegelein, SS Brigadeführer *in a conversation with Hitler about the Moslem* Handschar *division, 6 April 1944*

The high number of *Waffen*-SS units from foreign countries once again underlines its heterogeneity. There was not only a hotchpotch of ill-assorted front-line units; there were also special formations which, for part of the time at least, did not fight at the front but mainly concerned themselves with the frequently invoked 'enemies within'. In 1941–2, for example, the 5th *Waffen*-SS battalion achieved grim notoriety for its massacre of Jews in Byelorussia. These troops were later reassigned to various front-line units, such as the Death's Head and the Estonian SS Division. The *Waffen*-SS also contributed some 1,500 men to the notorious *Einsatzgruppen* of the SD and security police – men who after their murderous assignments returned to front-line duties. Furthermore, reserve units assisted in the deportation of Jews from the Reich, in the execution of civilians in Bohemia and Moravia and in the appalling destruction of the Warsaw ghetto in April 1943.

> After the first few days it was already clear that the Jews had no intention of being resettled voluntarily, but were determined to make a stand by all means possible and with the weapons they had available.
>
> *SS-General Jürgen Stroop, on the start of the uprising in the Warsaw ghetto*
>
> Something happened that exceeded our wildest hopes. Twice the Germans fled from the ghetto. One of our sections held out for 40 minutes, the other for more than six hours.
>
> *Mordecai Anielewicz, Jewish ghetto fighter, in a letter, 23 April 1943*

Stefan Grayek, a Polish Jew who at that time was one of the insurgents in the Warsaw ghetto, recalls: 'When we started the uprising, none of us believed we would survive. It wasn't our intention to stay alive – we only happened to survive because the Germans didn't manage to deal with all of us. Our intention was different: not to save our own skins but to react against the killing and to pay them back for it. It was the last opportunity to get our revenge on the SS for the murders they had committed in previous years. None of us expected to survive. But at least I wanted my revenge on the men who had murdered my family, my friends and my people.' The Jewish fighters could not hold out for long against the brutal onslaught of the SS and so SS *Brigadeführer* Stroop was able to report on 16 May 1943: 'The former Jewish residential quarter of Warsaw no longer exists. The main operation ended at 2015 hours when the Warsaw synagogue was blown up.' His men had killed over 50,000 ghetto inhabitants.

I don't believe anyone is capable of forgetting what happened. And if I can't forget, then perhaps I'm not adult enough to forgive either.

Tsvi Nussbaum, thought to be the 'Boy of Warsaw'

The battle was fought for every cellar, every building in the Warsaw ghetto and didn't end until the Germans dynamited one building after the other. In the end the ghetto was nothing but one big ruin, with no sign of human life.

Professor Israel Gutman, Polish Jew, then living in the Warsaw ghetto

One unit that attracted attention with its particular brutality to the rear of the front line was the Dirlewanger Brigade. Dr Oskar Dirlewanger, a dentist by profession, was imprisoned in 1935 for abuse of an under-age girl, but later, while on 'probation', fought with the Condor Legion on Franco's side in the Spanish Civil War. In 1940 Dirlewanger was given permission to establish a special unit of company strength, made up entirely of poachers. As the war progressed, more and more criminals joined it from prisons all over the Reich, men who had nothing whatever to with the noble profession of poaching. Initially, Dirlewanger's unit was not part of the *Waffen*-SS, but in autumn 1942, in the face of considerable internal resistance, it was integrated and deployed in the fight against partisans in Byelorussia. Here the unit became noted for murdering the civilian population in large numbers. Dirlewanger himself was particularly conspicuous for his brutal tactics in defiance of the laws of war, and later for his part in crushing the second, non-Jewish, Warsaw uprising in August and September 1944. In the house-to-house fighting against the Polish 'Home Army', the Dirlewanger Brigade took heavy casualties. As replacements he was given professional criminals and so-called 'anti-social elements' from the SS punishment camps, Wehrmacht gaols and concentration camps. The result was that the troops became completely ungovernable. Spurred on by Himmler's order to take no prisoners, they indiscriminately killed anyone who came into their sights. They were only surpassed in their atrocities by the SS RONA Brigade (the Russian National Liberation Army). This formation made up of Russians and Ukrainians was set up in 1942 to fight the communist partisans – a task in which they 'proved themselves' to the hilt. The unit attached itself to the German troops flooding back from the collapsing eastern front and, in the process of being re-formed as the 29th *Waffen*-Grenadier division, found itself assigned to putting down the Warsaw uprising. Here their thirst for blood took over completely. At first their German superior officers tolerated the continuous pillaging as 'normal Russian custom in war' and a 'necessary evil', and turned a blind eye to the mass rape of Polish women, to torture and to murder. But when German nurses, too, were raped and killed in a hospital, it became too much even for the SS to stomach. Even a mass murderer like Hermann Fegelein, Himmler's liaison-man with Hitler, was forced to admit when asked: '*Jawohl, mein Führer*, they're real ruffians.' At the end of August the unit was withdrawn from Warsaw.

It is not possible to assess a man from the *Waffen*-SS on the same terms as one from the party SS . . . If a *Waffen*-SS man is a particularly good soldier then in certain circumstances it will not be held against him if his knowledge of ideology is less than first-class.

Adolf Hitler

We do not expect you to become Germans out of opportunism. We expect you to subordinate your national idealism to a greater racial and historical ideal, that of the Greater German Reich.

From Himmler's speech in Charkov, April 1943

In 1943–4 the *Waffen*-SS had already turned into a ragbag of the most disreputable units. Yet to the outside world the image projected continued to be that of the highly effective panzer divisions, which formed the core of the front-line troops of the *Waffen*-SS and were among the best-performing combat formations in the entire Wehrmacht. The battles on the eastern front in 1943–4 have already been mentioned. However, in 1944 Russia was not really the principal theatre of war for the *Waffen*-SS, at least not for its panzer divisions. Since 1942 Hitler had been constantly worried that the Allies might land in France, even before the war against Russia was over. In November 1943 Hitler issued his Instruction no. 51, the last in which he dealt with the strategic situation. In it he refocused the conduct of the war from the east to the west. It was here, he believed, that the decisive battle of the war would be fought since, if the Germans succeeded in beating off attempts by the Allies to make a landing, all forces could be transferred to the east and the advance of the Red Army halted. If they failed, the war was lost.

Thus it was only logical for the *Waffen*-SS to concentrate its 'elite units' in France. The *Leibstandarte Adolf Hitler* and the *Das Reich* divisions were stationed there, as were the newly established Hitler Youth panzer division and the panzer-grenadier division *Götz von Berlichingen*, named after a medieval German hero. In April 1944 it had been necessary briefly to transfer the 'Hohenstaufen' and 'Frundsberg' divisions to the eastern front, but they returned to Normandy in late June. There, in July 1944, of the ten panzer and panzer-grenadier divisions in action, six belonged to the *Waffen*-SS.

Thus it is really possible to say that in this supposedly decisive theatre of war, the *Waffen*-SS formed the core of the defending troops. However, to be more precise, this was not true until the end of June, since immediately after the Allied landings only the Hitler Youth division – along with panzer divisions of the regular army – could be committed to the battle.

It is on the Hitler Youth division in particular that opinions are divided. It is often cited as a typical example of the rampant de-professionalisation of the *Waffen*-SS in the fourth year of the war. The seventeen- and eighteen-year-old soldiers had absolutely no battle experience; what is more, there were far too few officers and NCOs, and quite a number of those were not properly qualified. Some of the officers had not even got

I was 15 years old when my very personal part in the war began. In March 1944 an officer from the *Waffen*-SS appeared in our classroom at school. After giving an inspiring lecture he asked for volunteers for the *Waffen*-SS. My hand was the first to go up. You could say I grew up on National Socialism – it was all I knew.

Siegfried Schütze, a soldier in the 'Florian Geyer' SS cavalry division

as far as their school-leaving examination. To that extent this unit differed from the elite formations of the regular army, such as the panzer *Lehrdivision* (instruction division), which fought alongside it in Normandy. The explanation now seems clear: it was a hurriedly assembled division, in which boys who were still minors were sacrificed as cannon-fodder in Normandy. Wolfgang Filor, a soldier with the *Das Reich* panzer division of the SS, was then fighting side by side with the Hitler Youth: 'When we saw them fighting, at first we thought: my God, now they are starting to use children. I myself, as it happened, was in the Saint-Lô sector; I had an American tank in my sights and was about to knock it out. To my horror a German soldier suddenly raised his *Panzerfaust* (grenade-launcher) as a signal to hold our fire. Then the tank blew up and him with it. He'd sacrificed his life. He'd shot a hole in the tank from underneath with his *Panzerfaust*. The kids were like that.'

They could do that with us; we were still hardly more than children. We ran like lemmings straight for disaster. Thinking wasn't required. . . .

We thought we were something special. We're special heroes, we're the best division in the Wehrmacht.

Bernhard Heisig, soldier in the SS Hitler Youth division

It's a tragedy that these dedicated youngsters are being sacrificed in a hopeless situation.

Generalfeldmarschall Gerd von Runstedt on the deployment of the Hitler Youth division in Normandy, summer 1944

The casualties in the division are considerable. Given the situation, we have to reckon on the whole division being wiped out.

Kurt Meyer, known as 'Panzer Meyer', commander of the Hitler Youth division of the SS, 16 June 1944

There is no shortage of claims that the division was almost completely wiped out. It all sounds very conclusive – but the reality is rather different. In summer 1944 the Hitler Youth division was not, as has repeatedly been asserted, destroyed in its entirety. By September 1944 it had lost about 8,000 out of 20,000 men, in other words exactly the same proportion as the *Panzer-Lehrdivision* of the regular army. Nonetheless, as Bernard Heisig, who fought with the Hitler Youth in Normandy, puts it: 'Some of us considered those losses a proof of how tough we were, how hard they could push us in battle. It was a crazy mentality.'

The units braced themselves against superior Allied forces, but after six weeks of bitter fighting their strength was at an end and they were overrun. It is a well-worn cliché to say that the *Waffen*-SS and especially the Hitler Youth division generally fought with more fanaticism than any other units, but ultimately this does not stand up to examination. Nor does the ex-SS man, Wolfgang Filor, see boys of the HJ as the 'glorious heroes' that are honoured and celebrated today by SS veterans' organisations, though he does say: 'They were greater heroes than we were – for all their stupidity and inexperience. If you'd been at the front, been wounded, seen the corpses, then you knew what it was all about. I was shot up four times; the fifth time I didn't want to get into a tank again. Sometimes I wet my trousers. It was because of this fear that I recognised the dangers. Most of the HJ division didn't. They went bravely to their death, because they never thought about what could happen to them.'

The bare statistics are one thing, the memories of eye-witnesses on both sides are quite another. They often blur the differences between individual German units. In the hedgerows and copses of Normandy everyone was fighting a constant, almost hand-to-hand battle for every foot of ground. Ordinary infantry divisions were in the thick of it, just as much as the *Waffen*-SS was.

Of course, there were individual SS men whose martial exploits earned them a dubious fame. One of those was *Hauptsturmführer* Michael Wittmann who, in his Tiger tank, single-handedly shot up the British 7th Armoured Division. After this coup, Wittmann was hailed as 'Germany's most successful tank commander'. He was credited with destroying 138 tanks and 132 anti-tank guns. Yet it is easy to forget that in the heat of battle it is hardly possible to obtain reliable information about who has knocked out how many enemy tanks. These figures are to be treated with caution. They were mainly used for propaganda purposes.

For all the similarity between the regular army and the *Waffen*-SS in close combat situations, there was one thing that distinguished the two forces: in those instances of war crimes where there were survivors from a massacre of prisoners-of-war, or corpses were found with tell-tale bullet wounds – the finger almost always points to the *Waffen*-SS.

There is evidence that in the first days after the Allied landings the Hitler Youth division clearly acted on its orders to take no prisoners. On nine separate occasions SS soldiers shot dead a total of 115 defenceless prisoners-of-war. Doug Barrie, who fought against the Germans as a Canadian officer, offers this theory: 'Several officers insisted that Canadian prisoners should be shot. I guess they'd sort of gotten used to doing that while fighting in Russia – some of the officers and NCOs who'd served on the eastern front probably still thought that way. They were commanding the 12th Panzer division, the Hitler Youth, and passed on the idea – prisoners were a nuisance and the best thing was to get rid of them fast.'

You had to admit they were well trained. What's more they were determined to do all they could to inflict the highest possible casualties on us.

It was obvious that from boyhood onward they had been indoctrinated in the Hitler Youth. We thought many of them were fanatics, especially the officers and NCOs they had behind them. The ordinary soldiers knew they couldn't retreat or surrender – they'd have been shot. German prisoners told us that if they'd run away their families at home would have been in trouble. In any case they'd sworn to fight for Hitler to the end. They were very determined young men.

Doug Barrie, officer in the 3rd Canadian infantry division in Normandy

It would certainly be astonishing if only that division and, according to some suggestions also the *Leibstandarte Adolf Hitler* later on, but no other SS divisions, were involved in war crimes in Normandy. Why the order to take no prisoners was issued at all and why it was then rescinded, and why, despite such orders, enemy soldiers did sometimes fall into the hands of these units without being murdered – to this day none of these questions have been conclusively answered. Even though the details of these events may still remain in dispute, it is a fact that 115 Canadian prisoners were killed, and we know of no similar incidents in regular army divisions. It is also true that the Allies were guilty of killing prisoners on occasion, but not on the same scale.

Furthermore, the *Waffen*-SS did not shrink from excesses in their struggle against the French Resistance. As early as 2 April 1944 members of the Hitler Youth division massacred 86 inhabitants of a village near Lille, after claiming that shots had been fired from it at a transport convoy. A sharp protest from the Vichy French government was rejected by Field-Marshal Gerd von Runstedt as 'unjustified'.

After 6 June 1944 a sudden wave of attacks, ambushes and

dynamiting of railway tracks swept through France. These operations by the Resistance were intended to slow down the columns of German reserves that were being brought up to the western front. The SS *Das Reich* division was one of those affected. It was on its way to the Channel coast when it fell foul of the Resistance movement in southern France. Furious at the 'thoroughly shame-making helplessness' of the local Wehrmacht authorities, the division's officers demanded ruthless reprisals. On 7 June 99 Frenchmen were hanged in the town of Tulle in reprisal for the murder of 40 German gendarmes. On 10 June *Sturmbannführer* Dieckmann and an SS company went into the village of Oradour-sur-Glane in search of a fellow-soldier who had been abducted.

Jean-Marcel Darthout, who was twenty years old at the time, describes what happened: 'We were rounded up in the village square of Oradour. There the women and children were separated from the men. I kissed my wife and my mother and never saw them again. . . . Then I saw women and children being taken into the church. We men were lined up with our faces to a wall. The Germans asked us where we were keeping our weapons hidden. We had no weapons, but we weren't afraid either. Then they dragged us into a big barn and started to search everyone. Suddenly the soldiers began to sweep the floor with a broom, so that they could lie down on their stomachs with their machine-guns. Then everything happened very quickly. They fired again and again – then there was dead silence, a ghastly silence. The soldiers spoke to each other and came closer; I heard guns being cocked, click, click. I'll never forget that sound. Then more shots whipped through the rows of bodies – to finish them off. I felt feet on my shoulder, which was sticking up between the bodies, and another shot. It was for Joseph, who was lying on top of me. He saved my life.'

Dieckmann had about 180 men shot, and over 400 women and children were burned to death in the village church. Despite certain unexplained circumstances, the crime of Oradour is so blatant that even a publication of the veterans' association of the *Waffen*-SS had to admit after the war that in this case a company commander was guilty of excess. Soon after the massacre, Dieckmann and most of his men died in the fighting in Normandy.

I was luckily one of the first to fall to the ground. The others fell on top of me. I lay right underneath, and it was completely dark. They covered us with straw and brushwood. After a while I heard someone say: 'They're finished!' But they came back and started a fire, which quickly spread. With my hair alight, I crawled out from the pile of bodies. I was sure they would shoot me. But they'd gone. To them we were nothing more than a heap of corpses. That's how five of us survived.

Jean-Marcel Darthout, survivor of the massacre of Oradour

It is true that regular army units also followed the instructions to 'take ruthless measures', and that the combating of partisans more and more often deteriorated into the massacre of civilian populations who had no involvement with the Resistance. The general commanding the 56th Reserve Corps stated on 30 June 1944: 'In the course of combat operations against insurgent gangs our troops have committed irresponsible acts of looting, desecration and senseless destruction. This disgraceful conduct makes a mockery of the long-standing reputation of the honourable and clean-fighting German soldier.' The massacre of Oradour is thus far from being an isolated incident, but it is clearly exceptional.

This is true of all the war crimes committed by the *Waffen*-SS: their brutality was not unique, and the difference between Wehrmacht and *Waffen*-SS was certainly not so great as is often presented. Nonetheless the excesses of SS units generally overshadowed those of the Wehrmacht, whether in the war against the Resistance or the killing of prisoners-of-war.

By 20 July the unequal struggle on the invasion front against the far superior Allied forces was nearing its end. In a final effort, a few days previously, the *Leibstandarte Adolf Hitler* and the Hitler Youth division had fought off a major British assault on Caen. Now they too, like the regular army divisions, were exhausted. The commanders on the spot were all too aware of the situation. They knew that the crushing Allied advantage in arms and equipment would soon paralyse all resistance. Resignedly, the commander-in-chief of Army Group B, Erwin Rommel, admitted in a letter to Hitler: 'We are holding on, and if our situation is not fundamentally improved by reinforcements, we will have to die decently.' It was not only commanders like Rommel who recognised the absurdity of such orders. Even the senior generals of the *Waffen*-SS knew it could not go on like that. On the night of 15–16 July 1944 Rommel had a meeting with the CO of the 2nd SS Panzer Corps, Wilhelm Bittrich. Because of his biting criticism, Bittrich had long been a thorn in Himmler's flesh, but was considered indispensable as an army commander. Bittrich thumped the table: 'I don't merely know the situation in Normandy, *Herr Feldmarschall*. I also know how bad things are on the eastern front. There is no longer anything there that can be described as purposeful leadership. What's going on there is the most primitive kind of make-do-and-mend.' He went on: 'At the top they don't know the danger, because they have no proper view of the situation and so they can't assess it correctly. Day after day I myself see young people having to die needlessly, because they are being badly led from above. That is why in future I will no longer carry out nonsensical orders and will act as the situation requires.' Rommel's chief-of-staff, Hans Speidel, believed that even Paul Hausser and Sepp Dietrich were prepared to abandon Hitler. Does this mean that the *Waffen*-SS were willing to support the group of conspirators who nearly succeeded in killing Hitler on 20 July 1944? No, they certainly were not. In all the soundings taken by Rommel and others, what was discussed went no further than refusing to obey Hitler's insane orders to stand firm, and if possible relieving him of his *military* authority. No-one had considered staging a *coup d'état*, let alone an attempt on the Führer's life. For this reason Hausser, while not exposing his chief-of-staff Gero von Gersdorff, who was a member of the resistance circle, nevertheless made it quite clear that he himself, as an SS officer, still felt a sense of loyalty to Hitler.

Despite all the grumbling, the *Waffen*-SS did not refuse any of Hitler's 'instructions', no matter how absurd they were. Thus Paul Hausser, who on 7 August was promoted to commander-in-chief of the 7th Army, gave orders for a foolhardy counter-attack which was quickly crushed by fire from Allied fighter-bombers and contributed to the trapping of the bulk of the German forces by the Allies in the Falaise pocket. On this occasion, according to a statement by General Eberbach, Hausser took refuge in blind obedience – nothing else mattered to him. At virtually the last minute Bittrich and his SS 'Hohenstaufen' division managed to breach the encirclement and enabled some 40,000 men to escape.

> Of course we obeyed orders. Once one has accepted the obligation to obey, one must do so. There was no going against one's honour and loyalty to the SS. Cowardice in the face of the enemy was unknown among us. Anyone who was cowardly was dishonoured.
>
> *Erich Leffler, SS* Oberscharführer
>
> They never argued over orders. They behaved very correctly towards us, but if they'd been ordered to kill us, then they'd have killed us. Orders are orders.
>
> *Monique Corblet de Fallerans, a Frenchwoman, about her meeting with soldiers of the SS Hitler Youth panzer division*

The fact that Hitler had put the SS general, Paul Hausser, in command of an army in itself shows the prominence to which the *Waffen*-SS had risen. Hausser was even in the running to succeed Rommel as commander-in-chief of Army Group B, but his appointment was vetoed by *Feldmarschall* Kluge. On 1 August Hitler promoted his old war-horse Sepp Dietrich to *Obergruppen-führer*, equivalent to full general, and a few weeks later put him in command of the Sixth Panzer Army that was just being assembled. The closer the war came to its end – and especially after the 20 July 1944 assassination attempt – the more Hitler came to distrust the regular army and the more faith he placed in his supposedly reliable SS formations. At all events, when Himmler was appointed head of the Reserve Army, after the attempt on Hitler's life, the problems of recruitment to the *Waffen*-SS were over. Several thousand men were transferred in short order from the Luftwaffe and the navy, to fill the depleted ranks of those divisions which, in September 1944, withdrew in very poor shape to the borders of the Reich. Of all males born in 1928, and who were drafted in 1945, no less than 17.3 per cent were assigned to the *Waffen*-SS – more than in any previous year.

> In the SS, Sepp Dietrich was an outsider, the only man to oppose Himmler; but again, because of his relationship with Hitler, it was impossible for Himmler to remove him.
> *Albert Speer, during interrogation by the Americans, May 1945*
>
> He seemed to have no idea about the operations of his own panzer army in the Ardennes, and was unable to give a coherent picture of events, even at the most general level.
> *Robert E.Merriam, US interrogation officer, after questioning Sepp Dietrich, August 1945*

In September 1944 Field-Marshal Montgomery attempted a daring thrust through the Netherlands that would burst open the very gates of the German Reich. Three Allied airborne divisions were to secure the bridges over the Maas, the Waal and the Rhine. The 2nd SS Panzer Corps commanded by *Gruppenführer* Bittrich fought off the assault and at Arnhem wiped out most of the British 1st Airborne Division. During this action there occurred the kind of humane gesture that had become a rarity in this brutalised war; even before the battle was over, the British divisional medical officer asked Bittrich to give medical treatment to 2,200 British wounded. Bittrich agreed to this request. In a ceasefire lasting two hours the men were handed over and subsequently cared for by medical orderlies of the SS 'Hohenstaufen' division.

Despite the stout defence put up by the Germans, the Allies were now poised to invade the Reich at several points along its western frontier. Hitler himself had predicted that a successful landing by the Allies would decide the war. That battle was now lost, and Germany's defeat was all too apparent, even if in a final desperate effort the Allied advance could once more be stopped on the borders of the Reich. Even a fanatical SS veteran like

Kurt Meyer admitted, after being taken prisoner in September 1944, that it was now time 'to bring things to an end'. However, Hitler certainly did not think so – quite the contrary: ever since the retreat from France he had been toying with the idea of a major counter-attack in the west. As soon as the front had been stabilised, he switched determinedly to preparations for attack, taking personal control of everything. The army commanders in the field considered a successful breakthrough impossible on account of Allied air superiority and their own shortage of fuel. But the 'Greatest Military Commander of All Time' would not be told. He wanted to repeat the success of the western offensive of 1940. Then the German panzer divisions had made a surprise thrust through the Ardennes, crossed the Meuse near Sedan and brought about the collapse of the entire Allied front. Now he wanted to pull off the same trick again: 22 divisions, including 8 panzer divisions, were to march without warning through the Ardennes westwards as far as the Belgian port of Antwerp and bottle up the Allied forces in southern Holland. Hitler hoped that the severe winter weather would prevent the Allied air forces from operating. In addition, the advancing German troops would loot Allied fuel dumps and thus ease their own petrol shortage.

The Sixth SS Panzer Army was to spearhead the attack and, with its four divisions, would be the first to reach Antwerp. Hitler had ordered all men and weapons available in the Reich to be scraped together. Battle-weary units had new equipment and men assigned to them, new *Volksgrenadier* territorial divisions were established. For the first time a new model of tank, the *Königstiger* or Royal Tiger, was available in considerable numbers to blast open a path for the German troops. The *Leibstandarte Adolf Hitler* had created several battle-groups, which had to fight their way along the narrow roads of the Ardennes. The most potent fighting unit was that led by *Obersturmbannführer* Joachim Peiper, a typical young SS officer. On the eastern front he had earned a reputation as a tough and ruthless tank commander and had been decorated several times.

On the morning of 16 December 1944 the operation codenamed *Wacht am Rhein* ('Watch on the Rhine') began. The Americans were taken completely by surprise, mistakenly believing the Germans to be already beaten. The front line was soon overrun. Peiper's battle-group was able to ransack a US fuel store near Bullingen. His tanks and vehicles were refuelled up to the brim. But the Americans soon recovered from their initial shock and hurriedly brought up reserves. By 19 December Peiper was already encountering stiff resistance. What is more, their juice was running low and further progress was out of the question. The swift advance to the Meuse faltered. Peiper's group was trapped in the little Ardennes village of La Gleize, became embroiled in violent hand-to-hand fighting with hastily summoned American paratroopers and was pounded by heavy artillery. German aircraft flew over several times to drop supplies but nearly all the parachuted containers landed in the American lines. Peiper and his SS men were in a hopeless situation. In the end Peiper, with the 800 men he had left, decided they would fight their way back to the German lines, leaving behind their heavy weapons and the wounded. In the early hours of 24 December they broke out: the password was 'Merry Christmas'. Eight hours later the men reached their own territory, utterly exhausted.

The fate of Peiper's battle-group, in which such great hopes had been placed, is symptomatic of the entire Ardennes offensive. American reserves were soon able to bring the German advance to a standstill and wipe out the troops that had forged too far ahead. True, the Fifth Panzer Army made faster progress than the SS units, but it too failed to reach the Meuse, let alone Antwerp. On 26 December the Allies mounted a counter-offensive and, with effective air support now that the weather had cleared, pushed the Germans back to their starting-point. How greatly the picture had changed since 1940: this time the Allies did not, as they had done then, commit one blunder after another; in tactical and operational battlecraft they were more than a match for the Germans. The whole German offensive had been a desperate gamble that probably no-one but Hitler would have thought of taking.

If we consider the differences between the panzer divisions of the regular army and the SS units, we see a similar picture to that in Normandy: in combat they can scarcely be distinguished. On the other hand, the only documented war crimes were again committed by units of the *Waffen*-SS. For example, on several occasions the *Leibstandarte Adolf Hitler* killed American prisoners-of-war and Belgian civilians. The most notorious incident took place on 17 December 1944 at the Baugnez crossroads near Malmédy. Several SS men, put on trial after the war, claimed they had 'merely' shot at American prisoners who were trying to escape. However, William Merriken, an observer with the US Army's 285th Artillery Battalion and one of the 43 survivors of the massacre, tells a different story: 'We were standing around in smallish groups, waiting for some trucks to come along and pick us up and take us to a PoW camp. Parked on the road were two tanks and a half-track, which appeared to be guarding us. Then I saw a German in the half-track stand up and aim his pistol – he shot one American, then another, then a third. The two tanks raked us with machine-gun fire; I dropped to the ground, but I wasn't hit. They went on firing for a while and I heard bullets thudding into the bodies and the ground around me. Then it went quiet, till I heard two Germans coming in my direction. They stood directly over me. A body was lying across my legs. When the poor guy moved, one of the Germans shot him with a pistol. The bullet killed him and pierced my knee, but I didn't move.' A short time later he tried to escape towards the edge of the forest. 'I got up and hobbled across a field towards a house. As I got near the fence an SS officer came down the road. He aimed his pistol at me and pulled the trigger, but there was no shot. The officer ran along the road to stop other men who had escaped. I made it over the fence and hid in a woodshed.' Of the 72 men killed, 40 had been shot through the head at point-blank range.

News of the massacre spread like wildfire through the American troops, who for their part took no prisoners in the days that followed. After the war 73 members of the *Leibstandarte Adolf Hitler* were charged with war crimes and 43 of them condemned to death; 22 were sentenced to life imprisonment. When doubts were raised about the presentation of evidence, most of the sentences were reduced. None of the death sentences was carried out and the last defendant remaining in prison, Joachim Peiper himself, was released in 1956.

There has been much speculation about what led to this massacre. Several authors point out that, after an Allied air-raid which flattened the town of Düren, near Aachen, soldiers of the *Leibstandarte* had helped to pull the dead from the rubble, and that this was a reason for wanting vengeance. It is much more likely that once again, after all their experience on the eastern front and in Normandy, some individuals committed this atrocity, finding nothing reprehensible in killing defenceless, wounded Americans. Furthermore, it is striking that this incident is once again attributable to a 'core unit' of the *Waffen*-SS – which leads us to conclude that the indoctrination of these units was still finding its outlet in fanatical behaviour.

The Ardennes campaign exhausted the Wehrmacht's last reserves of energy but only succeeded in delaying the final Anglo-American offensive by six weeks. Wehrmacht troops were urgently needed on the eastern front, where in January 1945 the Red Army overran the German lines and were advancing relentlessly westward from the river Vistula. On 31 January the first Russian tanks succeeded in crossing the frozen river Oder. Berlin was less than fifty miles away.

However, that month Hitler did not despatch the battered Sixth SS Panzer Army to the Oder front to protect Berlin. Instead, he ordered it to Hungary. On 26 December 1944, while the Germans were still trying to break through the American lines, the Soviets had encircled Budapest. SS *Obergruppenführer* Karl Pfeffer von Wildenbruch defended the city for seven weeks with an odd assortment of different units, including two SS cavalry divisions. In January 1945 no fewer than three relief attacks were launched by, among others, the SS Death's Head and Viking divisions. None of the offensives came closer than twelve miles from the Hungarian capital.

By the beginning of February 1945 the defenders' strength was flagging. In the two SS divisions the Hungarian *Volksdeutsche* fought with no less determination than their Reich-German comrades, who were panic-stricken and literally fighting for their lives. For in 1941–2 those same soldiers had been in the SS cavalry brigade, creating appalling mayhem behind the lines and killing thousands of Russian civilians. Now they rightly feared the Soviets would take their revenge.

On 10 February, with organised defence on the verge of collapse, Pfeffer von Wildenbruch ordered the remaining 24,000 men to break out. It was a suicidal enterprise. They had no chance against the overwhelming superiority of the Red Army. The orderly break-out quickly fell apart and the men tried to scatter in small groups. They were quickly surrounded and mown down. The SS men often took their own lives rather than risk capture. Recent investigations show that of approximately 22,000 men who actually tried to escape to the west, some 19,000 died. In the days that followed no more than 700 completely exhausted men reached their own lines. Pfeffer von Wildenbruch did not have the moral courage to surrender with his beaten troops *en masse* and become a prisoner-of-war. Instead he led them like lemmings into the abyss.

On the very first day we lost 25 of our guys. Obviously that gives you plenty to think about.
> *Friedhelm Busse, soldier in the SS Hitler Youth division, on the fighting in Hungary in 1945*

The Führer believes the troops did not fight in the way the situation demanded and therefore orders the SS divisions, 'Adolf Hitler', 'Das Reich', 'Totenkopf' and 'Hohenstaufen', to remove their shoulder-flashes.
> *Order from Hitler, late March 1945*

In the confusion of the attempted break-out indescribable scenes were played out in Budapest. Here too the Red Army soldiers looted and raped, satisfying their thirst for revenge most of all on the Russians who had fought on the German side, but also against *Waffen*-SS prisoners. Countless numbers of them were executed by the Soviets. But even here the picture was not one of unrelieved brutality; humane standards had not been totally abandoned. For example, SS *Hauptsturmführer* Kurt Portugall describes his capture: 'After being interrogated I was offered a hunk of bread and some vodka. They said: You must be pretty hungry, you haven't had anything to eat or drink for days. I drank and ate, and then the unaccustomed warmth of the room made me sweat. The Russian major told me I ought to take off my camouflage gear. I did so and he looked with interest at my insignia of rank, the runic "SS" symbol and my war decorations. Then he said to me: I have great respect for the soldiers of the *Waffen*-SS. You will now be transported back to Russia. And there are just as many bastards in our HQ as in yours. I advise you to get rid of your SS badge and decorations. It'll be healthier for you.' It has to be said that this was a rare and isolated instance.

By the end, not even Sepp Dietrich was convinced any longer. I was with him in the last big German offensive in Hungary. The Sixth Panzer Army attacked south-east of Budapest with the latest equipment available, while the Russians had nearly reached the outskirts of Berlin. The terrain was completely unsuitable; it was a deep morass and many of the tanks got stuck. The Russians threw themselves at the extended flank of the attacking Sixth Panzer Army, which then went into hasty retreat. Afterwards Hitler ordered the removal of the SS shoulder-flashes, the symbol of their sovereign status. So at the end of the war the SS was demoted by Hitler himself.

Baron Philipp von Boeselager, officer in the Wehrmacht

Scarcely a month after the fall of Budapest Hitler launched his final 'great offensive', pretentiously codenamed *Frühlingserwachen* ('Spring Awakening'). The objective was to destroy the Soviet forces east of the Plattensee, the band of shallow lakes north-east of Berlin. The core of the attacking forces was still the *Waffen*-SS, of which a total of eight divisions took part in the offensive. But this operation failed too, after they had advanced a mere twelve miles. The divisions were in any case a shadow of their former selves. The SS had nothing left to put up against the Soviet counter-attacks. Hitler was beside himself with rage to see that not even the *Waffen*-SS were obeying his orders to hold their ground, but on their own initiative had begun retreating. He felt betrayed by his personal guard and on 27 March 1945 ordered that as a sign of its dishonour its personnel had to remove their shoulder-flashes. Sepp Dietrich ignored the dictator's instructions. Even among the SS, after the heavy fighting of the past few months, no-one was willing any longer to expose themselves to indiscriminate slaughter. All the strength and fight had gone out of the troops and they hurriedly withdrew. A little later the Red Army was at the gates of Vienna, and after a brief battle they captured the city on 14 April.

By now Hitler was sitting in the gloomy fantasy-world of his 'Führer bunker' beneath the Reich Chancellery, hoping for a second 'Miracle of the House of Brandenburg'. On 12 April 1945 the invalid American president, Franklin D. Roosevelt, died. But contrary to what happened in 1762 during the Seven Years War, the opposing coalition did not break up. On 16 April the Soviets started their massive onslaught on Berlin. After a hard and bloody battle the thin German defences collapsed. The encirclement of Berlin could no longer be prevented. Hitler had placed all his hopes on a relief attack led by SS General Felix Steiner. On 22 April Hitler kept asking anxiously: 'Where's Steiner got to?' However, Steiner had no intention of giving his threadbare troops the order to attack. When the Führer finally recognised the hopelessness of the situation, he broke down – for the first time ever. Everyone had betrayed him, he raged, first the Wehrmacht and now even the SS. The idea of National Socialism had been lost, there was no longer any point in living. He vowed he would never leave Berlin, but would die in his capital. Hitler wept, screamed and cursed. Then he slumped exhausted into an armchair. The tyrant was finally done with living. All attempts by his henchmen to persuade Steiner to attack, even at that late stage, foundered on the latter's sense of reality. 'No, I won't do it', he said. 'This attack is nonsense – it's murder.'

Germans in uniform were hanging from street-lamps, labelled as 'cowards'. At the very last minute they'd been hanged by fanatical Hitler Youth officers and SS men.

Günter Dunsbach, then in the Hitler Youth

On 25 April the ring of steel around Berlin closed and the Red Army launched their ultimate attack on the city. But even then a random collection of shattered divisions, elderly men of the *Volkssturm* and boys from the Hitler Youth forced the Red Army to fight their way through, street by street, in costly battles. The order to defend the city centre had been given to SS *Gruppenführer* Mohnke, a veteran of the *Leibstandarte*. Remains of the SS 'Nordland' division fought around the Tiergarten zoo, a battalion of French SS men defended Belle-Alliance-Platz and even Latvian SS men were engaged in the final battle for Berlin. And to the very end the SS showed no mercy. Franz Neuhüttler, a member of the SS Reconnaissance Regiment, tells us: 'We had returned from an engagement and there I saw, in front of the Reich Chancellery, two Russians sitting maybe ten metres from the entrance; they were prisoners. . . . From the gateway I watched the two Russians being made to stand up. The SS man drew his pistol and shot them both in the neck. I just asked myself: why?' On 30 April 1945 Hitler committed suicide. Two days later the murderous battle for the capital of the Reich was over.

Shortly before the end of the war we were holed up in a village in Upper Austria. When the Americans arrived some of our men hoisted a white flag. A court-martial was held and seven men were sentenced to death. We had to form up in a square, then a makeshift gallows was erected and the death sentences were carried out. At the time I felt that it was right for the men to hang, since they had stabbed us soldiers in the back.

Friedhelm Busse, soldier in the SS Hitler Youth division

Among the ruins of the Reich, the *Waffen*-SS met its doom along with the rest. On 30 September 1946 it was declared a criminal organisation. Before that, a dispute had already started about what the *Waffen*-SS had actually been, what had defined its character. Amid hostility on every side, a 'mutual aid association' for veterans was formed, with the initials HIAG. More than anyone, it was Paul Hausser who attempted to prove the unprovable: that the men of the *Waffen*-SS had been 'just like other soldiers' and had had nothing to do with war crimes or concentration camps. Some individual SS men may well have seen it like that, but it certainly bore no relation to reality. The *Waffen*-SS was an integral component of the state protection force, which had been charged with guarding the Nazi regime against real or imagined enemies, both external and internal. The close links with the general SS cannot be denied – particularly since there was such a large overlap of personnel. The officers were trained jointly, regardless of where they were to be deployed: in the concentrations camps, in administrative posts or on the front line.

In its short history the *Waffen*-SS went through an enormously rapid process of development. At the start it was clearly distinguishable from the regular army, by reason of its rigorous selection criteria, ideological indoctrination and the sense of being an 'elite order'. But the longer the war lasted, the more this distinction was lost. On one hand, the army itself became increasingly 'Nazified', and on the other the *Waffen*-SS, or at least its core units, gained in military professionalism. It would be an exaggeration to describe the soldiers of the *Waffen*-SS collectively as gangs of murderers. It is, however, a fact that some of the most ghastly war crimes were those committed by units of the *Waffen*-SS.

The occasional mythologising of the *Waffen*-SS, both in Germany and abroad, as the 'fighting elite of German soldiery' has little in common with reality, though it is a popular stereotype. Altogether there were 38 divisions of the *Waffen*-SS. Yet, among them, the gradient of performance was very steep. Certainly, the panzer divisions, in particular, were considered exceptionally effective in battle. But many other units were, militarily speaking, no more than average. Furthermore, we must not forget that there were also special forces in the regular army and the Luftwaffe. The *elite* of the Wehrmacht was certainly not the *Waffen*-SS. It is also important to note that, overall, the *Waffen*-SS did not suffer proportionately higher losses than the regular army. This may be further proof that the oft-cited but fatal 'spirit of self-sacrifice', was present to an equal extent in the army.

The myth of the high losses and superior equipment of the *Waffen*-SS grew up even *during* the war. The reasons for it are clear: the SS units regarded themselves quite simply as *the* elite and often acted that way in public. At the front they were easily distinguished from the Wehrmacht's field grey, by their camouflage fatigues, as well as the tattooing of their blood-group under their armpits. It is true that an elite division of the *Waffen*-SS had better equipment than an average division of the regular army. Not only to ordinary footsoldiers but even to officers, divisions like *Das Reich* often seemed like mobile armouries. All this gave rise to envy and feelings of rivalry. In August 1944, when the commander of the 2nd Panzer division was asked by men from the *Leibstandarte* for a vehicle to take their wounded divisional commander, *Brigadeführer* Wisch, out of the Falaise pocket, he simply replied: 'For the *Leibstandarte*? They've got enough transport; they're getting none from me!' On the eastern front the rivalry reached such a pitch that in 1942 the staff of the 2nd Army Corps deliberately delayed the relieving of the Death's Head division by regular army units, under the secretly confessed motto: 'Rather them than us.'

Admittedly, as the end of the war approached, this rivalry became less and less apparent. Finally General Guderian voiced the opinion that the longer the war went on, the more the SS units became 'our chaps'. In retrospect, that kind of statement reflects no glory on the Wehrmacht. It cannot, after all, do anything to change the peculiarly ideological character of the *Waffen*-SS nor the very significant differences between it and the regular army. They were *not* just soldiers like any others.

CHAPTER SIX

THE 'ODESSA' MYTH

The Germans who participated in the mass shooting of Italian officers or the execution of French, Dutch, Belgian or Norwegian hostages, or Cretan peasants, or were involved in the slaughter of populations in Poland or regions of the Soviet Union, which were then being cleared by the enemy, should be aware that they will be taken back to the scene of their crimes and that justice will be meted out to them on the spot by the peoples whom they treated so despicably.

The 'Moscow Declaration' by the Allies, November 1943

In the Peruvian capital, Lima, Judge Santos and some men from the *Guardia Civil* crept cautiously up to the house belonging to a certain Friedrich Schwend. The judge had been tipped off that this German was part of a Nazi network. He was also said to be involved in passing forged banknotes, in blackmail and perhaps even murder. As soon as he heard this, Santos quickly decided to order a search of Schwend's home. That was on 12 April 1972; but apparently the suspect had already been warned. Through a window the investigators could see him, still in his pyjamas, hastily burning papers in his ground-floor office. 'We seized the documents, and some were a bit charred', the judge says. 'Under a rug in the kitchen we found a trap-door leading to a cellar. There we found a vast collection of files, arranged on wooden shelves – the Schwend archive', Judge Santos recalls. Among these papers was a remarkable document, the minutes of a meeting; the 'Odessa File'.

The file relates to a secret meeting in the Spanish resort of Marbella, on a hot July day in the early 1960s. It tells us that about a hundred men gathered at a secret location. They had arrived from every corner of the world; from Iran and Iraq, from Latin America, the USA and Canada; from many countries of western Europe including, of course, Germany; and even from the Soviet Union. According to the minutes they had all come at the invitation of a notorious organisation, cloaked in secrecy. Its name was ODESSA, whose initials stand for *Organisation der ehemaligen oder entlassenen SS-Angehörigen* (Organisation of former or discharged members of the SS). According to the document seized in Lima, Odessa represented at this session 'all ex-members of the SS, without regard to nationality'. It seems that a number of leading figures in the criminal organisation at the heart of Hitler's state had survived the collapse of the Third Reich. They included 'representatives of the Central of Office of Reich Security (RSHA) and the Security Service (SD).' The identity of some of these shadowy figures was apparently so secret that it was even concealed from those present. The minutes mention 'six ex-officers of the SS, at present citizens of Israel, two of whom have managed to infiltrate the secret service of that country. Only the five Continental Directors of Odessa were permitted to know the identity of these comrades; they attended the sessions wearing masks, without taking part in the debate.'

The occasion for the meeting – assuming it did indeed take place – was the abduction of Adolf Eichmann from Argentina in 1960, by Mossad, the Israeli secret service, an event that went like a shock through the world community of ex-Nazis. It was now thought necessary to come up with a few Nazi 'home truths'. The minutes recorded that 'the signatories of the Atlantic Charter were nothing but irresponsible hypocrites and habitual criminals' and that 'the state of Israel, as an artificial and highly questionable creation, and as a state created after the Second World War, had never had any right to exist'. When the meeting discussed the seeking out and convicting of war criminals, the man whom they clearly had in their sights was the Attorney-General of the state of Hessen, Fritz Bauer. Bauer had made it his life's work to expose the crimes of the Third Reich, and since taking up his post in 1956 had launched a veritable campaign against the Nazi murderers. At his instigation the Auschwitz Trial, one of the biggest Nazi prosecutions in the history of the Federal Republic, began in Frankfurt-am-Main in

1963, with 20 defendants in the dock. The unspeakable crimes that were described in those court proceedings shocked world opinion, and for unreconstructed Nazis Bauer became the man they most hated and most feared. In Marbella the decision was made to 'pursue the execution of Bauer'. The abduction of Eichmann and the activities of Israeli hit-squads, real enough at that time, frightened the men of Odessa into deciding to 'create a secret service and a specialist commando, whose task would be to put a stop to the terrorist activities of the Israeli squads' and 'to secure the physical liquidation of every single Israeli agent, wherever they may be found'. The secretive debate lasted three whole days, then the group passed a resolution: 'Odessa declares war on Israel'. To round things off they sang the 'Horst Wessel Song' and in memory of the Führer gave a window-rattling triple *Sieg Heil*, 'which must have reverberated across to the British Rock of Gibraltar', as one of the participants reported enthusiastically.

The minutes of the mysterious Odessa meeting in Spain were taken from the private archive of Friedrich Schwend, a former SS operative and shady businessman who had gone to ground in Peru. The sensational document survived – despite his efforts to burn it. A paper attached to it proves that someone present at the conference had sent it to Schwend at his express request. However, there is no independent documentary evidence that the meeting ever took place. No names are mentioned in the minutes, and those who might have been there have maintained a cloak of silence. However, the possibility cannot be excluded that such a group did once meet and gave itself the name 'Odessa' – a name that stands for right-wing extremism and mystery-mongering. It is even used by neo-Nazi circles to confuse investigators. The 'Odessa' organisation is surrounded by a tangle of myths and legends. It is not even certain that it ever existed, let alone that it exists today. The files of the US Secret Service reveal that hints about the existence of Odessa were picked up as early as 1946. According to these clues, it was founded towards the end of the war as an escape organisation for members of the SS. With its help SS men were said to have been spirited away chiefly to Latin America and the Middle East. Rumour had it that in Soviet-occupied East Germany Odessa was also responsible for acts of sabotage aimed at preventing the

Russians from shipping out industrial plant. But was it a single organisation, or merely a blanket term for several similar bodies? In the mind of the Nazi-hunter Simon Wiesenthal, its existence is beyond question: 'I first heard of "Odessa" in 1946, from a former agent in the *Abwehr* (German military counter-espionage)', he says. 'It was a conspiratorial, secret SS organisation whose job was to smuggle war criminals out of Germany and get them to South America.' Wiesenthal, who provided the author Frederick Forsyth with the material for his political thriller, *The Odessa File*, is not at all surprised that the conspiracy remained secret: 'On the Nazi side they had professionals on the job – former undercover men, members of the security service, ex-agents, men who had played a prominent part in the administration of the Third Reich. Just as they had perfected the organisation of mass murder, they were now organising perfectly the escape of the mass murderers.'

When the war ended, there were some people like me who said: we must do something. But after three or four years I saw that I was the last, the only one left. And I couldn't come to terms with that. On one side millions of dead – and I never made any distinction between Jews and non-Jews – and on the other side some 150,000 to 180,000 guilty men, who had sneaked away to all parts of the world. People had simply watched it happen. But I made the decision then: I wanted to do something to restore justice.

Forget nothing! That way we help to prevent crimes against humanity from being repeated.

Simon Wiesenthal, Nazi-hunter

However, whereas Wiesenthal believes that, after successfully arranging these escapes in the 1950s, 'Odessa' was wound up, other informants have reported its continued existence to the CIA. They allege that a meeting was held in Beirut in 1960. In Peru 'Odessa' is said to have put forged dollar bills into circulation.

Its headquarters was thought to be located in Cairo. The leading figures in the organisation, it was said, operated out of South America, Spain and the Arab countries. To this day there is a strong presumption that even before the end of the war the SS shipped abroad vast amounts of currency, gold bullion and precious stones to finance their escape. In this way, through secret bank accounts and company shareholdings, the welfare of its members was assured. Under the protection of dictatorial and extremist regimes, former SS men could remain true to their ideals. They helped to build up organised terror and secret services, and in doing so steadily cultivated their own worldwide network. True to Himmler's watchword, 'Loyalty is our honour', and despite the lack of a Führer, 'Odessa' is said to have preserved its own sense of 'comradeship'. To this day, Odessa is believed to extend its tentacles, like a giant octopus, into the German judicial system, the extreme-right neo-Nazi movement, the prison service, into the secret services of many countries, into international financial circles, indeed all over the world.

> The most popular Nazi-smugglers were 'Odessa' and 'The Spider', although other mysterious groups were also named from time to time.
> *John Loftus, official in the US judiciary and Nazi-hunter*

Though this may all sound like fantasy, there is at least a kernel of truth in it. It is a fact that in the early days many SS perpetrators inexplicably escaped abroad. It is a fact that after the war Nazis like Otto Skorzeny, Johann von Leers, Alois Brunner, Friedrich Schwend, Klaus Barbie and Josef Mengele settled in Madrid, Cairo, Damascus, Lima, La Paz and Buenos Aires, and that from there they employed former henchmen in running businesses that were just this side of the law. It is also a fact that for years there were SS organisations whose influence was sometimes immense. Yet the existence of a tightly structured 'Odessa' organisation spanning the world is pretty improbable. The name 'Odessa' should rather be taken as an umbrella-term for a number of different SS networks and escape organisations – though even here the borders between rumour and reality were frequently blurred. 'Odessa' is the stuff of crime novels. How much of the 'Odessa File' is myth and how much reality?

> After the German army was defeated in the Battle of Normandy in June 1944, [Martin] Bormann took the first steps to put into effect the concrete plans for the Nazis' great escape. The first thing he had to do was get the vast Nazi wealth out of Europe and invest it safely.
>
> *Carl Oglesby, American journalist*

Still and dark, the tranquil Lake Toplitz lies in wild and romantic landscape near Bad Aussee in the Salzkammergut region of central Austria. It is surrounded by steep rock walls and can only be reached by a narrow forest road. Suddenly a robot submarine equipped with a camera comes humming up through the dark waters. With lights and ultrasound it has been combing the lake bottom yard by yard, in search of treasure – the legendary 'Nazi treasure of Lake Toplitz'. The diving operation by the Texan firm Ocean Advanced Technologies, in the year 2000, had financial backing from CBS Television and the Simon Wiesenthal Centre; it was at least the third one of its kind, and certainly the costliest. The bill is said to have come to over a million dollars. Yet the divers found nothing – except a few crates filled with bottle-tops, with a label reading: *Leider nicht* ('Afraid not.') Some jokers from the local inn had dropped them into the lake, just to annoy the treasure-hunters.

Yet Lake Toplitz is woven around with the wildest rumours. It is claimed that top Nazis, faced with the relentless advance of the Allies, sank a number of chests full of gold and jewels in its murky waters. The boxes were also thought to contain highly explosive papers from the Central Office of Reich Security, as well as documentation on the setting-up of companies and the transfer of SS funds to the safety of numbered Swiss bank accounts. They are said to prove what vast amounts of gold bullion and currency the Nazis shifted first to the 'Alpine Redoubt' in Bavaria and Austria, then to Switzerland and the wider world. The Nazi-hunter Simon Wiesenthal believes these illicit funds were intended for the building of a 'Fourth Reich'. Was 'Odessa', the escape-organisation for wanted Nazi criminals, financed with this money? Since the end of the war, treasure-hunters have been repeatedly drawn to the lake. When a young diver lost his life there in 1963, the authorities issued a strict ban on diving. The 300-foot-deep mountain lake with a layer of mud many feet thick on the bottom is just too dangerous. Drifting tree-trunks stretch out their branches like tentacles to entrap the unwary. Despite this, a number of relics of the Third Reich have been brought up from its depths: chiefly weapons, laboratory apparatus, rusty guns and rocket propulsion-units – remnants of a naval test station, which from 1943 carried out trials here of ammunition and undersea weaponry. The navy had completely sealed off the lake, a fact that gave rise to whispers among the local population and encouraged myth-making. However, the divers also found several dozen chests filled with forged British pound notes and the plates for printing them. What had been going on in this remote place deep in the Alps?

In 1944 the Allies were rolling relentlessly forward and Hitler's much-vaunted 'Fortress Europe' was dwindling to 'Fortress Germany'. Some of Hitler's followers hoped to evade defeat. While the twilight of the Nazi idols closed in on Germany, leading figures from the regime began converging from all parts of the Reich on the legendary 'Alpine Redoubt' – their final refuge. Myths surrounded this place, even before it existed. On 12 November 1944 a highly imaginative article appeared in the *New York Times* under the headline 'Hitler's Hideaway'. It stated that 'the whole district, 15 miles wide and 21 miles long, is mined and can be blown up at the press of single button. People say this fatal button is to be found on the desk of Himmler's underground office, which is located in a tunnel beneath the Führer bunker.' Among the Allies, horrific notions were circulating to the effect that Hitler and some loyal followers might put up bitter resistance to their last breath and perhaps take the war in a new and bloody direction. Rumours spoke of 'Werewolf' bands of fanatical Nazi partisans, who planned to go to ground in the mountains of southern Germany.

For a long time this last bulwark was thought to be a figment of Hitler's imagination. But in fact, as early as the end of May 1944, the SS chief, Himmler, was playing with the idea of establishing a defensible SS fortress in the mountains. Faced with imminent defeat, Hitler too grasped at this straw. Into the first months of 1945 he kept open the option of taking up a final battle position in the Alps, where he would wait until a clash between the Allies and Stalin's forces would blow apart the 'unnatural' wartime coalition. It was Hitler's hope that he could hold out in the Alps just long enough to be able, perhaps, to impose a separate peace on the Western Allies. In a 'Führer command' of 24 April 1945 he described the 'Alpine Redoubt' as a 'last bulwark of fanatical resistance'. 'Helped by the terrain, and in the south, through the construction of key strongholds' the redoubt was to stand firm to the last man against the onslaught of the enemy. But in the end the dictator decided otherwise. He remained in his Berlin bunker. On 30 May he and his mistress, Eva Braun, committed suicide.

'The news that Adolf Hitler was dead seemed incomprehensible to us at first. We had looked forward too much to his arrival in the fictitious "Alpine Redoubt"', recalls SS *Standartenführer* Otto Skorzeny in his memoirs. The commander of the SS *Jagdverbände*, or hunter units, and the man who was reputed to have 'sprung' Mussolini from his mountain prison in September 1943, had received orders to form the remains of his troops into the 'Alpenland' protection force. As the final battle for Berlin was raging, most of the staff, headquarters and supply facilities of the Wehrmacht and the *Waffen*-SS were already situated in the *Kernfestung Alpen*, the key Alpine stronghold. The leading figures of the Nazi party were now on the run and most of them made for the area around Bad Aussee in the mountainous lakeland of the Salzkammergut, south-east of Salzburg. This closed valley, between the Dachstein massif and the Totes Gebirge, or 'Dead Mountains', can only be reached by the 3,200 ft high Pötschen Pass. It was there that some of the most notorious mass murderers of the Third Reich felt safest. One of those who moved his headquarters to Bad Aussee in the spring of 1945 was Ernst Kaltenbrunner, who in January 1943 had succeeded Reinhard Heydrich as head of the Central Office of Reich Security. From Bad Aussee he intended to organise the defensive action. Parts of the Steyr munitions factory were to be transferred to the nearby caves and mine-tunnels, so that the production of weapons could continue underground. Top Nazis like Hitler's secretary, Martin Bormann, also arranged for important papers to be deposited in the caves and shafts of the 'Alpine Redoubt'. Valuable art treasures, thousands of paintings, engravings, water-colours and sculptures from all over Europe were also stored in the salt-mines of Altaussee, both to protect them from air-raids and also as bargaining-counters in any peace negotiations. These art treasures were later taken to safety by the American army.

> Experts estimate the wealth that the Nazis were able to hide in various parts of the world at one-and-a-half, or possibly two billion dollars. The list of those people who were and are entitled to have access to these funds must be one of the most important undiscovered secrets of the Third Reich.
>
> *Simon Wiesenthal, Nazi-hunter*

The 'Jewish expert' in the Central Office of Reich Security, SS *Obersturmbannführer* Adolf Eichmann, was another who found his way to the Salzkammergut. The 'bureaucrat of death', whose signature sent millions of human beings to the extermination camps, went into hiding in Altaussee, together with his wife and three sons. There, under orders from his boss, Ernst Kaltenbrunner, he was to 'organise resistance in the Höllengebirge' – the appropriately named Mountains of Hell. In the opinion of the former SD officer Wilhelm Höttl, Eichmann was 'one of the few who actually believed in the Alpine Redoubt.' He waited despairingly for orders from his chief, Höttl claims. On the other hand, Simon Wiesenthal said in an interview that the man who carried out the 'Final Solution of the Jewish Problem' had only sought out these remote mountains so that he and his accomplices could bury gold treasure beneath the high meadows of the Dead Mountains. Eichmann is said to have brought with him 22 crates filled with valuables stolen from his Jewish victims, as well as dental gold and gold wedding-rings from the concentration camps. The value of this 'Eichmann Gold', which has never been found, was estimated by the Vienna State Prosecutor's office in 1955 at 8 million dollars. According to an SS list, Kaltenbrunner is also said to have brought a veritable treasure-house to Aussee: five crates of jewellery and precious stones, 50 kilos of gold bars from the reserves of the German Reichsbank, several hundredweight of gold and gold coins in 50 boxes, 2 million US dollars, an equivalent sum of Swiss francs and a stamp collection worth 5 million gold marks. It is said that Skorzeny likewise brought 22 crates full of gold ingots to the 'Alpine Redoubt' and then moved them on to a neutral foreign country. 'All fairy-tales, all nonsense', says Wilhelm Höttl.

> Bormann came to the conclusion that the Nazis' only hope of surviving the military defeat lay in their own resources, especially in the cohesion of tens of thousands of SS men, for whom in the event of capitulation, only the gallows waited.
>
> *Carl Oglesby, American journalist*

Today, however, we have positive proof that, faced with defeat, high-ranking Nazis did move their wealth to safety abroad, though there is admittedly no documentary evidence about who was involved in planning this. On 7 November 1944 a French source informed the US Secret Service about a highly secret meeting of leading German industrialists, which was said to have been held on 10 August that year, in the Hotel Maison Rouge in Strasbourg. According to the French report, it was attended by the *crème de la crème* of armaments manufacturers and other leading firms, including Krupp, Bosch, Thyssen, Volkswagen, Rheinmetall, Daimler-Benz, AEG and Flick, along with big names from the Nazi party. The meeting was chaired by a representative of the Thyssen corporation. According to the report, he urged the German industrialists to prepare for a 'postwar economic campaign' and to 'establish links with foreign companies'. 'The NSDAP administration', he went on, 'is aware that after Germany's defeat some of its most prominent leaders may be convicted as war criminals. Measures must be taken to ensure that less prominent party officers are taken on as experts in different German companies.' Another speaker is then said to have stated: 'The party is prepared to advance large sums to industry so that each individual firm can set up a secret postwar organisation abroad. However, in return for this, the party asks industry to make available its financial reserves abroad, so that after this defeat a strong German Reich can arise once more.' It is believed that the president of the Reichsbank, Hjalmar Schacht, took charge of the economic side of the operation, while Otto Skorzeny of the SS handled the organisational details. Later on, it is said, funds for financing 'Odessa' flowed in through his office in Madrid.

There is no independent evidence to show that the meeting at the Maison Rouge took this form. Apart from the American report quoted above, we know of no documentation about the conference. Nonetheless it is consistent with the movement to transfer German industrial assets abroad, which can be traced from genuine existing documents. In 2001 an independent Swiss commission of experts found out that, from the beginning of the war, several hundred front-companies had been set up in Switzerland alone and that towards the end of the war the Swiss market was flooded with large quantities of precious stones, securities and currency plundered from occupied countries – not to mention forged British banknotes. The experts estimated the total value in 1946 of German assets deposited in Switzerland at over two billion Swiss francs. 'The transfer of German wealth to Switzerland during the war must have been considerable,' says the commission. 'Members of the industrial and political elite were faced with the question of how their material wellbeing and, in some cases, their personal safety, could be preserved in the postwar period. There is no doubt that, in the final phase, these activities increased and took on the form of a wholesale transfer of assets.' Unfortunately, this transfer of looted valuables and capital, with which the Nazi elite guaranteed their escape, can no longer be proved.

> The National Bank of Switzerland also discovered that from 1943 onward 'large and small batches of very cleverly executed forgeries' of British five- and ten-pound notes were offered for sale in Switzerland.
>
> *From the report of an expert commission, 'Switzerland in the Second World War', 2001*

In 1945, faced with imminent destruction, the Nazis were still making hasty arrangements in the mountains. Kaltenbrunner ordered the setting up of a complete forgery workshop in the 'Alpine Redoubt'. In 'Operation Bernhard', named after its SS boss, *Sturmbannführer* Bernhard Krüger, Jewish inmates of Sachsenhausen concentration camp had been employed since 1942 in supplying the Central Office of Reich Security with forged British pound notes, US dollar bills, postage stamps and documents. The idea had come from Reinhard Heydrich, who had initially intended to drop the pound notes over Britain from aircraft, in order to destabilise the country's economy. Now the SS wanted to exchange these duds for hard currencies abroad. As late as April 1945 Kaltenbrunner cherished the insane hope that the counterfeits would enable him to hold out in his alpine fortress for quite a long time. In the last days of the war the SS was also very interested in forged documents. Over the years these had been produced with great skill. Once an SS *Sturmbannführer* from the SD turned up in the forgers' workshop. He had with him the personal papers of an Argentinian, who had been arrested under some pretext. The documents had to be photographed and reproduced down to the smallest detail within 24 hours. The SD officer arrogantly assured us: 'Our agent will travel with these false papers to South America where, as an Argentinian citizen, he will find all doors are open to him', recalls Adolf Burger, a book-printer who was working at the time as a forger in Hitler's secret workshop. Burger and his wife had been dragged off to Auschwitz. His wife was murdered in Birkenau, and his parents also died in Auschwitz. It was only Burger's dextrous hands that saved him from the gas-chamber.

We were greeted by an SS officer named Krüger. He had been
in the Criminal Police, actually responsible for fighting forgery,
and now he was in charge of a forgery workshop with 142
specialists, counterfeiting millions of pounds sterling. He told
us, if we worked well, we'd be rewarded after the 'final victory'.

Adolf Burger, concentration camp inmate

The false papers would soon help not only agents but also wanted
war criminals to escape abroad. 'We printed Brazilian passports,
Tunisian identity cards, British and American military passes and
shipmasters' certificates', Burger elaborates. 'We even produced
metal dies. Once we forged Dutch baptismal certificates, then
there were official deeds from French cities or letterheads from
the Palestine Office in Geneva, with wording in Hebrew script.
We forged British marriage certificates and US army pay-books.'
They were the perfect means of changing identity. In the middle of
April 1945 the 141 prisoners engaged in 'Operation Bernhard' were
transferred to a satellite of Mauthausen concentration camp, on the
Danube in Upper Austria. There, in the cellars of a brewery, they
had to set up a new forgery workshop. They took with them crate-
loads of banknotes that had already been printed. The plan was that
they should finally move into the 'Alpine Redoubt', but this was
foiled by the arrival of the Americans, the prisoners in the forgery
team were liberated. But the 'funny money' had disappeared.

This simply fuelled the rumours about the 'Treasure of Lake
Toplitz'. Local people stated that, because of the swift advance
of the Americans, large number of metal boxes were shipped
up to Lake Toplitz and submerged in its waters. 'The Nazis
had to work fast. They were very nervous', Ida Weissenbacher
remembers. Soldiers of the SS forced Ida, then a 21-year-old
farmer's wife, to carry sixty crates with her horse and cart up
the narrow rutted track. There she watched the soldiers load the
freight into boats, row out into the lake and throw everything
overboard. She says that for 14 consecutive nights, in April
1945, heavy items of goods were carried up on carts drawn
by horses and oxen, and then sunk in the lake. In July 1959 a

team of divers discovered wooden chests beneath the waters of Lake Toplitz. When the lid of one was prised open with a crowbar, British £5 notes floated to the surface. This search yielded a total of ninteteen chests full of documents and forged banknotes. Lake Toplitz had apparently been the garbage-bin of the Third Reich. To this day, treasure-hunters hope it will also prove to be an Aladdin's cave. However, the fact is that to date there has been no trace of the fabled 'riches' that SS men like Kaltenbrunner and Eichmann were said to have dragged up to the 'Alpine Redoubt'. Even the search for secret documents has so far been fruitless, though an SS agent, who had taken part in those events, expressed the fear that sensational material might be brought to light from Lake Toplitz: 'If you just know the numbers of secret bank accounts, then you can find out which of the top men in the Third Reich are still alive. All you need to know is that someone has withdrawn money on behalf of Martin Bormann, then you can tell that he's still alive somewhere.' So wrote Friedrich Schwend in the Peruvian newspaper, *Correo*, in November 1963. He went on: 'There are many former Nazis today holding important government positions in Germany and Austria, who are opposed to the search for chests in Lake Toplitz. That is easily explained. There are secrets down there which would destroy more than one great political career of the postwar era." Even though Bormann was long dead, there was no limit to people's fantasies, and already some of the products of 'Operation Bernhard' had been recovered. Yet there are hints about what might have happened to the remainder of the forged banknotes. They tell a story that is worthy of any crime thriller. Once again the trail leads back to Lima and Friedrich Schwend.

Friedrich Schwend was the man chosen by the SS to exchange some of the counterfeit money for genuine currency. In doing so he does not seem to have accounted for every last *pfennig*, because after the war he was an extremely rich man.

Simon Wiesenthal, Nazi-hunter

What is definitely down there [in Lake Toplitz], provided it hasn't been swiped by Löhde, is the gold. This can't of course be destroyed or damaged, like letters or other documents can. . . . As you well know, a serving-wench in bed is sometimes better than Her Ladyship on the roof. In this affair let us exercise patience a little longer.

Friedrich Schwend in a letter to Heinz Riegel

According to observers at the time, Friedrich Schwend, alias Fritz Wendig, was an educated gentleman of distinguished appearance who, with his hooked nose and shining bald pate, could have passed as an antique dealer. In fact he was one of the craftiest and most disreputable figures in the Nazi network. A businessman, arms-dealer and smuggler, who sometimes passed himself off as an SS major, Schwend acted as chief salesman for the forged currency produced by 'Operation Bernhard'. On orders from the Central Office of Reich Security, he used counterfeit notes in various countries to buy gold, precious stones, jewellery and foreign currency, as well as real estate and apparently even paintings by Rembrandt and Picasso. As his headquarters he selected Schloss Labers, near Merano in the South Tirol, a castle set among vineyards and orchards. In the last days of the war Schwend hastily tried to get his valuables to a safe place. In May 1945 he was arrested by the Americans in Austria, but was released soon afterwards and, according to some reports, was employed as an agent in the US Secret Service, then called the CIC. In 1946 he was given permission by the CIC to travel with his wife to South America, under a Yugoslavian passport in the name of Wenceslav Turi, and settled in the Peruvian capital, Lima.

There he ran a chicken-farm as a cover for his criminal activities, operating as an arms-dealer, blackmailer, loan-shark, money-launderer and informer for the Peruvian secret service. His correspondence, which has been preserved, reads like a thriller. To 'Rudi, Klitsch and Hans' he writes: 'I would also be interested in some new or nearly new sub-machine-guns, with ammo if possible.' In a letter to the Swiss engineering firm, Oerlikon, we read: 'Please would you be kind enough to let me know whether you are in a position to supply us with medium-range rockets.' Shady financial deals are often discussed: 'I charged Spitz 40,000 Deutschmarks for the Rembrandt, payable in Switzerland as compensation for the swindle he pulled with the 600,000 Reichsmarks.' [This probably relates to the 1948 German currency reform, when the Nazi Reichsmark was withdrawn and replaced by the new Deutschmark. *Tr.*] Rumour had it that in Lima Schwend did everything he could to convert the remaining counterfeit pound notes, as well as property and valuables from 'Operation Bernhard' into hard currency to provide the financial basis for 'Odessa'. The 'deals' mentioned in his letters may have been part of this. Schwend himself freely admitted that after the war his entire fortune had been stolen from him – and mentioned among other things 80 kilos of gold, an original Rembrandt, a suitcase full of money and a valuable oriental carpet. But in any event Schwend found his involvement in 'Operation Bernhard' so exciting that he would have dearly loved to have seen it made into a feature film, as we learn from his letters. The only question was: 'How do we bring in the love-interest?'

One thing is certain, however; in the course of his criminal wheeling and dealing he kept in close contact with war criminals from the orbit of the SS, and provided a refuge for Nazis on the run. It seems that he received help in selling some gemstones from Otto Skorzeny, who by now had settled in Spain. On behalf of the former SS *Standartenführer* Walter Rauff, Schwend arranged passports for other 'old comrades' escaping justice. Rauff is believed to have invented the 'mobile gas-trucks' in which, behind the eastern front, 100,000 Jews, Russians and partisans suffered an agonising death by asphyxiation. Schwend was also in touch with Hitler's ace pilot, Hans-Ulrich Rudel, about whom we read in one letter: 'Rudel has the right connections, especially in Central America.' Schwend's most important business colleague in Latin America was one of the most brutal torturers in the SS: Klaus Barbie, alias Klaus Altmann. As the one-time Gestapo boss in the French city of Lyon he had murdered members of the Resistance and deported Jewish children, thus earning himself the nickname 'The Butcher of Lyon'. After fleeing from Germany he made his home in

Bolivia, but also owned a *pied-à-terre* in Lima. There is extensive correspondence with him as well. A certain man named 'Hieber' writes to 'Dear Herr Schwend and Herr Altmann', offering them money in exchange for 'Bolivian citizenship and a diplomatic passport'. A letter from Barbie to Schwend appears to threaten blackmail. Barbie mentions a 'Yid' he wants to 'deal with'. 'Your lawyer is to issue the charge and send it to the criminal police here. So let's do battle; that Yid has insulted us.' Schwend sat like a spider at the centre of a web of ex-Nazi connections. In April 1965 an informant of the US Secret Service did in fact link him with the mysterious 'Odessa': 'The secret organisation known as ODESSA was founded in 1947 in Buenos Aires by Hitler's secretary, Martin Bormann', the informant claimed. At the moment, the report continued, the network had its headquarters in Cairo, had a membership of 3,087 former Nazis and was financed by Nasser's government. The organisation was in possession of printing-plates for forging US dollar bills. These plates, according to the informant, had originally come from 'Operation Bernhard'. And: 'The head of Odessa in South America is Federico Schwend.'

> This whole state of being constantly watched and under threat from denazification and demilitarisation proceedings is extremely tiresome and over time prevents one getting any positive work done.
>
> *Hans-Ulrich Rudel, former colonel in the Luftwaffe*

As the war came to an end, prominent figures in the Nazi regime had every reason to prepare their escape. At regular intervals Allied radio stations uttered dire threats, like this one from the BBC: 'Anyone who is guilty of committing or inciting war crimes, mass murder or execution – be he an officer, other rank or member of the National Socialist Party – every guilty man will be pursued by the three Allied Powers to the ends of the earth and brought before his accusers, that justice may be done.' The punishment of war criminals and those chiefly responsible for the Second World War was a declared goal of the anti-Hitler coalition. As early as 20

November 1945 there began in Nuremberg the first trial by the four victorious powers, Britain, the USA, the USSR and France, of 24 'principal war criminals'. The SS was declared in general to be a 'criminal organisation', on the grounds that it 'was used for purposes that are criminal. These consisted of the persecution and extermination of Jews, brutality and killings in the concentration camps, illegal acts in the administering of occupied territories, the carrying out of forced-labour programmes and the maltreatment and murder of prisoners-of-war.' Himmler's elite order had finally become an 'army of the despised', as SS General Felix Steiner self-pityingly admitted.

When the advancing Allied troops liberated the concentration camps and finally saw the extent of the horror and the crimes committed, the search for the culprits intensified. Special forces now combed the country for war criminals. They carried with them lists of 'persons to be arrested automatically', in order to identify suspects from the Gestapo, SS and SD, as well as Nazi party mayors, Gauleiters and other senior officials. The Americans, occupying the west and south of Germany, were the most active in their search. In this they made use of the exhaustive 'wanted' lists drawn up by the United Nations War Crimes Commission (UNWCC) and the Central Registry of War Crimes and Security Suspects (CROWCASS), which was headquartered in Paris. These organisations drew up lists of the names of presumed war criminals who were on the run, and compared these with the names of over 8 million people who at the end of the war were being held in PoW and Displaced Persons camps. In this way hundreds of thousands of individuals were investigated and thousands were put on trial. Ironically it was precisely these CROWCASS dossiers of suspects which would soon provide a source that the American Secret Service could draw on when they needed to 'redeploy' former Nazis as US secret agents and informers.

The hunt for Hitler's executioners was on. Even the SS chief, Himmler, had attempted to escape his pursuers with the aid of an eye-patch and false identity papers. But Hitler's hangman was caught and then killed himself with a cyanide capsule. Only a few took that way out; the senior medical officer of the SS, Ernst

Grawitz, blew himself and his family to pieces with two hand-grenades. SS *Gruppenführer* Leonardo Conti took his own life while in prison in Nuremberg. Those SS officers who took refuge in the mountains found things getting too hot. When the German Army Group South-West laid down its arms in northern Italy, on 3 May 1945, not even the fictitious 'Alpine Redoubt' could be held any longer. Only a few scattered SS units still attempted to resist the formal surrender by the Wehrmacht on 8 May. Odilo Globocnik, an SS *Gruppenführer* and Lieutenant-General of Police, was a notorious mass murderer, responsible for the 'final solution of the Jewish problem' in occupied Poland. When he was tracked down to a mountain meadow near the Weissensee lake, and arrested, he bit on a cyanide capsule. Julius Streicher, publisher of the anti-Semitic smear-sheet, *Der Stürmer*, had fled to the 'Alpine Redoubt' in April and was posing as an artist. With his wife he hid in a farmhouse near Waidring in the Austrian Tirol. He was discovered there by the Americans and, on 1 October 1946, was condemned to death at Nuremberg. As the Allies came ever closer, even Ernst Kaltenbrunner abandoned his resistance plans and fled into the Totes Gebirge. He was captured by US troops in a mountain hut 5,000 feet up, then condemned to death by an Allied court and executed.

> We recognised all the SS men, even if they were disguised in another uniform, by the scar under their left arm, which was made when they tried to cut out their blood-group tattoo. We sent them to the Seventh Army in Augsburg, where all war criminals went.
>
> *Wolfgang Robinow, US interrogation officer*

But it was not just the Four-Power Tribunal in Nuremberg to which the top SS officers were answerable. In the American Zone alone there were twelve 'follow-up trials' under US military jurisdiction, involving among others the murder battalions of the SS *Einsatzgruppen* and the Gestapo. Other Allied trials were held for concentration camp guards, and the thugs and murderers who ran the camps. In the western zones of Allied-occupied Germany, a total of 5,025 people were convicted. Of the 806 death sentences passed, 486 were carried out. In one prison for war criminals, Landsberg in Bavaria (where Hitler himself was briefly imprisoned in 1923–4), the Americans carried out 255 executions. In the Soviet occupation-zone the number of trials is estimated at 45,000. In countries outside Germany as many as 60,000 people were convicted of Nazi crimes. In Poland alone 1,214 Germans paid for their misdeeds with their lives, among them the commandant of Auschwitz, Rudolf Höss. According to figures from the Federal German Ministry of Justice, a total of 80,000 Germans have been convicted of Nazi crimes, 12,000 of those in the former GDR (the communist East German republic).

In April 1945, as Stalin's troops were closing the ring around Berlin, SS officers with good connections were already cobbling together new 'pasts' for themselves. 'A senior officer brought with him hundreds of sheets of paper with all kinds of different letterheads on them', Eichmann later recounted. The officers were given forged 'testimonials' with fictitious and innocent-sounding jobs that they had been given during the war. When the Third Reich collapsed in rubble and ashes, the bulk of the SS officer corps were taken prisoner. Certainly a number of Hitler's thugs succeeded in vanishing among the millions of German PoWs. But for many, the former sign of their membership of the elite SS was their nemesis. The blood-group indicator, tattooed under their left armpit, was intended to guarantee SS men preferential treatment in hospital. Now it provided their pursuers with an easy means of identification. By the end of 1945, in the American occupation-zone alone, some 100,000 people, classified as dangerous, had been interned.

It was in the chaos of the internment camps that the 'Odessa' myth took shape. 'In the PoW camps there were always two or three SS men who belonged to the organisation', claims Simon Wiesenthal. "Odessa" was their password. If one of them asked: "What on earth are you talking about?" they could always reply: "About a mutual friend who comes from the city of Odessa."' According to Wiesenthal, the purpose of the organisation was to provide SS war criminals with a route out of Germany and get them to South America. In 1947 an American agent was infiltrated into the Nazi network under the codename 'Operation Brandy'; he reported that as well as the 'Brotherhood' and the 'Spider' there was an underground network called 'Odessa'. The letters, he said, stood for '*Organisation der ehemaligen* (i.e. 'former') or *der entlassenen* (i.e. 'discharged') *SS-Angehörigen*' ('members of the SS'). The head of this group was said to be Otto Skorzeny. This is the first time that the name of the most legendary daredevil of the Third Reich had been mentioned in connection with 'Odessa'.

I spent two years searching for the monster Mengele in South America. I know what lies behind that name.
  Zvi Aharoni, of Mossad, who spent years hunting the SS doctor, Josef Mengele

Mengele felt so secure that he even applied for readmission as a medical practitioner.
  Beatriz Gurevich, head of the research project 'Proyecto Testimonio', run by the Argentine–Israeli association, Daia

---

The disappearance abroad of some of the most wanted Nazi thugs further fed the myth of a secret escape organisation called Odessa. For years these men haunted the minds of Nazi-hunters, historians and journalists. The SS doctor, Josef Mengele, disappeared apparently without trace. In reality the trail of the 'Auschwitz Angel of Death', who carried out cruel experiments on concentration camp inmates in which twins in particular met agonising deaths, led through Argentina and Paraguay to Brazil. Mengele was never caught. He drowned in 1979, while swimming near Sao Paulo. Another who disappeared was the Gestapo chief and SS *Gruppenführer* Heinrich Müller. The technocrat of terror had sent hundreds of thousands of Jews to the death camps of the Holocaust. 'Gestapo Müller' was last seen on the day after Hitler's death in the bunker beneath the Reich Chancellery. In May 1945, Müller was thought to have gone into hiding in Altaussee under the alias of '*Leutnant* Schmidt'. After that his trail vanished. Adolf Eichmann also seemed to have disappeared into thin air. Not until 1960 was he abducted from Argentina by the Israeli secret service, Mossad, tried in Israel and executed. It took until 1983 for Klaus Barbie to be tracked down in Bolivia, from where he was extradited to France. Hunters are still on the trail of Alois Brunner, Eichmann's 'best man' for deportations. When last heard of he was living in Damascus. To put it mildly, the escape routes and subsequent movements of these men are cloaked in mystery. Yet they were *not* planned by a single, globe-spanning secret league called 'Odessa'. The reality was more complicated than that. After the collapse of Hitler's Reich and the start of the Cold War, there was suddenly a whole series of networks, institutions and governments which had an interest in helping SS criminals. Thus, what emerges is that many roads lead to 'Odessa'.

One of these roads led through Rome, the favourite destination for Nazi 'pilgrims'. On 15 May 1947 a US security official named Vincent La Vista sent a top-secret report to Washington, stating that the Vatican was the 'largest single organisation involved in the illegal movement of emigrants'. It was helping people of all political persuasions, the report said, 'as long as they are anti-communist and in favour of the Catholic Church'. La Vista named a series of Catholic organisations that had assisted in illegal escapes, including the Austrian and Croatian Aid Committees, as well as bodies in Latvia, Poland, Romania and elsewhere. As long as the Vatican keeps its relevant archives under lock and key, the extent to which the Catholic Church and even the Vatican itself were involved in helping Nazis to escape will never be entirely clear. But it is a fact that perpetrators like Adolf Eichmann escaped to South America via Rome. Yet the murderers were not alone – immediately after the war, armies of uprooted people were on the move, people whose greatest wish was to leave the devastation of Europe behind them; released or escaped prisoners-of-war, slave-labourers, people driven from their homeland, Jewish survivors of the Holocaust – as well as their fleeing executioners.

Rome acted as a magnet for those seeking help. They all hoped the Church would help them on their way, with food, clothing, money, accommodation and above all documents enabling them to set sail from Italy's international ports of Genoa and Naples. In a spirit of generosity the Catholic institutions took them in. In the chaos of those days it was very possible that Nazi criminals were able to mingle with those seeking help, and to remain unrecognised. Yet there were also a number of high-ranking ecclesiastical officials, who quite deliberately helped Nazi perpetrators and in so doing made use of a dense and finely woven network. Whatever success 'Odessa' might claim in smuggling Nazis, compared to the Catholic Church it was an amateur operation.

Closer investigation revealed that in the Latin American countries, where the Church represents a controlling or dominating factor, the Vatican has put pressure on their embassies in Rome, with the result that they have adopted a positive attitude to the immigration of former Nazis and fascists into their countries, just as long as they are anti-communist.
Secret report of the US State Department, 1947 (La Vista Report)

The Vatican has always maintained that it was unaware of the identity of the people who merited its humanitarian assistance. Yet a good many influential clerics not only knew who the Nazis were, they deliberately sought them out and ensured they were given preferential treatment.
John Loftus, official of the US judiciary and Nazi-hunter

A driving force in this network was the Austrian bishop, Dr Alois Hudal, Rector of the Collegio Teutonico Seminary of Santa Maria dell'Anima, the national church of German-speaking people in Rome. The concentration camp commandant Franz Stangl told Gitta Sereny in an interview: 'I escaped from the interrogation prison in Linz on 30 May 1948. Then I heard that Bishop Hudal at the Vatican in Rome was helping SS officers, so I drove to Rome.' Stangl had been in command of the Sobibor and Treblinka extermination camps, where 900,000 human beings had been put to death. When the Third Reich fell apart, he went to ground in an Austrian village; though disguised as a civilian, he was picked up by the Americans as a member of the SS. At that time, no-one had yet heard about the mass murders in Treblinka, and apparently the Americans did not know who they were looking at. It is not known how Stangl managed to escape and get over the border into Italy. Simon Wiesenthal believes that 'Odessa' had provided him with identity papers. In Rome Stangl found his way to Bishop Hudal. 'The bishop came into the room where I was waiting, stretched both hands out to me and said: "You must be Franz Stangl. I've been expecting you!"' Stangl went on to tell Sereny how Hudal arranged accommodation for him in Rome, and fixed him up with a Red Cross passport and a visa for Syria, as well as a job in Damascus. He made his home in Syria for a while and finally emigrated with his family to Brazil. Not until 1967 was he extradited to Germany and sentenced to life imprisonment.

> Had Stangl stayed in Syria, he would probably, like his accomplice Alois Brunner, still be safe and free today.
>
> *Simon Wiesenthal, Nazi-hunter*

Hudal was a man of diminutive stature, 'who for that reason always tried to act big', a former colleague commented maliciously. As a patent admirer of the Nazis, the bishop dreamed of a kind of 'Christian National Socialism', and when he published his book *The Foundations of National Socialism* in 1936, he personally dedicated it to Adolf Hitler, 'the Siegfried of Germany's greatness'. Faced with the surging tide of refugees, Pope Pius XII placed the welfare of prisoners and refugees in the hands of a 'Papal Aid Commission' (the *Pontifica Commissione Assistenza* or PCA), which in turn set up national sub-committees. Hudal was in charge of the Austrian section, the *Assistenza Austriaca*. However, he helped all German-speaking people and made special efforts on behalf of Nazis being held in Italian prison camps. The 'brownshirt bishop' had in effect made it his job to prevent German fugitives from falling into Allied hands. In his memoirs he openly boasted about helping the much-feared governor of Lvov, in the German-occupied Polish region of Galicia: 'He died in my arms in Rome's Santo Spirito hospital. The man I cared for to the end, Baron von Wächter, Vice-Governor of Poland, *Generalleutnant* and *Sturmbannführer* in the SS, was being hunted everywhere by Allied and Jewish authorities. At the same time as his superior, *Generalgouverneur* Hans Frank, was being tried and hanged in Nuremberg, Wächter managed – not least through the touching and selfless help of Italian monks – to live in Rome for months under an assumed name, before dying of blood-poisoning.' Apparently Hudal had even made a secret deal with the Italian police whereby wanted Nazis were not arrested, but were taken to churches and monasteries nominated by the bishop.

I recalled with deepest gratitude the help I received from Catholic priests when escaping from Europe, and decided to pay tribute to the Catholic faith by becoming an honorary member of it.

Adolf Eichmann, 1959

I am a priest, not a policeman. . . . It was my duty as a Christian to help any refugee from communism. I can neither confirm nor deny that Eichmann was among them. No-one confessed to me about their past in the Third Reich, and at that time pictures of Eichmann had not been seen.

Bishop Alois Hudal, 1961

May God give his blessing to the revival of Germany.

Alois Hudal, December 1948

Yet hiding-places were not enough. What SS men on the run needed above all were money and travel documents, so that they could escape overseas. It was here that another organisation came into play, one which set itself the goal of helping all those in need of protection, regardless of their political attitude. This was the International Committee of the Red Cross (ICRC). Whether by accident or design, the Red Cross became the clearing-house for illegal journeys to Italy and onward from there. Here the escapees received those urgently needed documents that were issued to everyone 'compelled by war for one reason or another to leave their country of residence in conditions where they lack a valid passport, and are unable to obtain a new one, which permits them to leave their country of residence and enter the country to which they wish to travel'. The papers were issued in any name at all. The Papal Aid Commission vouched for the identity of the applicant, and often the recommendation of a churchman like Bishop Hudal was enough. It was the dream of every wanted criminal who needed a new name – and knew some benevolent dignitary. Gertrude Dupuis-Marstaller, a Red Cross delegate in Rome described the chaotic situation: 'Every day people were queuing up in their hundreds. Sometimes we had to call in the police to keep order. Of course, people claimed endorsement by everyone from God Almighty downwards, but for some reason we always relied on the Papal Aid Commission. And how could we doubt the word of a man of the cloth?' As the US agent La Vista reported, there was a flourishing black market in these documents. 'We will never know how many dealers were operating in Rome, repeatedly getting new Red Cross passports issued in invented names.' Admittedly, by the late 1940s the Americans were less concerned about escaping Nazis than 'that the communists are exploiting this opportunity to send their agents into the relevant countries'.

> There are large groups of German Nazis who come to Italy with the sole purpose of obtaining fictitious identity papers, passports and visas, so that they can then travel directly on via Genoa and Barcelona to Latin America.
> *Secret report of the US State department (La Vista Report)*

Ironically, it was from the Americans that Hudal received the money to pay for visas and steamer tickets. After the war, the National Catholic Welfare Conference in the USA injected financial aid directly into the national sub-committees of the Papal Aid Commission, and thus to Hudal as well. Then, all he had to do was obtain entry visas from hospitable countries. For these, Hudal usually applied to Argentina, whose dictator Juan Perón had always had a weakness for Nazi Germany. A Nazi counter-intelligence officer, Reinhard Kops, who had also fetched up in Rome, helped the bishop in this work. As Kops wrote in his memoirs: 'Bishop Hudal used me to sift through the new arrivals, as criminal elements had to be kept out, as far as possible. The onward transport of the others was then coordinated. In this connection, it was fortunate that at that time, as part of an extensive immigration agreement with Italy, the Argentine government of General Perón sent a man to Genoa as secretary. This man hailed from the [German-speaking but Italian-governed] South Tirol and had been a German officer during World War Two; his name was Franz Ruffinengo. The hand that Franz extended from Genoa, I grasped in Rome.' Franz Ruffinengo, a former officer, not in Hitler's army but that of Mussolini, worked in Genoa as secretary of the Argentine Immigration Commission in Europe (DAIE), an organisation secretly known among fleeing Nazis as an easy touch. What is more, the archbishop of Genoa, Guiseppe Siri, who held a protective hand over the refugees, had set up a committee specifically to get people out to Argentina. According to a report by a US agent, the Archbishop paid particular attention to the emigration of anti-communist Europeans to South America: 'This general classification of anti-communists applied, of course, to fascists, Ustashi and similar groupings.'

The Ustasha was the Croatian fascist organisation headed by Ante Pavelic, ruler of the (predominantly Catholic) 'Independent State of Croatia', which had been set up in 1941 with the blessing of Hitler and Mussolini. Backed by Ustasha battalions, concentration camps and other brutal means of repression, the regime had suppressed and murdered thousands of Serbs, Jews and Moslems. In 1945, the Ustashi abandoned Croatia in a headlong flight from Tito's partisans and sought help from the Papal Aid Commission in Rome. The man who took responsibility for them was Monsignor Krunoslav Stjepan Draganovic, a theologian at the Illyrian College of San Girolamo. Draganovic was an imposing figure: tall and dark-haired, always dressed in a long soutane, flowing overcoat and broad-brimmed clerical hat, he made a sinister and unnerving impression. 'There was something about his smooth and unctuous manner that I found very repugnant', remembers someone who met him in Rome at that time. 'He had snake-like eyes and a

In that unstable postwar period there were not many people who followed an unerring and righteous path. But there was surely no-one who greeted the young postwar emigrants with such generosity of spirit, such clear authority and unshakeable helpfulness as His Excellency Bishop Alois Hudal.

From the expatriate magazine Der Weg *(The Way), 1948*

The next day we discussed with the Genoese friends of my protector from the South Tirol, about how to board a ship illegally, without papers, as a so-called 'blind passenger'. It soon emerged that this was not as easy for the merchant-princes of Genoa to arrange as it had looked from a distance. Even calling in two ships' captains produced no solution. It turned out that the port of Genoa was then receiving the undivided attention of the Italian police. In the weeks that followed, some comrades of mine would discover this to their cost.

Juan Maler, alias Reinhard Kops, escape helper

wary look. I didn't like him at all.' During the war Draganovic, as a colonel in the Ustasha, had himself been responsible for the deportation of Jews and Serbs, and in 1944 had decamped to the Vatican. This poacher-turned-gamekeeper became a key figure in helping Nazis to escape.

Draganovic's contacts with Bishop Siri and the Genoa branch of the International Red Cross were worth their weight in gold. His most prominent protégé was Ante Pavelic himself, whose escape to Argentina he arranged. Draganovic had succeeded in persuading the Argentine immigration authorities to grant a quota of several hundred people from Croatia, whose entry was permitted without much checking. Mixed in among this group, with the approval of Draganovic, there were also some German Nazis. Hudal and Draganovic worked hand in hand, obtaining Red Cross passports, and establishing contact with consulates and port and shipping authorities. And if all else failed, the conspiratorial Bishop Hudal would make a personal appeal to Perón, as he did in a letter dated

31 August 1948. In it he asked for 5,000 visas for German and Austrian 'soldiers'. These were not refugees, Hudal declared, but fighters against communism, men whose 'self-sacrifice' had rescued Europe from Soviet domination during the war. Put in more direct language, he was requesting visas for German and Austrian Nazis.

> The first thing was to get hold of papers. Some friends found out that the easiest way was through a release-form from the British. It wasn't all that hard to get one, nicely stamped and signed, but with the rest blank. I added the details that I was from a Wehrmacht unit in Norway and was being freed and sent to Hamburg. I could even add any name I wanted. Just for a change I chose 'Hans Behrens'.
>
> *Juan Maler, alias Reinhard Kops*
>
> Roman Catholic priests, mainly Franciscans, helped 'Odessa' to smuggle escapers from monastery to monastery, until they could be received by the Caritas organisation in Rome.
>
> *Simon Wiesenthal, Nazi-hunter*

This was how hundreds of SS men were spirited away to Latin America, via what was known as the 'Monastery Line'. They included a number of the worst war criminals. In 1950 Adolf Eichmann, who was being hunted all over the world, escaped, in his own words, 'with the help of a Franciscan father in Genoa, who arranged a refugee passport and an Argentine visa for me in the name of Riccardo Klement'. The monk who signed his Red Cross passport was probably a Hungarian, Fr Edoardo Dömöter of the Community of San Antonio in Genoa, a close associate of Hudal. In 1948, Walter Kutschmann of the SS, who was accused of murdering thousands of Jews in Poland and of taking part in deportations from France, was given assistance by a Spanish Carmelite order. Disguised as a Carmelite monk he escaped through Spain to Argentina. It was probably Bishop Siri of Genoa who helped Walter Rauff to disappear to Syria. Another SS man, *Hauptsturmführer* Erich Priebke, was given identity papers by the Papal Aid Commission, in the name of Otto Pape. With these he was able to acquire a Red Cross passport. 'Of course I couldn't travel on my own passport', he explained later, 'which is why Bishop Hudal in the Vatican obtained a blank passport for me from the Red Cross.' Priebke had been a very close associate of the head of the Gestapo in Rome, and was involved in the massacre at the Ardeatine Caves near Rome, on 24 March 1944. In the worst wartime atrocity on Italian soil, 335 civilians were shot in the neck in reprisal for a partisan attack on SS soldiers of a South Tirolean police regiment. To this day there is also speculation that others whom the Church helped to escape included the concentration camp doctor, Josef Mengele, and Eichmann's 'top man' for Jewish deportations, Alois Brunner. Hudal later noted with pride in his memoirs that after 1945 he had 'devoted his entire charitable work principally to former supporters of National Socialism and Fascism, especially so-called war criminals . . . and quite a number I plucked from the hands of their tormentors, with false papers that enabled them to escape to happier countries.'

Either he helped many people, and among them some important Nazis, without knowing who they were; or he helped a few other people – and we know, of course, that he did do that – but concentrated on the Nazis in full knowledge of who and what they had been.

Bishop Jakob Weinbacher, Hudal's successor in Rome

Bishop Hudal was very close to Pope Pius XII – there is no doubt about that; they were friends.

Bishop Jakob Weinbacher

Bishop Hudal was not very close to the Vatican. He operated on the outer fringe. And he was certainly not close to the Holy Father. . . . People didn't take him seriously.

Fr Burkhart Schneider, Catholic historian

It is not known whether Pius XII himself helped any wanted SS men to escape along the 'Vatican Line' or the 'Monastery Line', or even whether he had any detailed information about this. The charge of helping Nazi escapers must still be laid chiefly at the door of Bishop Hudal. There was a network of various individuals and organisations in Italy, who maintained contact with senior office-holders in the Church and with Vatican institutions. The author Uki Goñi comes to the conclusion, in his latest investigation, that certain cardinals such as Giovanni Battista Montini, who later became Pope Paul VI, used their influence to smooth the path for escaping Nazis, and offered, as 'moral justification' for this, their sometimes pathological hatred of communism. Goñi writes: 'Bishops and archbishops like Hudal and Siri did after all make the necessary arrangements possible. Priests such as Draganovic, Heinemann and Dömöter signed the passport applications. In view of such unambiguous evidence as this, the question of whether Pope Pius XII was fully in the picture, is not only unimportant, it is also absurdly naïve.' At all events, every identity document signed by a man of the Church carried the crucial entry: 'Religious faith: Catholic.' Hitler's air-ace, Hans-Ulrich Rudel, wrote gratefully from Argentina: 'There were some of us who trailed through the Alps from monastery to monastery, dressed in monk's robes. One may take what attitude one likes to Catholicism. But the fact that, in those years, so many valuable members of our nation were rescued from certain death by the Church, and especially by individuals of outstanding personality within the Church, must rightly be remembered for ever!'

> On its own authority the Church let a great many people travel overseas. So in a quiet way, within the scope of what was possible, they counteracted the crazed thirst of the victors for revenge and retribution.
>
> *Hans-Ulrich Rudel, former colonel in the Luftwaffe*

The skill of the Church in helping Nazis on the run was admired in an unexpected quarter. Although the US secret service, the CIC, had identified Draganovic as a 'fascist and war criminal', it ended up doing business with him. The CIC needed travel documents and visas for agents whose disappearance from Europe was helpful to them. For a fee of $1,000 to $1,400 per head, Draganovic was happy to provide assistance. In return, the CIC turned a blind eye whenever the Croatian smuggled his Ustashi fascists out of the country. As early as 1947 the CIC had set up an escape route for its agents; in secret service slang it was known as the 'rat line'. When the Iron Curtain descended across Europe, the route was used to extract agents at risk in Eastern Europe and the Soviet-occupied zone of Austria. The 'rat line's' brilliant organiser was Jim Milano. Working with the CIC from its base in Salzburg, he billeted the agents in 'safe houses', fixed them up with false papers where possible, then smuggled them across the border to the Italian ports of Genoa or Naples, and on to a ship taking them overseas. 'It actually wasn't a problem getting passports that were either second-hand or belonged to people who'd died. You could buy them anywhere', said Jim Milano in a TV interview. 'The key was the visa.' However, when the 'rat line' was increasingly obstructed by the suspicious Soviets, the Americans called upon Draganovic's professional assistance. 'A colleague of mine came and told me: "Hey, there's a priest who can get hold of Red Cross passports." He was ideal for our needs. We called him "The Good Father".'

It was not until 1983 that their cover was blown, when it emerged that one of the agents on the CIC payroll had been Klaus Barbie, the Gestapo chief in Lyon, who had escaped along the 'rat line' and reached Bolivia in 1951. The 'Butcher of Lyon' was notorious for the barbarous interrogation methods he employed to extract confessions from his victims. He would submerge them in a bath of icy water, beat them with a whip or cudgel, administer injections, burn the soles of their feet with red-hot irons, stand them against a wall in mock-executions, or ram needles under their finger-nails. His speciality was electric-shock torture, in which electrodes were attached to the victim's nipples or testicles and a high-voltage current was shot through them. 'Barbie was a monster,' said one of his torture victims in the Resistance. 'He always had a whip in his hand. He beat people without a second thought, and ordered others to do the same. He conducted the interrogations in person. It really amused him to see others suffer.'

An honourable man, both intellectually and personally; totally
without nerves or fear.

From an internal CIC evaluation of Barbie

Mr Barbie is very important to the United States. He does
things that are dangerous.

Dick Lavoie, member of the CIC, 1948

As an SS *Hauptsturmführer*, Barbie was on the wanted lists of
both the French and the Americans when, in spring 1947, he
had the idea that would save him: he would cut a deal with the
Americans. The omens were favourable. The Cold War between
east and west had begun, and the fear of communist infiltration
suddenly made Himmler's former secret service and police
professionals of particular interest to the west. Jim Milano recalls
the precarious situation at that time: 'We simply knew very little
about the Russians, about their army, their tactics, battle-plans
and so forth, and there was a good deal of pressure on the secret
service to get hold of this information. The general attitude at
that time was that almost anything was permissible, in order to
gather intelligence.' Barbie made himself known to the CIC
(Counter-Intelligence Corps) of the US Army, who promptly hired
him as an informer. His initial assignment was to 'infiltrate the
Bavarian Communist Party'. Thus began a macabre double game,
in which US agents were, on one hand, zealously hunting down
war criminals for trial at Nuremberg, but behind the scenes were
tacitly making sure that 'valuable' men eluded their prosecutors.
Barbie soon became known as a jack-of-all-espionage-trades and
a brilliant interrogator. 'In view of the great value he was to our
organisation, we had no great pangs of conscience', one of his
American colleagues recalls. But when France called more and
more forcefully for Barbie's extradition and French detectives were
hot on his heels, the Americans found an elegant solution: they
arranged for Barbie, their now embarrassing agent, to disappear.
He quickly made contact with old SS comrades in Latin America,

worked closely with Friedrich Schwend and acted as adviser to the Bolivian secret service. Gradually it emerged that Barbie was far from being the only SS officer on the CIC's payroll. Since 1998 the CIA, successor-organisation to the CIC, has been releasing its documents on war criminals. Of the fourteen Nazi thugs whose personal dossiers were recently made public, nine had been in contact with the US secret services, including none other than the head of the Gestapo, Heinrich Müller. The documents show that after the war Müller was held in two different US internment camps and had been interrogated by the Americans for weeks on end. Then all trace of him vanishes.

The Americans in particular had an incredible talent for being taken in by tall, blond, blue-eyed Germans, simply because they looked exactly the way American officers used to look on the screen.

Simon Wiesenthal, Nazi-hunter

We knew what we were doing. It was absolutely necessary to use any sonafabitch we could. All that mattered was that he was anti-communist.

Harry Rositzke, Russian expert with the CIA

A complete exposure of Barbie's work . . . would admittedly not reveal any current secret service operations; it would, however, show the French that we have directed similar operations against them.

Note from the Office of the US High Commissioner for Germany, June 1950

Yet the secret services of the USA were not the only people to apply a double standard in respect of useful Nazis. In the summer of 1945, only weeks after the German surrender, the Supreme Command of the US Army decided 'to make new use of exceptionally bright Germans, whose continuing intellectual output we may be able to exploit'. Those they chiefly had in mind were experts on U-boat construction, military medicine, chemical warfare and rocket technology. The Americans wanted to tap the knowhow of these German experts before the Soviets did. That is how hundreds of Nazi scientists started a new career in the USA, instead of ending up in the dock at Nuremberg. They included Wernher von Braun and his entire team, who had designed and built Hitler's 'miracle-weapon', the V2 ballistic missile. The facts that von Braun, who headed the rocket research-centre at Peenemünde, was an SS officer, and that thousands of slave-labourers had been worked to death in the underground missile factory at Dora-Mittelbau, were scrupulously ignored. Yet even without official endorsement it was often relatively easy for 'anti-communists' to enter countries like the USA or Canada. A former member of the *Waffen*-SS explained how in 1950 he obtained a visa from the Canadian Consul-General, 'as I was a Christian and against the Bolshevists'. In 1953 a friend of Friedrich Schwend invited him to visit him in Los Angeles. 'There are really no longer any political worries', the friend wrote. 'On the contrary, we Germans are flavour of the month, regardless of whether we are former Nazis or not.' It was not until 1979, when the US Department of Justice set up the Office of Special Investigation (OSI) to hunt down Nazis in hiding, that a chill wind began to blow for Nazi war criminals living in the States. Fifty-six of them were expelled and a further sixty-eight were deprived of their citizenship. At the time of writing seventeen US citizens are on trial for war-crimes and another hundred and seventy cases are being investigated. Immigration bans were imposed by the USA on tens of thousands of former Nazis, including the former Austrian president and Secretary-General of the UN, Kurt Waldheim. Thus, almost six decades after the war's end, the USA is busy uncovering the network of escape routes for SS men that puts in the shade any secret organisation like 'Odessa'.

Today, the USA is not the only country to have confronted its 'murky' past. With a blessing from 'on high', Argentina had also been turned into a hideaway for fugitive Nazi criminals. The role

After the war I lived in Italy illegally. In late 1947 I was hiding in an Italian monastery. One day an American officer, who had found out where I was, came and said to me: 'We have more important things to do than look for you. We now have a common enemy. Do you want to work with us against international communism?' That was obviously a way out for me. The officer took me to Austria, where I worked with a CIC unit. I interrogated people, military personnel, who were escaping from Eastern Europe. Some of them were sent back to gather information about the political and military situation in the territories occupied by the Russians.

Karl-Heinz Hass, former SS man

that Argentina, and most of all its president, Juan Domingo Perón, played in helping Nazis to escape justice, has been described by the Argentinian writer Uki Goñi as 'the real Odessa'. In both world wars the country had harboured certain pro-German feelings. Juan Perón, who had been president since 1946, had a thoroughly benevolent attitude to Hitler and the Germans in general. He regarded the opening of the War Crimes Tribunals by the Allies with obvious distaste. Perón called Nuremberg 'an infamy' and 'the greatest monstrosity, which history will not pardon'.

Argentina was the most civilised country in Latin America. What is more, there had always been very close links between Argentina and Germany – there was a large German colony there. That is why it was so attractive.

Fabian Philipp, German journalist in Buenos Aires

The dictator set himself the objective of rescuing as many Nazis as possible from punishment. In this, a key part would be played by Perón's secret service chief, Rodolfo Freude, whose 'Information Bureau' was in the Casa Rosada, the presidential palace in Buenos Aires. Freude was a young, fair-haired Argentinian of German extraction. His father Ludwig, a German businessman, had been in close touch with the Nazis during the war, and especially with Germany's foreign intelligence service. He was also a close friend of Perón. Immediately after Perón took power a 'National Ethnic Institute' was founded, which was unmistakably anti-Semitic in character. Its staff looked into ways of preventing communist and Jewish emigrants from entering the country. Working hand-in-hand with this institute, Rodolfo Freude's secret service set about organising the escape of Nazis.

The most important figure pulling the strings behind these operations was a former SS *Hauptsturmführer*, a German-Argentinian named Horst Carlos Fuldner. Shortly before the end of the war, in March 1945, as a member of the German foreign SD (security service) he travelled to Madrid to explore escape-routes for SS men. In 1947, when the Allies demanded his extradition, he fled to Argentina. There he became an agent in Freude's 'Information Bureau' – with special responsibility for 'German immigration'. Among others he recruited Nazi 'technicians' for the Argentine air force. This was how Hitler's top airmen, like Adolf Galland, General of Fighter Aircraft, and Hans-Ulrich Rudel, the most highly decorated member of the Wehrmacht, found their way to Buenos Aires. But together with a series of war criminals from western Europe and Croatia, the most important task entrusted to Fuldner was rescuing Nazis, including German SS men. The Belgian, Pierre Daye, who was under sentence of death for collaborating with the Nazis in Brussels, wrote later: 'All those foreigners had been sentenced to death in their own countries. President Perón knew that, and I admire his independent spirit and the courage with which he received us at the presidential palace.' At the end of the operation, Fuldner could claim credit for facilitating the escape of such SS perpetrators as Adolf Eichmann, Josef Mengele, Erich Priebke, Josef Schwammberger and Gerhard Bohne.

It is said that Perón's beautiful and controversial wife Evita had prepared the ground for the 'rescue operation'. As a woman who loved elegant clothes and expensive jewellery, she had a thoroughly selfish interest in allowing high-spending Nazis into the country, or so rumour had it. On her trip to Europe in 1947,

> I ask timidly if it is all right to use my proper name. No, that would obviously not do. Half joking, I then say that the name 'Hans Meier' would be all right by me, or even Paul or Saul. The main thing was to get some kind of document together, so that I could travel to South America. The very next morning they bring me a document with the fine-sounding name of Emilio Meier! Well, I *had* said they could call me Meier if they liked. So now my name is Emil Meier and with this name I set off for Argentina.
>
> *Hans-Ulrich Rudel, former colonel in the Luftwaffe*

she made sure of a warm welcome from General Franco in Spain, from the Swiss and from Pope Pius XII. The Nazi-helper Horst Fuldner also arrived in Europe in December 1947 and made himself useful in the Argentine Immigration Office (DAIE) in Genoa, the port of departure for ships to Argentina. However, the headquarters of the Perón rescue team was set up in the Swiss capital, Bern, at Marktgasse 49. Officially it was there to recruit German 'technicians' for military projects in Argentina. After the war, German know-how in military technology, not to mention secret service contacts and underground work, was rated very highly in Buenos Aires. The Argentine military were discussing plans for building arms factories, war-planes and even nuclear weapons. Perón's great ambition was to turn Argentina into a major military and industrial power. 'Germany was defeated, we knew that', said Perón in 1970. 'And the victors wanted to take advantage of the enormous technological advances that the country had achieved over the previous ten years. The manufacturing plants could no longer be exploited, as they had been destroyed. The only thing they could make use of was the people.' Since approval from the Allies was required before men who had held office in the Axis Powers could be brought to Argentina, they would have to be smuggled in secretly. But these men were not just technicians, scientists and arms experts. The truth is that those running the 'Argentine Emigration Centre' were notorious Nazi sympathisers, who helped many SS men to escape. Their operations were financed by German and Austrian industrialists. Hardly any of the escapees were ordinary refugees from war. The Swiss authorities – in particular the Minister of Justice and the Chief of Police – turned a blind eye. Even the fact that many of these 'technicians' first had to be smuggled illegally out of Germany or Austria and into Switzerland before they could travel on to South America, did not worry the Swiss. Transit visas for the 'illegals' were issued without demur. When the office was finally closed down in the spring of 1949, Fuldner had enabled some 300 Nazis to escape, but of those scarcely 40 were genuine technicians.

Unfortunately, first-class Luftwaffe pilots are often lumped together by anti-German propaganda with Eichmann, Mengele, Schwammberger and other concentration camp personnel – the flotsam of war washed up on the shores of the Rio de la Plata. Here they had to survive as best they could. Eichmann was an ordinary worker in a car-factory outside Buenos Aires. None of them came to Argentina with a contract from Perón or even with support from secret organisations like 'The Spider' or 'Odessa'. I didn't either.

Wilfred von Oven, long-time assistant to Goebbels

Perón's 'Odessa' route could not have been simpler: first, an entry permit had to be obtained from the immigration authorities in Buenos Aires. This could be applied for by the escapee at any Argentine consulate in Europe. Nazi war criminals needed nothing more than a reference from someone working in Perón's 'Information Bureau', in order to obtain an entry permit in the required name, whether genuine or assumed, It is certainly no coincidence that Erich Priebke, alias Otto Pape, applied for his entry permit in 1948, at precisely the time when Carlos Fuldner was processing the papers at the Argentine Immigration Office in Genoa. On the same day, and with the consecutive number, the entry application for the 'Auschwitz Angel of Death', Josef Mengele, alias Helmut Gregor, was lodged with the immigration authorities in Buenos Aires. Since, at that time, something like

500 entry applications were arriving in Argentina every day, it is probable that Fuldner telexed both names simultaneously to Freude's office in the Casa Rosada. The precise route taken by these war criminals will admittedly remain for ever a secret; in 1996 the Argentine government ordered the destruction of all the relevant files. The writer Uki Goñi, who uncovered the whole process, wrote: 'It was at this moment, when two SS criminals simultaneously received their papers, that Perón's Nazi escape organisation most resembles the fictional "Odessa" of novels and films.' Only a few weeks later Adolf Eichmann and Josef Schwammberger applied for entry to Argentina.

In total, about 2,000 passports and 8,000 identity documents were issued.
Pietro Bianchi, member of Perón's diplomatic service and today defence counsel for the former SS man Erich Priebke

Most of them came under false names. They all had Red Cross passports with names like Meier, Kunz or Schmidt. But their real names were quite different.
Fabian Philipp, German journalist in Buenos Aires

In those days, human rights and morality meant absolutely nothing.

Fabian Philipp

The immigration authorities in Buenos Aires now had to telex their approval to the relevant consulate. The applicant could then go and pick up his permit. For SS war criminals on the run, this was usually arranged by emissaries of Perón's team in Europe, or by henchmen like Draganovic and Hudal. Armed with their permit, the escapees could apply to the Red Cross for a travel document, on which the consulate in turn stamped its visa. The last bureaucratic hurdle still to be surmounted was the Argentine Immigration Office in Italy, the DAIE. But as a rule no difficulties were encountered there either. The man who ran the DAIE office in Rome from 1946 onwards was a Salesian monk, José Clemente Silva. He had been given express instructions to organise the immigration of 4 million Europeans, in order to realise Perón's dream of an economic and social revolution. In Genoa, where the DAIE subjected would-be immigrants to a final medical check, the South Tirolean Franz Ruffinengo, of whom mention has already been made, acted as a Robin Hood figure to those who claimed to have been 'deprived of their rights'. With that the way was open for the journey to Argentina, new identity and all. Not only did more than 2 million immigrants ultimately find their way to Perón's Argentina; as an escape route for SS perpetrators it functioned brilliantly. On 23 October 1948 the steamer *San Giorgio* left the port of Genoa – carrying with it Erich Priebke and his family. On 19 July 1949 Josef Mengele travelled to Argentina; in his luggage was a small case containing his 'research' notes from Auschwitz. On 14 July 1950 Adolf Eichmann, alias Riccardo Klement, landed in Buenos Aires, the 'gateway to hope' of a new life.

When I think about it, I'm convinced in the end that to have held out any longer in Germany at that juncture would have done us no good whatsoever.

Hans-Ulrich Rudel, former colonel in the Luftwaffe

To tell the truth, they were all dirt poor. The exception was Mengele. He came from a family that owned a factory making farm machinery. There was money there and his father supported him.

Fabian Philipp, German journalist in Buenos Aires

The notion that these refugees from the SS had set up a branch of 'Odessa' on the Rio de la Plata belongs to the realm of fantasy. Nonetheless, it is true that contact between 'old comrades' was not broken off, even in the New World, which meant that the rumour-mill kept on turning. In May 1948 Franz Ruffinengo also arrived in Argentina. He decided to profit from his contacts and opened a travel bureau in Buenos Aires. It soon became very popular in German-Argentinian circles, and business boomed. As Reinhard Kops, who now called himself Juan Maler, wrote: 'This success was, of course, immediately interpreted, in a series of cooked-up stories on both sides of the Atlantic, as conspiratorial activity by the "Argentine Nazis". It was supposed to have its origins in a totally fictitious organisation called "Odessa", which had helped the criminals to get to South America.' Kops, who was a close collaborator of Hudal's in helping Nazis to flee, had himself managed to escape to the sunny climes of Argentina in September 1948. He found employment with a Nazi magazine called *Der Weg* (The Way), the favourite rag of Nazi fugitives, with a clearly anti-Semitic slant. Its main function was to glorify the SS.

Der Weg was published by the Dürer publishing company, whose premises were a popular rendezvous for SS men on the run. *Der Weg* kept in touch with prominent Nazi criminals like Josef Mengele and Adolf Eichmann and was a mouthpiece for racists, such as the former editor of the National Socialist organ, *Wille und Weg* (Will and Way), the anti-Semitic agitator Johann von Leer. It was emigrants from the *Waffen*-SS who had particularly selected the magazine as their campaign platform. For a while a group of SS veterans used to meet regularly in the Hotel zur Post in Buenos Aires. Two hundred former members of the SS supported each other with help and advice, gave warning of international search operations, and promoted National Socialist ideas. With extremist rhetoric they attempted to rehabilitate the *Waffen*-SS in the pages of *Der Weg*: 'We men of the *Waffen*-SS do not care a damn about the right to vote, the rule of law, democracy and the four freedoms, so long as the memory of thousands of our comrades is preserved in the much-vaunted "lawful states". For us the rule of law still begins with iron bars.' *Der Weg* was soon selling 20,000 copies per issue – with circulation in Germany and Austria – and gained the reputation of being the organ of the 'Fourth Reich'.

Because of his close connections with Nazi war criminals, the 'Comrades' Welfare' society founded by Hans-Ulrich Rudel was also widely regarded as a 'Nazi front organisation in Argentina'.

Simon Wiesenthal even equates it with 'Odessa'. The purpose of the association was to support imprisoned war criminals and their families in Germany. In Argentina and Chile Rudel collected money from 'willing and generous donors who were concerned about the fate of the ostracised and reviled, yet often the most loyal sons of their country, who were simply victims of victors' justice'. The proceeds went towards legal costs, and paid for parcels of food and clothing. 'It was not long before the good heart of the overseas German community showed itself', wrote Rudel. 'By Christmas 1951 we were able to send off 1,500 parcels.' Among the families receiving 'care parcels' like this from Argentina were those of Hitler's deputy, Rudolf Hess, and the man who briefly succeeded him as Führer, Grand-Admiral Doenitz. There is no doubt that 'Comrades' Welfare' was imbued with Nazi thinking and campaigned for a general amnesty for political prisoners in Germany. Rudel himself was a good friend of Perón and a successful businessman. His closest associate was the SS man Willem Sassen, who had been sentenced to death in Belgium. As advisers and arms-dealers the two maintained excellent relations with Latin American dictators like Paraguay's Alfredo Stroessner and Augusto Pinochet of Chile. In conjunction with Josef Mengele, Rudel investigated the market in Latin America for the agricultural machinery built by Mengele's family firm in Bavaria. The Nazi elite in Argentina remained loyal to each other, chatted over coffee and cakes and toasted the 'good old days' at 'brownshirt' parties. However, there is no available evidence to prove that 'Comrades' Welfare' did anything more than send parcels and provide social support.

Another front organisation for helping Nazi fugitives was the CAPRI Group. With the support of President Perón and businessmen of German ancestry, the conspiratorial Horst Carlos Fuldner set up an industrial development company called the *Compañia Argentina para Proyectos y Realizaciones Industriales*, or CAPRI for short. The firm employed expelled German engineers and other specialists on government-funded energy and irrigation projects. Nearly all the senior staff of CAPRI were postwar German immigrants. What is more, CAPRI also provided the perfect cover for SS officers and political fugitives on international 'wanted' lists. Such people were not required to offer any specific skills. For a while Adolf Eichmann was employed by CAPRI under his assumed name of Riccardo Klement.

I have seen that swine Eichmann, who pushed the Jews around. He lives near Buenos Aires and works for a water company.

Anonymous tip-off, 1952

I knew as early as 1953 that Eichmann was living in Argentina. I just didn't have first-hand evidence. Finally in 1954 I found someone who was willing to identify Eichmann. But for that I needed $1,800. I had $1,300. I only needed another $500. So I wrote to the then president of the World Jewish Congress, Nahum Goldmann, asking him for the money. But Goldmann and his colleague, Rabbi Abraham Kalmanowitz, believed Eichmann was hiding in Syria. They considered the risk of lending me the $500 too great. So they refused.

Simon Wiesenthal, Nazi-hunter

But the man who painstakingly organised the deportation of millions of Jews to the death camps proved to be pretty inept; he was soon out of his depth and turned in sloppy work. 'In technical work he was a complete washout', says a former colleague of his, Heinz Lühr. One day when Lühr asked Eichmann's wife, in some surprise, why her husband was so tight-lipped about his past, her reply was: 'Leave him in peace. He's been through some difficult times, very difficult.' Eichmann never managed to establish himself successfully in South America. He kept his head above water doing odd jobs, and before he was abducted by Mossad on 11 May 1960 he had been making a living as a car-mechanic, foreman and rabbit-breeder in the pampas. The word 'remorse' was unknown to him. In 1956 he confessed to a fellow-Nazi, Willem Sassen: 'I'm gradually getting tired of living as a vagrant between different worlds . . . I would be only too ready to present myself to the

German authorities, if it wasn't for my concern that their interest in the political side of the matter might not still be too great for a clear objective outcome to be achieved. . . . I was nothing more than a loyal, proper, correct and hard-working member of the SS and Central Office of Reich Security – motivated only by the ideals of my Fatherland, to which I had the honour of belonging. In my own mind I was never a bastard, nor a traitor. Despite conscientious self-examination I have to conclude that I was neither a murderer nor a mass murderer.' The fugitive Eichmann sought refuge in concepts like 'oath to the flag' and 'performance of duty'.

Looking at the people at CAPRI who came from the SS, you could tell they had once worn the black uniform. And there was even a rumour that my personnel manager, who had been an SS officer himself, wanted to command an SS *Standarte* again.

Heinz Lühr, Eichmann's boss at a water-works in Buenos Aires

My guilt was obedience.

Adolf Eichmann

He was the book-keeper of death.

Simon Wiesenthal, about Eichmann

Even though the SS community demonstrably kept up contact with each other and gave each other mutual help and protection, no such thing as a tightly organised secret network ever existed. As long as Perón held a protecting hand over the Nazi criminals, they really had no need of an 'Odessa'. In July 1949 the dictator went as far as issuing a general amnesty for foreign residents who had entered Argentina illegally. No questions were asked about their past. One of those who then showed up at the immigration authorities was Otto Pape, who claimed that up to the end of the war he had been in hiding in the German embassy in Rome. Thus Otto Pape once again became Erich Priebke, and all quite legally.

He settled in one of the many colonies of German immigrants in Argentina, which had turned into sanctuaries for Nazi fugitives. Priebke chose San Carlos de Bariloche, a picturesque ski-resort in the Andes, where Reinhard Kops had already settled, and Josef Mengele often came to stay. Here Priebke enjoyed a peaceful existence, opened a delicatessen and even became chairman of the German-Argentine Cultural Association. He travelled around the world often, even to Germany, and regularly renewed his passport at the German embassy in Buenos Aires. Everything went well until 1994, when he openly admitted to an American television crew, who were actually looking for Reinhard Kops, that he had taken part in the massacre at the Ardeatine Caves in Rome, and described how he had shot two Italians with his own hand. 'Things like that happened then', he said. 'In those days, young man, orders were orders. D'you understand?' The interview produced an outcry across the world. An extradition request from the Italian government quickly followed, and was granted by Argentina in November 1995. On 7 March 1998 a court in Rome sentenced Priebke to house-arrest for the remainder of his life. Since then the SS men still living in Argentina have become more cautious.

> For the past twenty years he has moved around in complete freedom. Everyone knew who he was, where he was going and where he came from.
> *Andreas Schulz, Priebke's lawyer in Berlin, 1996*

One of the most charismatic figures in the web of legend spun around the 'Odessa' myth is Hitler's 'miracle weapon', Otto Skorzeny. To this day the rumour persists that he was the head of 'Odessa' in Spain. Born in Austria, he was one of the first people in his country to join the Nazi Party. In 1939 he signed on with the SS *Leibstandarte Adolf Hitler* and later fought in the SS *Das Reich* division in France, Yugoslavia and on the eastern front. Finally he was appointed by the Central Office of Reich Security as a special agent engaged in sabotage behind enemy lines. Surprise attacks, abductions and murder were everyday activities for Skorzeny's strike-force, whom the Allies dubbed

'Hitler's Commandos'. Six foot tall, with a duelling-scar from ear to chin, the SS *Standartenführer* achieved ultimate fame as the 'audacious hero' on 12 September 1943. On that day, according to the propaganda, he led a team of German paratroopers who spectacularly freed Benito Mussolini from a mountain hotel in the inaccessible Gran Sasso massif, where he had been imprisoned by the new Italian government. 'I have been sent by the Führer', he is said to have announced to a dazed Mussolini. For this operation, Hitler personally decorated Skorzeny with the Knight's Cross. However, the paratroopers who had taken part were furious, claiming later that Skorzeny had just come along for the ride; and only after the Duce had been liberated did he step into the limelight and seize the honour for himself. Be that as it may, the 'Hero of Gran Sasso' became an icon to all those who hoped that daring commando raids like this would turn the war in Germany's favour again. Furthermore, he became a propaganda mouthpiece for all the fanatical slogans about fighting on to the death. Skorzeny carried out an equally daring abduction of the son of Admiral Horthy, the ruler of Hungary, whom Hitler wanted to blackmail into maintaining his alliance with Germany. Then in the winter of 1944–5, during the Ardennes campaign, Skorzeny led a group of saboteurs behind enemy lines, dressed in US army uniforms. Among his comrades-in-arms he finally achieved near-legendary status.

In the last days of the war Skorzeny withdrew to the 'Alpine Redoubt'; there, in May 1945, he fell into the hands of the Americans, who charged him with the murder of US prisoners-of-war during the Ardennes offensive. However, in August 1947 he was acquitted by a US military court. While in prison Skorzeny had been interrogated by American intelligence officers for hours on end, and the transcripts fill several ring-binders. Then, as he still had to go through a de-nazification process, he was detained in an internment camp near Darmstadt. According to later statements by Skorzeny, both the US and Soviet secret services offered him the opportunity to collaborate with them. At that time a request for his extradition had already been issued by Czechoslovakia, where he was to be put on trial for war crimes. Many years later, Skorzeny was keen to explain in considerable detail how he managed to escape from prison. As he wrote in his memoirs: 'I am reluctant to go on talking about my "escape". On 27 July 1948 I set off on my own; I got away without wire-cutters or a rope-ladder, without bribery or help from others. I took a determined step towards a new life, towards freedom.' Yet shortly before he died in 1975, Skorzeny told his biographer, Glenn Infield, a different story: three SS officers, whom Skorzeny had contacted earlier, apparently drove up to the prison in Darmstadt, dressed as US military policemen, in a car with American number-plates. 'We've come to collect prisoner Skorzeny for tomorrow's hearing in Nuremberg', they explained to a confused guard, and took Skorzeny away without further ado. It was as easy as that. In his cell Skorzeny left behind a farewell letter with the portentous words: 'I believe it will be impossible for the court to come to a just decision, because it will have to bow to stronger pressures from outside. I have but one wish, and that is to live with honour in this my Fatherland.'

It seems that, even during his imprisonment, Otto Skorzeny had already begun building up an underground SS organisation, which appears in the files of the US secret service, first as the 'Skorzeny Movement', than as the 'Brotherhood', and finally as 'Odessa'. In one confidential report by the US military police to the European headquarters of the secret service we read: 'A group of former SS men and paratroopers have formed an underground movement headed by Otto Skorzeny. According to reliable sources its headquarters are located in the Tirol, Austria. This movement has two objectives. Firstly: active resistance against Bolshevism. Secondly: removal of the western occupying powers.' Later, an undercover agent pointed to the existence of 'Odessa' in a top-secret report dated 20 January 1947: 'The leader of this group is Otto Skorzeny, who runs it from the camp at Dachau, where he is interned. The men who take their orders from Skorzeny are being helped by the Polish guards to escape.' For the onward escape-route from Germany to Italy, Skorzeny had allegedly created the organisation known as 'The Spider', in which his accomplices had developed an elaborate system of 'safe houses' throughout Germany. According to Simon Wiesenthal, the fugitives were transported around Austria and Germany in the very same US army trucks that were used by German civilian employees to distribute the American army newspaper *Stars and Stripes*. 'That meant that a military policeman would at most take a quick look in the back of the truck and see bundles of newspapers. What he didn't see were the men crouching behind the bundles, holding their breath so as not to be heard; what he was unaware of was that the truck-driver was a member of "Odessa"'. Initially, the escape-route was said to run through southern Germany to Austria or Switzerland and then to Italy. Later it went from the port of Bremen directly to Rome or Genoa.

Despite his acquittal by a US court, Skorzeny's name was still on the list of those wanted by the UN. The details of Skorzeny's escape, narrated by Glenn Infield after interviewing him in person, sound pretty far-fetched. In 1949 he apparently travelled to Argentina in order to stake his claim to the secret treasure of the Third Reich: the money, gold and jewellery that had belonged to the Jews murdered in death camps, and which Hitler's secretary, Martin Bormann, was said to have entrusted to Juan Perón. According to Infield, the dashing SS officer even succeeded in seducing the beautiful Evita and what is more, managed to secure part of the 'Nazi hoard' for himself and for 'Odessa'. Infield does not name his sources for this information. We must presume that Skorzeny was simply pulling the author's leg.

In 1997, a later president of Argentina, Carlos Menem, was forced by public pressure to set up a Commission of Enquiry into Nazi Activities in Argentina (CEANA). Its remit included an investigation of the legendary 'Nazi gold'. But after two years of research the commission was only able to show that Argentina had been a refuge for at least 180 Nazi criminals, although the unofficial figure is vastly higher than that. Of 'Nazi gold' there was not a trace. However, since most of the files in Argentina had been destroyed, and given the doubtful independence of a commission answerable to a Peronist government, this does not say much. At all events, in 1950 Skorzeny finally arrived in Madrid, where he operated under the name of Rolf Steinbauer, both as a representative of German and Austrian industrial companies, and as an arms-dealer. He travelled widely and kept in touch with the 'old comrades' of the SS. In addition to the fact that the Austrian 'likes to drink his whisky almost neat', even the US secret service could only establish that it was 'very possible that Skorzeny knows the whereabouts of many wanted Germans, who have left Germany by secret routes in order to conceal their identity'.

Before long the devious Otto Skorzeny was given an opportunity to extend a helping hand to one of the most brutal mass murderers of the Third Reich. In 1953, Egypt's ambitious new ruler, Colonel Gamal Abd el-Nasser asked the Americans to help him build up a military intelligence service and an internal security force. The CIA had long since ceased to have any scruples about making use of Nazi criminals in their covert activities. The case of Klaus Barbie was not an isolated one. Yet it was not always opportune to publicise American involvement, particularly when it concerned the crisis-torn Middle East. Hence, in particularly sensitive matters, the Americans preferred to call on the services of a former general in the Wehrmacht, Reinhard Gehlen, whose organisation – the forerunner of today's Federal German Intelligence Service – they had been backing since 1946. Since the defeat of Nazi Germany, Hitler's spy-chief for the war in the east, together with his files of explosive information, had been at the service of the USA. His espionage network in the Soviet Union, not to mention his links with former SS men, were worth their weight in gold to the Americans. The man Gehlen picked for the job in Egypt was Otto Skorzeny. In the course of the next year and a half Skorzeny activated his lines to the SS escapee groups and Nazi associations and recruited some 100 Germans for the Egyptian secret service. Most of these were former SS or Gestapo personnel. According to research by the American Nazi-expert, Christopher Simpson, one of the recruits was a man named Alois Brunner. After Adolf Eichmann, Brunner was the most notorious 'final-solutionist' of the Third Reich and one of the most wanted war criminals of them all.

Brunner's career leaves a trail of blood all across Europe. In 1938 he was Eichmann's closest associate in the 'Centre for Jewish Emigration' in Vienna. Under Eichmann's instructions he organised the deportation of Austrian Jews to the extermination camps. Soon he became Eichmann's 'clearance expert' for difficult cases. Whenever there was a hold-up in deportations somewhere, Brunner was sent into action – be it Salonika, Paris, Nice or Bratislava. Wherever he turned up, he was shortly able to report proudly to his chief that the city was 'free of Jews'. In all, Brunner sent more than 120,000 human beings to their death. His precise escape-route remains uncertain to this day. At first he went to ground in Germany for a few years, using the name Alois Schmaldienst. Even when imprisoned by the British and Americans his cover was not blown. For a while he even worked as a driver with the US occupation forces. At the beginning of 1954 he was sentenced to death in France – *in absentia*. When things got too hot for Brunner, he left Germany. His friend, a former SS *Hauptsturmführer* named Georg Fischer, gave him his passport. After some minor cosmetic surgery Brunner even looked like Fischer's passport photo. The new Georg Fischer then took a train to Amsterdam and from there fled to Rome. Exactly who helped him in the Eternal City remains a matter for speculation. But we may assume that Bishop Hudal believed the injunction to 'love thy neighbour' included Brunner too. At all events, Brunner travelled direct from Rome to Cairo on a tourist visa.

Egypt was an ideal refuge for Nazi criminals, as indeed was the whole Middle East. The saying there was: 'He who is an enemy of the Jews is our friend', particularly as the foundation of the state of Israel in 1948 was regarded by the Arabs as an affront. Thus German experts were welcome in the secret services, the military and propaganda ministries. However, after three months Brunner's visa expired and he made his way to Syria – another safe haven for stranded Nazis. In Damascus the murderer set up home and began working on shady business deals, including arms-trading. When Brunner was finally hired by the Syrian secret service in 1960, he knew he was safe from extradition. If Brunner is still alive, he has escaped prosecution to this day. In postwar Germany the wheels of justice have ground slowly and with little enthusiasm. Too often the need for just retribution has been forgotten. It is true that in the early 1960s Austria issued warrants for Brunner's arrest and made an extradition request to Syria, but the half-hearted efforts to find him petered out. Investigations in Germany dragged on endlessly. In 1984 the Public Prosecutor in Cologne finally issued an arrest warrant followed by an extradition order, but they produced no result. However, others clearly knew where he was hiding: in June 1961, when a parcel was handed to him at the main post-office in Damascus, the bomb inside it exploded. Brunner survived but was seriously injured and lost his left eye. Twenty years later, in July 1980, another parcel-bomb blew off both his hands. In 1985, when the wanted war criminal had the effrontery to give an interview to the German picture-magazine, *Bunte*, it provoked a storm of outrage among Brunner's surviving victims. The Federal German judiciary took no action; not even a 'wanted' poster was printed. Brunner has been declared dead several times already – but the hunt for him is still on. Many similar cases can be documented. They are the result of a fatal policy towards the past: aiding fugitives by default.

I am prepared to stand before an international court and answer for myself. The only country that will never get me is Israel. I refuse to be another Eichmann.

Alois Brunner, 1985

If Eichmann drafted the staff plan for the destruction of the Jews, it was Brunner who made it happen. They are like twin stars of death. . . . Of all the criminals of the Third Reich who are still alive, Alois Brunner is without doubt the worst.

Simon Wiesenthal, Nazi-hunter

The Federal Republic owes me a whole lot of pension.

Alois Brunner, Damascus, 1985

From the outset, there were German protests against 'victors' justice' and de-nazification by the Allies. But with the intensification of the Cold War and the beginning of the Korean War, 'cleaning up' ceased to be a priority even for the Allies. The rearmament of Federal Germany and its integration in the Western Alliance were now at the top of the agenda. Among the groups concerned with the welfare of Nazi criminals the most prominent was the SS veterans' association, *Stille Hilfe* (Silent Aid). After working covertly for years it was officially founded on 15 November 1951. Its board of directors was made up of high-ranking former SS officers together with luminaries of the Evangelical and Catholic churches. The first president of the association was Princess Helene Elisabeth von Isenburg, affectionately known as 'Mother of the Landsbergers', referring to the ex-Nazi inmates of Landsberg jail.

A strict Catholic, who had once been classified by a local branch of the Nazi party as 'politically reliable', she discovered a fellow-feeling for the war criminals locked up by the Allies in Landsberg Castle. There were some 1,600 prisoners there; they had been sentenced in the trials that followed the Nuremberg Tribunal, and included members of SS *Einsatzgruppen*, the Gestapo and the German general staff, as well as leading industrialists. The princess tirelessly pleaded the cause of the 'victims of victors' justice', even with the Pope himself – with active support from Hans-Ulrich Rudel's 'Comrades' Welfare'. This brought her under suspicion of helping Nazi fugitives and of being a part of 'Odessa'. Her contacts with overseas SS groups, such as the one in Scandinavia, fed the rumours. At all events 'Mother Elisabeth' was successful: under vociferous pressure from the German federal government, as well as from lobbyists of *Stille Hilfe*, almost all the high-security prisoners in Berlin's Spandau jail were released after a time. In February 1951, following a decree of clemency by the US High Commissioner, John McCloy, 92 of the remaining 142 convicted Landsberg prisoners were released, though there was a storm of protest in Germany when the last 7 war criminals were hanged in Landsberg on 7 June 1951.

> In silent, positive assistance, to help all those who, as a consequence of wartime and postwar conditions, have forfeited their liberty through imprisonment, internment or similar circumstances where they cannot speak for themselves.
> *From the articles of association of 'Silent Aid'*

> A true mother to those abandoned by everyone else.
> *Hans-Ulrich Rudel, about Princess Helene von Isenburg*

However, the old SS comrades in Germany continued with their intrigues. A new network was founded under the name *Hilfsgemeinschaft auf Gegenseitigkeit, Bundesverband der Soldaten der Ehemaligen Waffen-SS* (Federal Mutual Aid Association of Former Soldiers of the *Waffen*-SS), or HIAG for short. In this society old members of the SS were able to glorify the Nazi regime and boast about their war experiences to their heart's content. They could sound off with such pearls of wisdom as: 'Life is a battle in every way – and the world is merciless enough to trample over anyone who is not ready and willing to accept that law of life.' In 1956 HIAG also gained official recognition as a registered association. Within a very short time it could claim hundreds of local and regional groups. For many years its president was the SS general, Kurt Meyer, affectionately known as 'Panzer Meyer'. Until his death in 1961, he campaigned for the rehabilitation of the *Waffen*-SS. HIAG took the view that members of the *Waffen*-SS had been soldiers like any others and had had nothing to do with the crimes of the general SS. 'We knew nothing about the atrocities,' said a spokesman for HIAG, 'and we are grateful to the government in power at the time for maintaining effective secrecy.' Right up to the 1970s the SS association had considerable influence on ex-army and nostalgia societies, as well as on political parties. For many years, a former member of the *Leibstandarte Adolf Hitler*, Hans Wissebach, sat in the federal parliament, the Bundestag, as a deputy in the right-of-centre Christian Democratic Union. Wissebach was a spokesman for HIAG. True, HIAG was dissolved in 1992, but its journal, *Der Freiwillige* (The Volunteer) is still published. In 1952, alongside HIAG, the 'Viking Youth' was founded on the lines of the Hitler Youth, to ensure the growth of a new 'brownshirt' generation. It was not banned until 1994.

This sniffing out of Nazis has got to stop.
Chancellor Konrad Adenauer, 1952

There can be no future unless light is shed on the past.
Efraim Zuroff, Nazi-hunter

The foundation of the Federal Republic seemed to offer the Germans a welcome opportunity to draw a line under the past, as they supposed. For Germany's first postwar chancellor, Konrad Adenauer, the re-integration of many active supporters of the Nazi regime was a prerequisite for rebuilding his country. 'You don't throw away dirty water when you have no clean', was how he rationalised it. That was why former members of the Nazi elite were among those given office and honour in the young Federal Republic. As early as 1952 the so-called '131st law' enabled former Nazi officials, even members of the Gestapo, to be accepted in the civil service. The climax came in 1954 with the Law on Exemption from Punishment. In the opinion of the historian Norbert Frei, this law meant that by the mid-1950s scarcely anyone needed to fear 'being pestered by the state and the judiciary about their Nazi past. Almost everyone was now absolved of their guilt.' What followed was a 'creeping' amnesty. In 1960 the Bundestag confirmed the statute of limitation for crimes of manslaughter under Nazism, and in 1968 this was even extended to being an accessory to murder. At that point the trials of some 300 former members of the Central Office of Reich Security had to be abandoned, even though those in Eichmann's department had organised the Holocaust. Had Eichmann been put on trial in Germany instead of Israel, he would possibly not have been convicted. However, the investigation of Nazi crimes in Germany was still very actively pursued by the Centre for the Prosecution of National Socialist Crimes, in Ludwigsburg. It is true that after the war over 100,000 criminal prosecutions were initiated, but only 6,500 people were ever convicted; of those only 12 received the death-penalty and 163 were sentenced to life imprisonment. Many criminals got away with it. Quite a number of them are still living as free citizens today.

Finding this intolerable, Nazi-hunters have been active all over the world, in the hope of bringing the war criminals to justice. The Israeli secret service, Mossad, made headlines in 1960 when it abducted Adolf Eichmann from Argentina. The paper-pushing manager of the Final Solution was tried and sentenced to death in Jerusalem and executed in Tel Aviv on 1 June 1962. Hunting for Nazi criminals was also the life's work of a married German couple, Serge and Beate Klarsfeld. It was their dogged research that led to the arrest of Klaus Barbie in 1983. When Serge Klarsfeld was the victim of a bomb-attack in the 1970s, a letter claiming responsibility was received from 'Odessa'.

My assignment in March 1960 was quite simple; I was given a street and house-number in Buenos Aires and had to see if it was true the Eichmann family was living there. That was all. I drove over there and saw right away that the house was standing empty, and if Eichmann *had* ever lived there, he was gone. But then I heard later that the Eichmanns had lived in Chacabuco for years, and had moved exactly two weeks before I got there.

Zvi Aharoni, Mossad agent

An escape organisation like 'Odessa' wasn't really necessary – the Nazi war criminals were able to go on living in Germany unmolested.

Beate Klarsfeld, Nazi-hunter

A New York private detective named Steven Rambam describes himself as only a part-time Nazi-hunter. But he is a successful one: his investigations led to the conviction in 2001 of the SS officer Julius Viel, for the murder of Gestapo prisoners in Bohemia. But probably the most legendary of all Nazi-hunters is the death camp survivor, Simon Wiesenthal. According to his figures, his documentation centre has brought a total of 1,200 fugitive Nazi perpetrators to trial.

Tracking down Nazi criminals is 'a race against time', says Wiesenthal's successor, Efraim Zuroff, who runs the Simon Wiesenthal Institute in Jerusalem. The guilty men are dying off. Zuroff does not look like a Nazi-hunter, more like an office manager, with his smart suit and tie, neatly parted hair and slightly tinted glasses. He sees himself as pursuing Nazis from behind his desk, accurately and relentlessly uncovering their past, over many years if necessary. When fugitive SS perpetrators hit the headlines, Zuroff has often been behind it: he was the one who found out that, contrary to all the rumours, the Auschwitz doctor, Josef Mengele, had died in Brazil. Currently Zuroff is mainly active in eastern Europe. 'The Holocaust was a Europe-wide phenomenon,' he says. He is a long way from giving up: 'There are still Nazi perpetrators alive who have probably killed six times as many people as Osama bin Laden has; they all ought to be convicted.' In the last few years the hunt for the remaining Nazi criminals has gained momentum everywhere. Even German investigators have displayed growing determination. In 1987 the former SS *Obersturmführer* Josef Schwammberger, who once ran a death camp in Poland, was arrested in Argentina, and in 1992 was tried in Germany on multiple murder charges and sentenced to life imprisonment. In 2002, Friedrich Engel, former head of the security police in Genoa, was sentenced to seven years imprisonment for the brutal killing of Italian prisoners in May 1944. Wiesenthal once summed up the motivation for his implacable hunting down of the criminals in a kind of parable: 'In the Hereafter we Jews will meet the victims of the Holocaust. The victims will ask: "What did you do in life?" One of us will say: "I was a lawyer." The next: "I was a school-teacher." And I will say: "I did not forget you."'

It is quite natural that if you belong to the SS, you're part of a big family. Whether you're now in Greece, Germany, Holland or Denmark, it makes no difference. By now we're all over eighty, and young people are joining us, but the hard core keeps together like the Cossacks used to do.

Florentine Rost van Tonningen, widow of a Dutch Nazi leader

Today there is a kind of 'brownshirt solidarity' that makes sure the memory of the perpetrators is not allowed to fade either. The soul of the SS 'Silent Aid' society is embodied by a woman named Gudrun Burwitz. As the daughter of Heinrich Himmler, she holds court among her admirers at events put on by old and neo-Nazis, for example at the annual memorial ceremony for old comrades of the *Freikorps und Bund Oberland*, held at the Bavarian lake resort of Schliersee, or the gathering of SS veterans at Ulrichsberg in southern Austria. Every October Nazis young and old from all over Europe make a pilgrimage to this ancient site of Celtic worship, to pay homage to the 'ideals' of National Socialism. To the woman whom Himmler called *Püppi* (Dolly), her father is still a hero.

> One does not begin a new life with a lie. I am still Gudrun Himmler.
>
> *Gudrun Burwitz in the 1950s*

True to the SS motto 'Loyalty is our honour', the 'Silent Aid' society, which was finally deprived of its charitable status as recently as 1999, still provides support for imprisoned war criminals and arranges money and legal counsel for its members. Among those who benefited from the charity of this network was the former SS *Oberscharführer* Anton Malloth. Back in 1948 he was sentenced to death in Czechoslovakia for the murder of concentration camp inmates, and was subsequently pursued all over Europe for having supervised the police jail known as 'The Little Theresienstadt Fortress'. It now emerges that from 1988 onwards, with support from 'Silent Aid' he lived in an old people's home near Munich, untouched by the German judiciary. Not until 2001 was he sentenced to imprisonment for the remainder of his life. But 'Silent Aid' still looks after him. And it continues to stand by other 'victims' such as Josef Schwammberger and Erich Priebke, who, since his conviction in 1998, has been under house-arrest in Italy. As 'Silent Aid' explained: 'Upright and soldierly, Priebke shows the world what a true German is.'

By now the search for runaway Nazis is turning into a ghost-hunt: if still alive, Alois Brunner would be more than ninety years old, and 'Gestapo-Müller' would have passed his century. But anyone who believes that with the death of the last perpetrators the SS networks have been broken up, is making a mistake. At an early stage the old SS associations were cultivating a new crop of brownshirts. Modelled on 'Silent Aid', the 'Aid Organisation for National Political Prisoners' (HNG) was founded in 1979 to look after imprisoned neo-Nazis. According to the German constitutional authorities, the sympathies of the HNG are expressly for prison inmates 'who have, out of political conviction, committed acts of arson against accommodation for asylum-seekers, inflicted bodily harm or been guilty of other criminal behaviour'. Providing them with 'welfare' is a perfect cover for the recruitment of new neo-Nazi troops. These young thugs also draw their exemplars from the past, in SS men like Erich Priebke and Josef Schwammberger. The fact that '"Silent Aid" has always had the function of providing an example to the extreme right', was once confirmed by Christian Worch, a neo-Nazi with several previous criminal convictions. A former officer in the BDM (the girls' equivalent of the Hitler Youth), Gertrude Herr, and her adopted son, the extreme right-wing lawyer and neo-Nazi leader Jürgen Rieger, are both active promoters of neo-Nazism among Germany's youth. Together they have founded a number of dubious societies and set up hostels, which the constitutional authorities have classified as 'the most significant centres for the training of old and new Nazis from inside and outside Germany'. In her speeches Gertrude Herr has imposed her pernicious views on eager disciples: 'No Jew was ever gassed in Auschwitz. Camps for gassing people simply did not exist.'

The SS in particular adopted a policy whose aim was Jewish emigration. The fact that this emigration could only take place to a limited extent, is attributable to the consequences of the war – which had not been caused by Germany. In the course of the war the decision was taken to evacuate the Jews to labour-settlements in the east. In this connection it should be remembered that world Jewry had declared war on Germany as far back as March 1933.

From an extreme right-wing web-site

As a substitute for the banned 'Viking Youth', an association called the 'Friends of Ulrich von Hutten' was set up under conditions of the utmost secrecy. The founders were the former BDM officer Lisbeth Grolitsch, and Otto Ernst Remer, who once commanded the *Grossdeutschland* guard battalion. To this day the 'Friends' association upholds the ideals of the SS and is especially active among the younger generation. It openly circulates militant propaganda material, organises conferences for right-wing extremists, spreads its front organisations all over the German-speaking area and selects promising young 'stars' for ideological training. In its publication, the *Huttenbriefe* (Hutten Letters), it promulgates openly anti-Semitic hate-propaganda, Holocaust denial, militant racism and glorification of the Third Reich. 'The great questions of the human race cry out across the ages and cannot be ignored. Adolf Hitler showed us routes to their solution', rants the *Huttenbriefe*. 'The Fourth Reich remains the goal of the Germans.' As meaningless as such fantasies may sound in our pluralistic society, they nevertheless show that the poisonous ideology of the SS persists to this day – and bears fruit not least among adolescents. Even today there are thousands of web-sites on which the SS is glorified. Even today, youths who model themselves on the SS stride through the streets in jackboots.

> Every Jew is a walking advertisement for the next Holocaust.
> *From an extreme right-wing web-site*

Even today people are tormented on the street in broad daylight, or their homes are fire-bombed. One only has to think of the case in 1992, in a suburb of the east German port of Rostock, when the mob ran wild for three whole days and set fire to a hostel for foreign workers, while neighbours and police looked on. Even today people are publicly defamed as 'Yids'. Even today the word 'comradeship' as it existed in the SS is a synonym for concerted violence. As long as parts of Germany represent a trap for 'strangers', as long as the country's disabled are physically abused, and intellectual fire-raisers demonise democratic values, as long as computer-games with names like 'Concentration-camp rat-hunt' lower the threshold of inhibition – so long will the sinister spirit of the SS remain with us. Thus the story of the SS will always be a warning from history.

APPENDIX

Ranks of the SS, and their equivalents in the regular German and British armies

SS	German Army (Heer)	British Army
Oberstgruppenführer	Generaloberst	General
Obergruppenführer	General der Infanterie (etc)	General
Gruppenführer	Generalleutnant	Lieutenant-General
Brigadeführer	Generalmajor	Major-General
Oberführer	N/A	Brigadier
Standartenführer	Oberst	Colonel
Obersturmbannführer	Oberstleutnant	Lieutenant-Colonel
Sturmbannführer	Major	Major
Hauptsturmführer	Hauptmann	Captain
Obersturmführer	Oberleutnant	Lieutenant
Untersturmführer	Leutnant	2nd Lieutenant

Non-commissioned Ranks

Sturmscharführer	Stabsfeldwebel	Staff Sergeant
Hauptscharführer	Oberfeldwebel	Sergeant-Major
Oberscharführer	Feldwebel	Senior Sergeant
Scharführer	Unterfeldwebel	Sergeant
Unterscharführer	Unteroffizier	Corporal
Rottenführer	Obergefreiter	Senior Lance-Corporal
Sturmmann	Gefreiter	Lance-Corporal
Oberschütze	Oberschütze	Private 1st Class
Schütze	Schütze	Private

INDEX

Note: bold page numbers refer to major entries. Major entries are in chronological order, where appropriate.

Aachen 277
Abwehr (intelligence service) 103
Adenauer, Konrad 53, 337
adoption, forced 101–2, 168
Aharoni, Zvi 304, 339
Albanian SS unit 260
Alpine Redoubt 290–3, 295, 302, 330
Altaussee 292
Anschluss 135
Anthropoid, Operation 117–18
anti-Semitism 65, 73, 80, 129–30, 193–4, 225, 257
  in literature 67–8
  post-war 320, 325
Antwerp 274
Ardeatine Caves massacre 313, 329
Ardennes offensive 274–7
Argentina 285, 305, 309–10, 311, 312, 318–29, 332, 340
  Emigration Centre 321–2
  Immigration Office (DAIE) 321, 322, 323–4
  Nazi Activities inquiry (CEANA) 332

Arnhem 273
art treasures 292, 298, 299
  see also Nazi gold
Artamen League 70–1
Auschwitz Trial 285–6
Auschwitz-Birkenau 96, 170–1, 174, 175–6
  building of Birkenau 214
  as death camp 186, 205–20, 214, 295
  doctors at 217–20, 226–7
  personnel at 183
  regime in 206–8, 224–5
  slave-labour at 184–5
  torture/beatings at 210–11, 225
Austria 289, 319, 322, 331–2
persecution of Jews in 135–6, 137, 333–4

Babi Yar massacre 197–9, 200–1
Bach-Zelewski, Erich von dem 55, 95, 166, 204, 247
Bad Aussee 291–2
Bade, Wilfried 20
Balkans 249–50
banknotes *see* currency
'Banner of Blood' 14, 18

Barbarossa, Operation 186–7, 192, 241
Barbie, Klaus 288, 299–300
  in South America 305, 315–16, 339
Bauer, Fritz 285–6
Baugnez crossroads massacre 276–7
Bavaria 8–9, 11, 13–15, 73, 303
Beck, Ludwig 106
beer-hall putsch 8, 9–10, 13–14
Beirut 287
Belgium 141, 274
  SS troops/collaborators from 240, 242, 320
Belzec death camp 61, 186, 216
Berchtold, Josef 6, 9
Bergen-Belsen camp 183
Berlin 24, 108
  Allies' assault on 280–1
  political struggle in 20–2, 25–7
Bernhard, Operation 295–6, 298, 299
Bialystok atrocity 193–5
Birkenau see Auschwitz-Birkenau
Bittrich, Wilhelm 271–2, 273
Blaskowitz, Gen 233, 234
Blobel, Paul 152, 186, 199–202
Blume, Walter 144
Bohemia see Czechoslovakia
Bohne, Gerhard 320
Bolivia 15, 26, 299–300, 317
Bonhoeffer, Deitrich 58
Bormann, Martin 2, 23, 32, 44, 100, 162

and Himmler 101
and Odessa organisation 289, 292, 300, 332
Bosnian Moslems 259–60
Bothe, Hertha 183
'Brandenburg' unit 233
Brandy, Operation 304
Brazil 307, 340
Bromberg 139
brothels 133–4
Brown House 30, 31
brown-shirts see SA
Browning, Christopher 187, 195
Brunner, Alois 288, 305, 313, 333–5
Buchenwald concentration camp 29, 174, 181, 183, 227, 245
Budapest 277–9
Buenos Aires 288, 319–20, 322–3, 325
Burckhardt, Carl Jacob xiv, 62, 129–31
Burger, Adolf 295–6
Burwitz, Gudrun (née Himmler) 97, 340–1
Byelaya Tserkov 151–2
Byelorussia 102, 249, 262
  murder of Jews in 260
  SS volunteers from 257, 259

Caen 270
Cairo 288, 300
Canadian PoWs 267–8
Canaris, Admiral 103, 132
Capesius, Dr 226–7
CAPRI group 326–7, 328
Carmelite monks 312–13

Catholic Church 305–14, 336
Chamberlain, Houston Stewart 67
Charkov 251
Chelmno death camp 186, 216
Chile 326
Churchill, Winston 104
CIA/CIC *see* secret services *under* United States
Cold War 315–18
collaborators 177–8, 186
communism/communists 18, 29, 115, 146, 263, 314
'Comrades' Welfare' society 325–6
concentration camps 5, 33, 39–40, 80, 93, 129, 173–86, 301
    doctors at 98, 217–20, 226–7
    Eicke and 179–80, 185
    liberation of 228
    personnel 179–81, 182–3, 185–6
        domestic/social life for 211–12, 223
        Jewish 177–8, 222–3
        post-war trials of 302
    prisoners work in 177–8, 186, 222–3, 225
    slave-labour at 183–5
    system 175–8, 181–2, 223–5
    see also individual camps; and see death camps; Holocaust
Cossacks 259
Courland pocket 258
Croatia 250, 310, 311
    SS volunteers from 260

CROWCASS (Central Registry of War Crimes & Security Suspects) 301
currency 289–90, 293
    forged 287, 294–7, 299, 300
cyanide *see* Zyklon B
Czechoslovakia 113–14, 159–68, 261, 341
    resistance in 114, 115–18, 159–60, 163–4

Dachau concentration camp 23, 39–42, 57, 85, 174, 206
    Eicke and 179–80, 234
    human experiments in 98
    liberation of 228
DAIE 321, 322, 323–4
Daluege, Kurt 25
Damascus 288, 307, 334, 335
Darmstadt 170, 172, 330–1
Darré, Walther 71, 82
Daye, Pierre 320
death camps 93, 96, 186, 205–20, 245
    doctors at 217–19
    forced labour in 222–3
Death's Head units *see Totenkopf*
death's-head symbol x, 7–8
Defamation Law (1934) 127–8
Denmark, SS volunteers from 240, 242
DESt (*Deutsche Erd–und Steinwerke GmbH*) 183
Deutsche Bank 97
Dieckmann, *Sturmbannführer* 269
Diehl, Karoline 99–100

Diels, Rudolf xi, 36, 46, 126
Dietrich, Sepp 45–6, 48, 50,
        55, 166, 233–4, 271,
        272, 278, 280
    and Himmler 243, 273
Dirlewanger Brigade 262–3
Dirlewanger, Oskar 262
doctors, SS 217–21
    see also Mengele, Josef
documents, forged 295–6, 305,
        306–7, 308–9, 315
Draganovic, Krunoslav Stjepan
        310–11, 314–15, 323
Drossel, Karl-Heinz 196

Eastern front 61, 71, 89–93,
        100, 104, 244, 251–3,
        264
    German retreat on 263, 277
    SS brutality on xv, 142–55,
        188–97, 267
Egypt 333–4
Eichmann, Adolf 135, 136,
        140, 156–9, 165, 206
    role in Holocaust 205, 216
    post-war 285, 292–3, 305,
        308, 320, 322, 323,
        324, 338
Eicke, Theodor 41–2, 46, 54,
        178–81, 185, 234, 256
    and Death's Head units 235,
        238
Einsatzgruppen ('action
        squads') 187–201, 246,
        260–1
    character of men in 179–81,
        201–2
    composition of 187–8
    in post-war trials 302

Engel, Friedrich 340
Erich, Else 183
Estonian SS division 256–7,
        260
eugenics 29, 69, 76–7
euthanasia 228

Falaise pocket 271–2, 283
Farben, I.G. (chemical
        company) 179, 184–5
Fegelein, Hermann 246–7, 263
Ferencz, Benjamin 190, 192,
        196, 200
Fest, Joachim 53
Filor, Wolfgang 245
Finnish SS units 241, 256
First World War 7–8, 11, 35, 66
Flanders 240
Flossenbürg concentration
        camp 181, 183
France 141, 235–6, 237, 238
    German retreat from 264–72
    in hunt for ex-Nazis 316
    murder of Jews in 114–15
    PoWs murdered in 238–9
    resistance in 114, 268–70
    SS volunteers from 241, 242,
        281
Franco, Gen 321
Frank, Hans 155
Fransiscan monks 312
freemasons 129–30, 133
Frei, Norbert 338
Freikorps units 11, 207
Frenzel, Karl 209–10
Freude, Rudolfo 319–20
Frick, Wilhelm 35–6
'Friends of Ulrich von Hutten'
        342–3

Fritsch, Karl 208
Fromm, Fritz 47
Frontbann organisation 15–16, 24
'Frundsberg' division 253, 264
Fuldner, Horst Carlos 320, 321, 322
Füss, Karl 8, 10

Gabëik, Josef 117–18, 167
Galland, Adolf 320
gas 184, 204–5
    buses/trucks 114–15, 188, 205
    chambers 95–6, 205, 209, 212, 221–2, 226
Gehlen, Reinhard 333
Genoa 306, 310, 312, 315, 321, 324, 340
German Army xi, 13, 35–7, 232–3, 236, 238
    Armies
        Army Group Centre 61
        Fifth Panzer 275
        Sixth 251
        Sixth Panzer 274–5, 276
    brutality in 248–9, 250
    in defense of Germany 274
    fight alongside SS 264, 265, 266
    soldiers' attitude to SS 196–7, 254, 282–3
'Germania' unit *see* 'Viking' unit
Germany
    civilians in 2, 37–8
    defeat of 108–11, 278–81, 293–5, 300–1
    invasion of 273–81

persecution/murder of Jews in 137–8
recession in 8–9, 19, 21, 120
state terror in 5, 19–23, 32–4
post-war 296–7, 334–5, 337–8
Gerstein, Kurt 215, 222
Gestapo xi, xiii, 125–9, 143
    brutality of 167
    in post-war trials 302
ghettoes 137, 139, 140, 148, 155
Gildisch, Kurt 3–4, 52, 55
Giordano, Ralph xiv, 128–9, 132, 226
Gleiwitz radio station, attack on 138
Globocnic, Odilo 61, 175, 302
Goebels, Joseph 18–19, 23, 24, 44, 51, 82, 103
    as head of Luftwaffe 84
    on Heydrich 114
Goerdeler, Carl 105
gold *see* Nazi gold
Goldmann, Nahum 327
Goñi, Uki 314, 319, 323
Göring, Hermann 2, 9–10, 44, 46, 51, 103, 125, 136
Götz von Berlichingen division 264
Graf, Ulrich 13–14
Grawitz, Ernst 301–2
Greater German Reich 114, 239–41, 263
Greece 250
Gritschneder, Otto 4, 8, 14, 21, 22

Guderian, Gen 283
gypsies 80, 146

Handschar division 259–60
Hass, Karl-Heinz 319
Hassell, Ulrich von 85
Hausser, Paul 234, 251, 271–2,
    281–2
Heiden, Erhard 17
Herbert, Ulrich 191
Herr, Gertrude 342
Hess, Rudolf 10, 53, 56, 326
Heydrich, Bruno 117, 118–19,
    123–4
Heydrich, Heinz 123–4
Heydrich, Lina (née von Osten)
    112, 119, 120, 131–2,
    138–9, 145, 159, 160,
    166
Heydrich, Reinhard xi, 44,
    112–69
    character xiii, 119, 129–32,
        141–2
        arrogant 162–3, 166
        loner/outsider 120, 122
    family 112, 122, 138–9,
        160
    Jewish ancestry 120, 123–4
    hobbies
        fencing 155–6
        flying 140–2
    early life 119–21
    rise to power xii–xiv, 113,
        122–3, 124–6
    in France 114–15
    in Czechoslovakia 113–16,
        160
    and Gestapo/SD 125–6,
        132–4

    in Poland 138–40
    and concentration camps 40
    and Himmler xii–xiii, 30, 89,
        121–2, 141, 165
    and Hitler 115, 142, 164,
        165–6
    and Jews 129–30, 131–2,
        134–5
        role in Holocaust xii, xiv,
            156–9, 208
    murders ordered by 2, 3, 52,
        125
    in Nazi party 121
    plots against 115, 117
    death xiv, 163–9
Heydrich, Silke 112, 160
HIAG (mutual aid association)
    281, 337
Himmler, Gebhard 64–5, 72
Himmler, Gudrun *see* Burwitz,
    Gudrun
Himmler, Hans 85
Himmler, Heinrich 13, 32, 44,
    60–111, 247
    character xi–xii, 30, 61–4,
        74–6, 84–5, 97, 104
        animal lover 97
        anti-Semitism 67–8, 91–2
    and concentration camps 80,
        181–2
    contemporary opinions of
        61–3, 91, 243
    family 97, 100–1
    health/illness 65–6
    early life 64–71
    and Heydrich *see under*
        Heydrich
    and Hitler 89–90, 103–6
    and Holocaust xii, 40–1,

58–9, 61, 83–4, 91–5,
108–9, 203, 215–16
and human experiments 98
and Nazi ideology xii, 29–
30, 63–4, 67–70, 76–7,
80–3, 263
crackpot theories 86–9,
90, 158
racial obsession 85, 92,
100–1, 232, 240
in Nazi Party 71–2, 76, 78
and SS ix, x, xi–xiii, 2, 28–9,
37–8, 48, 103, 172
and *Volkssturm* 106–7
and *Waffen*-SS 231, 240,
255–6
in Germany's defeat 108–11
negotiates with Allies xii,
104, 108–9
plans Alpine Redoubt
291
capture/death 111, 301
Himmler, Marga (née Siegroth)
73–4
Hindenburg, FM von 35, 47
Hitler, Adolf 23, 47–50, 53,
56, 159–60, 263
rise to power x, 5–6, 9, 10,
12–13, 16, 32
criticisms of 24–5, 251, 253–
4, 271
hesitancy 48
and Eicke 179–80
and Holocaust 93–4, 146,
154, 155, 175, 212–13
loyalty to 7, 9, 172
mythology surrounding
82–3
plot against 105–6

strategies 251, 264, 273–4,
275, 279, 330
and *Waffen*-SS 239–40
defeat of 108–9, 278–81,
290–1
Hitler Youth 229, 254–5,
264–7, 268, 270
loyalty/fanaticism of 266,
272, 281
HNG (neo-Nazi aid
organisation) 341–2
Höcker, Karl 226–7
Hoepner, Gen 238
'Hohenstaufen' division 253,
264, 271–2, 273
Höhne, Heinz 28, 38
Holland *see* Netherlands
Höllengebirge mountains
292–3
Holocaust ix, 58–9, 83–4,
91–5, 108–9, 144–55,
189–201, 205–28,
333–4
denial of 342
perpetrators' attitude to 192,
195–6, 201–4, 218
perpetrators' motives for
174–5
planning of xii, 114–15,
155–9, 186, 214–15,
335
homosexuals 80, 85
Höppner, Rolf-Heinz 155
Hörbiger, Hans 86–7
Höss, Rudolf 71, 93, 109–10,
184, 205–7, 303
role in Holocaust 206, 209,
213, 215, 221, 223,
224

Höttl, Wilhelm 123, 292, 293
Hudal, Bishop Alois 306–10, 311–14, 323, 334
Hungary 277–9, 330
 SS volunteers from 256, 277

ICRC *see* Red Cross
Infield, Glenn 331, 332
inflation 8–9
intelligence-gathering xiii, 30, 103, 121, 126
 in brothels 133–4
Isenburg, Princess Helene Elizabeth von 336
Israel 285, 334, 338
 police of 158, 286
 see also Mossad
Italy 250, 306–10, 313, 319, 329, 332, 340
 DAIE offices in 321, 322, 323–4

Jäger, Karl 144–5, 148, 189
Jews
 expulsion of 135–6, 137–8, 140, 157
 persecution of 134–7
 see also anti-Semitism; Holocaust
Jung, Edgar 45
Junge, Traudl 80

Kaduk, Oswald 226–7
Kahr, Gustav von 9, 13, 55
Kaltenbrunner, Ernst 291, 293, 295, 302
Kamenz-Podolsk 252
Kershaw, Ian 5

Kersten, Felix 38, 62–3, 84, 90, 93–4, 97, 105, 141–2
Kiev 115, 197–9, 200–1
Klarsfeld, Serge/Beate 338–9
Klausener, Erich 3–4
Kluge, FM 272
Kögel, Max 205
Kogen, Eugen 178, 180
Kohout, Pavel 113, 161, 163, 167
Kops, Reinhard 309–10, 312, 325, 329
Krebs, Albert 30, 75
Kripo (criminal police) 140, 143
Kristallnacht 136
Krosigk, Schwerin von 137
Krötz, Robert 8
Krüger, Bernhard 295, 296
Krüger, Friedrich Wilhelm 61
Kubis, Jan 117–18, 164, 167
Kursk 251
Kutschmann, Walter 312
Kyffhäuser League xvi, 38

La Paz 288
La Vista, Vincent 305, 309
Landsberg prison 303, 336
Langbehn, Carl 104
Langbein, Hermann 175–6, 224–5
Latvia 147–8, 153, 189, 305
 SS units from 256–8
Leers, Johann von 288
Leibstandarte Adolf Hitler 3, 231–2, 235, 246, 249, 251, 329
 on Western front 264, 270, 274, 283

Leningrad 244
Less, Avner 158
Lidice 167–8
Liepaja (Libau) 147–8
Lima 284, 288, 297, 298, 300
Lippert, Michael 54, 55
Lithuania 147, 189
Litten, Dr Hans 23
Lodz ghetto 155
looting/corruption 96–7, 134,
        135
    see also Nazi gold/treasures
Lorenz, Erika 60
Lublin-Majdanek concentration
        camp 183, 186, 205
    death camp at 216
Ludendorff, Erich von 9, 13
Luftwaffe 84, 141, 272
Lutze, Viktor 37, 49
Lvov 149–50, 307

Madagascar 92–3
Madrid 288, 320, 332
Maison Rouge meeting 293–4
Majdanek see Lublin-Majdanek
Malloth, Anton 341
Malmédy 276–7
Malsen-Ponickau, SS-
        Oberführer von 40–1
Mandal, Maria 183
Manstein, Erich von 233–4,
        249
Marbella, Odessa meeting in
        284–6
Masur, Norbert 108
Maurice, Emil 6–7
Mauthausen concentration
        camp 181, 296
Meine, August 60

Menem, Carlos 332
Mengele, Josef 217–18, 288,
        313, 320
    post-war 304, 313, 320,
        322–3, 324, 326, 340
Meyer, Kurt 266, 337
Middle East 286, 288, 333–5
Milano, Jim 315, 316
monks/monasteries 312–13,
        314, 319
Moravia see Czechoslovakia
'Moscow Declaration' 284
Mossad 305, 338
Mountain divisions 249–50,
        256
Mulka, Robert 226–7
Müller, Heinrich 154, 158,
        304–5, 317
Münch, Hans Wilhelm 176,
        216
Munich 49
    putsch 8, 9–10, 13–14
    SS origins in 5–7, 15
Mussolini, Benito 9, 330

Naples 306, 315
el-Nasser, Col Gamal Abd
        333
Nazi gold/treasures 289,
        292–3, 298, 299, 332
    see also currency
Nazi ideology xii, 63–4, 68–71,
        80–9, 131
    as pretext for Holocaust 150,
        175
    in SS recruitment x, 28–30,
        191, 200
Nazi Party 12, 19–20, 79, 181
    power struggles in x–xi,

2–5, 12–13, 15–16, 19, 24–7
Nebe, Arthur 95, 144, 187–8, 196
neo-Nazis 340–3
Netherlands 141, 240, 273–5
Neurath, Konstantin von 159–60
Night of Long Knives 51–6
NKVD (Soviet secret police) 149
Normandy 264–71
Norway 141
    SS volunteers from 240–1, 242
Novgorod 244
NSDAP *see* Nazi Party
Nuremberg 20
    trials xiv, 55, 189–90, 192, 201, 202, 219, 301, 319

'Oberbayern' unit 233
Oberheuser, Herta 219
Odeonsplatz, Munich 13–14
Oder, River 277
'Odessa' organisation **284–343**
    funding for 294, 299
    hiding places/escape routes 306–10, 319–23, 331–2, 334
    influence of 288
    meaning of name 285, 304
    meetings of 284–6, 287
    mythology of 286, 324–5, 329
    origins 286–7, 331
    structure 305
Ohlendorf, Otto 144, 189–92, 202

Oradour massacre xv, 269–70
Oranienburg concentration camp 24, 33
Orpo (police units) 187
Orth, Kariun 181

Palestine 138
Panesky Brezany (Heydrich's estate) 112
Papal Aid Commission (PCA) 307, 309, 310, 313
Papen, Franz von 43, 47
Paraguay 326
partisans 249–50, 258, 259, 263
    Nazi, rumours of 290
passports *see* documents, forged
Paul VI, Pope 314
Pavelic, Ante 310, 311
Peiper, Joachim 274–5, 276
Perón, Evita 320–1, 332
Perón, Juan Domingo 309–10, 312, 319–20, 323, 326, 332
Peru 284, 286, 287, 297, 298
Phleps, Arthur 259
Pinochet, Augusto 326
Pius XII, Pope 307, 313, 314, 321
pogroms 146–55, 189, 193–5, 249
Poland 61, 89, 91–2, 138–40, 233–4, 305
    children stolen from 102
    ghettoes in 139, 140, 155
    persecution/murder of Jews in 93, 138–40, 233–4, 340

war crimes trial in 303
  see also Warsaw
police forces 79, 121, 124–5,
    140
  combine with SS 187–95,
      202–3, 235, 239–41,
      244
  see also Gestapo
Polishchuk, Ludmilla Sheila 199
Potsdam 35
Potthast, Hedwig ('Häschen')
    100–1
Prague 116–17, 118–19,
    160–1, 163–8
Priebke, Erich 313, 320, 322,
    324, 328–9, 341, 342
Pripet marshes 246–8
prisoners-of-war 208
  murdered 238–9, 246,
      267–8, 276–7
propaganda 39, 138, 150, 171,
    266, 330, 343

Quedlinburg Cathedral
    ceremony 80–1

railways 216
  sabotage of 115–16
Ramban, Steven 339
Rasch, Otto 144
Rascher, Dr Sigmund 98–100
'rat line' 315
Rauff, Walter 299, 312–13
Ravensbrück concentration
    camp 108, 168, 181,
    219
Red Cross 129, 308–9
  passports 311, 312, 313,
      315, 323

Reich, Das division 249, 251,
    258, 269, 283, 329
Reich Security, Central Office
    of (RSHA) xiii, 140,
    143, 155, 285, 329
Reichenau, FM von 152
Reichswehr see German Army
resistance movements 113,
    114, 117–18, 159–60,
    247, 268–9
RSHA *see* Reich Security,
    Central Office of
Ribbentrop, Joachim von 60,
    134
Richter, Eberhard 2
Riedweg, Franz 29–30
Rieger, Jürgen 342
Riga 148, 149
Röhm, Ernst 10–12
  as head of SA 26–7, 34–5
  and Himmler 72, 77–8
  and Hitler 3, 11–12, 15–16,
      26, 31, 36–7, 42–3, 47,
      50
  homosexuality of 30–1, 44
  plots against 31–2, 43–51
  murdered x–xi, 53–4, 180,
      234
Roman Catholic Church 72
Romanian SS units 25, 256
Rome 305–6, 309–10, 333
Rommel, FM Erwin 271
RONA Brigade 263
Rosenberg, Alfred 71, 82, 256
Rosenwink, Alois 7, 18
Rostock 343
Rostov-on-Don 244
Rubenstein, Richard L. 228
Rudel, Hans-Ulrich 299, 300,

314, 320, 321, 324,
    325–6, 336
Ruffinengo, Franz 310, 324,
    325
Runstedt, FM Gerd von 268
Russia see Soviet Union
Russian National Liberation
    Army see RONA

SA (Sturmabteilung) x–xi, 5,
    42–3, 232
  brutality of 19–23, 32–4,
    45
  in power struggles x–xi, 2–5,
    19, 24–6, 36–7, 42–55
Sachsenhausen concentraton
    camp 138, 174, 181,
    295
Salomon, Franz Pfeffer von 19,
    25
Salon Kitty 133–4
Santos, Judge 284
Sassen, Willem 326, 327–8
Scandinavia 336
  SS volunteers from 240–1,
    242
Schacht, Hjalmar 294
Schellenberg, Walter 43, 82,
    90, 122, 132
Schenk, Ernst–Günther 62, 64,
    85, 91, 110
Schleicher, Gen Kurt von xi, 3,
    4, 44, 51–2
Schmid, Dr Willi 4, 57, 58
Schmidt, Wilhelm 50
Schneider, Pipo 193–4
Schneidhuber, August 50, 51
Schreck, Julius 6
Schulz, Paul 1

Schwammberger, Josef 320,
    323, 340, 341, 342
Schwarze Korps, Das (SS
    journal) 4–5, 131, 137
Schwend, Friedrich 284, 286,
    288, 297–300, 317, 318
SD (SS security service) xiii, 38,
    46, 132–4, 140, 143,
    200, 320
selective breeding 29, 69, 76–7,
    99–100
Serbia, murder of Jews in 250
Siberia 169
Siegesmund, Hermann 31
Siemens 97
'Silent Aid' society see Stille
    Hilfe
Simpson, Christopher 333
Siri, Guiseppe 310, 311,
    312–13, 314
Skorzeny, Otto 288, 291, 294,
    299, 304, 329–33
slave-labour 183–5
Smolen, Kasimir 173, 225
Sobibor death camp 186, 210,
    216, 306
South America 15, 26, 286,
    288, 295, 299, 304,
    312, 316–17, 326
  see also individual countries
Soviet Union 71, 104, 142
  army of 277–81
  in Cold War 333
  invasion of 186–7, 241, 244,
    251, 264
  murder of Jews in 92–3,
    96, 115, 144–55, 157,
    189–95, 203, 246–8
  prisoners-of-war from 208

SS volunteers from 263
see also Eastern front
Spain 284–6, 288, 312, 320,
    332
Spandau prison 336
Speer, Albert 2, 62, 88, 145,
    162, 273
Speidel, Hans 271
'Spider' organisation 288, 331
SS (*Schutz-Staffel*)
    origins ix–xi, xvi, 5–29
    character of men in xiv–xvii, 8,
        11, 58, 170–6, 179–81
    and concentration camps
        40–2, 79–80, 170–1,
        175–8, 179–80
    in concentration camps *see*
        Totenkopf units
    corruption in 96–7
    discipline in 18, 223–4
    foreign units in 107, 240–3,
        256
    ideology/mythology in 4–5,
        14, 28–30, 71, 80–4,
        204, 282–3
    insignia/motto/oath ix, x,
        7–8, 28, 77, 88–9, 173,
        341
    Mountain divisions 249–50,
        256
    murder squads *see*
        Einsatzgruppen
    recruitment/selection x, 17,
        29, 65–6, 76, 107, 178
    role 16–17, 38
    solidarity in 195
    songs of 18, 19
    tattoo 303
    training 84, 172–3, 182,
        187, 234
    academies 258
    women in 182–3, 218–20,
        342
    veteran's associations 335–7,
        340–3
    see also Odessa
        organisation
    see also Waffen-SS
SS-*Verfügungstruppe* (rapid
    reaction force) 231,
    232–5
Stahlecker, Dr franz Walter
    143, 150
Stahlhelm (Steel Helmet)
    organisation 35
Stalingrad 100, 251
Stangl, Franz 306–7
Stark, Hans 170–4, 225–6
Stauffenberg, Count von 105–6
Steiner, Felix 253–4, 280, 301
Stennes, Walter 25–7
Stille Hilfe (SS veteran's
    association) 335–6,
    340, 341, 342
Stosstrupp Hitler (Hitler
    Shockforce) ix–x, 5–6,
    8, 12–13, 14
Strasbourg 293–4
Strasser, Gregor 45, 72
    murdered by SS xi, 4, 55
Strasser, Otto 73
Streicher, Julius 302
Stromberger, Maria 219–20
Stroop, Gen Jürgen 261
Svoboda, Karel 117
Switzerland 321, 322, 332
    Nazi bank accounts/treasure
        in 289–90, 294

Syria 307, 313, 334, 335
T4, Operation 186
Tacitus 68–9
Tcherkassy breakout 252
Theresienstadt camp 108, 161
'Thüringen' unit 233
Thyssen corporation 293
Tollmann, Paul 5, 11, 21, 41
Toplitz, Lake 289–90, 296–7
Torbräu 9
Totenkopf units **170–228**, 261,
    277, 283
  character of men in 189–92,
    225, 227–8
  in concentration camps
    170–1, 173–8, 180–6
  illusion of normality in
    223–4
  in Poland 233, 234–5
  in Russia 244–5, 251
  training 237
Treblinka death camp 186,
    216, 306

Ukraine 102, 149–50, 151–2,
    246
  SS volunteers from 257, 263
Ulrichsberg 340–1
United Nations 332
United States
  Nazi scientists in 318
  Office of Special
    Investigation (OSI)
    318
  secret services of (CIC/CIA)
    286, 287, 293, 298,
    304, 314–17, 330
  employs Nazis 301,
    316–17, 319, 333

troops massacred by SS
    276–7
Ustasha organisation 310–12,
    315

Vatican 305, 311, 314
Versailles Treaty 8, 170, 172
Vienna 135–6, 333
'Viking' unit (prev 'Germania')
    232, 240–3, 246, 249,
    256, 277
Volkdeutsche divisions 256, 258,
    277
völkisch ideology 63–4, 68–71,
    83–4, 95
Volksgrenadier divisions 274
Volkssturm 106–7
von Braun, Wernher 318

Wacht am Rhein, Operation
    274–5
Wächter, Baron von 307–8
Waffen-SS xiv–xv, 103, 104,
    143, **229–83**, 325, 337
  brutality of xv, 152, 229,
    246–8, 262–3, 267–70,
    275–6
  character of men in 229–30,
    262–3, 281–2
  foreign units in 240–3,
    255–61
  in France 264–72
  in Holland/Belgium 274–6
  loyalty to Hitler 271–2
  military achievements of
    245–6
  officer shortage in 255,
    258–9, 264–5
  origins 230–3

Panzer divisions 251–2, 256, 266, 272, 274–6
recruitment/selection 236–7, 240–3, 253, 254–6, 272
reputation of 252–3, 263–4, 279, 282–3
Sixth SS Panzer Army 274
strength 230, 232, 235–6, 253
expansions of 230–3, 240, 252–3, 255–7
training 258, 259
in Germany's defeat 278–81
see also Hitler Youth; Leibstandarte Adolf Hitler; Reich, Das
Wagner, Alfred 39, 49
Waldheim, Kurt 318
Wannsee Conference 157–9, 214
war criminals, hunt for 300–2
Warsaw 91
ghetto 154, 214, 261–2
uprising 262–3
Weg, Der (pro-Nazi journal) 325
Wehrmacht see German Army
Weisthor, Karl Maria 87–9

Wessel, Horst 20, 286
Wiesenthal, Simon 204, 287, 290, 292, 306, 307, 312, 317, 326, 331–2, 339
and Eichmann 327, 328
motive for Nazi-hunting 340
Wiking unit see 'Viking' unit
Wildenbruch, Karl Pfeffer von 277–8
Wildt, Michael 132
Wiligut, Karl Maria (aka Karl Weisthor) 87–9
Wittmann, Michael 266
Wolff, Karl 44, 60–1, 89, 90, 95, 104
Worch, Christian 342
'world ice' theory 86–7, 90
Worm, Hardy 6
Wormhoudt massacre 238–9
Worysch, Udo von 55

Yugoslavia 249–50
murder of Jews in 250
SS volunteers from 256

Zuroff, Efraim 337, 339–40
Zyklon B 96, 184, 209, 212, 221, 222, 226